A Life of Learning and Other Pleasures:
John Meisel's Tale

A Life of Learning and Other Pleasures: John Meisel's Tale

And gladly wolde he lerne, and gladly teche.

The Canterbury Tales, Prologue

WINTERGREEN
STUDIOS PRESS

Wintergreen Studios Press
Township of South Frontenac, PO Box 75, Yarker, ON, Canada K0K 3N0

Wintergreen Studios Press (WSP) gratefully acknowledges the financial support received from Queen's University, Sean Conway, Victor Rabinovitch, John and Phyllis Rae, and several anonymous donors. WSP also thanks the following for permission to reprint previously published material:

> John Meisel with portrait (2004) by Barry Kaplan, previously published in *Profile Kingston*; Meisel quits CRTC by Frank A. Edwards, previously published in the *Kingston Whig-Standard*; Canadian Content by Frank A. Edwards, previously published in the *Kingston Whig-Standard*; Knights and MPs by Terry Aislin (1982), commissioned by the CRTC.

Every effort has been made to contact the copyright holders, artists, photographers, and authors whose work appears in this text for permission to reprint material. We regret any oversights and we will be happy to rectify them in future editions.

> Book and cover design by Rena Upitis
> Editing and indexing by Teri-Ann McDonald
> Front cover photo: Photographer unknown
> Back cover photo: Rena Upitis (2011)
> Composed in Book Antiqua and Candara, typefaces designed by Monotype Typography and Gary Munch, respectively

Library and Archives Canada Cataloguing in Publication
Meisel, John. 1923 –
A Life of Learning and Other Pleasures: John Meisel's Tale/John Meisel

ISBN: 978-0-9865473-3-1

1. Autobiography—Personal Memoirs, General, Historical, Political, Cultural Heritage. 2. Political Science—General, Canadian Politics, International Relations. 3. Political Process—General, Elections.

I.   Title. A Life of Learning and Other Pleasures: John Meisel's Tale.
Legal Deposit – Library and Archives Canada

In memory of Mami, Tati, Rose and Murie.

And for Hanna, Victoria, Karl and all my students, colleagues and other friends. In my mind, as I retraced my steps, many of you looked over my shoulder.

Other Books and Monographs by John Meisel

The Canadian General Election of 1957
University of Toronto Press, 1962.

Papers on the 1962 Election, (ed.)
University of Toronto Press, 1964.

L'évolution des partis politiques canadiens
(comprising No. 2 of
Cahiers de la société canadienne de science politique, 1966)
Quebec City, 1966.

Ethnic Relations in Canadian Voluntary Associations
(with Vincent Lemieux), No. 13,
Documents of the Royal Commission on Bilingualism and
Biculturalism,
Information Canada, Ottawa, 1972.

Working Papers on Canadian Politics
McGill-Queen's University Press, Montreal, 1972, 1973, 1975.

Cleavages, Parties and Values in Canada
Sage Publications, London and Beverly Hills, 1974.

Debating the Constitution (ed. with Jean Laponce)
University of Ottawa Press, 1994.

As I Recall/Si je me souviens bien
(with Guy Rocher, Arthur Silver and IRPP staff)
(Six introductions and a conclusion.)
McGill-Queen's University Press, Montreal, 1999.

Contents

Foreword

John Meisel's life is the story of Canada but Canada also defines the story of his life. The one mirrors and shapes the other so that the two become inseparable. It is this symbiosis that makes this story so compelling.

The autobiography begins innocently enough with the young boy whose father was a senior official with the Bat'a Shoe Company in the interwar period. Europe was still the centre of the universe, at least for Europeans, but the Bat'as had built one of the few large multinational enterprises with branches all over the world. Hailing from newly independent Czechoslovakia, a small European country born out of the Austro-Hungarian Empire and caught between the continent's giants, the Bat'as nevertheless had a global sensibility unusual among middle Europeans. John Meisel was fortunate that his father worked for the Bat'as. As a Bat'a official, the Meisel family travelled to the periphery of a Europe that was seething and beyond to Africa.

The family was Jewish and after 1933, Europe was no place for Jews. As John tells the story, their Jewish identity sat lightly — they were not a religious family and they identified as Czech rather than Jewish — but that would have been no protection at all had they remained in Czechoslovakia. The Meisels left central Europe not because they were Jewish but to work for Bat'a, but how lucky were they to be ahead of the river of blood that would wash over the continent.

The war broke out when John was an adolescent. He was not drafted and was never a combatant. Nevertheless it must have been subliminally frightening for a young man to watch the country he grew up in occupied by the Nazis. This early part of the autobiography is surprisingly gentle, fleeting, and almost indirect, but the thin skein of horror that runs underneath is never far from the surface. The Meisel family was but a hair's breadth away from the Nazi rallies in the stadiums, from the marching boots, and from the Panzer divisions that rolled across Europe with almost no opposition. There, but for John's father's job, would they have been. Although John writes with humour about his adolescence — his lightness of being infuses the whole manuscript — between the lines one senses his deep awareness that his adolescence was marked, as he puts it, by being "at the margins of possible extinction. The advent of Nazis next door and the growing power of Germany," he tells us, "endowed the Jewish reality with a terrifying, nearly paralyzing dimension and immediacy."

This sensibility of the fragility of existence had, I suspect, a profound effect on the making of John's life as a political thinker and doer. His early and sustained commitment to political pluralism, the deep interest in the machinery and the mechanics of democracy, the continual preoccupation with national unity, all of these can be understood as the unconscious perspective of someone who, so young, had seen and lived a very different European experience. For these children of that Europe, nothing was, is, or ever can be, wholly secure and nothing can be taken for granted. Beneath John's unfailing optimism and exceptional good humour runs this thin awareness of horror.

It is a young John Meisel who comes to Canada in 1942, a Canada so different from the one we know today. The Bat'a family softened and eased the welcome. The Meisel family did not struggle with Canadian officials who felt that "none was too many," that refugees from Europe, particularly Jewish refugees, were unwelcome. The Meisels came to Ontario, then overwhelming white, monocultural, where everyone ate sliced white bread wrapped in plastic packaging and knew the history of the United Empire loyalists, even if they were not loyalists themselves.

The story that John tells of his welcome into this community is disarming and quite wonderful. Speaking English with a charming accent but an accent nevertheless, one would think that this young man might have had a difficult experience at the hands of the establishment. Not so. The gregarious, intellectually curious, young John is welcomed first into private school, where he does astonishingly well, and then into the bastion seat of Canada's English cultural empire, the University of Toronto.

It is at university that John becomes essentially Canadian in his perspective. The University came alive in the post-war period, particularly in the humanities and the social sciences where it was home to some of the greatest men of letters. The University was not yet fully conscious of its mission to educate Canadians about Canadian literature or Canadian politics. The giants looked to England, sent their best students to Oxford, and had more than a whiff of nostalgia for the mother country. But Canada was stirring, and a Canadian sensibility was beginning, especially at the University of Toronto.

It is no accident that this University made Canadians of so many who had come — and would come — to Toronto. Peter Newman, Peter Munk, Anna Porter, and successive waves of immigrants and refugees would tell essentially the same story as does John, although of course the texture changes from one to another. They all marvel at the welcome they received, at the openness of their fellow students, at the invitations to dinner, at the sociability, at the ease. To their utter astonishment, they discovered that their fellow students — who "were" Canadian — thought of them as Canadian. And so, they became Canadian, almost forgetting to hold their breath. But not quite. They carried with them that extra sensibility, that sense of gratitude to Canada, a tangible sense of obligation. In this as in many other ways, John foreshadows those who come after him.

After his graduation, John quite remarkably makes a seamless transition to Queen's where he joins the faculty as a young instructor. A graduate student reading this story today would be transfixed. There was no formal competition for the position, no requirement of a doctoral degree, today's certificate that is an essential rite of passage. The most senior faculty member — who had met and liked John — hired him. This would be inconceivable at any university in Canada today where the watchwords are fairness, openness, transparency, and process. But not then. John paints a marvellous portrait of a tiny academic community, in the heartland of English Canada, where a small number of men all knew each other, were largely of similar cultural background, usually spoke only English, and liked their scotch and cigars if not their sherry. A small number of senior faculty simply hired their own or each other's students to fill the growing demand for teachers as the universities grappled with the post-war growth in students.

It is easy, indeed sometimes irresistible, to caricature this society of great white men. But John's story does not permit this kind of easy fun, because this singularly like-minded group welcomed him so easily and without hesitation into their inner sanctum. John was multilingual, not unilingual, he spoke with the faintest trace of an accent, not with an English Ontario twang, he brought with him a whiff of central Europe, not Oxford, and he was a passionate and committed teacher, with little of the dry wit and sarcasm that so amused the old guard. Despite all these differences, John moved seamlessly into Canadian academic and political life.

The autobiography is quite remarkable because there is an almost taken-for-granted quality to the story as John tells it. Yet how unusual it is. It is here that John's story is most strongly the story of Canada's becoming, of the future rather than of the past. His story is the opening of Canada, an opening which occurs over and over again in subsequent generations, of a capacity not only to absorb but to change, to expand, to grow, to encompass. And those Canada welcomed enriched Canada in turn. It is this symbiosis that weaves between the lines of this remarkable autobiography, a subtext that can be shared by so many who are less known and less loved than is John Meisel.

I will not say much in this foreword about John's work because he says it so well. He takes us on an intellectual journey of his preoccupations, interests, and worries about the country he loves. I will say only that John embedded himself at the centre of an academic community in a country in transition, in the process of leaving its colonial concerns behind and beginning to grapple with the meaning of its independence, its connectedness to North America, and its role in the world. John was one of those, as one of his students told me, who helped to rewrite the rules as the country reimagined itself.

John Meisel's early path-breaking work on electoral behaviour laid the foundation for Canada's polling industry and the study of political parties. He was the first English co-editor of the *Canadian Journal of Political Science* as the new discipline separated from Economics and shaped its own principles and practices. As tensions grew between French and English Canadians, John led significant research for the Royal Commission on Bilingualism and Biculturalism, arguably among a handful of the most important royal commissions of the last several decades. He was President of the Royal Society of Canada, a society of Canada's most distinguished academics.

John also went beyond the academy, as few of his generation did. He describes in fascinating detail his growing interest in culture and cultural policy, at a time when most of his colleagues were infatuated with the prospect of making politics a "hard" science. It was no accident that John developed such a deep interest in culture and its regulation and published groundbreaking work on cultural policy. First and foremost, he brought his European sensibility, a deeply civilized appreciation of the importance of culture to public life. In addition, cultural policy was a fault line running between French and

English, an abiding interest throughout his career. And finally, English Canada, where he lived and worked, struggled to articulate its sense of itself in the face of the powerful pull of American culture and the proud and self-assured culture of Quebec. When he became Chairman of the Canadian Radio-Television and Telecommunications Commission (CRTC), he oversaw the introduction of pay television and pushed forward debates about Canadian content in the face of rapidly evolving technology. As a scholar, he did the pioneering work on the political context of culture and on government policy toward the arts. After his term at the CRTC, John wrote and taught about the politics of regulation, an important new area that attracted growing numbers of students.

As I was writing this foreword, I sought out a few of John's thousands of students to better appreciate what John was like as a teacher. Rana Sarkar responded this way: "What makes John Meisel so extraordinary are his human qualities — discipline, insight, and effectiveness are met in equal measure by charm, empathy, and an unrivalled capacity for friendship. Woven into his story is the warmth and generosity he extended to his many thousands of students, colleagues and friends around the world. He remains a mentor, trusted friend, and sometimes advisor to generations who were lucky to come across him, giving wise advice on issues of personal and national significance. His immense influence on generations of scholars, journalists, and public officials is his lasting and ongoing legacy." A teacher could wish for no finer accolade.

Most of John's teaching career was in the predigital age. Next door to his office, he had a library of materials collected over the course of his career that he opened to any student who asked. This treasure trove of studies, reports, student papers, and dusty pamphlets opened many minds and sparked countless debates and discussions. His wonderful spiral house, built in the woodlands on a lake, which John bequeathed to Queen's, has been and continues to be an open house to the legions of former students who come back again and again for advice, ideas, and wisdom.

In the later stages of his career, John once again mirrored the evolution of his beloved Canada. He became increasingly involved with the development of the International Political Science Association and was the founding editor of the *International Political Science Review*. Convinced that Canadian scholarship had much to contribute to the world and that it had much to learn from the world, John travelled the world promoting shared research and scholarship that crossed cultures. Here too John and Canada moved together along the same path. Canadians now understand far more deeply than they ever have the myriad networks of connections that link people living in Canada to countries all over the world, and the global platforms that Canadians are building in the private, public, and not-for-profit sectors.

I came to know John decades ago. I was never a student, nor a colleague at Queen's, his beloved university that is the object of his unswerving loyalty and generosity. I do not work in his field. Yet we have become academic friends, bumping into one another for shorter or longer periods, at conferences, at workshops, in Moscow or in Kingston. I was drawn to John, as were so many, by that lively and inquiring mind, but not only by the quality of the mind. John has a deep appreciation of culture and a lovely sense of history. But so do others. What then sets John apart? The twinkle in his eye, the sense of humour, and the grace and charm that undergirds the humour. John Meisel is fun. Of how many great Canadians can we say that?

Janice Gross Stein,
Director, Munk School of Global Affairs,
Toronto, February 6, 2012

A Life of Learning and Other Pleasures:
John Meisel's Tale

Jenda 1935—John 2004. Echoes of Dorian Gray?

Overture: An Alien Voice?

Curiously, my voice, when I hear myself speak, is free of any "foreign" accent. I sound to myself as the quintessential Anglo-Ontarian—one who has had some schooling abroad maybe, but who nevertheless managed to absorb the vocal style of his peers. To others, however, there are unmistakable echoes of a polyglot background. There was one exception: Murie, my late wife. Always eager to bolster the old morale, she insisted that I did not have an alien way of speaking, merely a slightly unusual intonation. But, as so often happens in marriages, she probably came to share some of her husband's perceptions (and I, hers), including the way he sounded to himself. So her evidence was suspect.

The polyglot school, I am afraid, is correct, and not surprisingly. I began life in central Europe, with German and Czech as my initial languages, delved seriously into British English in my teens only to switch to French, before reverting to English again, but this time of the central Canadian kind. I arrived in Canada in 1942, aged nineteen, having previously inhabited Austria, Czechoslovakia, England, Holland, Morocco and Haiti.

In the light of this geographical and linguistic miscellany it is appropriate that I begin the recollections and reflections which follow by sketching where I acquired my manner of speaking and how I got here.

Until she married, my mother lived in the tiny town of Weipert (Vejprty in Czech), in the Sudeten area of Northern Bohemia, right, but really right, at the border with Germany, as specified by the Versailles Peace Treaty four years before I was born. One could walk from my grandmother's house along the street in Weipert and, before long, unwittingly stumble into Saxony. The dominant language was German, as was my mother's upbringing. She eventually married my father, who came from Moravia—Czechoslovakia's predominantly Czech speaking central province, lying between Bohemia and Slovakia.

My father—*Tati* as he has always been to me—was equally comfortable in Czech and German but his hometown, Zlín, was Czech speaking. So my mother (*Mami*) learnt Czech, which eventually became her principal language. But soon after the end of the First World War my parents moved to Vienna, where they stayed

ten years and lived mostly in German. I was born during this
Austrian interregnum in 1923 and, to my subsequent great chagrin
and, yes, shame, suffered for years the humiliation of hailing from
that imperial city. The reason for the discomfort will come to light by
and by.

The critical point is that German was my first language and that I
went to a German-speaking Montessori kindergarten, and then
completed the first grade in Vienna, before the parents returned to
Zlín. There, my schooling and the total ambience of life were Czech.
When my parents, in an effort to prevent my forgetting the language,
spoke to me in German, I invariably and pointedly replied in Czech.
We shall see why.

Another linguistic shift soon occurred, however. After
completing public school, I entered a secondary institution where the
prescribed Czechoslovak high school curriculum was offered largely
in one of French, English or German. Some subjects — Czech
grammar, literature, geography, history and crafts for some arcane
reason — were taught in Czech but all else, in my case, in English.
After completing the required three years, at age 13, I was sent to
boarding school in England. My sojourn there was rudely
interrupted by two near-cataclysmic events, to be revealed anon.
What mattered on the accent front was that in 1939 I joined my
parents, who had moved to Casablanca; then, a year or so later, I
accompanied them to Haiti. My schooling, consequently, continued
in French until 1942, when I came to Canada and reverted to English.

All this to-ing and fro-ing inevitably affected the linguistic
baggage I brought with me when I arrived from steaming Haiti in
frigid Toronto, congealed in a –20°C cold snap. The climate shock
induced a very high fever, apparently prompted by my having
acquired malaria while in the tropics. I cannot, alas, remember in
which language I hallucinated. The other latent and unwitting of my
imports was the sort of accent a teenager would acquire while
immersed in an English public school, tinged by a German base, and
adorned by Czech overtones imposed by the most important and
formative of his languages. My immediately preceding two years of
French education, while handily equipping me for the newly
unfolding life in Canada, left only trace elements, I suspect, on the
idiosyncratic treatment I bestowed on prevailing canons of
pronunciation. The result is that while everyone hearing me knows
at once that I am not native born, no one can quite identify the
flavour, other than that it is European. But, as I admitted, my inner

ear is quite impervious to all that. To me, I sound like a Canadian, born and bred.

In pecking out this confession about my ambiguous voice, I realized that the cosmopolitan layers providing the ground coat of my Canadian speech are probably much more significant than I knew. Speech defines the man. The foregoing gloss about the evolution of my speech is an hors d'oeuvre, easing the reader into the meatier fare of how I came to Canada. Why did I become a Canadian and not the citizen of some other haven or, infinitely worse, yet another Holocaust statistic?

Originally, when gearing up to deliver myself of this book, I meant to dispatch the story of my life lightly and in passing. The focus was to be Canadian folkways, issues, institutions and events, tackled within the perspectives of my experiences with them. This intention was inspired by an observation made in *his* memoir by my great mentor, J.A. Corry, "...Narcissus, gazing in fascination at his image in the pool, was underemployed."

A great many of my friends, and even mere acquaintances, have persuaded me otherwise. They have found sufficiently intriguing the oral autobiographical scraps I would from time to time toss off, to press for a coherent record of the whole story. Honest, they really have, and still do!

Some confessors pretend that they are reluctant scribes, dragged towards reminiscence and the computer by an acute sense of duty and a clamouring, thirsty public. I cannot make this claim (I am loving the exercise no end so far) and am unaware of a raucous *public* clamour — possibly, I tell myself, because I am a bit deaf. Still, quite a few pals have gently suggested that they can wait for the wise reflections on Canada's triumphs and travails elicited by my career, but that they would like to see the personal stuff. So I have resolved to do both — a very Canadian solution, you may say. The intended short bio is hence longer than planned, and the musings about the country more marginal.

Part I starts in Vienna and shows how I made my way — or, more precisely, was carried by events — from the banks of the Danube ultimately to the shores of the St. Lawrence, the locale and base of so much of my life. Way stations on three continents will detain us en route as well as a few incidents and events affecting the passage. From Vienna we'll move to Zlín. Thereafter these will be some of the subjects claiming our attention: an early pedagogic sojourn in Britain; taking the waters in Vichy; first steps as a fourteen-year-old man of the world in an adventure, à la Somerset Maugham, on board a P & O Liner en route from London to Tangiers; a lengthy and perilous bout with an awful illness; the casbah in Casablanca, prompting an emotion-laden evocation of Rick's Bar; a hair-raising flight from Tangiers to Lisbon; a transatlantic crossing on *Cabo de Hornos*, while it was conveying, sardine-like, refugees from Europe to America; a relatively short sleepover in a Panamanian prison; attending school in Port-au-Prince; reaching North America at Baltimore, on board a Standard Fruit banana boat: and "much more," to adopt huckster talk. Finally, we shall enter Canada uncharacteristically by train at Fort Erie, to begin the translation of a much-buffeted Czech boy into a grizzled Canuck.

Part II sees me plunge into education, first as a schoolboy and student, then as a junior and, eventually, as a qualified university instructor. I begin, in a Quaker-inspired boarding school, with dreams of pursuing a career as a fruit farmer. But my romantic intention falls prey to the realistic counsel of the headmaster, who senses that I might be better suited to the groves of academe than to apple or pear groves. He also cleanses me of a visceral phobia of everything German. I then obtain a prof's qualifying papers at the University of Toronto and Britain's London School of Economics (LSE). A brief engagement, during this period, as the lowliest of low ranking junior instructors at Queen's gets me hooked on university life.

Upon entering Part III, we undergo a sea change as we move from the chronological personal mode to my professional life: teaching, researching and writing, performing myriads of related tasks (The Third Pillar), including a serious engagement as a regulator when I served as Chairman of the Canadian Radio-Television Telecommunications Commission (CRTC: The Human Side of Czardom), and finally some memorable engagements outside Canada (Foreign Affairs). Purely academic concerns imperceptibly spill into the policy area.

PART I: Departures and Arrivals

I

Vienna

It was really Karl Meisel's doing that the place I first set foot on in this world, so to speak, was Vienna. My grandfather had a fruit-importing and jam-making business, operating both in Zlín and the Austrian capital, and Tati worked for him in Vienna for a while after the First World War. His job required frequent trips to Serbia, where he bought plums for grandfather's *Powidl* (*povidla* in Czech), a jam much favoured in central Europe. One of the benefits of these trips was that they cured him of smoking. The Serbs he dealt with were a friendly lot and kept offering him cigarettes which they deftly rolled with the fingers of one hand. To make the paper stick they spit on it and then "glued" the two sides together. The only inoffensive way Tati could think of for turning down the unsavoury weeds was to say he did not smoke. So he didn't and never resumed the habit.

According to vague, never amplified remarks by my parents, the relations between father and son were often difficult, and Tati left the Meisel firm to become the general manager of an Austrian bank. I never knew much about the details of his work at that time but do recall two salient aspects which affect our story. The bank job must have been a good one, for he had the use of a car and a chauffeur and could afford to build a lovely villa with a huge garden in Döbling, an attractive residential part of the city. But there also was a downside, as I was told when I was older: the bank went bankrupt, as did innumerable other firms during the Depression, which led to the parents' return to Zlín. I believe that its demise was related to the fatal misfortunes of the Rumanian oil industry which, according to comments I overheard, also cost my father a pretty penny.

While growing up in Zlín, Tati was a classmate of Tomáš Baťa, whose family had been shoemakers for generations. Tomáš was a genius who phenomenally raised the scope and scale of the family trade. The Baťa Shoe Company ultimately grew into the largest multinational shoe manufacturer in the world. For many years after the German takeover of Czechoslovakia, its headquarters were in Toronto and Zurich. My father joined his former classmate's enterprise during the War in a senior managerial position, before moving to Vienna. Ten years later, after the Austrian bank fiasco, he rejoined the company in Zlín, becoming the Export Manager. This must have been about 1929.

But I am getting ahead of myself. The menu for this chapter is my life's beginning in the city of Sachertorte, *Schlag* (Austrian slang for whipped cream), the incomparable Philharmonic and Strauss waltzes. I was, given my age, largely oblivious of these and other allurements. Tati, Mami and my sister Rose, our garden, some of the parents' friends and relatives, our maid Dolfi and her husband Polo (who was also our part-time gardener) and eventually kindergarten and my first year of school — these loomed largest on my horizon.

The earliest event I recall from the Viennese beginnings is, in a sense, my first encounter with freedom. It gave rise to a gentle shower of vivid impressions and emotions which left an undying mark. I cannot pinpoint my age at the time, but must have been four or five. It was the first time I was allowed to skip my afternoon nap; instead, I was bundled off into the garden. On that autumn day, moist I think, I exuberantly waded through mounds of leaves exuding a powerful, pleasing perfume. I can still smell it and, when strolling or hiking in the fall, am occasionally reminded of it and that exhilarating afternoon so long ago. This is the first episode I recall of a smell intensely evoking the memory of an experience, person or happening. When I became infatuated with Proust, many years later, and read of the importance he attached to young Marcel's reliving the taste of the famous little *madeleine* he ate with his mother, and the emotions evoked by this seemingly trivial interlude, I knew and felt exactly what he was talking about. And I realized that not only taste but also smell enables us to relive privileged moments in our lives. I now understand that there are physiological reasons for this.

Long after voicing the speculation that one's disposition may be inherited, I came across a fascinating discovery of some British scientists, reported in one of my favourite newspapers, the *Neue Zürcher Zeitung*, in the spring of 2010. Whether one sees a glass of water half full or half empty depends on a gene, 5-HTTLPR. It affects serotonin, a neurotransmitter known to contribute to feelings of well-being. Only 97 subjects participated in the experiment but, following my temperament, I am inclined to believe that the findings point in the right direction. Irrespective of the genetic link, however, I am certain that the upbeat nature of my make-up has a lot to do with the circumstances of my childhood, starting in Vienna and then shifting to Zlín and, ultimately, to an English school.

Another reason I found that autumnal afternoon so memorable is that, at some point, I surprised a little creature with a cute pointed snout who, when it spied me, rolled itself into a prickly ball. My first hedgehog. They are nocturnal and this fellow had no business — like me, perhaps — being awake. I do not remember what followed but was told that I ran into the house in a state of high excitement, and announced that there was a sweet animal outside, wearing a hood (an early hoodie?). I still acutely recall how absolutely delighted I was by this apparition. Ever since, I have harboured a special affection for hedgehogs, badgers and similar creatures, even the much larger Canadian groundhog and its western and mountain cousins. No doubt various British children's books, delightfully (and, alas, anthropocentrically) humanizing this menagerie, have augmented my affection for it.

Ever since coming across Erich Fromm's *Escape From Freedom*, I have been aware of freedom being both a blessing and a burden. It liberates but also imposes the often onerous necessity of making choices. On that leaf-drenched afternoon, however, although I could not have realized the implications of my feelings, I felt exceptionally happy about not having to go to lie down after lunch and being allowed, instead, into the garden. I now *know* that the removal of a constraint and the opening up of unanticipated opportunities (the hedgehog?) induced in me feelings of excitement and extraordinary happiness.

This afternoon represents an unusual high — a moment of singular exhilaration and bliss — and its uniqueness grew out of the intensity and degree of my reactions. I was normally a most happy and sunny child. There were, naturally, anxieties inevitable in the process of growing up, perhaps particularly in a household where the children were subjected to pretty strict discipline. But overall I greatly enjoyed life — even during a later phase when I suffered considerable discomfort and pain. It is also likely that, being blessed with a positive disposition, I have over the years forgotten much of the bad and retained more of the good, a characteristic I still exhibit, sometimes to the irritation of my less sanguine friends. In short, all my life I have been blessed with the happiest of temperaments.

My immediate family was extremely close. I do not recall any hostility between Tati and Mami. If there was any — and, marital squabbles being unavoidable, occasional disagreements seem likely—my sister and I were shielded from such events. But I do remember incidents attesting to the loving relationship between the parents. Two stand out: Mami, who was manually dexterous, painstakingly making charming Plasticine or marzipan mini sculptures for Tati on special occasions, such as his birthday or his return from a long trip; and Tati, when the season allowed it, daily greeting Mami at the breakfast table with a rosebud he fetched from our garden. We regularly saw the grandparents, various aunts and uncles, cousins and a few friends, but the ties among the four-part nuclear family were much more important. This was enhanced colossally after the outbreak of the Second World War, when the four of us followed a roundabout trajectory from Europe to Canada.

As Rose was four years my senior, we enjoyed few shared interests or activities during those early years. We got along well, and she was usually kind and helpful to her little brother, but we were not particularly close during my early childhood. The bonds grew tighter later, particularly during the family's emigration. Both of us were extraordinarily well behaved. Mami insisted on a rigid code of exemplary behaviour. Corporal punishment was rare; I remember being spanked (Tati's unenviable task) only once. I may be idealizing the situation a bit and must admit that while Rose was an exemplary child, her brother was a bit livelier and hence more prone to land in trouble. But this occurred seldom.

Members of families were expected to love one another, and so we did. But we really did feel strong emotional attachments. And why not? The parents, from all accounts, were kind, fine upright people, widely liked and respected. We enjoyed the amenities of a very comfortable, middle-class existence, including plenty of attractive space indoors and out and very congenial servants.

Among the latter, two stood out and rivalled the parents in my heart. Dolfi, the general maid was nearly as dear to me as Mami. It was Mami who brought us up, but Dolfi's role was in part that of a nanny. After we left Vienna, when I went to visit from Zlín, it was Dolfi and Polo I stayed with, rather than relatives. Polo's full-time job was that of gardener for the City of Vienna, where he was member of a radical union. He was either a Communist or Socialist, but certainly "Red." His and Dolfi's apartment later fell victim to the infamous cannonade which "Black" Chancellor Dolfuss ordered against subsidized workers' flats in Vienna.

I loved the outdoors, the garden, and Polo. The proud possessor of miniature tools, I was under the impression that I helped him in his work, although there were moments of play as well. I remember being given a ride in his *putna,* a wooden, tubular, shoulder-carried container used for spreading manure. I recall a particularly thorough bath afterwards but do not remember any recrimination from the parents for the somewhat odorous aura I must have exuded upon returning to the house. Polo and I talked an awful lot as we "worked," and he became a close confidant.

One of our conversations still sticks in my mind, almost certainly because the parents were sufficiently amused by it to repeat it to friends. Starting school was a terrible bind for me, partly because it interfered with the gardening and the loving company of Mami and Dolfi. After the first few school days, Polo asked how I liked it. "I am going to resign from this club," is as closely as I can translate the reported response.

Polo was also quite special because he had an amazing skill which provided Rose and me with one of the most cherished moments of the week. He knew how to read the invisible print he insisted is present between the lines in each newspaper, but is hidden from the untrained eye.

Cooling off in the garden in Vienna with Mami and Rose.

So, after our Sunday bath (only thorough ablutions were in order on weekdays), Polo would come to the nursery, newspaper in hand, and would "read" the most wonderful stories, week after week. Compared to the usual children's classics and other fare read to us on weekdays (which we loved, to be sure), Polo's offerings were as the pungent lines of Dylan Thomas are to the egregious poesy of William McGonagall.

I may have devoted too much space to Dolfi and Polo, but they were so much loved and so important that they earned it. Indeed, they serve to highlight an important feature of our childhood. The parents were true egalitarians. Although the then usual forms of address between employer and servant prevailed in our house, the parents, by example, saw to it that we accorded exactly the same respect and civility to our staff as to all adults, including relatives and friends of whatever status. This was not articulated in any special way but was simply assumed to be the normal custom followed by the parents, and so also by us.

In my fifth or sixth year, I attended a Montessori kindergarten, which I adored. Despite having had relatively few contacts with other children until then, I was neither intimidated nor delighted by this exposure to other kids, and I liked the "Aunt" who ran the show and rewarded good behaviour with delicious junk candies. This was likely anathema to strict Montessori principles but did not, insofar as I can tell, permanently demolish my character. I learnt a lot more about the Montessori method later, when Rose took a course in London from Mme. Montessori herself, assisted by her son.

As my exchange with Polo about my reaction to school shows, this rather idyllic pre-school exposure to semi-formal education, which was really play outside the home, came to an abrupt and unwelcome end when I entered the first grade of school. A big part of my problem was that Rose had preceded me in the same school and established the reputation of an exemplary pupil both in terms of academics and comportment. The teacher thought the world of her and found her brother less appealing, no doubt for good reason. She was honest enough not to hide this.

In her I first encountered someone who did not exude love, or at least neutrality, but rather an austere distance. The chemistry between us, as we say nowadays, was not joyous — a situation likely exacerbated by my having not yet learnt the rules of Austrian school decorum. Informed by the deep psychological insight purveyed by *The Reader's Digest* and family journals available at supermarket checkout counters, I now suspect that I may have had a light case of ADHD — attention deficit hyperactivity disorder. At least, a faux pas I committed on one of my first days of school points to this diagnosis. I saw a bird or some other intriguing object fly past the classroom and so naturally got up from my desk and approached the window to get a better look. This spontaneous gesture, no doubt triggered by an early urge to make a scientific observation, was not welcomed by Frau Overbeck, the teacher. She let me know that no one got up without her permission and that my sister would never lapse into such unacceptable behaviour. This sort of invidious comparison became a fairly common feature of my first grade experience. The bird episode was of sufficient gravity that my mother was informed of my dereliction. My irritating curiosity did not lead to the case being reported to the school doctor or nurse (there wasn't one) or land me on a psychiatrist's couch. Ritalin was still unheard of. The problem was resolved by my learning that one had to display a certain degree of self-discipline. Done!

Although I learnt how to behave in school, and was a reasonably good student, I never approached Rose's exceptionally high academic performance. We never again, in fact, went to the same schools. But, as we saw, trouble in the Rumanian oil fields indirectly freed me of the prolonged exposure to this dour teacher. I learnt my lesson; either the regime in Zlín was less strict or my future teachers were more relaxed. Whatever the cause, I had an easier time in school after Vienna.

II

Maturing in Zlín

My still-smouldering disappointment over lack of rapport with Frau Overbeck has trapped me into giving you a distorted impression. Despite the one darkish cloud, which may, uncharacteristically, have thickened and aggrandized in the mind as time elapsed, I was very happy in Vienna and even liked some parts of school.

The location of our new home differed dramatically from the cosmopolitan ambience of the old Austrian capital. Zlín, for centuries a sleepy provincial Moravian town, was being transformed before our eyes into the ever less important appendage of a colossal industrial complex. The Baťa concern played a major part in all aspects of life, from the dominant architecture of the new parts of town, to health services, entertainment, dominant mores and even schools and municipal politics. In contrast to the pattern evident in North America, and now also in parts of Europe, the old buildings and streetscapes were left largely undisturbed, and the new was placed in adjacent land. While the ever-growing Baťa facilities, built in their characteristic red brick, modular style, kept getting bigger and bigger, the old core remained more or less intact. Alas, after the war the Communists plunked into the middle of the old square a massive, jarring building in the overbearing and gloomy design characteristic and representative of Stalinism.

Another difference between Vienna and Zlín affected me. The possible impact of this only occurred to me as I was assembling the memory castle in your hands. It brings us disquietingly close to psycho-history—a form of inquiry I view with both fascination and skepticism. Our Viennese villa was enclosed by a high wire-mesh fence. At quite some distance from the house, there were two gates: one, rarely used, for cars; the other for pedestrians and cyclists. The smaller entrance could be opened electrically from the kitchen, outside of which there was a mirror so placed that it permitted seeing the distant entrance. It was the cook, Resi, who controlled this access to the house. The complicated arrangement resulted in my feeling when at home that I was screened on all sides by some sort of enclosure. I never thought that danger was lurking outside or felt I was locked in, but nevertheless sensed being separated from the world beyond. I was in a cocoon.

In Zlín, everything was open. The company-owned residences were usually demarcated by two wires, one above the other, which could be tightened by means of a spool. I loved playing with it. These only suggestive fences encouraged crossing rather than stopping, and bestowed the sense that one was a part of a larger community.

Am I being altogether too fanciful when I allow this Vienna/Zlín divergence to remind me of one strand in the literature on Canadian identity? Did I, when in our Austrian house, experience a smidgen of the garrison mentality ascribed by some cultural historians to our Canadian forefathers? Is it too farfetched to be reminded in this context of one of Northrop Frye's suggestive insights? In *The Bush Garden*, he argued that an important element in the formation of the Canadian mind has been the absence of any frontier, except to the South of us. And even it, in his day, was slender. There is only seemingly unlimited space stretching north, west and east with no obstacles in the way. This, he thought, created a distinguishing mental map among Canadians, affecting our national character. I have, of course, perpetrated a cruelly simplified summary of Frye's more nuanced observation. It struck me, however, as I was musing over the relocation to Zlín, that as an *individual* my mental state may have been affected by the physical opening up of space and the abandonment of a somewhat cloistered ambience and life. Our house was ever so much more integrated into the neighbourhood than the Viennese villa.

The facade of a house on the square in the centre of Zlín boldly announced to one and all that it was the site of grandfather's jam business. Having the name MEISEL emblazoned in such a public way drove home that I was now living where we had roots, and where many people were familiar with the family name and some of its members. This was a far cry from the anonymity bestowed by the metropolis on the Danube — not that anonymity robbed me of much sleep during my first six years, or later for that matter.

It did not take me long to realize that I had to watch my step. For I shared not only a name, but also a striking resemblance with my father, despite the age difference. The first time I was made aware of this was when my pals and I were reducing an orchard keeper's workload by helping ourselves to an apple or two. He happened to come along at the wrong time and was not delighted by our assistance. To my great distress, he announced that he recognized me and would in the evening report my criminal activity to Frýda — as my father was known to his friends and many Zlínites. He did, and I was given a lesson about private property.

This starching of my moral fibre was, in effect, unnecessary. There was, in the current, ugly phrase, zero tolerance for even the slightest lapses. Rose and I were brought up to embrace and practice the most rigid canons of honesty. Even the whitest of white lies were infra dig. Once, while still in Vienna, I came across a chewed pencil stub on the street and made a fuss because Dolfi did not try to find its owner. So the orchard raid presented a horrible dilemma for me. My gang, with whom I spent most of my play and sports time, and who were the essence of my extra-familial life, launched this caper, and I was caught in the squeeze between moral precepts and peer pressure, as well as the intense desire to be accepted by my friends. This was perhaps my first encounter with *realpolitik*.

Zlín was a great place for us kids, partly because we were a privileged lot. It was, as I indicated, something of a company town, but not at all in the same way as many one-industry dominated locations in Canada. The Bat'a company developed diverse extensive areas. Some were residential, some industrial and commercial, whereas others provided various facilities — a cinema, hospital, a hotel, a department store and a museum. There was, needless to say, a splendid shoe shop.

The advent of so many employees, and the wish to attract and keep a satisfied and efficient work force, as well — no doubt — as an active social conscience, prompted the company to build attractive and comfortable rental homes for everyone. Many recruits came from surrounding farm areas which were far from opulent. The quality of the dwellings was, consequently, far above that to which many newcomers had been accustomed. But even the pronounced egalitarian outlook of Tomáš Bat'a did not lead to the provision of uniform accommodation for everyone. We are, after all, going back to the 1920s and '30s — a much less equitable age than the twenty-first century. There were multiple unit dwellings, duplexes and single-family homes of varying size, although the differences between them were moderate.

When we moved from Vienna, the house provided had to be adapted a bit from the usual design of the senior executive homes so as to accommodate the parents' furniture, including Mami's baby grand piano. It was therefore brand new, and situated at a corner lot in *Nad Ovčírnou* ("Above the sheep pen"), a pleasant neighbourhood of managers' families, on an incline overlooking much of the huge, attractive factory area.

Clowning in Zlín, circa 1934.

Nad Ovčírnou also overlooked a section of town housing the *Internáty* — large, several-storied residences for single apprentices, of whom there were hundreds. The buildings, faintly resembling benign and friendly barracks, and their grounds provided extensive sports facilities which, on working days, were available to the boys in the neighbourhood. So we had lavish recreational opportunities. These were supplemented by the billiard/ping-pong room in the nearby ten-storey company hotel — our own skyscraper — that towered over all other buildings. We had no interest in playing pool (and likely would not have been welcome at the tables), but were dead serious about ping-pong. It became one of my favourite games. To top off all this manna from heaven (or the company), our neighbours, the Čiperas, (he was the company's General Manager) had two boys roughly my age and a tennis court, which also doubled as a skating rink and hockey pad in winter.

No wonder, in light of all these recreational opportunities, that my parents had trouble making a reader of me. I became one later, after an illness restricted my sports. Until then, while I was not quite a boy jock—other things did interest me—life with a troop of neighbourhood cronies, much of which occurred out of doors, filled most of my free time. And then, of course, after the first summer in Zlín, there was school.

Public school in Czechoslovakia took five years. On the basis of my start in Vienna, I was allowed to enter the second grade, which posed no serious problems. Nor did the switch to Czech. No one compared me to my sister and although I was not a brilliant scholar, I managed to sail through the work without a hitch, with only one exception—Art or "Drawing" as it was called! In that subject I received a passing but low grade. My parents promptly put me in the hands of a drawing tutor whose task it was to pull up my graphic socks. He succeeded in improving my mark but not my skill. Later I became a passionate amateur of the plastic arts. "Amateur" in the sense given by the *Canadian Oxford Dictionary* as "a person who is fond of (a thing)." Sketchbooks are wasted on me; my only hobby in this general area is a lifelong involvement in photography.

Central European schools were rigid, strict and excellent. The government in Prague (and not the "provincial" Moravian authorities) prescribed the curriculum in detail; standards and content of courses were uniform throughout the land. So far as I remember, there was no local school board. Teachers were employees of the Czechoslovak state. This structural context, as well as the inevitably lingering traditions of the defunct Austro-Hungarian Empire, imposed on school life a formality and rigidity reminiscent of Vienna, which differed substantially from my later experiences in British and Canadian schools.

Music, art, crafts and gym were an integral part of the program and every bit as important as the academic subjects. We did an hour or so a week of gymnastics and played soccer, ice hockey (weather permitting) and the English brand of handball. No one ever changed clothes for the athletic program. We just wore our ordinary outfits. Before, during and after. Since deodorants were unknown to us, we must have exuded a powerful aroma after these exertions.

While public school was pleasant enough (sweaty children notwithstanding), it was not as much fun as my subsequent schooling. There were moments of levity, as when lice invaded some folks' hair. All the girls were subjected to boyish brush cuts and we fellows received shaved heads. There were also slightly terrifying scenes, however. One of our teachers, habitually gloomy, must have suffered from melancholia. Once, while talking of the likelihood of another war, she informed us that at least half the boys in the class would eventually be killed in it.

Relations between pupils and teachers were formal but friendly. I remember chatting quite often with Mr. Horák, the principal, because we walked to school along the same route. No one was ever driven or bused. He knew Tati—they may have been schoolmates— and on one occasion he indiscreetly shared one of our exchanges with him. The Baťa company had a factory and many stores in India and had similar undertakings in numerous other countries in the Middle East, Africa and Asia. My father was deeply involved in these enterprises. In the early 1930s, Tomáš Baťa, accompanied by Tati, flew to India and beyond in a twin-engine company Fokker, making numerous business stops along the way. Such initiative was unheard of at the time, and of considerable interest to the Czech public gripped by the vicissitudes of the Depression. Accordingly, the Czech press regularly reported the progress of the journey. Everyone knew about it.

On one of our talks on the way to school, Mr. Horák asked me what I would like Tati to bring me from India. This question had never occurred to me, but I did not wish to appear flat-footed. "A small elephant," first popped into my head, obviously not quite considering the mammoth problems such a pet would cause. Anyway, this response greatly amused the principal who, upon his return, regaled Tati with it.

Architecturally, most Zlín schools shared the style favoured by the company. It had developed a building technology, relying on uniform reinforced concrete parts which were poured into forms and used in all large Baťa construction. The walls were of red brick with plenty of windows. Although the particular design of each edifice varied somewhat, in relation to its function, there was a certain uniformity giving the town its characteristic airy, light and pleasant look. The process was amazingly efficient. Any floor of a large factory building, hotel, hospital, *internát* (apprentices' residence) or *škola* (school) could be erected in one week and the interchangeable metal moulds were transported easily and used over and over again. Several schools, designed in this matching style but diverse in shape, were grouped together into the school quarter with some common sports facilities and an *aula* (great hall) for formal shared events. The centrepiece was the Masaryk Secondary School. My memory may be playing one of its occasional pranks here but I recall it taking about fifteen or twenty minutes to get to school from home — a little longer returning because it was uphill. When I finished public school (the idea of any sort of commencement celebration to mark this milepebble was utterly unthinkable) and returned after the holidays, it was, geographically, only a short step from the old to the new school. But as a leap towards a new life, it was colossal. This was not primarily because high school was more advanced than the first five years, but because of the kind of school it was.

Zlín. The Masaryk High School dominates the school quarter, including my foreign language academy behind it.

Baťa spanned the world. The firm's far-flung operations required personnel fluent in many languages, and certainly the international tongues of commerce. So Zlín boasted not only the large Czech High School, which dominated the pedagogical quarter, but also the *Cizojazyčná Škola Města Zlína* — the Foreign Language School of the Town of Zlín. Since its curriculum was taught in three streams — English, French or German, the teachers were cosmopolitan. In addition to the Czechs proficient in one of the privileged tongues or responsible for "Czech subjects" — language and literature, history and geography — there were instructors from lands or areas where the three main school languages were spoken: Czech- and German-speaking citizens of Czechoslovakia (but no Slovaks, I believe); some francophones, likely from France, Switzerland or Belgium; and two Brits, Mr. Gibbs and Mr. Grubb.

Paní Sedláková (*Paní* is Mrs. in Czech—I no longer remember her first name and Paní Sedláková was what we called her) taught Czech grammar (a formidable challenge, given the complexity of the language) and also literature. She combined two, not always reconcilable, traits: she was a communist and a Czech nationalist. Her outlook which, without proselytizing, she in no way concealed, made her teaching always socially conscious and responsible. And her love of Czech poetry and prose was infectious. Although she instilled in us an appreciation of the works studied (along with their failings), she was not content to let the matter rest there. Literature, being the product of the historical and social ambience of its time, reflects the lives that created it. The early teenagers in her hands learnt to share the experiences, challenges and traditions of their ancestors and their society through the eyes of enduring poets and prose-smiths. By sharing with us her social concerns, and her love of our country, she reinforced, through her highly respected office and authority, sentiments echoing some of Tati's inclinations. She helped make me a patriot.

To find instructors thoroughly at home in English, the school authorities advertised in the London *Times* for teachers, willing to ply their craft in what Neville Chamberlain, after he betrayed us, referred to as "Czechoslovakia—a far-off country of which we know little." The response must have come largely from adventurous, recent graduates of Oxford—at least these were the kind of people engaged by the school authorities.

The parents occasionally invited some of our teachers for dinner; I remember both Englishmen and Paní Sedláková being guests— occasions I always enjoyed a lot. Rose met Mr. Gibbs at one of the dinners and they dated from time to time when she was in Zlín. I approved (not that anyone asked me) because it enhanced, so I thought, the pupil's capacity to reconnoitre the thinking on the other side of the divide. It appears that I was not above making comments in class which revealed to Mr. Gibbs (but no one else) that I was aware of his having been on a date with my sister. I might, for example, have said that a particular project was late because I needed my sister's assistance for it but she was nowhere to be found. Since Rose must have been sixteen at most, at the time, these trysts were no doubt of the most innocent kind (remember, this was 1935 or 1906), but my oly digs were always reported to Rose and then relayed to the culprit.

John Grubb was a highly creative, free-wheeling and imaginative son of a Church of England bishop. Since none of the subjects taught according to the official curriculum had appropriate textbooks in English, he produced ours more or less from day to day, by writing and then running off copies on the Ditto machine. The Dittoing was a cumbersome process involving the laborious brushing and cleaning of previously used, metal-covered master blanks which were re-used over and over again. John Grubb allowed some of us to assist by cleaning the blanks and cranking out the required copies. I was lucky to have been included among his helpers because it gave me the opportunity to get to know him well.

The Czech school system was typical of those prevailing in central Europe at the time: authoritarian, strict, academically impeccable. There was not much fun except for the pleasure we derived from the study of the prescribed subjects and a couple of hours of music and gym a week. John Grubb, while no slouch in the upper storey, and serious about his academic responsibilities, was decidedly fun. Blessed with a straight-faced but potent sense of humour, he managed to bestow on his teaching a strong element of joy and relaxation. In addition, he allowed his irreverent nature to peek through. This resulted in many of his charges developing, on their parts, a capacity to scoff a bit at the rigidity and formality permeating the school. It is hard for a twenty-first century North American to imagine the awe and respect for authority instilled in my generation of central Europeans by the educational system. John Grubb managed to crack that shell and so launch us on a course of less shackled development. Ironically, as we shall see, in this way he unwittingly enhanced some of the philosophical goals underpinning the values of the young Czechoslovak democracy. Or perhaps it was not unwitting at all.

But from the personal point of view, the most telling contribution to my *épanouissement* resulted from his casual suggestion that I write a book. I was twelve at the time and flabbergasted by this audacious idea. Only famous and respected sages did this sort of thing, not mere schoolboys. I cannot remember whether the subject chosen was his or mine (probably the former), but it was one that offered free rein to the author's imagination: life on Mars. I started this project, and got part way into it, before other concerns led to its avowed suspension but actual abandonment. Despite the aborted outcome of this enterprise, I derived immense benefit from it. That anyone should think that I could pen a book was explosive and the act of writing something completely "out of my head," liberating. I am experiencing the same sense of welcome freedom as I key these memory-based recollections. At any rate, John Grubb's Mars project, though incomplete, began a lifelong habit of scribbling, one which has provided me with immense enjoyment and satisfaction.

One example of the Grubb wit and spirit also portrays the political climate in the school. Our classrooms had an internal window facing the corridor from which one gained entry. It made a showcase, visible from inside and outside the class, in which the pupils' work was normally displayed. As the class teacher, Mr. Grubb was responsible for its content. Part of his tenure in Zlín coincided with the Spanish Civil War between the leftist government and the Fascist rebels. Our English section of the school and its British teachers (and likely all of the Czechs, as well) sympathized with the government and abhorred the right-wing forces wishing to topple it. The same held for the French stream. But the German faculty, composed of Sudeten Germans, i.e., Czechoslovak citizens from the German speaking parts of the country, tended to sympathize with the uprising, which was supported by the Nazis and Hitler's Reich. The head of the school's German section was one of them. His class faced ours and he often examined our exhibits with dour distaste, possibly because he lacked a sense of humour and because there was no love lost between him and our John Grubb. He was utterly bamboozled by the window confronting him one day after the Spanish Fascists lost an important battle with the government forces.

The window was empty except for four items: a collection of Spanish coins surrounding some nuts, followed by the numeral 2, and a capital U. Herr X (Dr. Freud has made me forget his name) took a few days to decipher the pictogram and particularly to figure out its English slang. When he did discover "nuts to you," he was anything but amused, as we learnt from our spies. We, of course, basked in our superior knowledge of English, and the (regrettably short-lived) defeat of the Spanish Fascists.

Although we were only school children, we were deeply conscious of the international crises threatening peace and the integrity of Czechoslovakia. Hitler had come to power in 1933, the Fascists were in ascendancy in Spain and Italy, and the League of Nations, which was popular in our country, was less and less capable of living up to the high expectations the world had of it. Politics was in the air, and our teachers in various classes — history, geography, Czech literature — made us politically aware to a degree undreamt of in North America at the time, or even today.

The lore presented to us on the history of Czechoslovakia accepted, as a given, that the Protestant Czechs remained a subject people until their liberation in 1918. They had been defeated in the Battle of the White Mountain in 1620 by an alliance of the Holy Roman Empire, the Catholic League and Spain, and then annexed by Austria. The three hundred years of governance from Vienna were marked, we learnt, by more or less forced Germanization and conversion to Catholicism. As a result, the Czech language and the Protestant population had practically disappeared from the towns and cities, until both were reinvigorated by the nationalist revival in the nineteenth century.

Whatever the subtleties of the case, what I heard in school convinced me that the Austrian experience had been harmful to Czechs and that in a sense we were, or had been, enemies. The dissonance between the two nations was exacerbated by the particular legacy of the Hapsburg Empire with all its imperial trappings: an aristocracy, court, titles, orders and suitable "refined" manners. The Czechoslovak republic — greatly influenced by Masaryk who, like a later successor, Václav Havel — enormously affected prevailing thought and championed democratic and egalitarian ways, was much less elitist.

The differences between the legacy of Austria's imperial past and the succession Czechoslovak republic can easily be exaggerated. But even today it is visible when Vienna and Prague are compared. Both are magnificent, but the city on the Danube is "grand"; its history as the proud centre of a powerful dominion is evident in its broad avenues, massive monuments, huge palaces, and street names recalling ancient battles and victories. Prague, on the other hand, even with the huge Hradčany Castle towering over everything, is informal, intimate, bourgeois, and down to earth. The opulence, dripping privilege, and class nature of the famous annual Viennese Opera Ball, still a going concern, widely and vicariously enjoyed on television, are unthinkable in Prague.

A vignette says it all. It was the custom, in the old days before the birth of the Republic, for well brought up gentlemen to kiss a lady's hand, to refer to people by title, and to call middle and upper class women *Gnädige Frau* (gracious lady). After 1918, these practices largely continued in Austria but there was no doubt whatsoever that, in the new Republic's ethos, there was no place for them. Our teachers made sure that we learnt that in a democratic society, all citizens are equal. To say *Ruku líbám milostivá Paní* (I kiss your hand, gracious lady) was unacceptable. People were to be called by name, not some sort of rank or occupational moniker. And kissing a hand is obsequious, old-fashioned and, what's more, unsanitary. So there!

Austria, and particularly Vienna, and what they stood for, were thus to be, if not despised, then at least censured and avoided. This cast an awful pall over me, since I was suffering the indignity of coming from there. Usually I have no trouble reconstructing an experience in words, but I must admit defeat when it comes to describing the shame and embarrassment my birthplace caused me. They were overwhelming. I would do almost anything except lying—that was never an option—to conceal my horrible provenance. Despite having relatives there, including my grandparents, uncles, aunts, nieces and nephews, I only returned twice or three times before I grew up, in part to see Dolfi and Polo. They, being pretty far on the political Left, were not tainted by Austria's imperial past. I knew that, even at a tender age.

Increasingly, after Hitler's advent to power in 1933, anti-Austrian and anti-Hapsburg feelings were matched by anti-German sentiment. Czechs and Germans had rarely, collectively, been great buddies, but the expansionist gestures and threats of the Third Reich, as well as the antithesis between Nazism and Masaryk's liberal democracy, greatly exacerbated distrust and hostility. Resentment of Austria was joined and ultimately exceeded by hatred of everything German. In the end, Austria and Germany were lumped in the same bag as enemies of Czechoslovaks. After all, they spoke the same language and after the 1938 *Anschluss*—Germany's annexation of Austria—they became, effectively, one country. The fact that so many Austrians had welcomed the German Nazis and their ways made this oversimplification plausible and palatable.

So, the Zlín years made me, on the one hand, quite anti-Austrian and viscerally anti-German. That subsequently Germany, supported by the overwhelming majority of Sudeten German, dismembered Czechoslovakia, persecuted patriotic Czechs, plunged the world into a bloody war, and behaved with unspeakable brutality to Jews and others, further inflamed the hatred. It was only much later in a Canadian school that I learnt how to manage the feelings spawned by all that and how to place Nazism, Austria and Germany into a rational context.

Life in Zlín by no means fostered only negative attitudes. It also brought important life-guiding positive consequences. Czechoslovakia, more than any other Austro-Hungarian succession state, abolished many of the unpopular practices associated with the former Empire — autocracy, bureaucratic chicanery, pronounced class distinctions. This goal was somehow transmitted through the educational system. Consequently, one of the most significant benefits of the Zlín years was that they drilled into our heads the virtues of a tolerant, moderate and fair society.

Tatíček (little father) Masaryk, as we called him, the towering architect of our country, and head of state, sought to ensure that his values penetrated the minds and fabric of the new republic. He had been a professor of philosophy and authored a large and impressive oeuvre dealing with nationalism, sociological problems, Marxism, "the Czech Question," Russian literature and ideas, and other ethical and socio-political issues. A deputy in the Austrian Parliament before we achieved independence, he espoused the cause of Czechoslovak statehood.

We adored the President and he personified the general dogmas propagated by the school. Years later, the memory of my boundless admiration of him made me revisit the scene. In the late 1940s, I decided to do my M.A. thesis on Masaryk, which provided the opportunity to verify whether he really was as magnificent as we were led to believe. Although some specks of clay attached themselves to his feet in this process, he stood up well, and still serves as a model academic, politician and statesman.

His colossal impact on me found expression in a mini lecture, years later at a party I hosted to celebrate — sit tight — the 60th anniversary of my briefcase. More about this caper is coming up in a later chapter, "Ottershaw College."

A page or so back, I noted that two experiences provided the dominant, formative ideological legacies of the Zlín schools: growing into a Czech with distinct anti-Austrian and anti-German attitudes; and espousing the social and political values of a liberal democrat, *à la* Masaryk. There were others, of course, some related to our family life and some to the increasingly intrusive and menacing impact of international politics. Anglophilia, for example, began under the sway of John Grubb, and the ever more searing fear of an impending world catastrophe both left their marks on my subsequent positions on international affairs.

A third important outlook evolved in Zlín. The shortest way of identifying it is to call it the "Bat'a spirit." An incident encapsulates it: in the summer of 1936 I was sent to an *Imka* (YMCA) camp near Prague. An additional tennis court was badly needed, so another boy from Zlín and I, led by a counsellor, buckled down to building it. This was a huge task. When someone expressed surprise to the counsellor that two campers would volunteer to take this on, he replied "Oh, they are Bat'a boys," or words to that effect, meaning that we were brimming with the characteristic Zlín work ethic.

The town, or at least the dominant Bat'a districts, comprised a colossal shrine extolling and almost sanctifying human labour. The working day was from seven in the morning to five or six in the evening, (only noon on Saturdays), with an hour's break for lunch. A powerful siren, mimicking clocks on church towers in more traditional settings, informed us of the factory's shift changes. The walls along the streets leading to the factory were plastered with slogans encouraging efficiency. I remember only one which strikes me as not very helpful. "THE DAY," it read, "HAS 86,400 SECONDS." Toil was also celebrated in the name of the principal square outside the factory gates: *Náměstí Práce* (The Square of Work).

That hard work was an essential and noble feature of the human condition was drilled into our heads, as was the notion that all honest workers were equally worthy members of society.

No wonder that an article in *The National Geographic Magazine* (August, 1938) called Zlín's inhabitants "the Yankees of Central Europe," undoubtedly intending this to be a compliment.

While the work fixation was clearly driven by secular motives, it reminds me of the Protestant work ethic, observed in the classic analyses by Max Weber (*The Protestant Ethic and the Spirit of Capitalism*) and R.H. Tawney (*Religion and the Rise of Capitalism*). They noted that some Protestant sects saw work as a form of prayer, bestowing grace. In Zlín the fervour with which toil was seen as a paragon of human experience displayed more than just a whiff of religious zeal. The Bat'as and most others in the leadership of the company were Catholics, so Protestantism scarcely explains the Zlín ethos. But its intensity made it a potent secular religion. Whatever the origins, it was a pervasive force that no one in Zlín could escape.

One of the company's more puritanical dogmas chafed our friend John Grubb: its rejection of anything to do with alcohol. In the ten-storey, fancy, Bat'a hotel, there was not a drop to be had of anything stronger than *limonáda*. Or perhaps I should say *"officially not a drop to be had."* Czechs are not only among the finest brewers of beer in the world but also among its more enthusiastic consumers. As was Mr. Grubb. Like many of his compatriots, he was fond of unwinding in the local towards the end of the day, which was not easy in Zlín. There were NO pubs, or anything like them, anywhere on Bat'a property. The only such place I knew of, the shabby-looking *Balkán*, was tucked away in the corner of the old town square. Sometimes, I was told, slurred versions of Czech songs and alcoholic odours emanated from this establishment. It is to here, *faute de mieux*, that our form teacher had to repair in search of a pint or, more likely, litre. We thought metric, after all.

This short detour on our path shows that while we were imbued with the Bat'a spirit, we were also made aware — as our knowledge of John Grubb's tippling reveals — that exceptions often vary even official dogma. John Grubb taught us this, through his comportment in the strict school environment and also in his private behaviour. But although he may have deviated from one local norm, he had to work exceedingly hard to produce our lessons. So, as I noted earlier, in the big picture, he lived up to, and reinforced, Czech democratic values and the Bat'a work ethic.

Was I being groomed to becoming a workaholic? Yes and no. During most of my adult years I worked exceedingly hard. But I saw being a prof as embracing more or less in equal parts (but not always at the same time) teaching and forming students, researching and writing, generally advancing the academic enterprise, assisting the policy process and, in as much as possible, making of myself a fully faceted person. I thus did not pursue scholarly ends so doggedly as to make me a lop-sided, partly stunted human being, incapable of relating to my students. All of this receives greater attention in chapters to come. The Zlín years and the Bat'a tradition, embodied by Tati, lingered on for decades. They shaped my attitude to work and its relation to duty. One had to tackle tasks and challenges put before one, even if this meant difficulty and possible trouble.

A former student, Derek Burney, wrote a memoir entitled *Getting it Done*. He meant, by this title, that when he had to do a job, he'd do it, sooner rather than later. Reading his book, and its nagging title, was the match that finally ignited my resolve to deliver on a promise made ten years previously, and reiterated tiresomely ever since. Thus, I began to write these reminiscences and reflections, though perhaps without Mr. Burney's characteristic expedition. I have always tended to cogitate, procrastinate and meet deadlines by a whisker. Indeed, Jean Van Loon, a one-time collaborator and now author, paid me the dubious compliment of writing at one point "(F)rom you I learned that submitting drafts on time is not always essential." But being socialized in the Bat'a school, so to speak, made me accept tasks dutifully and unflinchingly, even if they were daunting and even if their completion was sometimes delayed.

To sum up and repeat, Zlín made me a Czech nationalist, an adherent to Masaryk's democracy and a follower of the Bat'a school of hard work. But there was, given my background, a significant omission. What did it *not* do? Why did it foster a visceral adherence to, and identification with, the Czech nation but none at all to Judaism? My family was Jewish, but this had little effect on how I saw myself and who I thought I was. Jewishness was a religious category and not a group definition or a racial matter. And even as such it was most muted. We were brought up to believe in God and always said our evening prayers but these were generic, rather than denominational. With only a minor exception, we had no exposure to a religious body, Jewish or otherwise. The Zlín setting, in which there was only a smattering of Jews, failed to ignite any kind of Jewish consciousness.

When rereading this chapter, a suspicion started nagging at the back of my mind. Have my long years of plying the social sciences partially anaesthetized my memory, leading unwittingly to distortion? In seeking to identify youthful influences, I saw primarily societal, institutional and general conditions, as a social scientist would tend to do, and perhaps undervalued the more intimate and familial aspects. This imbalance requires redress.

What was the effect of family influences? After all, one's self-definition in ethnic and religious terms, and numerous other personal traits, is normally the product of parental and family exposure. The religious question (the title of one of Masaryk's books, by the way) just noted provides an easy entrance to this dimension of my youth. Tati, Mami, Rose and I were, of course, fully conscious of being Jews, and my paternal grandfather was practising and Orthodox. But, insofar as I was concerned at the time, these were small things which had few consequences. Along with a few Protestant kids (Bohemian Brethren—the descendants of the Hussites), I was excused from the religion classes in school, taught by a priest. On Yom Kippur we did fast part of the day and attend a portion of the religious service in the local Jewish prayer room, which had originally been the chapel for the noble family residing in the local castle. The surrounding park boasted many chestnut trees; after leaving the service, I loved collecting the fallen, gorgeously coloured and lustrous fruits peeking out of their green, bristly robes. We knew the religious significance of the atonement theme associated with this greatest of Jewish holy days, and took it seriously, but I must confess that the chestnuts were equally important to me. I still, whenever I can, pick up these maroon jewels in the autumn.

Almost all our relatives were Jewish, as were many of the parents' friends. But all *my* friends, schoolmates and teachers were gentiles, insofar as I knew, and the question of what religion anyone belonged to was unimportant and largely unnoticed. We celebrated Christmas which was an important annual event, but entirely secular. So I grew up aware of belonging to a group which was in some ways different from others, but there was no emotional content in this realization. I strongly identified with the Czech nation and shared a religious link with Hebrews. Being a Czech was a powerful, emotional feeling identifying me; being Jewish was a descriptive category.

The advent of Nazis next door, and the growing power of Germany, dramatically changed all that and endowed the Jewish reality with a terrifying, nearly paralyzing dimension and immediacy. But it did not alter my group adherence.

Our little foursome—our nuclear family, as I later learnt the textbooks called it—constituted the focus of our family life, despite Tati being away a lot on business and Rose studying in Brno, about 100 kilometres away. Zlín did not have a *gymnasium* (a secondary school leading to the matric), so she had to leave home, as other Zlín kids had to, to receive the highest levels of academic education. This affected our little ménage.

We readily displayed our feelings. There was occasional friction but the dominant atmosphere I recall was one of harmony and affection. The day-to-day management of the household, including the upbringing of the children, fell to Mami. After all, she was there all the time and Tati was not. And she *was* my mother; in those days it was the mums who invariably assumed the lioness's—or even the exclusive—share of nurture. In the area of comportment, however, the parents practised what studies of federalism call "divided jurisdiction." Tati became involved only in cases of the most serious disciplinary breach. He was called upon in this capacity very rarely, both because such lapses occurred exceedingly seldom and because a hint that a matter might be referred to him was invariably enough to cause the collapse of any obstreperous impulse.

I suspect that the division of labour between my parents did not result from planning and strategic thinking, but emerged as the natural arrangement between them, given their circumstances and personalities, and the conventions of the times. One thing was absolutely clear: the parental front was a united one. I do not recall a single instance of their not being in complete agreement about an issue affecting us children. Playing one parent against another, which I witnessed in some other domestic situations later, was utterly unthinkable.

Mami was a constant and reassuring presence. In addition to providing overall guidance, she had very good taste, preferring simplicity and aesthetic design. She was a competent pianist who fostered, in her children, a love of music. I recall not only her playing but also the most handsome, blue-cloth bindings she provided for her complete set of the Beethoven piano sonatas. Her baby grand was also an important part of my life: as a young child I adored sitting under it and playing with the pedals. Later I tinkled on it a bit and, with two fingers, made up a very simple tune. My sole venture into composing.

Mami liked attending concerts; from time to time she travelled to Vienna to hear favoured performers and, particularly, her hero violinist, Bronislaw Huberman. When she learnt that he was apparently unfaithful to his wife, she stopped these excursions. This was a mistaken confusion of relevant and irrelevant categories, as I realized years later. While running the Queen's concert series, I learnt that some of the most outstanding performers were anything but admirable human beings.

Culturally, Zlín was a desert. A lot of amateur music went on, but there was little by way of theatre, plastic arts or ballet. The company ran a large and successful movie theatre which, very rarely, offered a musical event. The Moravian Teachers Choir, a famous ensemble, performed there and I heard Dvořák's *Rusalka* and Smetana's *Bartered Bride*. We also received a visit from the famous (and wonderful) puppet theatre of Špejbl and Hurvínek, which still operates in Prague. Despite these exceptions, after Vienna, my mother was hard put to quench her cultural thirst.

Much later, when the parents lived in Toronto, they were faithful subscribers to various series at Eaton Auditorium and Massey Hall. Towards the end of their lives, strangers apparently wondered who that very old couple was who attended so faithfully, rain or shine, ice pellets or thaws.

Tati was by no means totally absent from the scene. He exerted considerable influence on my tastes and views. More interested in the visual and literary arts than Mami, he had in his youth acquired works by Czech artists and collected specially illustrated and rare editions of Czech classics and works of contemporary writers, painters and photographers. Tati's old friend, Pan Ulehla, was also the local bookseller; he supplied not only all our books but also our magazines, and even *Lidové Noviny*, the pro-Masaryk daily newspaper, which was delivered by his son. He, I recall, had a bad limp but needed the job. He was also responsible for bringing my *Mladý Čtenář* (Young Reader), a periodical to which I was addicted. It always arrived later at the house than in the stores and I agitated for a different form of procurement. Tati would not hear of it, pointing to the broader social implications of supporting a local bookseller and his handicapped son.

As a Czech nationalist, my father had, before Czechoslovak independence, been an active member of *Sokol* (Falcon), the patriotic Czech gymnastic organization and a focus of young nationalists. After his return to Zlín, he continued to belong but was too busy to attend. Still, he induced me to join and take the important gymnastic classes. This reinforced my nationalist inclinations and, no doubt, my muscles, and exposed me to more apparatus work than I had bargained for, and more, certainly, than I was good at. The *Sokolovna* (Sokol Hall) was at the other end of town from *Nad Ovčírnou*; I remember walking interminably to and from the weekly meetings.

Tati was an assiduous newspaper reader until his ripe old age, when he served as my reliable clipping service. No wonder I ate up public affairs. An interest in politics was also fanned by the encroaching and ever more menacing world crisis which we tracked with the aid of several newspapers as well as, first, a crystal set and, later, an ever-crackling radio.

For a time, my father served on the municipal Council and sat as a Social Democrat. I am ashamed to say that I knew virtually nothing about this part of Zlín or his life. I *assume* that the Council was likely controlled by the Baťa company and that most, if not all, members were acclaimed and picked by the management. I do not understand how Tati could represent any party other than Masaryk's and can only assume that the party was not active in local politics. Whatever the answer, Tati was certainly on the moderate left of the political spectrum and on the moderate nationalist side.

Since this was so, one important aspect of his work in Zlín later truly astonished, even shocked, me. In the mid 1930s, we were in the throes of the deepest economic depression, with families hurting very badly because of the massive, ubiquitous layoffs and catastrophic unemployment. The Bat'a works were threatened. During one period Tati spent a lot of time in Rome, trying to sell the Italian government a large order of army boots. These, and this is where the shock comes in, were intended for Mussolini's armies in Ethiopia, which the Fascists had cruelly and unlawfully invaded in 1935. Tati, like most Czechs, opposed the aggression, and applauded Hailie Selassie's moving and historic speech at the League of Nations in Geneva, which protested Italy's invasion of his country. Yet Tati engaged and persisted in the difficult negotiations, in the end coming away with the critical contract. These proceedings received a lot of attention; when Tati returned to Zlín, he was greeted by a huge procession of workers who carried him on their shoulders to the Square of Work.

By the time, years later, when I fully contemplated the moral dilemma posed by this episode, I was living in Kingston and somehow never talked to him about it. He was a quite exceptionally upright, principled and moral being, universally recognized as such, and the Italian contract must have caused him enormous anguish and soul searching. His welcome home by the workers made it clear that, to them, it was a saving godsend. And Tati may have told himself that there were plenty of others all too willing to provide the boots, had Bat'a not done so. But I never asked.

For the Meisel family, the affair had a silver lining. One of the critical persons involved in the negotiations was a Signor Mario Rocco, a high government official. He was, presumably, a member of the Fascist Party but also apparently a most decent, humane person. He and his German (but anti-Nazi) wife became very friendly with the parents. They visited one another, in Rome and in Zlín, although the relationship clearly had to be circumspect. Mr. Rocco's true mettle came to light in connection with Uncle Polda. Tati's brother practiced law in Vienna. After the German occupation of Austria, his family's safety was in jeopardy and they had to flee—an extremely difficult and risky business. It was Signor Rocco who, through his government connections, enabled the family's escape to England via Italy.

One might think, reading this, that politics permeated every aspect of my childhood, but that was not the case. I was, at various times, preoccupied with friends, lessons, games, and girls. On this last front, my parents were of little help: they neglected to reveal to me the mysteries of what is so inadequately called "the facts of life." I started acquiring this lore from the *Nad Ovčírnou* irregulars and then did more advanced research when at boarding school in Britain. Very early inklings of some realities appeared on my radar because Rose and I used to be bathed together when little. This brought *la petite différence* to my early attention in a most natural way. I also dimly connected the presence of a bidet in the bathroom to this phenomenon but my chief interest in the artifact was that it was possible to balance a ping-pong ball on its vertical jet, which I greatly enjoyed doing when nothing better engaged me.

On the matter of lessons, however, my parents were more involved. I cannot remember whether they first broached the subject of music lessons or whether the impetus came from me. My closest friend Ládík Ungr, who lived more or less kitty-corner from us, started learning to play the cello and this may have given me ideas. Although I never became anything like a good fiddler, taking lessons for a few years and then playing a bit was tremendously enriching. It not only provided the unique experience of being intimately engaged in a close activity with others, when playing in an orchestra, but also enhanced the enjoyment of listening to music.

But there were problems. My first teacher, reputed to be a fine musician, came to the house for the lessons. He was an ogre who, among other things, gouged Mami's piano with deep pencil scars produced by ill-tempered beating of time or expression of wrath. A caricature of the central European, autocratic schoolmaster, he terrified me. I was so scared of him that I asked Mami to be present at all our encounters. She agreed, thereby exposing herself to a doubly excruciating torture: my scraping and the frequent onslaughts on her boy.

After the grating introduction to the world of Paganini, I was entrusted to another teacher. The reasons were never articulated but were tacitly shared. My new instructor taught in the municipal Antonín Dvořák Music School, located in the chestnut-blessed castle which harboured the Jewish prayer room. He was a gentle, kindly soul and the first violin in the quartet that introduced me to chamber music. His first task was to help me unlearn some of the bad habits acquired earlier. The chief of these was not placing the finger squarely and unequivocally on the spot of the string intended to produce the desired note. I had become so petrified that I acquired the disastrous habit of moving the digit up and down a bit until it produced what I thought I could hear as the right note. This defence against my choleric teacher's displeasure created an excruciating mess that even I found hard to endure. Although his successor managed to go some way towards eradicating the uncalled for *glissando*, it was not until I continued violin lessons in Britain a couple of years later that I managed to rid myself of it.

Despite Tati's inflated work habits, we managed to enjoy what some manuals now refer to as "quality family time." Since the factory operated at full blast even on Saturday morning, the weekends were short, but Sundays were devoted to family activities. Very often we visited the surrounding rolling and partially wooded countryside; our expeditions invariably led us to visit a scenic town or village, a church, castle, chalet, hut, or some other attractive site.

Neither parent drove then. We did not own a car, but had the use of one. Tati financially enabled a Mr. Opavský to acquire a large *Praga* car for his limousine service. He, in turn, met all our conveying needs. No money ever changed hands. I assume that the cost was simply deducted from his debt. People walked a lot more in those days, and Mr. Opavský was called upon only on special occasions. He was, naturally, the link with the nearest train station in Otrokovice, about 15 km away. Zlín was not on a rail line.

The agenda of the Sunday outings followed a well-established pattern: drive to the target site, usually on narrow dirt roads (there were hardly any paved ones) through small, very poor farm villages overrun by geese and other farm critters; stop at a suitable establishment for coffee or juice and what the French so pleasantly call *une pause santé;* traverse forests; explore local attractions and hike a bit; have a meal in a nice hostelry; maybe walk again; and return home, dead tired. On many occasions there was no special attraction and the principal activity consisted of walking and admiring the scenery. Occasionally some friends or visiting relatives joined us. Wine was seldom if ever consumed, not because of any principle, but because my parents were by nature abstemious. Still, no meal was complete, at least for the adults, without a glass of *Plzeňské* — Pilsner.

Because she was away from home, studying at the gymnasium, Rose joined these expeditions only rarely. But she came home during holidays and was with us one Sunday when the parents entertained guests. At one stage she and I abandoned the rest of the crowd gathered in the living room, to talk in the winter garden. I loved this sunny room, enveloped by windows, with its tile floor and many flowers and other plants. Given the difference in our ages, and the great dissimilarity in the way we lived, Rose and I had somehow drifted apart. There was no chasm or disagreement between us, but neither was there any great intimacy. We liked one another but lived largely in separate worlds. But that long talk in the winter garden changed everything.

The timing and site predisposed me (perhaps us) towards a special encounter. It was Sunday afternoon, a time which during my childhood and even beyond, often produced a slight melancholy. I have no idea why this should have been so. Whatever the cause, the setting and circumstance of this occasion led to a meeting of souls.

One of the themes of our conversation was nothing less than immortality. I was desperately afraid of dying, partly because of not being sure of what would follow and partly because I enjoyed life so very much. But at the same time, the idea that things would go on and on forever and ever, without end, equally filled me with profound apprehension and anguish. An intolerable prospect. The dilemma between the two possible outcomes was not exactly a nightmare — it arose in the conscious mind while I was awake — but it was a theme causing intense dread. I shared it with Rose on that occasion.

That Sunday afternoon redefined our relationship. Thereafter, we enjoyed a powerful intimacy which was greatly enhanced a couple of years later when Tati, Mami, Rose and I, encased in a family-centred security blanket, escaped Europe. But even before then, in the summer of 1936, Rose and I spent a richly companionable and magnificent month in Britain, where we were sent to improve our English. Our first absence together from the parents and central Europe cemented our new bond.

III

Ottershaw College

It never occurred to anyone, including myself, that I might eventually go to university. This exalted option was still quite uncommon in the central Europe of the 1930s. Tati had taken a business course. The very notion of a university offering so mundane a program as business was unthinkable at that time. Mami, after she left middle school, was sent to a finishing school, a quaint institution which has not survived those well-bred days. My Canadian Oxford Dictionary defines it as a private school, especially for girls, "for completing a student's education with a strong emphasis on the social graces." Her artistry at the piano, and with crayons, brushes, scissors and paste, and flower arrangement was honed there.

No definite plans for my career had emerged, but two possibilities were vaguely mooted: hotel management or business. A thorough command of English was considered an essential precondition to either and was expected to result from my attendance at the Cizojazyčná Škola Města Zlína. But despite the rudiments acquired there, and the brief immersion in Britain subsequently, my command of Emily Bronte's mother tongue was still far from perfect. This shortfall likely led to the notion that I might go to an English secondary school. Mr. Grubb and Mami's English teacher were called upon for advice and she eventually set out for England to explore suitable colleges.

The two leading candidates ended up being Dulwich and Ottershaw. The former is an ancient and well-known public school, famous for its art program and fine gallery—a great plus in Mami's eyes. She found the place impressive and congenial. Ottershaw stood in dramatic contrast but eventually won out. It was virtually unknown, having been founded only a few years previously. It was also mildly radical: no fagging, no caning, a somewhat innovative approach to pedagogy. Unlike other such schools, it had no Officers' Training Corps; instead, the boys participated in a farm program and helped maintain the large, attractive school grounds. All this appealed to Mami a lot but the pièce de résistance, if this term may be applied to so charming a person, was the headmaster, the

Reverend Mr. Jeffreys. He, and his ideas of what made a good school, completely won her over. The fact that his wife was a violinist ready to continue my lessons confirmed the good fit. So Ottershaw it was, and in September 1937, Mami and I set out for London and the third major educational turn of my life.

We spent a few days in London readying me for my new career as an English schoolboy and visited Kinch & Lack, School Outfitters, the shopping Mecca of boys and girls entering a boarding school. This large shop, located on the impressively named and situated Buckingham Palace Road (or was it Gate?) possessed complete lists of *all* clothing (inside and out), and other non-academic equipment, prescribed by various so-called public schools. Much later I was reminded of this merchandising convenience when I learnt that love birds in North America, entering wedded bliss, deposit similar lists with fancy stores to assist relatives and friends pursuing wedding presents. Not a single item of the worldly possessions accompanying me to school had a provenance other than K & L, also known by schoolboys as Pinch and Stack.

At the core of this scholastic trousseau was the school uniform. Among its principal features were the dark blue blazer with the schoolcrest embroidered in silver on the upper left pocket, the school tie, grey flannels and shorts, white flannels for tennis and special occasions in the summer, a navy blue suit for Sundays, a mac — the ubiquitous navy blue raincoat — several shirts (grey flannel for daily use in winter, white cotton for summer and Sundays), and blue and grey heavier ones for rugger. In addition to these staples I received replacements for items ranging from such intimate utensils as a comb and tooth- and hairbrushes to two pairs of black shoes and a kit to keep them polished — part of the school code enforced during a daily inspection after chapel. There was a plaid wool blanket to go over the regulation beige issue on the dormitory beds and an undreamt of novelty, a tuck box.

This object, utterly unknown to me earlier, became something of a survival kit. A wooden crate, about the size of a small trunk, it was intended for goodies to supplement school meals. The latter — to digress for a moment — were so meagre that every night, after we tucked ourselves into the beds, Mr. Perreira, the gym master, would enter just before lights out to present some, but only some, of the boys with a supplement to their diet in the form of tablets. They were known as "energy pills" and were certainly (these were the 1930s!) innocent tonics, compared with the performance enhancing drugs made notorious years later by the Olympic Games, the Tour de France, and other competitive so-called sports. The lucky recipients of the gym master's favour were exclusively members of the school's first rugby team.

Every item in my K & L treasure trove had to bear the owner's name. Arrangements were thus made for all to acquire ample supplies of woven CASH name labels which were sewn on every single item of our clothing. Our name was also engraved, embossed or etched on any object suitable for such identification. I still own a beautiful clothes brush whose handle of light brown polished wood has J.MEISEL in black letters neatly burnt into it, not to mention a few rolls of the famous CASH name tags. Another relic of Buckingham Palace Gate which, unlike my blazers, has not been ravaged by moths and still serves, is the plaid rug. The school tie has also survived but is so spindly, as was the custom in the 'thirties, that it now looks grotesque. It has, in any case, since been joined by many cravats of other institutions to which I have links.

Another life companion, contributed by the outfitters and originally having my name on it, is still serving me daily. It is a small brown suitcase. It is made of an indestructible, rubber-based, lightweight substance—vulcanite—no longer used for luggage. The reason may be that it is so tough that manufacturers, noticing that replacements were never needed, stopped making it. Capitalism is guilty of far worse and more stupid decisions. While my name on it has long since worn off, the suitcase has nonetheless attained some modest fame because of its longevity and its capacity to evoke the past. It was originally intended for "away" games when we travelled to other schools, carrying sports clothes and other necessities. A dozen years later, when I started lecturing at Queen's, I found that it both fitted perfectly into the basket in front of the handlebars of my bike and resisted scuffing better than leather. It was reborn as the bearer of my lecture notes and other items indispensable to a prof. I have, at times, owned awesomely respectable briefcases, but they were too good for my bike. So I periodically reactivated the Ottershaw bag, particularly after I reached the age when I ceased caring whether people thought that I was approaching eccentricity. In the last twenty years or so, the bag and I have become inseparable.

In 1997 it dawned on me that the case and I had been together for sixty years and that it deserved special recognition. So I threw a huge party at the Agnes Etherington Art Centre called the "Valise Valedictory," at which I announced its retirement. In naming the party I could not resist the alliteration, but I actually thought of the event as a 60th birthday celebration, not a farewell. The valise is still in service. It was not only the age and usefulness of what had become my battered briefcase that called for notice, but also the timing of its acquisition. It encapsulated a profoundly meaningful episode in my life. In the middle of the festivities, I gave a half-hour, illustrated lecture (the invitees were warned before deciding whether to come) in which I discussed the intensely emotional impact of the days in London when the valise entered my life. Here is the historical and emotional context.

For a Czech patriotic boy, keenly involved in world affairs, those were tense days indeed. Hitler had begun to show his demonic self and it was clear that Germany, playing the "blood is thicker than water" card, vis-à-vis the Sudeten Germans, had become a life-threatening menace to Czechoslovakia, peace and world order. Waves of alarming rumours affecting war and peace, life and death, rolled our way and fed the Angst marking the times. And then, in the middle of this, a day or so after we arrived in London, an event made my blood freeze. The grim, black news broke that T.G. Masaryk, our dear *tatíček* Masaryk, had died. This was an ominous development, likely heralding the end of a happy era and the beginning of a new uncertain, horrible one.

My valise powerfully evoked the foreboding of what Winston Churchill later aptly called *The Gathering Storm*. The "birthday" lecture sketched a background of this in words and slides, but focused on the sense of loss and the anxiety occasioned by Masaryk's death. I dwelt on his critical contribution to the founding of a viable democracy in central Europe and drew a parallel between Masaryk and Havel. My concluding point was that the small countries of Europe, like Czechoslovakia, make valuable cultural and intellectual contributions which are either unknown to, or ignored, by those immersed in the artistic, intellectual and political world of the larger, more powerful countries. The train of thought was influenced by "Prague: A Disappearing Poem," (in *Granta, 17*) by Milan Kundera, the Franco-Czech writer who never tires of reminding us of the uniqueness and importance of small countries.

In addition to bequeathing a few treasured mementos and artifacts still in my possession, London's shopping spree also fashioned some life-long sartorial habits. Ever since 1937, and to this day, my basic wardrobe includes a dark blue suit, two or three pairs of grey flannels, and a mac. The latter's trademark may have shifted from Mackintosh to Burberry or Aquascutum (the current model; Burberries have crept out of my price range). Life without such articles of clothing is unthinkable. I have noticed that several colleagues of a certain age who also studied in the UK display similar tastes. We have been known to stroll out of a cloakroom with someone else's trench coat but, since we all know one another, reparations quickly follow.

Two items one would expect to find there were *not* on the K & L list. One was a school cap, widely associated with British schoolboys. Ottershaw, for reasons I never discovered, did not have one. So I continued to sport a beret, the headgear of choice ever since I learnt how to walk. It was common in central Europe at the time and because it could easily be rolled into one's pocket when not in use, undoubtedly saved a forgetful cuss like myself a lot of money at the hat shop. During the brief post-adolescent stage when I favoured the famous Borsalino *chapeaux* discarded by Tati, I more often than not forgot my hat somewhere. Ever since, berets have been the thing.

The other missing item was a bathing suit. The school had a fine pool which I, and a few other hardy souls, used quite early most mornings. I must have been emboldened to embark on this regime by a desire to consolidate the swimming foundations laid at camp. To my surprise, coming from the more prudish culture of predominantly Catholic Czechoslovakia, bathing suits were forbidden. This was something of a shock and led, at first, to a serious misconception. I could not believe how very many of my schoolmates were Jewish. It was only later that I learnt that, unlike in Czechoslovakia where only Jewish boys seemed to be circumcised, in Britain this practice was quite common among gentiles. Anyhow, skinny dips and skinny swims immediately became the norm. Years later, when I had my own lake, and there were no easily offended guests about, I always swam in my angel suit, deriving satisfaction from the thought that if any passers-by objected, they had only themselves to blame; they were trespassing.

Ottershaw's permissive attitude to early morning swims was a bit of an anomaly—school life was closely regulated. Hardly a minute of the day was unprogrammed. An even more astounding departure from the rigorous pattern of our lives came to light in our mathematics classes. These were taught by Mr. Hartley, a genial man who played the bassoon in the BBC Orchestra, taught and collected most wind instruments and conducted the school's instrumental ensemble. His method of teaching was in my experience unique. He rarely conducted a formal class. Our timetables provided for daily maths periods which we spent working in his classroom. At the beginning of term he handed out the assignments we had to complete by its end in Arithmetic, Algebra and Geometry, as well as the relevant references in our textbooks. We were free to work on whichever of the three subjects we felt like at any time, so long as we completed all the assignments in the end. When our texts failed to guide us adequately to the solution of a problem we went up to Mr. Hartley's desk where he guided us to victory. If a particular difficulty caused widely shared anxiety, he would conduct a class to deal with it. Our math instruction was, therefore, conducted largely on a one-to-one basis and was driven by our own priorities and needs.

The school was situated in a massive country house in the middle of a huge, park-like estate. It was apparently built by a wealthy English entrepreneur to impress the King of Belgium. The lord of the manor intended, so the story went, to obtain lucrative concessions in the Belgian Congo (diamonds?) for which the consent and support of the King (Leopold? Albert?) were essential. The mansion was to furnish a sufficiently regal and congenial setting to induce the King to oblige. Fate decided otherwise. Soon after the owner and his spouse moved in, the chatelaine died. The widower was so distraught that he left the place never to return.

I wrote the preceding paragraph by hand and bereft of my computer in 2007 while on a skiing holiday in Austria. Upon our return home I stumbled onto *An Illustrated History of Ottershaw Park Estate – 1761-2011* written by a magnificently thorough amateur historian John Athersuch. Not even a breath of a murmur of the romantic story of the school building's construction, nor of the Congo and the King. I can only conclude that what was widely circulating as history by the school community was nothing but a *canard*. But it was what I was led to believe, and it became an integral part of the mental image of Ottershaw I harboured for seventy years!

According to the aforementioned *An Illustrated History of Ottershaw Park*, the mansion was first completed in 1762 and underwent a great many changes, under a succession of owners, before it was bought by the school. In my time it sat on countless hectares of gorgeous, partly treed, rolling Surrey countryside. There was a charming, typical English country church very near, linked to the school, astonishingly, by an underground passage. It was, in effect, a Potemkin village church. It had never been a house of

worship and merely accommodated the school's laundry facilities
To conceal its crassly utilitarian mission, it was masked in
ecclesiastical garb better to fit into its rural setting. That, at least, is
what I was told, but...

And now a confession: for the sake of convenience and also
because of a spotty memory this chapter resorts to a sort of poetic
licence. I have collapsed *two* sessions at Ottershaw into one. I started
there, as noted, in September 1937 but in late November fell ill and
eventually returned to Czechoslovakia. I came back to Ottershaw
only in September 1938 and remained until the summer holidays just
before the outbreak of the war. My illness and its aftermath form the
subject of the next chapter. In the meantime memories of both the
Ottershaw phases are telescoped into one.

Mr. Perreira, among his many hats, wore that of boxing
instructor. Pugilism was an option within the gym classes. For
reasons I do not understand, since I am a pretty mild and un-
combative type, I signed up for it. When I informed the parents of
this Mami was terrified and Tati—as peaceable a soul as I—was
surprisingly very pleased, noting that I ought to learn how to stand
up for myself. At any rate, I enjoyed boxing, particularly with Kubín,
my permanent sparring partner, who hives on the scene again in a
moment. At the end of term, my boxing report pleased me greatly
and caused considerable merriment at home. The Ottershaw reports
were one of the many aspects of the English school system I
preferred to what I had known at home. There, the only assessments
parents received assigned a numerical mark in each subject—1 was
tops and 5, disaster. No further comments. At Ottershaw each master
wrote a verbal evaluation of the student's work and performance.
Mr. Perreira's judgment read, "Because of John's unusually long
reach, he has the makings of a useful boxer." It was the "useful" that
the parents found unexpected and hilarious.

In addition to his unusual style of mathematical instruction, Mr.
Hartley revealed a side of British (Ottershaw?) education which was
at odds with the formal character of Czech schools. In England,
teachers somehow managed to establish fairly relaxed and personal
ties with their students, perhaps because those I encountered taught
in a progressive boarding school. Mr. Grubb had imported this free-
wheeling way to Czechoslovakia, thus creating an exception. As
conductor of the school orchestra, Mr. Hartley worked with its
members in a setting quite distinct from a classroom. Once a year, he
and his wife held a tea for the orchestra members in their home. To

be invited to a teacher's home was novel and delightful but its impact was surpassed by what was a tradition at these gatherings. The tea took place in cherry season and several bowls of the shiny, ruby balls were scattered about the room. At a certain moment and, apparently according to plan, a battle broke out between the string and the wind players. The weapons were the pips of the cherries we ate. These were rapidly squeezed between two fingers and so propelled at a member of the section of the orchestra other than one's own. That such a messy frivolity was tolerated, indeed encouraged, in a school setting was utterly incongruous to me and I have wondered since how our hosts dealt with the inevitable cherry stains pock-marking their beautiful home.

My English master was Mr. E. His name escapes me. He was one of my favourites, so it is quite bizarre that my brain misfiled it. A little less flamboyant than some of his colleagues, he nevertheless contributed much to my knowledge, training and enjoyment. I no longer remember to which literary works he introduced us. One was certainly a Shakespeare play; he was hence the first of several teachers who aroused my Bardolatry. On one occasion he expressed surprise over the quality of my written work, considering that English was not my first tongue, and encouraged me to write a lot, an advice he repeated strongly on his report card. Following the earlier launch by John Grubb, Mr. E steered me towards a life in which words played a big role. I felt thoroughly comfortable in his presence and in the unspoken mutual awareness of our being, at some level, kindred souls. Any teacher who can instill this kind of feeling in a pupil does a lot more than just earn his keep.

Neither of the two members of the school's staff who were most important to me taught me in regular classes. They were Mr. and Mrs. Jeffreys. As my headmaster and as my violin teacher, they filled a huge space in my life. "Jeff," as we called him, although not to his face, exuded charm and *joie de vivre*. While there never was the slightest doubt about his authority, he was approachable and friendly, displaying a genuine interest in, and concern for, every one of his flock. He was well aware of my anxiety about the world's political crisis in general, and that of Czechoslovakia in particular. He was by no means one of Britain's appeasers and sympathized with the plight of my country. On one occasion, when Chamberlain gave a major speech on radio, probably around the time of his Munich betrayal, Jeff offered us boys a choice of either listening to it, or to a special broadcast of Beethoven's Ninth Symphony. I chose the music, a decision I now find incomprehensible except, perhaps, that I feared the worst from Hitler's Munich pal and thought that I could not bear the torture. At that time I greatly loved the Ninth and its Ode to Joy — a musical taste which has changed since, despite its high repute among so many musical cognoscenti.

It was important to me at that stage in my life to be liked by people in authority — a concern which vanished as I grew older, and for which I am now ashamed. That Jeff took an interest in me, and seemed to like me was, therefore, very important and reassuring. He had, I am certain, the same effect on all the boys which, no doubt, contributed to the easy power of suasion he exercised over us.

The adult I felt closest to was Mrs. Jeffreys. The contrast between her and my first violin teacher (an ogre, as you will remember) could not have been greater. She was gentle, caring, and empathetic. That she was a woman, probably about the same age as Mami, must also have enhanced her appeal; she probably filled an important niche in my life *in loco parentis*.

One of the Jeffreys or some other school nabob prized the island's cultural figures so highly that each of our dormitories bore the name of one of them. During my first landing, the dormitory celebrating the composer Delius became my nest. I had never heard of him before but have come to love his melodic sense and pleasing evocations of British soundscapes. My second pad was Galsworthy, a much more familiar name.

It was Mrs. Jeffreys who discovered that I needed spectacles, as we called them. It seems that I consistently made certain errors in reading music. She guessed that the cause was a sight problem. She consequently took me to an optometrist in a Staines, a nearby town, where I was issued with a pair of perfectly round, horn-rimmed specs, of the kind favoured by Harry Potter. They came in a luxurious case, far superior to the standard issue in Czechoslovakia, but not as ostentatious as those now peddled by optical firms which, it seems, have been captured by the fashion industry.

Mrs. Jeffreys bore remarkably well the rather mechanical communication I maintained with the fiddle and brought me into Mr. Hartley's orchestra. Here she kept close watch over me by arranging to have me share her desk. This taught me a lot and shored up my courage. Her solicitude and maternal concern added much to my comfort and diminished what would otherwise have been painful loneliness and homesickness.

A more constant and important factor in assuaging the wrench of being abroad and away from the parents was Jarek Kubín. He also came from Zlín. Our dads, being senior Baťa men, were acquainted; Mr. Kubín, aware that Frýda was about to send his boy to an English boarding school, did likewise when he was transferred to the large Baťa factory in Tilbury, east of London. We became fast friends and were, no doubt, sources of amusement to the other boys because of our national idiosyncrasies. We helped one another accommodate to the novel and often startling ways of an English boarding school and to find relief from total English immersion. The opportunity to lapse into Czech from time to time and to talk about "home" was bliss.

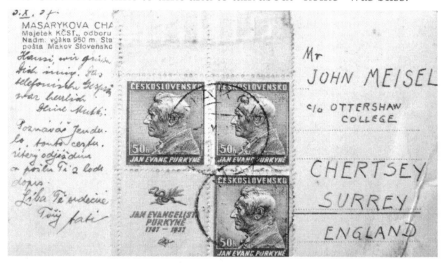

A bilingual greeting from Mami and Tati from a scenic hut, marking a now forgotten special philatelic occasion.

My illness and then the war forced us to go separate ways; I have always greatly regretted this since I was very fond of him and am sure that we would otherwise have become lifelong friends. I feel the same way about some Zlín companions, particularly Ládík Ungr, my closest pal there. Geography and the disruptions caused by war came between us. But I also wonder whether some lack in me is to blame. A bit of effort after the war could have revived the bonds between us. I even have a vague sense that some desultory exchange took place with Ládík but that it petered out. Each of us was probably so utterly affected by our respective, dramatically different experiences, that the former bonds failed to survive. But I wonder if this is the case, since I wallow in friendships and have been amazingly lucky in the number I have made and kept since coming to Canada. Perhaps the art of keeping friends was something I learnt in the New World. Although I was at Ottershaw almost a year and a half, I have no recollections of a single close friend, other than Kubín.

Such friendly relations as I did entertain with chums were, so to speak, functional. They emerged from shared, sustained activities and were, for the most part, confined to them. One of these centred on the Camera Club. I loved taking pics with my very cheap but adequate Voigtländer 4 x 4 reflex camera. At Ottershaw I learnt how to develop, print and enlarge my negatives. When one of my enlargements was reproduced in the college magazine, I gained some confidence and pursued photography, particularly dark room work, with considerable zest. This interest dovetailed nicely with my having to give up sports because of the injured leg. My first "published" work was a trite close-up of my violin and bow. I loved the instrument's shapely lines and the warm glow of the wood which were captured by the camera even though we only used black and white film in those days.

Working in the dark room introduced me to a lot of the popular music of the era. *Alexander's Ragtime Band* was a hit at the time, as were the songs of Jack Hylton. One of my fellow enthusiasts—a photo friend whose name I recall as Morden—always brought a portable radio along, which introduced me to one small segment of British popular culture. I was greatly impressed by Morden, and some others in the club, for the professionalism they brought to their photography. They were most knowledgeable about shortcuts and equipment available to us shutterbugs and darkroom amateurs. They read periodicals in the field and spoke with awesome ease about the problems we encountered and their possible solutions. I detected similar depth among boys pursuing other hobbies and interests. These relative experts were the precursors of the "professional amateurs" I would later meet in London.

My crowd in Zlín was not as sophisticated and I now wonder why this should have been so. Was it because Britain was what we would later have called a more developed country, with a higher standard of living? Or is the difference, if indeed there was one, to be ascribed to Zlín being a small Moravian town, less advanced than the metropolitan London ambience? Had I lived in Prague or Brno, my experiences might have been different. Age may also have been a factor. I was probably losing some of the characteristics of childhood and beginning adolescence, an age which, despite its troublesome tensions, also marks the advent of adulthood. Most of my English companions also came from financially quite comfortable families, whereas the background of my schoolmates at home was more mixed. Whatever the reasons, I learnt that hobbies and leisure pastimes could involve much knowledge and a certain level of professionalism. They could become so thoroughly absorbing as to displace one's work—a notion utterly incompatible with the work ethic I had absorbed in the Bat'a dominated Zlín.

During our free time, I particularly enjoyed the bicycle rides some of us took to the two nearby towns of Woking or Chertsey. Five or six of us would set out to go to a cinema (with the permission of the headmaster) or just a tearoom for those much-loved British staples, tea, scones and sweets. I no longer remember how the membership of each sortie was chosen. I must have been, with Kubín of course, a member of a friendly cohort that did things together, but these friendships were of a group and not an individual sort. It was through this network of comrades that I got wind of a three-speed, second-hand bicycle available for 12/6, i.e., twelve shillings and six pence. This sum was, even then, ludicrously low, the equivalent of less than five current dollars.

I also became quite engrossed in sports. These were much more important at Ottershaw than in Czech schools, partly because of its residential nature, I suppose, but also because of a cultural differences. I doubt whether the Zlín school authorities considered the gym classes and limited school games relevant to our character formation. Not so in Britain. Here the development of skills, the desire to excel and a commitment to fair play were on a par with our academic life.

Although cricket was popular at Ottershaw during the appropriate season, I never succumbed to it. Tennis was my game. I had already started in Vienna and then continued on a neighbour's court in Zlín. The big innovation, after boxing, was rugger. It was compulsory at Ottershaw and, in the autumn and winter terms, comprised the centrepiece of the athletic program. I enjoyed it and would have been hard pressed to choose between it and the much more familiar soccer. It was played without any protective gear. Later, when I encountered the panzer outfits donned by my Canadian schoolmates playing football, I could hardly keep a straight face. I nevertheless must admit that it was an injury suffered during one of the regular rugger practices that led to my illness and prevented my ever again engaging in any contact sport.

During my second phase at Ottershaw I consequently benefited, twice weekly, from free afternoons to myself. These were filled primarily with two pastimes. School rules, sensibly no doubt, forbade anyone remaining in the buildings during the time allocated to rugby practice. This led to my frequently taking long walks through the school grounds and the surrounding countryside. Although I enjoyed these, there were times when I dared to defy the school's marching or, more precisely, running orders. I noticed that the common room, during these afternoon periods, was rarely visited by prefects, let alone masters, and so provided an opportunity to catch up on my extracurricular reading.

It was during one of these deliciously illicit moments that I made a wonderful literary discovery: *Lilliput*. As the title suggests, it was a small, almost pocket-sized magazine, whose covers each month featured a drawing by Walter Trier. I had for a long time relished his illustrations of the novels by Erich Kästner, all of which I devoured even at the stage in my life when reading was not a top priority. Each month, Trier's light-hearted, droll portrayal of a threesome — a man, a woman and a little black dog — shone with good humour and subtly set the tone for what was to follow. *Lilliput* contained short stories, innovative photographs, and lots of material on the arts. It pioneered a new form of journalism, one which combined the written word with art. Its left-of-centre perspective and strong anti-fascist stance dovetailed well with my own outlook. I subscribed to it for years after I left Ottershaw.

Although the state of my health prevented me from engaging in activities involving vigorous body contact, it did allow me to join the Scouts. I was an enthusiastic, if somewhat clumsy member of the Kingfisher patrol. This was exciting but I cannot say I brought glory to our troop. My membership raised one small problem: the initiation ceremony involved swearing an oath of loyalty to His Majesty the King. I could not imagine that this would ever conflict with my obligations as a Czechoslovak citizen, but the possibility of some future conflict could not be ruled out. Characteristically, I chose to overlook this and hoped for the best. A clash of loyalties never materialized.

Many of my fellow followers of Lord Baden Powell had their shirts plastered with badges attesting to various accomplishments. Partly because of my medical problems and the short time of my attendance, but also because of lack of dexterity, I sported only one badge. It attested to my mastery of the Morse code. I was quite proud of it but also hoped to win additional skill and kudos by learning to tie the prescribed knots for the badge in this vital sphere. But butterfingers and the advent of the war frustrated my ambition. I also let the side down in another matter. On one of our overnight outings, Kubín and I found that the temperature in our tent was so cold as to prevent us from falling asleep. Since the campsite was not terribly far from the school, we ran to our dorm, crawled into bed and then returned early next morning with no one being the wiser. This was, without doubt, a major breach of the honour code but we managed to assuage our consciences on this account.

A couple of special events at Ottershaw are indelibly imprinted in my memory. One is my first encounter with Guy Fawkes. I may have heard of him in Zlín (his annual "celebration" is the sort of feature of British folklore Mr. Grubb would have wanted to share with his pupils), but it was not until 1937 or 1938 that I had the chance actually to participate in the commemoration of the 1605 gunpowder plot. To mark the anniversary of an historical episode by lighting fireworks and burning the effigy of the villain was a real novelty, but what really got to me was that the dummy committed to the flames was not that of a seventeenth-century rebel but of Hitler. Such irreverence towards a leading political figure — even a despised one — was unheard of and shocking. It was also exquisitely gratifying, since Adolf was indubitably the Czechoslovaks' enemy No. 1. That my British school and its masters and pupils shared our hatred was a most welcome sign of solidarity.

The other notable experience diverged in nature, but not in character. It too revealed a striking irreverence that would not have been found in Zlín; it too was politically most congenial. A visiting theatrical group offered *The Birds* by Aristophanes. I had never heard of him, nor had I ever seen or read Greek drama before. I found the interplay between the solo actors and choruses intriguing, and the plot a bit complicated. But what was completely unexpected and gripping was that the text was laced with allusions to contemporary British and world politics and politicians. The production was particularly unflattering to Neville Chamberlain which suggests that I must have seen it in 1938, after the Munich pact. Any denigration of the treacherous British prime minister would, at that time, have been most gratifying to me. That a school presented a play first performed in Athens several hundred years before the Christian era was amazing and that it poked fun at the government then in office was fantastic. Such *lèse mujeslé* would never have been possible in my Zlín school.

Lest the foregoing suggests that we were being indoctrinated, it is fair to say that the atmosphere was pretty even-handed. Although the Common Room contained "progressive" publications like *Lilliput*, and I think, *The New Statesman*, many more centrist and conservative voices were about. *The Times* and *The Daily Telegraph* were everywhere and were important providers of news.

I left Ottershaw in 1939 for the summer holidays and Casablanca, where the parents were then living. I was to return for the Michaelmas term and packed accordingly. But the war broke out and the school was eventually closed. Someone kindly sent my effects to Morocco, but I did suffer some losses. I have never seen my precious bike again, and my tent, stored in my locker, also became a war casualty, at least in so far as I was concerned. I hope that someone was able to make good use of it. But the abandoned possession that triggered the most subsequent thought was an item safely stowed away: a Hungarian salami. They have a long tuck-box life and I expected to nibble at it after my return. There was no return and I have from time to time wondered how long it remained undetected and how its abandoned existence finally came to light. Answers to these questions are among the most trivial casualties of the war.

IV

Osteomyelitis: Coping with Staphylococcus Aureus

The affair started innocently and without menace. While running to the afternoon's Farm Service exercise in mid-November 1937, I did not feel quite up to snuff and sensed some discomfort in my right thigh. As the afternoon wore on, I became feverish and experienced real pain. Mr. Going, the master supervising our fieldwork sent me to the school nurse who, he anticipated, would issue the chit allowing me to be excused. For reasons best known to herself, she decided that I was either malingering or exaggerating my pain. Contesting decisions by those in authority, no matter how preposterous, was not my style. I slouched back and conveyed the verdict to Mr. Going. He was also our Geography master and his subject was one of my favourites. He knew me a lot better than the nurse and believed me. He bid me to just sit nearby and then return with the others when they finished.

My condition worsened rapidly and by evening even the harridan had to concede that something was wrong. I have a vivid recollection of being carried late that evening on a stretcher down the baronial main school staircase en route to the nearby Weybridge Cottage Hospital. Through the feverish haze enveloping me, I felt a mild sense of triumph. The school rules which I, miraculously, still have, and even more miraculously, found, were unequivocal on the matter of stair use: "'Seniors' may use the Main Stairs; 'Juniors' the back stairs; No one the Marble Stairs." So there, nurse! I was conveyed to the ambulance in style, far exceeding that befitting a callow Junior.

Dr. Sam Beare, the school doctor, lived in Weybridge and had attending privileges in the hospital. He diagnosed my problem as osteomyelitis, an acute bone infection which can, as it did in my case, develop into a chronic illness lasting intermittently many years or even the whole life of the patient. The infection can be caused by trauma anywhere in the body and is carried, particularly in children, into one of their bones. The causal villain is usually the dreaded *staphylococcus aureus*, who, these days, causes many of the outbreaks of mass infections in hospitals. My problem was probably caused by a hard hit in the thigh while playing rugger. In 1937 neither sulfa drugs nor antibiotics were available, and the only treatment was to open the site of the infection surgically, clean as much of it as possible, and sew it up. The best scientific follow-up was to drink a lot of fruit juice and keep one's fingers crossed.

I did not dread many things as I was growing up, but one BIG FEAR concerned hospitals. The word itself evoked a massive, dark-walled and ominous, hulking structure. I likely passed such a place in Vienna while still quite young and associated it with death and pain. The memory stuck. Fortunately I was too feverish and delirious on the way to Weybridge to take in much of what was going on and was thus spared the deep anxiety a conscious trip to a hospital would have caused. After a few days' residence, when my mind had cleared, and particularly towards the end of my stay when my temperature returned to normal, a completely different perception formed. Although I had suffered pain and anxiety, the memory I now have of the hospital is a pleasant one.

I had a bright private room filled with flowers. Mami arrived from Czechoslovakia and was, at first at least, a 24-hour companion. The Jeffreys and others from the school visited occasionally, but the most important person on the horizon, by far, after Mami, was Dr. Beare.

There is no doubt in my mind that I owe my life to him. My physical condition was desperate. I had developed abscesses in different parts of my body and ultimately the staphylococci reached and settled in my lungs. Pneumonia set in which was seen, by far, as the most life-threatening of my afflictions. Walter Marmorek, a family friend studying architecture in Britain, initiated a consultation with one of Britain's top specialists, Lord Horder, who was also the King's physician. He came down from London, examined me, and is alleged to have said, "There is nothing you can do for this boy."

Despite feeling miserable and uncomfortable, I was not aware of how grave my condition was. In the absence of any available medication, my attitude and will to live were critical factors in a possible recovery. Dr. Beare was nothing short of heroic in his efforts to keep up my spirits. He had a son my own age and, in addition to being a caring physician, strongly sympathized with my plight and that of my family. On many occasions he dropped into the hospital as often as four or five times a day to see me and to cheer me up. He succeeded in engaging my attention and in imparting a sense of optimism. Mami and some friends did a lot to help, but he, partly because of his authority as my doctor and partly because of his winsome ways, played a critical role in my ultimate recovery.

Over twenty-five years later, while in London working on my Ph.D., I bought my first car and my wife, Murie, and I drove to Weybridge to see him. We had stayed in touch via Christmas cards. He lived in a lovely apartment in a converted country house, approached by a large circular drive way. As we drew up at the appointed hour, he came out of the front door towards our shining Morris Minor, and with outstretched arms said with a heavily foreign accent and a huge grin on his face, "Dr. Beare, vot can you do against my vinds?" This was a reminder that among my numerous afflictions while in his care had been severe intestinal discomfort for which I constantly sought relief.

Dr. Beare was greatly respected and loved. So I was not surprised when, some years after this last encounter, I learnt that among the many units which now make up the greatly enlarged Weybridge Hospital, one is the Sam Beare Hospice Ward. He had eventually specialized in palliative medicine and his contribution to it was obviously great enough to justify naming it in his honour.

Most of the Weybridge details have now vanished but one, though trivial, is still very much with me. It is linked to my love of flowers. Mami and my friends made sure that my room always contained cheerful pots and vases. One day a really special specimen arrived I had never encountered before. It was a Jerusalem Cherry. Surrounded by deep green foliage, its bright red balls resembled the fruit after which it was named. I was enchanted and have been a fan ever since.

There is another, rather embarrassing memory which concerns Jeff — not the headmaster but a dog. I now realize that although I bore up remarkably well under my ordeal, it did spoil me a little. Given my precarious and uncomfortable state, everyone tried to humour me by granting such requests as I might occasionally voice. There were not many of these, at least I do not remember any. But at one point I allowed that I would really love to have a dog. This was, under the circumstances, a preposterous idea. But in the end Mami did go to London to acquire a Scotch terrier, my choice for a canine companion. The little pup was delivered to the hospital and after consultation with Mr. Jeffreys, who acceded to my request, he was called Jeff — the greatest honour I could bestow on both man and beast. Since I was bed-ridden during the whole of our short-lived acquaintance, I never looked after him. He must have been a headache in the hospital and certainly was one when Mami and I eventually returned to Zlín.

I have made no mention of Tati so far. He was suffering from his own great affliction: extreme workaholicism. He did come to England once or twice to see me. But I remember little about his being there. His job commitment was colossal and I did not find it at all strange that he could not spare more time. He wrote and phoned and I found all this quite normal. Also, as I mentioned in the Zlín chapter, Mami was much more the hands-on parent than he. In a way, I suspect that at that fraught moment in my life, my mother's constant presence was probably more important to me.

Once the pneumonia subsided and I recovered sufficiently from my operation, I was moved home to Zlín. This was accomplished by means of the twin-engine Fokker company plane in which Mr. Bat'a and Tati had flown to India 1932. Mami, Jeff and I, plus all the essential gear, were picked up at London's Croydon airport and whisked (at 1930s speed) to the airport near Zlín. For many years I assumed that it was the kindness of the Bat'a family that enabled us to use this plane. It would have been much more difficult to make the journey by ambulance, train and boat and the idea of enduring the Channel crossing on the ferry gives me the willies. Later it occurred to me that Tati must have paid the costs which does not, however, diminish the debt I feel I owe the Bat'as.

I continued to be bed-ridden for months, waiting for my right femur to restore itself sufficiently to bear my weight. When a new infection subsequently developed, I was admitted to the Bat'a hospital in Zlín, where I was once again operated on.

World affairs took a turn for the worse at this time and began to transform the Meisels from your traditional middle-class European family to globe-trotting quasi-refugees and, ultimately, contented Canadians. On March 12th, 1938, German troops moved into Austria and, with the consent of the Austrian government, annexed the country. The top management of Bat'a held an emergency meeting which lasted well into the night. It decided that central Europe would likely fall to Hitler and that the worldwide operations and holdings of the company were, thus, in danger. Bat'a was a tightly centralized enterprise: when even a mere pair of shoe laces was sold in one of its Indian or other foreign stores, a bookkeeping entry was made in Zlín. To avoid probable future disaster, the decision was taken then and there to move the nerve centre of the foreign operations abroad. Tati's export department started the next day moving to Holland, where Bat'a had a large factory in Brest near Eindhoven.

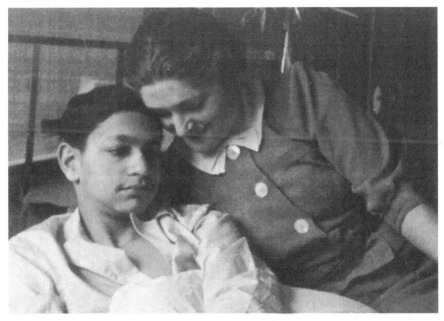

Zlín, March 1938. Hoping to heal enough to travel.

But there was a problem—two in fact. Rose was in her final year of the *gymnasium* in Brno and the parents decided that she should stay there and finish. If a crisis loomed, she would be able to get away. And Jenda's bones were not yet ready for the journey. So Tati went off alone while Mami and I stayed in Zlín, and Rose in Brno. In April, my progress was sufficient to warrant a walking cast, permitting me to hobble around a bit. Mami and I entered Holland on May 24th, my passport tells me. I had by now spent two months in Weybridge and three bed-bound in Zlín.

The journey was not without excitement and colour. In those threatening times, some Czechoslovak citizens tried to ensure their future security by spiriting valuables abroad. There were strict regulations governing what prized objects, and in what form and quantities, could be taken out of the country. Given these circumstances, my cast posed a peculiar challenge: some astute person raised the question of whether it might be suspected of harbouring diamonds or what have you. A few days before our departure customs officers were, therefore, in attendance in the hospital, when a surgeon applied a huge walking cast stretching from my waist down the leg to a hook at the bottom of my foot. The official responsible for controlling the export of valuables, plastered (sorry) my cast with official stamps attesting to its innocence. I was also provided with a formidable-looking document describing the method used and ensuring that I was clean.

A more romantic episode resulted from the fact that I had to change platforms at the Prague railway station. I could not walk more than a few steps at the time, as I was just learning to lug my cast around and to manoeuvre with two sturdy wooden crutches. I had to be lifted and carried most places. Facilities for people who were then called "handicapped" did not exist. Wheelchairs were a rarity, reserved only for those suffering serious, permanent afflictions. We are now much more tolerant of, and helpful and accommodating to people with disabilities. This is one item on my balance sheet of human advances and regressions in which the former outweigh the latter. Human resourcefulness made up for the absence of fancy equipment. I was lifted from the train when we arrived in Prague and hoisted onto an ordinary wooden chair which was placed in the middle of a huge, man-drawn luggage wagon. A most exciting adventure followed. I was taken by a huge lift into labyrinthine corridors and through eerie subterranean nooks and crannies until we rose, in another cage, to the departing platform. I can best convey the feeling I had while being pulled through what seemed so danger-filled a maze by referring to the 1935 classic film version of *Les Misérables,* which I saw many years later. It strongly evoked the atmosphere created by the Prague railway cellar. The terror of Charles Laughton (Javert) mercilessly stalking Frederick March (Valjean) was absent, but in all other regards, the sinister setting of my subterranean Prague transfer vividly recalls the ambience of the film.

My condition continued to improve after we settled in Eindhoven and caused only two difficulties: one medical and one psychological. In efforts to see something of our new locale, we often took Sunday excursions to various interesting sights. This being Holland, most of these were not very far away. Tati engaged taxis on these occasions, into which the family and my cast could be squeezed relatively easily. The cramped and often joggling quarters nevertheless took their toll. On several Monday mornings I discovered that the previous day's half sitting, half lying position in the jostling car had caused a crack to develop in my cast, running from the hip to the groin. Repairs were made in the St. Josef Ziekenhuis where new plaster-laden bandages were applied around the impaired area. This worked for a while but eventually new fissures appeared after delightful outings. The method of dealing with this was identical to the first one: apply more plaster. As a result, the size of my leg's carapace kept growing until I had to procure much larger sized pants. Furthermore, the weight of the cast was also rising. This made walking increasingly awkward and demanding.

I had been instructed to use my legs as much as I could and so regularly hobbled along streets in our neighbourhood. There were lots of kids about, some of whom followed me, in near-regular formation, shouting rhythmic, incomprehensible rhymes which sounded like invective. They were certainly not meant to encourage. I found this inexplicable and quite disconcerting. I felt like a Pied Piper whose wires had gotten crossed and who haplessly attracted a hostile following. But there was nothing I could do about it. The experience coloured my impression of Holland. While I liked a great many things in this tidy, clean country, and while the prevailing concern about German intentions matched mine, I found the behaviour of the kids offensive and cruel. On the other hand, my visits to the hospital, including yet another (minor) surgical intervention, were more than satisfactory. But the unwanted street scenes gave me a glimpse of one of the psychological costs of being a cripple, to use a forbidden but still current word.

Whatever the impact of Dutch urchins on my morale, the body mended well in Eindhoven, and I was able to return to Ottershaw in the autumn for the 1938–39 school year in reasonably decent health. Body contact sports were a thing of the past and I had to adjust to a somewhat new life. Exercises were prescribed to restore the capacity to bend the right knee which involved doing innumerable painful knee-bends. The suppleness of my youthful frame and my perseverance enabled me to recover almost the normal use of the right leg. Much later, when I became a cross-country ski enthusiast, I gave profound thanks to whoever it was that guided me to restored knee action. Nevertheless when I returned to England I limped. Mr. Perreira, the gym master, was puzzled by this, since there no longer was an apparent physical cause. A determined bloke, he had me walk along the proscenium of the school auditorium-theatre, while he sat in the front row and watched me pace from stage left to stage right and back again, ad nauseam. We held several such diagnostic séances without any breakthrough until he finally noticed the cause of my uneven gait: whenever I took a step, I failed to lift my right ankle. Many weeks in a cast had somehow made me forget something I had learnt as a toddler—how to walk properly. As soon as this was pointed out to me, I either remembered the trick or just restored the lapsed reflex. I lost the limp in no time.

* * *

Things were quiet for a while and the old enemy, *staph.*, left me alone. I was able to lead a reasonably normal life. It was not to last, however. Late in 1939, a new abscess formed in my leg which had to be lanced. This task was performed by a Dr. Sacuto who ran a surgical clinic in Casablanca, where, as a later chapter reveals, I joined the parents just before the outbreak of war. Despite occasional swellings and fevers during our stay in Casablanca I was, with only short exceptions, able to swim in the Atlantic and even to play volleyball with Tati's co-workers and their families. Mind you, volleyball in those days was, like tennis, less vehemently played than now. So although not in perfect health, I was well enough, when another Meisel move became necessary, to embark with Rose and the parents on a circuitous journey to Haiti.

Once settled in Port-au-Prince, my medical welfare was placed in the hands of Dr. Jalowec, a competent, meticulous and genial Austrian general practitioner. Elevated temperatures, occasional flare-ups in my leg and blood tests revealed that I was still in trouble. Abscesses kept appearing on or near the original site on the outside of the right femur. Eventually a swelling also developed on the left side of the leg, above my knee. These boil-like spots had to be opened. It was clear that a bone-scraping exercise was called for but Dr. Jalowec, who knew local conditions well, strongly advised against entering a Haitian hospital. Sanitary conditions there were such that the consequences of a bone operation would likely have been disastrous. Since it was probable that we would eventually leave Haiti, he devised a holding strategy. A heavy regimen of vitamins C and D was prescribed and sulfa drugs administered, when necessary. He came to the house regularly to disinfect the affected areas as much as possible by irrigating the wounds. For a spell this produced a comical (disgusting?) situation when the disinfecting liquid, introduced by a syringe on the right side of the thigh would emerge through the wound on the left above my knee, the abscesses having linked up inside my leg. These measures enabled me to wait for proper treatment once we gained access to an acceptable hospital. Eventually one or both of these lesions healed, only to act up again later. ·

The good doctor (and he was one) proved right. At the beginning of 1942 we left Haiti for El Dorado — Canada. I entered Pickering College almost immediately in Newmarket, where everything was fine for a while. I even managed to skate a few times but the old pattern recurred and the nurse (much nicer than the one at Ottershaw) arranged for me to see Dr. Case. He was an important figure at Pickering not only because he was the school physician, but also because he had an attractive daughter who attended the nearby high school. He took one look at my records and extremities and knew what to do. "Go to Toronto and see R.I. Harris in the Medical Arts Building on Bloor Street," he announced. Harris was the head of orthopedic surgery at the University of Toronto and a person of some presence and eminence. After many pokings and squeezings, not to mention X-rays and blood tests, he told me that an extensive operation was required which, however, could wait until the holidays. It would require a lot of time in the operating room and for the rehabilitation.

A date was set for early summer, but had to be missed. I developed scarlet fever and Dr. Harris insisted on a long recuperation period because he wanted me in top condition for the operation. I went through an intensive period of daily long walks, swims and tennis games, so the skin Dr. Harris finally confronted bore a pitch-dark tan. In those days we thought that spending a lot of time in the August sun was a benign and healthy equivalent to a goose being fattened up before a feast.

The operation confirmed that my right femur had turned into a mere shadow of its former self. Large areas resembled lacery, out of which huge, neat holes had been chewed by some dainty but marauding beast. Parts of it looked like a hardened sponge. I know this not because I saw the *before* and *after* X-rays but because of a wonderful spiritual daughter of Florence Nightingale. Miss Marjery E. Talmay was my principal nurse for several weeks. At first she must have spent virtually all her time with me. Throughout, she showed devotion to her vocation light years beyond the call of duty. She kept Dr. Harris's booty — the excised pieces of bone — in a fridge and, once I recovered somewhat from my ordeal, asked whether I would like to have them. I became the owner of a 14 cm x 7 cm x 5 cm cardboard ossuary, containing the thoroughly cleaned fruit of Dr. Harris's labours. A neat label, made of adhesive plaster reads "BONES with compliments of M.E.T." I kept it for many years on the mantelpiece, shocking adult guests and delighting visiting children. The Museum of Health Care at Kingston haughtily declined my generous offer to donate it and it now is in the hands of Victoria Wilcox, my splendid niece who has immense family loyalty and a macabre sense of humour.

So much bone had to be removed that a great fear emerged that what was left of the bone would break while or after I returned from the operating room. This would have called for an amputation. A light cast was applied as soon as possible and replaced later with a more sturdy model, enabling me to walk. In due course, the femur restored itself to normal proportions and strength.

Dr. Harris was able to supplement his legendary surgical skill with another crutch, if I may test your endurance with yet another corny play on words. By the time of my operation, sulfa drugs were in common use, at last providing a weapon in the fight against *staphylococcus aureus* and other enemies.

Although my early encounters with Dr. Harris led to his most thorough and intrusive attack on my problem, it was by no means his last ministration. During the years from 1942 to 1949, while studying at Pickering College and then at the University of Toronto, I succumbed to new attacks, not all of them in my leg. But by this time sulfa drugs were supplanted by antibiotics as the most effective way of coping with the infections. To combat these new attacks, Dr. Harris prescribed penicillin which, at first, could only be administered by injections every three hours and later by continuous intravenous drips. Eventually, a suspended form of penicillin was devised which required only one injection a day, and therefore eliminated the mandatory confinement in hospital. Sometimes, when a joint was affected, a cast was applied immobilizing the area. The usual sites of trouble were my right elbow and the left shoulder. An encouraging sign was that these attacks occurred at ever greater intervals until they ceased altogether. By the time I reached my mid-thirties, this phase of life came to an end; osteomyelitis no longer loomed threateningly on the horizon.

During most of my "osteo years" in Kingston, our general physician was a close friend, Dr. Malcolm Brown, who later became head of the Medical Research Council of Canada in Ottawa. Being a friend, he knew a great deal about me not necessarily related to my health. On one occasion, when my right elbow was acting up again, he astonished me by asking, after examining the painful site, "When are you giving this paper you have been sweating over?" I was in the process of drafting my first major presentation to the annual meeting of the Canadian Political Science Association. The research on which it was based was massive, and the occasion of the greatest professional significance. What Malcolm had noticed, but never mentioned before, was that my outbreaks tended to occur in periods of stress. Once he raised the issue, I recalled that while at U of T, a big flare-up coincided with examinations. All this is likely old hat to the medicos but it was news to me, reinforcing the impression I had of Dr. Beare as my saviour. The patient's state of mind is of the greatest relevance to his physical state and recuperative powers.

Osteo, or rather the treatment it at one time called for, produced a side effect years after the illness had abated. I discovered its link to osteomyelitis by a curious accident. When I was in my middle fifties, I reported to Murie that my students were increasingly incapable of articulating clearly. This was evident particularly in my large classes. She ever so gently raised the possibility that the problem might not have been the students' mumbling but my hearing. Accordingly, I hotfooted it to Dr. Malcolm Williams, the Head of Otolaryngology at Queen's, a friend and great tease. He assured me, after his audiologist performed her explorations, that there was nothing to worry about, my problem was merely advancing senility. Yes, and there was a loss of hearing, but hearing aids were not yet needed. Eventually, however, they came to constitute an absolutely essential part of life.

Some years after I had first raised the hearing problem, I was hospitalized for a hernia operation. Some minor glitch occurred and I had to wait in an antechamber of the operating theatre. There I was, bored on a stretcher and bereft of anything but the regular issue nightie. Casting about for a distraction, I discovered a file containing the correspondence between my GP and the surgeon, containing a letter that had somehow strayed into this folder by mistake. It was the report from Malcolm Williams, the ear man, to Don MacNaughton, my GP, written after the first ear examination. It described the extent of hearing loss and then added an intriguing thought. It was likely, it volunteered, that this impairment was caused by the heavy doses of sulfa drugs John had been given while suffering from osteomyelitis.

The only other physical remnants are hypothetical. Both a pronounced scoliosis and a deformity in my right leg may trace back to the bone disease. Tailors notice that one of my legs is a couple of centimeters shorter than its mate. My dreadful posture has adjusted to this so that I do not limp, except, for some reason, when I am tired.

Despite such minuscule inconveniences, I have managed to lead a pretty active life. I walk a great deal and avoid escalators and elevators as much as possible. Until I moved to live in the country, I played tennis regularly. In my forties, Ned Franks, a former student and current friend introduced me to cross-country skiing, an activity which I have indulged in ever since. When I go for pleasant walks or glide along on XC skis—activities requiring the use of my legs—I often remind myself of how extraordinarily lucky I am to be able to do so.

Early fears, spawned by my illness, have greatly informed my character. One such fear was that the staphylococcus infection might settle in my brain and thus cause my demise. I did not ask Dr. Beare or any of his successors about this and may have been on shaky medical ground. But whether realistically based or prompted by ignorance or fever, I had the notion that I might die on short notice. Every day, therefore, was a wonderful gift I sought to make the most of. This approach, not uncommon among people in similar circumstances, made it a lot easier to cope with the challenges presented by the disease. And it has stayed with me even after my recovery. Living every day as if it were your last is not a bad prescription although, admittedly, it is not always easy or even possible to remember.

A by-product of this perspective was that I acquired the habit of not being too upset by small things or by things I could do absolutely nothing about. In view of my long-standing and abiding interest in politics and public affairs, there have always been enough really BIG problems and wrongs to fill the day. At one point I wondered, however, whether I had carried my practice too far. Dr. Delahaye, a Kingston physician whom I knew because we were both active in the local branch of the Canadian Institute of International Affairs, gave me a medical examination needed for an insurance policy. He asked me how I was doing, and I told him that I was maturing, that I was learning to put up with a great many things I abhorred. A wise gent, he said "Don't learn it too well," an admonition that is still imprinted indelibly on my mind.

The ailment affected not only the body and mind but also, particularly during its early years, my socialization. Being on crutches or bed-ridden for long periods interferes with normal behaviour. I never learnt properly how to dance, for instance, and virtually all my early girlfriends were nurses, whom I met while lying in bed. Time and advent to university changed the latter but not, alas, the former. Still, I cannot complain that the early handicaps damaged the ease with which I was later able to interact with people. On the contrary, enforced absence from the busy hurly-burly of adolescence vividly brought home to me how dependent we are on the goodwill of others and how dependent that goodwill is, in turn, on how we treat them. The easy sociability I acquired as a young child was thus probably enhanced by having been so ill.

The most important non-medical effect by far of osteo was, however, that it turned me into a reader. The parents had tried hard, before my illness, to introduce me to attractive children's literature in both Czech and German; I greatly loved some of it and was also committed to the daily paper and to a children's periodical. But, as well, I loved participating in all the games played by my Zlín pals and that left relatively little time for reading.

Much has been said and written about how reading affects our lives. The inverse receives less attention. How does life affect our reading? When I was immobilized in bed, the handicap of playground distractions disappeared and reading became an extremely important component of the day and, often, the night. Having been given this start, the habit took, and I was hooked. I have wondered whether I would have drifted into an academic career had I not had this forced bookish immersion.

Committing memories to paper brings with it the urge to evaluate phenomena touching our lives. Accordingly I keep wondering whether, despite the obvious hardship it inflicted on me and my family, I owe a debt to *staphylococcus aureus*.

In the long run, and after the misery has passed, I believe that my life was amazingly enriched by my sickness. In addition to causing misery, it provided opportunities and several of its aftermaths have constructively altered the path I tread.

V

The Gathering Storm and a Break in the Clouds

My health had improved substantially by 1938, but the same could not be said of world affairs. Crisis followed crisis, as Germany kept pushing the world relentlessly toward the abyss. One positive development, however, unrelated to the larger scene, reunited the Meisel family. Rose graduated and eventually Mami and I joined Tati in Eindhoven. Now we were all under the same roof, producing, among other things, many giggles as we practiced speaking Dutch together.

We also went on what was our last joint sojourn in Czechoslovakia. During my holidays, the parents decided to spend a brief vacation in Slovakia's Tatra Mountains. The experience, while scenically gorgeous, was eerie and upsetting. Our hotel was not anything as posh, but I was reminded of it, years later, by the imposing hostelry figuring in *Last Year at Marienbad*, the stylish, but also quite sinister, French film.

The blackest gloom suffused our mood. Germany was mobilizing its armed forces, as was Czechoslovakia, and Hitler threatened to invade unless further concessions were made. The vast majority of Czechoslovak Sudeten Germans had turned Nazi and appealed to Hitler for release from the Czech "yoke": they wanted to join the German Reich. Our hotel resembled a purple-martin house in late autumn. Guests vacated the hotel at an alarming rate, until we were the last holdouts. The staff, wanting to close the place, daily presented us with increasingly menacing and horrendous accounts of the latest developments. They pressed us urgently to depart. For reasons I cannot even begin to imagine, we tarried a day or two longer before leaving. All this was terrifying and totally uncharacteristic of Tati, who was caution personified. Even a mere a gossamer's weight of prudence dictated that we pack and leave.

The Slovak interlude gave me a small taste of what so many European targets of Nazi venom—Poles, Czechs, Jews, Roma, homosexuals—felt before confronting the world of Dachau,

Auschwitz, Belsen, Terezín, Buchenwald and the like. We mercifully escaped, but it gave me an inkling — only an inkling — of the horrible anguish, dread and impotence that engulfed so many millions of Hitler's actual and potential victims.

Soon after my return to school the parents moved again, this time abandoning Europe altogether. Relocating the Export Department to the Netherlands, the company realized, was not a whit more secure from German takeover than Czechoslovakia. Bat'a decided to decentralize the control and management of its worldwide activities by creating a number of regional headquarters. Casablanca was to be the control centre for Africa and Tati was to be the head of it.

Just after Rose's and my school terms ended in the summer of 1939, Tati developed gallstones and his Casablanca doctor recommended that he take the famous cure in Vichy. He complied, and the parents came to London for a few days before all four of us took off for the French spa.

Vichy, soon to become the home of the infamous, Nazi-collaborating regime of Maréchal Pétain, was still, in July of 1939, a comfortable city brimming with spas, hotels, parklands and entertainment sites for folks bent on restoring or preserving their health. Tati took the prescribed baths and the whole family regularly attended one of the many grand halls housing fountains supplying the salubrious waters. The health-pilgrims approached these with their own drinking vessels encased in a wide variety of wicker or leather cases. The setting and the rituals were elegant and may have contributed to Vichy's curative effect. Who was to say whether Tati's problems were alleviated by Vichy's treatments or by its psychological effects?

My recollections of the town are spotty and trivial. It was only years later that I realized that Vichy is in the Auvergne and that, had we been more with-it, we might have made an effort to hear, in their native habitat, some of those wonderful local songs Joseph Canteloube later made world-famous. Murie and I were to virtually wear out the grooves of an LP record by Salli Terri, accompanied by Laurindo Almeida, which introduced us to this music. Another missed opportunity also came to light only later, in an Outrement restaurant, a favourite hangout of René Lévesque and his crowd (one of whom I was interviewing there). The owner, who was an *Auvergnat,* insisted that his region produces by far the best sweetbreads in France, a dish he adopted as his *spécialité de la maison.*

It *was* terrific; we had clearly missed something while in Vichy by not partaking of this delicacy.

Sometimes quite insignificant matters stick in the mind, whereas weighty ones vanish. I have no recollections whatsoever of our hotel and meals but remember a frivolous pastime which greatly amused Rose and me; we never forgot it. We discovered the *pédalo*, a two-seater watercraft rentable at a boathouse on the Allier, the river running through the town. Like a bicycle, it is propelled by pedals. I have no idea why we thought them so funny, but we did venture out in them quite often, admiring the town from the river.

Like all spas, Vichy provided its visitors with numerous distractions to while away the time between medical assignations. We avoided the Casino but often attended concerts given in the parks in bandshells and other suitable venues. One of these was of particular interest to a growing boy. It was offered by an all-female orchestra — the first one I had ever heard or heard of. The musical quality seemed high, a judgment confirmed by Mami, who knew whereof she spoke. But while they were most decently and correctly attired, there was a slight element of eroticism in how they were turned out. Nothing blatantly provocative about it, you understand, but to a boy my age certain curves and contours made a sufficiently deep impression to remain for life.

These minor flashbacks are dwarfed by the oppressive gloom that ceaselessly weighed on us, caused by the deteriorating international situation and the ever-darkening prospects for the world's imminent future. Several catastrophes had taken place earlier in the year which bode ill for what might follow. Germany, assisted by Poland and Hungary, had by now annexed parts of Czechoslovakia. This perfidy was made possible by the Munich Pact in which Britain and France contravened their treaty obligations, betrayed Czechoslovakia and shamelessly appeased Hitler. Neither Czechoslovakia nor the USSR were invited to the discussions, although mighty Italy was there. Next spring Hitler blatantly ignored *his* undertakings and created the Czechoslovak Protectorate — a de facto annexation. For us Czechs and most Slovaks this was the end. Only a military victory could rectify Hitler's wrongs. But who could possibly wish for that? Memories of the senseless slaughter of the First World War were still in most people's minds. The likely advent of another such bloodbath and its unimaginable horrors cast a tragic pall over humankind.

Tati completed his treatments towards the end of August, and we sailed from Marseilles to Algiers and Morocco. While en route the news broke that the arch-enemies, Nazi Germany and Communist Russia, signed a ten-year non-aggression pact freeing Germany for its next European adventure, the invasion of Poland. This occurred on September 1st, a few days after our arrival in Casablanca, plunging the world into war.

Despite the months of threatening skies, there were a few bright spots amid the strain. In 1981 the government of Quebec issued a poster to mark the Year of the Handicapped. It shows a fatally broken sturdy branch of a tree, but above the break a slender new growth glistens in the sun. "La vie continue," (Life goes on) is the caption. It hangs on one of my walls and is a most attractive and evocative reminder that even amid disaster, there usually is reason for hope and optimism. And so it was on the eve of the looming conflagration: during those days of gloomy foreboding, the 1939 Easter holiday, spent with Tati and Mami in Morocco, offered a welcome respite.

I set out for our latest home on what was then the most exciting, colourful and romantic experience of my life. Since my preceding years had not been exactly drab, that is saying something. The trip involved leaving Ottershaw by train via London to Tilbury, a long boat ride to Tangiers and another rail jaunt through Spanish Morocco and the North African desert and ended in Casa, as we came to call it. Scenically, socially and emotionally, this explosive experience still reverberates in my head.

A train departed from St. Pancras for Tilbury with the sole purpose of conveying passengers intending to board RMS *Cathay* for its journey to India and beyond. My destination was the first stop, Tangiers, at the north-western tip of Africa, opposite Gibraltar. The idea of a boat-train, as it was called, was highly romantic, promising to lead to far away, magical places.

The fifteen thousand ton *Cathay* seemed a floating palace of luxury. I never saw the First Class quarters and had a hard time imagining their splendour since *my* class, the Second, was opulent beyond anything I had ever seen. One distinction between the two classes, I surmise now, was that my lot did not put on a dinner jacket for the evening feast although we certainly changed into our best togs. The ship belonged to the Peninsular and Oriental Steam Navigation Company, known to frequenters of the Raj as the P & O. Its furnishings, routines, and personnel plunged me into a world I had so far encountered only in the pages of books by Conrad and even more so by Somerset Maugham and Agatha Christie. The officers were, needless to say, white but most of the folks routinely looking after us were Indian.

My first close encounter with the cabin steward occurred in the morning after we left port. Someone knocked exuberantly on the cabin door at an ungodly hour and woke me and my cabin mate with trays bearing hooded pots of tea. Quite a bit later, the steward was heard splashing about in a nearby bathroom from whence he emerged, bidding me to enter. After I had sat in the tub and scrubbed myself in salty water, he came back, suggested that I pull the plug and poured a bucket of fresh water all over me, forestalling an itch from sea salt. A sumptuous breakfast was served in the dining room later, assuaging my fear that I would have to make do all morning with just a pot of tea, no matter how delicious.

It was not only the Indian cabin crew who initiated me into the ways of sea travel; my cabin mate — whose name, improbably, was Mr. Greenhorne — kindly took me under his wing. He rolled his R's, and when we first met I found his accent not unlike that of my fellow Czechs. His provenance, however, was not central Europe but Scotland. He became a friend and guide. I gleaned my first impression of him from his luggage. When, upon boarding, I found our cabin, no one was in it, but half the floor was strewn with well-travelled suitcases and trunks adorned with a profuse crop of labels of hotels and steamship lines from all over the world. The whole looked awesomely cosmopolitan. There was also a rather outsize wooden case whose contents were revealed only later. It was full of guns. My partner, it turned out, was an explorer and hunter. Mr. Greenhorne showed me the ropes of life on board. He and a group of equally well-travelled and knowledgeable cronies, who had obviously known one another before, foregathered every evening in a certain corner of one of the bars to natter about their globe-trotting lives. They invariably invited me to join them and, despite my tender age and relatively sedentary life, included me in their gang. You can imagine how the accounts of their adventures captivated their young companion, who really *was* a greenhorn. I picked up a lot of lore I thought might come useful to The Kingfisher patrol of the Ottershaw Scouts. One such gem still lingers in my memory bank: the best powdered milk for safaris was KLIM, "Milk spelt backwards, you know."

During their post-prandial séances the explorer/hunters clung to whisky, whereas I opted for orange juice. They successively treated one another to drinks and unfailingly covered my tab as well. Since both the price of fruit juice and my consumption were modest, this did not tax their pocket books unduly. They always signed a chit and I had no idea of what it all cost. I wished to play my part, however, and on the eve before our arrival in Tangiers requested the privilege of taking care of the next round. This was met with mirth and argument which, in the end, I won. In doing so, I ran into a problem. Tati, a seasoned traveller, filled his letters before I sailed with useful advice for the trip. One matter he stressed was always to pay cash, and never to sign anything. This, remember, was well before plastic money. He thought that this policy would avoid possible fraud and impulsive expenditure. So when it came time to pay, I produced a couple of those white, insignificant-looking five-pound notes, which looked like everything but money. I knew that they would easily cover the bill. We were in 1939, remember. But the steward politely refused, insisting that I sign a chit. I am not sure whether this was P & O policy or a desire not to sully his hands with filthy lucre. I had no choice but to settle my one-item account later at a time and place specified by the bursar.

Tati had also told me that I would be able to rent a folding chair and a rug on one of the decks, which would be assigned to me throughout the voyage. I did so and thus was able to read or sleep outside during the day and to watch the ever-changing colours, movements and patterns of the billows. When the sea got rough and intimations of nausea began, it was often a bit easier to lie outside than in the enclosed cabin.

I must admit that even on this fine voyage and on board a much larger craft than the Channel ferries, I succumbed. The Bay of Biscay, which we traversed while passing the Western coast of Spain, is known for challenging queasy tummies. I did miss a meal or two and suffered the indignity and discomfort of *mal de mer* (the French sounds so much more impressive than its English equivalent). And although it was neither pretty nor hygienic to find relief at the railing rather than inside, it was more direct and less likely in heavy seas to cause being knocked against walls and stairs while staggering towards the toilets. It was also, at times, unavoidable.

Apart from the hours when I was, perforce, feeding the fish, the time outside was most enjoyable. I read a great deal, wrote little sketches of the people I had encountered, and strode briskly around the deck, which had signs posted at regular intervals from which one could deduce how many yards or miles one had walked.

The trips to and from Tangiers featured another miraculous aspect: their cost. The return fare from London to Tangiers was incredibly low. The figure of £15 sticks in the mind but even if it was more than that, it was apparently derisory.

Enchantment marks the next short phase of my Easter holiday. The very idea of Tangiers fascinated me quite apart from the town's intrinsic charm. It was a political entity new to me: an international zone, administered jointly by France, Spain, Britain and Italy. I was obliged to stay there for a day or so before catching my train to Casablanca, enabling me to look around a bit.

My introduction to an Arab town and to Mediterranean climate and vegetation was stunning. The luxuriant botanical opulence hit home the most, although the vitality, bustle and oriental mystique of the place certainly also made a big impression. The weather was perfect. My room in a small, bright, beautiful hotel had a balcony overlooking the blue, blue Mediterranean: white walls, many tiles, magnificently shaped and textured pottery vessels, terraces, an immaculate small garden with alcoves containing diverse clusters of seats, and charming winding paths, but most of all a profusion of bright flowers everywhere, surrounded by leaves in varying shades of green and in contrasting textures. The greenery and flowers were overwhelming.

As so often when recalling a powerful feeling or experience, I am driven to compare it to a book or film. In this case, although the differences are far, far greater than the similarities, the *atmosphere* of Tangiers was somehow recreated for me while watching *To Catch a Thief*, the 1955 Hitchcock film with Cary Grant and Grace Kelly, in which the scenery of the Riviera is the major attraction, despite the eminence of the two stars. Tangiers was less dramatic, but the luminosity and lush vegetation of Hitchcock's north shore of the Mediterranean also marked its south-western extremity. It was the most beautiful and romantic town I had ever seen and my small hotel the most perfect place I had ever stayed in. That's impressionable youth, for you, although both really were delightful, and still are, even to the jaundiced eye of an old man who has since seen a great many other places which have made the heart sing.

VI

Casablanca

Upon arriving in Casablanca, we pondered whether I would be able to return to my school after the holidays and, if not, what would become of my education. War conditions and the closing of Ottershaw provided the answer: a return to England was out.

An alternative strategy was devised, complicated by occasional eruptions of osteomyelitis and other time-consuming detours. I made no bones about being less comfortable with maths than with what the French call "the human sciences." And although I had started private French tutorials in Zlín, and continued with regular classes at Ottershaw, my French was still not as strong as it might have been. Arrangements were made for me to become an occasional student in a local school, while also taking regular private classes in Algebra and French. My maths teacher was Victor Sutton and the language coach a young chap called Palacci. My address book reveals that his first name was Beno, but this word was never used. Victor originally hailed from Syria and Palacci from Lebanon.

I did not benefit much from the school encounters, which were curtailed by illness, but learnt a great deal from both my tutors, some of it related more to cultural practices than to scholarship. Oddly, two surprises in the latter category relate to bodily functions. I was quite shocked, when reaching M. Sutton's apartment for a morning class, that on the floor near his bedroom door there stood a liquid-filled chamber pot. This turned out to be a regular phenomenon in the mornings but never later in the day. I kept speculating about the hour at which the maid arrived to take care of things. As for Palacci, most of our conversational lessons took place while we were walking to various interesting sites in Casa. On one such sortie, we passed a public convenience. As we approached, he said with brutal directness, "Voulez-vous pisser?" I found this shocking despite having attended a boys' school.

Palacci helped vastly to improve my French and, oddly, also enriched my knowledge of English letters. One of his assignments consisted of translating into French a delightful fable by James Thurber, the beginning of a love affair that has continued ever since.

Casablanca provided another valuable pedagogical experience. Tati bought a car—a Dodge or Plymouth—and engaged Djilali, a mechanic in a nearby garage, to drive us occasionally on our weekend excursions, visits to major Moroccan cities and other errands. He was very intelligent and spoke French well. On one occasion he invited us into his home to a family dinner. Sitting on the floor, popping lamb meatballs into our mouths from a significant but safe distance and eating everything with our fingers, we enjoyed a mouth-watering repast and an extraordinarily pleasant and interesting dinner. Among the many delicacies was the very best roasted corn I have ever eaten in my life. It was done on an open fire.

It fell to Djilali to teach me how to drive. This he did with great patience and exceptional attention to detail, manifested in, among other things, the precision of his instructions. He always indicated when it was time to sound the horn—an operation more frequently resorted to in Latin and Arab countries than in Canada, and particularly in a cluttered city like Casa. He told me when to sound the horn and specified at whom. He would, say *"Klaxonnez pour le Juif,"* (sound the horn for the Jew) or...*l'Arabe,* or...*le Shluh* (Berber mountaineer) or...*le chameau* (camel). Ethnic identification was facilitated by the pedestrians' or bike-riders' headgear: Jews wore black fezzes, Arabs red ones, and Berbers white small turbans. Camels were usually bare-headed. Djilali was a good teacher, but I failed my first driver's test. This, apparently, was a routine occurrence prompted by a desire to increase municipal revenues. I was not obliged to continue filling Casablanca's coffers after the second test, however.

Most of the indigenous population of Casa was Arab, but there were also numerous Shluh and a significant number of "native" Jews (distinguished from their European co-religionists by not being called *Juifs* but *Israéalites*). We came to know our cleaner and cook, Ahmed, better than any other local resident. He was a Shluh. Mami, who was almost fanatical about cleanliness, said that he was the most pristine person, by far, she had ever encountered. His white robes and turban were always impeccable, no matter what he did, and he regularly washed the soap in the bathroom. He taught me how, when cooking an omelette, it is stylish (and fun) to turn it over by tossing it into the air—the only attraction I experienced, at that time, to culinary pursuits. We lived in an apartment on a street called—ironically, given the unfolding events *rue de l'Aviation Française*. At some point it came to light that Ahmed had taken up residence in a structure on the roof of our apartment building which also housed various utility spaces and elevator machinery. His "cell" was minuscule and there were no sanitary facilities. How he managed to maintain his immaculate status under these circumstances, we never discovered. He asked the parents to conceal his place of residence since the management would certainly have evicted him.

We all liked Ahmed a lot and thought that he was happy in the service, so to speak. But one day he told Mami that he would be leaving. He came from a remote village in the Atlas Mountains and his mother had sent word that she found a suitable bride for him; it was time to return and marry her. He had, of course, never met the lady but was certain that his mother's choice would work out well.

The "European" population was predominantly of French descent, and its language and cultural context were overwhelmingly French. Since Casa was the site of Bat'a's African headquarters, there were quite a few employees, including a small but cohesive Czech colony. There was little mingling with the local, non-Czech European population, let alone with the various native groups.

An important part of the Czechs' social life took place on some of Casablanca's many nearby gorgeous beaches, where the European co-workers—both blue- and white-collar—and their families spent part of Saturday and Sunday. During the 1939–40 so-called phony war, gas rationing was not in effect, so weekend junkets were still possible. The principal pastimes were swimming, fishing (sardines were used as bait), playing volleyball and soccer, drinking, and just taking in the breathless view of seemingly unending sand beaches, flanked by the massive rolling waves of the Atlantic Ocean. Being Czech, the group was also absorbed by the preparation of substantial, often heavy meals. The pleasant beach life was, of course, marred by continuous fretting about the imminent explosion of "real" war.

Some of our Czech Bat'a crowd joined a local volleyball league and actually won the Moroccan championship—a feat particularly impressive to those unaware of the weakness of the opposition. Despite my leg, I was able to play with the team from time to time and so later boasted to my Varsity friends with a straight face that I had been on the team that won the volleyball championship of Morocco.

Given the setting and the circumstances, it is not surprising that there was a good deal of drinking during our beach outings – more of it than met the eye. Some folks continued imbibing well into the night and beyond. The beverage of choice was called "*mlíčko*" (small milk). It was absinthe which gained its affectionate name from the fact that when water was added, it turned a milk-like white. Tati worried about the popularity of this concoction and other libations, because on Mondays the plant suffered from serious absenteeism which sometimes spilled even into the next day.

Rose and I chummed together with a small group made up of youngish Bat'a office workers. We went to films and concerts and, fairly regularly, drove to nearby Camp Boulhaut, where in a seaside café we drank coffee, chatted and played bridge – my only, and short-lived, exposure to the game. Cards bore me.

I am struck now by the fact that our whole life was spent so much in isolation from the large colony of francophone Europeans and from the Arab population. That evening at Djilali's was the only time we spent in the home of an Arab Moroccan. We had some social contact with the Suttons but it, too, was slender.

When France fell in June 1940, the atmosphere and activities in Casa changed dramatically. An influx of refugees began arriving, including some Czechs and Slovaks, few of whom had any ties to Bat'a. Mr. Kundrát, the Czechoslovak Consul, with whom we were on very friendly terms, did what he could to help them, but his means and powers were limited. As the head of the largest local Czechoslovak enterprise, Tati was very much involved helping many of our fellow countrymen.

A fallout from this situation left an ineradicable impression – one that resurfaces from time to time, not to haunt me, but to send a delayed chill down the spine. Word came one evening that a group of Czechoslovaks hoping to disembark in Casablanca was on board a ship moored just outside the local harbour. They would be allowed to disembark their imminently departing ship only if some creditable person guaranteed their bona fides and their not becoming a burden to the local authorities. Failing that, they would either become perpetual floating refugees barred from landing anywhere – such cases were not unknown – or they would be returned to a French port from whence they would fall into Vichy and, ultimately, German hands.

Tati, Mr. Kundrát and some Bat'a colleagues set out on that dark night to the harbour where they explored what could be done. I was allowed to come along and so was exposed to the heavily atmospheric, salty ambience of the port of Casablanca and the smoke-filled office where the negotiations with the local authorities took place. These were tense, but a small boat was eventually dispatched to fetch our Czechs from one of the ships lined up on the horizon. After a lengthy examination of passports and searching interrogations, the Czechs were allowed to stay.

Our rescue mission is one of the most dramatic recollections of my adolescence. I do not know to what extent I have superimposed subsequent impressions of various ports on this one, including the sinister Hamburg port in the BBC's famous adaptation of John LeCarré's *Smiley's People*, or is it *Tinker, Tailor, Soldier, Spy*? But what I recall now is a highly atmospheric jumble of cranes, massive ships, coils of rope, the shriek of sirens, the sound of waves lapping the nearby wharves, bare light bulbs shrouded in a damp mist, and lit-up port holes here and there attesting to an ongoing life on the sea. All of this bathed in a mixture of smells of the sea, fish, sweat, far-away blossoming trees, and an occasional whiff of tobacco smoke, presumably emanating from the bearded salt who used to adorn packages of *Players* cigarettes. The overall impression was one of awe, excitement and, also, of fear. I felt myself to be in the presence of something cosmic and immensely powerful, and at the same time beckoning, intriguing and full of the promise of undreamt-of adventure. In addition to the physical setting, the human context makes this episode so indelible. For some of the passengers, the outcome was a matter of life and death.

Not all Czechoslovaks arrived in Casablanca in so dramatic a fashion. Some trickled in overland from Algiers or Tangiers, others arrived on regularly scheduled boats. Almost all escaped fallen France. Two groups stood out. One group, refugees in the strict sense, sought a safe haven and an opportunity to get on with life. The other group, also driven from France, was composed of Czech airmen. Their primary goal was to get to Britain, so as to continue fighting in the war. They hoped to join Czech air force units regrouping in Britain in conjunction with the Royal Air Force, and continue fighting the Germans. Although at this stage travelers were still able to obtain exit visas, there were severe restrictions: male nationals of military age from Allied countries were precluded. Czechoslovaks, with their London-based government-in-exile, were clearly on the Allied side. Hungarians and Rumanians, whose governments had thrown in their lot with Germany, were allowed to leave.

How can one speak of Casablanca without recalling *Casablanca*, the much-loved film? In the language of cyber-lovers, it is a perfect link to my Casa days. Pure fiction, it has nevertheless unwittingly become a telling documentary of the tense atmosphere and the trapped souls whose very lives depended on the ability to obtain a visa in a largely corrupt world. Neither Rick, his American Café, nor its colourful denizens ever existed, of course, but one character, Captain Louis Renault, Prefect of Police, had a close double. There *was* a chief of police, not immune to an occasionally greased palm, who decided who obtained an exit visa. How to persuade him to do so in the case of our Czech aviators?

Rose, immortalized by my Voigtländer camera.

Enter Rose, my bookish sister. I do not know how she came to play so perilous and critical a role but play it she did. She was perfectly suited for it, although totally bereft of any prior training. An attractive young woman (although no vamp or femme fatale), she was very bright, linguistically skilled, endowed with a sense of humour and clearly a quick-witted actress. I suspect that Mr. Kundrát, the consul, may have had a hand in her recruitment. The trick was for the prospective traveller to produce a birth certificate, or some other document, indicating that he was born in some preferably unpronounceable and unheard-of place. Chaps who first saw the light of day in Prague, Brno or Bratislava were out of luck. My sister would make an appointment with the police chief (whom she came to know fairly well, given the number of visa applicants), present him with the documents and the persuasive argument that the village of origin was in Hungary or Rumania, and engage in pleasant conversation. Both smoked. At one stage, the prefect would rise, excuse himself for a moment and push towards her a beautiful cigarette box made of the root of a Moroccan tree. When she opened it, it was empty. This caused no surprise and Rose knew what to do. The appropriate bribe was placed in the box which was then shoved to the other side of the desk. When "Captain Renault" returned, the conversation resumed and he in due course casually opened the box. If he liked what he saw, the *Visa de Sortie* was issued. There is no question that the prefect was on the take. But he needed to be careful and to cover his flank. Hence the charade about the Czech's place of origin. And one never knew whether, like so many French and Moroccan officials, he sympathized with the Allies and was glad to thumb his nose at the Colonel Strassers and their ilk.

We saw quite a bit of the small cluster of Czech newcomers. Most were artists, although there was also an extremely bright and kind agronomist. He was a Communist with an intense interest in the socio-political and economic underpinnings of the world crisis. Novotný took quite an interest in me and persuaded me to start writing analyses of the current political scene in Britain which we then discussed at length. Another instance of an adult encouraging me to put thought on paper.

One of three artists we befriended was Pelc, a well-known caricaturist. He presented us with a cartoon of me in boxing shorts, arms and huge boxing gloves resting on the ropes, and a bowl with what looked like dentures on the floor of the ring. Rose must have leaked info about my brief immersion in pugilism. Kopf was a landscape artist. He had lived in Polynesia which was evidenced in much of his work. But the two strong black ink drawings he gave us in no way evoked Gauguin's luscious paintings. They were lovely but also expressed something of Czech dourness, and likely the worries darkening our lives. Another member of the group was Adolf Hoffmeister; though primarily a writer, he was a multi-talented, versatile artist. He was famous, but we found him less congenial than the others for his manner was patronizing, probably because Tati was "in trade" and Hoffmeister, an aesthete.

One day Tati announced that he had received a cable instructing him to leave Casablanca. Germany's stranglehold on France was becoming more evident, and no one knew how much longer the flimsy legal mote of the Moroccan Protectorate would last. There was a chance that German control would become absolute. Our Jewish background made us extremely vulnerable, and the company advised that we leave.

The family held a council of war to decide how to respond to the cable from HQ which was, at that time, in Brazil. Tati was given a choice among five possible sites. I have forgotten two of them but recall that Manila in the Philippines, Honolulu in Hawaii, and Port-au-Prince in Haiti were offered. There was great irony in the situation. Mami, who always suffered terribly in the heat, had apparently said when she married Tati, that she would happily follow him anywhere, except to a hot climate.

I acutely remember our council of war. The parents, Rose and I sat around the dining-room table; I was flabbergasted that I, still a schoolboy, was included. This was the first time that our family made a major decision together. After considering heaps of relevant, and some irrelevant factors, one dimension emerged as decisive. We were, as I noted in previous chapters, all great anglophiles and Haiti, while less interesting than the other possible places, and certainly no less hot, was much closer to Canada. And Canada was part of the British Commonwealth and was in many ways British. Perhaps, if Tait accepted the position in Haiti, to run Bat'a's Central American enterprises and manage a small shoe factory, and if we went to Port-au-Prince, a further move to Canada might eventually follow. This seemed possible, as there was a large Bat'a enterprise there, run by Tom, the old Chief's son. So Haiti won.

Another Czech member of the Casa Bat'a team, Mr. Stein, was also racially tainted in German eyes. He was invited to accompany us to Haiti, where he would act as my father's senior secretary, a role for which his Moroccan duties prepared him well.

We now shared some, but by no means all of the problems and anxieties of other Casablanca refugees, as depicted in *Casablanca*. We needed a permanent visa for Haiti and several transit visas for the countries to be traversed on the way there. We also required exit visas from Morocco — a tough nut to crack, given the sex and ages of three of our party. Permission had to be obtained to cross Spanish Morocco which, given that Franco was in the saddle in Madrid, was de facto in enemy hands.

Although confronting some of the problems of refugees, our position was incomparably less disquieting and tragic than that of other migrants. We had a place to go to, no obstacle in obtaining a permanent Haitian visa, a multinational corporation backing and funding us, and could, for the time being at least, stay in Morocco until we were ready to depart. And in Mr. Stein we had a travel companion whose duty it was to take care of many of the challenges arising during the trip. It took no less than two months to get to Port-au-Prince. All this notwithstanding, the long voyage was in many ways also enjoyable, instructive and beautiful, so we had a lot to be thankful for. Not least, that getting out of the Vichy Protectorate might have saved our lives.

VII

A Long Journey

As the seagull flies, the journey from Casablanca to Port-au-Prince is straightforward. In 1940, however, this avian opportunity was not available to humans, and our trip was consequently a stuttering process full of obstacles and detours.

The longest segment of the trip — traversing the Atlantic — was achieved on board a notorious Spanish liner from Lisbon to Santos, Brazil. *Time* magazine (December 1, 1941) later noted that the ship and its sister vessels, were known in Latin America as "the Whitened Sepulchres." The transatlantic lap, however, was only the meat in the sandwich. The two pieces of toast on each side were the journeys to Lisbon and from Brazil to Haiti.

The reason we chose this route was partly logistic — the Atlantic had to be crossed somewhere and its northern half was a treacherous theatre of war. It was also business-driven. The head of the Baťa organization at the time was Jan Baťa, the founding Tomáš's half brother. Mr. Baťa invited Tati to confer with him in Brazil about Tati's upcoming duties in Haiti and Central America. So the way to Haiti was charted via Brazil.

Our first challenge was to get out of Casablanca and reach Lisbon. Two barriers stood in the way: Czechoslovak citizenship precluded an exit visa for the military-aged men and made traversing Franco-controlled Spanish Morocco hazardous. We could not get to Tangiers by train. The only option was to suppress our Czech passports for this trip and obtain substitute travel documents. Consul Kundrát procured passports for us issued by the government of Morocco. They were a special kind which described our nationality as *Apatride*, i.e., "without a country" or "nationality." Since these were the official documents enabling us to leave Morocco and admitting us to Tangiers, they also contained the visas, permits and immigration notations we obtained for the entire trip to Haiti. Mr. Kundrát assured us that this stratagem would not jeopardize our Czechoslovak citizenship. As soon as we arrived in Haiti, we checked in at the Czechoslovak consulate to register our genuine passports and revert to using them.

The subterfuge worked and we made it safely to Tangiers. The foregoing lovely sentence was so easy to jot down just now. But at the time, the moments when the French-Moroccan and Spanish-Moroccan officials examined our papers and permits were excruciating. Would we get away with it? What would we do if not? What if some of us were permitted to pass through and others not? What if we were deported to German occupied territory? The whole procedure took very much longer than anticipated and our overnight train arrived four hours late. I was terror-struck during the first *étape* of our voyage.

Although the source of the dread resided elsewhere, the next segment of our escape was equally tension-filled. British and Canadian navies were confronting German and Italian surface vessels and submarines everywhere and the Battle of the Atlantic was in full swing. The only feasible way to get from Tangiers to Lisbon was to charter a plane from Air France, an airline not enjoying a high reputation and scathingly known as *Air Chance*. Still, *faute de mieux*, as they would have said in Paris, there was no other available means of quitting Africa. To make matters worse, the plane we squeezed into was minuscule and the weather during the flight, treacherous. At one stage we encountered a spectacular and hair-raising thunderstorm. Not at all a comfortable trip.

Hotel Frankfort provided shelter for the three days we spent in Lisbon. The time of year, indifferent weather and our circumstances led to the hotel and the whole city making a dark and heavy impression. Years later, in happier times and a sunnier season, I found Portugal's capital radiant. In 1940, most of our time was devoted to completing our travel arrangements, gathering more stamps and signatures for our spurious passports, and receiving inoculations. Hours and hours were devoted to sitting and waiting in various offices for grave and grey officials to discharge endless arcane formalities. A number of Czechs came to see us, about one of whom I later wrote a short story — Guilt — which describes a poignant and painful dilemma characteristic of his and our plight in those times. A more cheerful and totally unexpected encounter took place in the hotel lobby. I bumped into Santyana, the only Portuguese pupil at Ottershaw. He was older than I and we did not know one another closely but it was astonishing and cheering to meet him. We both wore our school ties!

On October 4ᵗʰ, we embarked on the *Cabo de Hornos*. Our voyage took a little over two weeks: we stopped in Cadiz, Spain, to pick up additional passengers, then at Teneriffe in the Canary Islands, before setting sail for Rio de Janeiro. From Rio it was just a short hop to Santos, the port for Sao Paulo, our destination.

Our cabins were in the First Class and, while a bit shabby, were more than adequate. But we soon discovered that, as a major conveyor of refugees, the boat inhumanely crammed an incredibly large number of them in the hold. Many possessed worthless visas to various countries sold by crooked officials. Some were compelled to roam the world in these hellish ships and possibly even be returned to Nazi Europe and death. Frederic Charles Blair, Mackenzie King's notoriously Jew-hating immigration chief, had soulmates throughout the world. None died on our crossing so far as we knew, but a few, according to reports, did so on previous trips, earning the vessel, and its sister ships their sinister nicknames.

Upon landing in Rio we were greeted with newspaper stories reporting that our ship had been strafed by the Royal Air Force during the crossing and that there were five mortal casualties. This was a complete fabrication, likely planted by Axis propagandists. It is also possible that five individuals — passengers or crew — did die on the way and that the fabricated RAF attack was a convenient scapegoat. After a short stop in Rio we left for Santos, from where a short trip overland took us to Sao Paulo.

The days in and around Sao Paulo have merged in my mind into a kaleidoscope of superficial impressions, without rhyme or reason. The landscape was stunning, with precipitous roads snaking from the sea high into the adjacent plateaux and down again, offering breath-taking views of the mountains and unlimited vistas of the sea. But it also provided smaller brilliant patches of gaudy colour of tropical vegetation. If the gardens of Tangiers and Casablanca appeared to be shouting exuberantly in their splendour, those of Brazil shrieked with uncontrolled excess. They were bursting out of their optical seams. There was nothing wrong with them but they took getting used to. I also recall fragments of magnificent parks and museums, a huge greenhouse filled with orchids, a stadium entirely constructed of immense beams and curved struts of wood, unending expanses of sandy beaches and cornucopias of wonderful fruit. If I had to choose one word to capture my first impression of South America, it would be "vibrant."

After about two weeks, it was time to move on. Poor Tati had missed much of the fun because of his business commitments, and he was anxious to reach Haiti and start his new job. But once again, even though we were now largely outside the war zone, a straight line between Santos and Port-au-Prince was not available. No direct connections existed and we had to sail to Panama and from there take yet another ship to complete our journey.

The first vessel was a far cry from the *Cabo de Hornos*. The *Brazil Maru* was a Japanese luxury liner operated to earn its owners US dollars. It and a sister ship sailed literally around the world, ferrying passengers for a stiff price in American currency. Mr. Stein had once travelled on the *Normandie*, France's super-elegant equivalent to Britain's *Queen Mary*, and observed that the Japanese liner was every bit as stylish. We would have preferred to avoid so politically unsavoury a ship, but no alternative was available.

We boarded in Santos for a two-week trip to Balboa at the Pacific Ocean end of the Panama Canal. I had always thought that getting from the Atlantic to the Pacific by sea involved travelling from East to West but learnt better. Panama links Costa Rica and Colombia by creating a sort of east-west land bridge, an isthmus, roughly from the southern tip of North America to the northern point of South America. The canal starts on the Atlantic side at Colon and runs southeast towards Balboa and Panama City on the Pacific.

Because of the magnificence of the boat and the excellence of the service, the passage was extremely pleasant. Compared with the opening portion of our journey, it was relaxing and uneventful, although not entirely bereft of noteworthy incidents.

One day Tati received an invitation to visit the Purser's office. Upon arrival, he was presented with a bill for an astronomical amount. It turned out that an alleged Baťa employee had booked a passage on one of the *Brazil Maru's* sister ships. Because of his nationality, whatever it was, he was refused admittance to his intended destination. Unable to secure entry to any country, he was compelled to stay on the ship for months, despite having paid for only a single short passage. He was still there at the time of our trip. His current employment status was ambiguous but he had had some link with Baťa in the past. Tati, the shipping company knew, was a Baťa executive and it held him responsible for the tab of this modern-day Odysseus. It was a good try for which the purser deserved Brownie points, but it failed. Tati, with Mr. Stein by his side, managed to weasel out of what at first seemed an alarming fix.

Sojourn on the Japanese craft assisted my acquisition of social graces: I learnt how to eat with chopsticks — the dining room steward was an amused teacher — and I found out how to eat an olive. After one of the ship's many social events, Rose asked whether there was something wrong with me. I said "No," and inquired why. "You did not seem yourself this afternoon," she replied, "you did not talk much." My response was "What did *you* do with the olive stones?" I had never encountered these delicacies before and found no suitable receptacle for the pips, so stored them in my mouth.

Crossing the Panama Canal took a whole day, about eight or nine hours, and involved at least two lock operations. The ship was raised quite a height in the first, and then lowered again in the second, further along. Among the interesting views, one, alas, elicited some base instincts. A smallish, male group of passengers stood out among the passengers because of their objectionable behaviour. They were loud, threw their over-weight around, and — here's the crunch — loudly spoke German. They stood on the forward deck and watched practically the whole set of navigational manoeuvres. The day was sunny and hot, and as it wore on, the complexions of the Axis nationals kept turning redder and redder until they resembled lobsters. No one warned them that this was happening. Worse, and I confess this with only a speck of shame, we observed the process with glee and a healthy degree of *Schadenfreude,* to use the unique term bequeathed the world by their ancestors. We were at war, after all, although the country of the ship's flag was still neutral.

When we arrived in the evening at Balboa, we were immediately punished for our moral lapse: the immigration officials showed concern over our visas and told us that we would have to spend the night quarantined in a prison, pending, it was hoped, the resolution of the problem. We did have Panamanian visas, but they were invalid unless counter-signed by the United States consul. The reason for this precaution almost certainly was that there were so many honorary Panamanian consuls selling invalid visas all over the world; thus, some control was necessary. The timing of our arrival sunk us. It was close to American Thanksgiving and the consul had gone to his home in South Carolina, I think it was, to shoot grouse, turkeys or whatever. But not to worry, we were told, he would return in a few days; in the meantime, we could rent First, Second or Third Class accommodation in jail. We opted for the First and found the premises tolerable, if not luxurious.

Tati wanted to do some work with the manager of the local Bat'a store which posed no problem. He was allowed to absent himself from the premises. And next day they informed us that we could go to a hotel if we wished, but that we could still not legally change ships in Panama until the American signature was secured. Though the conditions in prison were quite simple, they were adequate and so we stayed another day until we were released from technical incarceration. Although there were a few tense moments during all this, the most serious challenge just then was that Rose came down with a very high fever caused by malaria. We worried that this might endanger the outcome of the consular problem, but her condition remained undetected and quickly improved.

The consul returned to his post and authenticated our visas, and we continued the journey as planned. We travelled overland to Colon on the Atlantic side of the canal and spent the night in a hotel whose name reminded us — as if we needed it — that we were now in a new geo-political sphere of influence. It was the Hotel Washington. Next morning, only three days after our arrival in Panama, we sailed to Port-au-Prince on a smallish efficient American ship, the SS *Panama*. We landed three days later, fifty-eight after we left Casablanca. The only fragment of information available about the final leg of our long journey in my memory or files is this unsurprising entry in my diary for November 24th, 1940: "Seasick."

VIII

Haiti

Haiti offered the first opportunity, since Ottershaw, to attend school in anything like a regular fashion. Immediately upon arrival in Port-au-Prince, I entered *St. Louis de Gonzague*, a respected *lycée* for boys run by the well-known Catholic teaching Order, the *Frères de l'instruction Chrétienne*. Except for classes in Haitian history and geography, the curriculum was more or less identical to that offered in such institutions in France. Academic standards were high.

Our "class brother" — who also gloried in the title *Préfet de discipline* — and I were the only white people in the class. Most of the students were mulatto, to use a term still current at the time, a nice mix of white and black. The ruling class in Haiti, other than the tiny group of Americans, was composed almost entirely of such hybrid Haitians. They spoke impeccable, even elegant, French and enjoyed a vigorous, rich cultural life. But they also mercilessly exploited their economically marginalized, mostly black, compatriots, thus creating a society plagued by huge income disparities. Most of the poor were only a banana skin away from subsistence, and usually below it. These conditions are endemic to Haiti and have been exacerbated by the catastrophic earthquake of 2010 and subsequent disasters.

The Catholic Church played a dominant role through its pervasive presence. It also, through schools like mine, contributed to the very high cultural standards of the local elite. While we were in Haiti, the Church also engaged in a vigorous campaign to reduce the influence of voodoo which seemed to coexist happily with the Roman creed and practice. A scandal received much press coverage soon after we arrived. A prominent socialite fainted while attending Mass. When good Samaritans sought to loosen some constricting garments, they discovered that below the outward layers of her attire she was festooned with all sorts of voodoo amulets. This, although it was not acknowledged in public was, apparently, not uncommon. What the Church was not involved in, insofar as we could see, was a vigorous effort to alleviate the social and economic plight of the people.

Our house in Port-au-Prince. The donkey, carrying a rider of either sex, was a common sight.

Several features of local life emerged as we settled in our house in a downtown, middle-class neighbourhood. The family next door was presided over by a judge. Their water, like that of everyone else, was heated by metal barrels on the roof, where they were baked by the sun. The shower, unlike ours, was outside as well, enabling us to hear the musical accompaniment of the judge's ablutions. He had a fine deep voice and a pleasing repertoire, not confined to musical offerings. Blessed with fabulous memory, he recited long passages from classical French plays by Corneille, Racine and Molière. These were rendered with moving passion or tenderness, as the occasion required. Since at *St. Louis de Gonzague* we had a daily hour of French literature, focusing on the seventeenth century golden age of drama, he unwittingly provided vivid complementary illustrations of some of the works I was studying.

He offered testimony to more than the elevated cultural level of the neighbourhood by providing a glimpse of prevailing relations between the sexes. Altercations next door between husband and wife were frequent, particularly when he was showering, and always one sided. He lectured and verbally abused her from inside the shower enclosure, while she attentively stood outside saying relatively little. She never took advantage of their respective spatial dispositions. Not once did I see her enter the house and leave hubby to his soap, harangues and soliloquies. One-sided male dominance of this sort was the norm in Port-au-Prince, we were told.

Our relationship with these and other neighbours was quite different from what it would have been in Canada. On the rare occasions when we saw one another in front of our homes, we politely acknowledged our respective presence, but no more. We knew no one in the neighbourhood. Astonishingly we failed to establish any kind of social relationships with the locals. This pattern resembled what had evolved in Casablanca, and both contrast sharply with the parents' outlook and disposition. They were friendly egalitarians as free of xenophobic or racial prejudice as one could be; the reasons resided elsewhere.

One was simply linguistic. Tati's French was pretty good but he was not a natural linguist and never felt totally comfortable in either spoken French or English. Mami, likely because of her good ear, handled languages better, but her forte was English rather than French. So it was natural that they found it more relaxing to associate with Czechs and other Europeans. We knew no Americans. My parents were not, in any event, particularly gregarious; Mami was perhaps more outgoing than Tati, but neither constantly needed the company of people. They everywhere felt most at ease with a small group of friends and family. During what was in some sense our exile, at least at first, Baťa co-workers were prominent in it. Most of them had known one another in Zlín and shared not only the Baťa experience there but also the challenges of moving abroad. They *were* all members of an extended family.

I also suspect that the friendly, relaxed social relationships we later found natural and common in Canada simply did not exist in the same way in Haiti. Prevailing mores were different. One kept one's distance and did not invade alien space. The fact that our neighbours' children and I did not attend the same schools probably also contributed to our failure to develop closer contact. In fact, I do not remember any of the neighbourhood children. Quite aside from the heat, osteomyelitis prevented me from engaging in sports, which removed another possible road to friendships.

Why did I not establish any close ties with any of my schoolmates? We arrived at the college, attended classes, and then immediately dispersed to our homes, spread throughout the city. I was never invited into a classmate's home, nor did I invite any one into mine. Prevailing cultural patterns no doubt had a lot to do with it, quite apart from the particular background and situation of our family. Our non-participation in the local religious life may also have played a part.

The close-knit nature of our family was powerfully enhanced by the intimacy and isolation imposed by forced exile. Eindhoven, Vichy, Casablanca, the long journey — they all placed us in close spatial proximity with one another while simultaneously holding us at a linguistic remove from others, at a time when the enveloping atmosphere was crushingly heavy with catastrophic news and rare, often tragic, messages from our homeland. No wonder the four Meisels had unconsciously forged themselves into a tiny defence league slightly aloof from others. Surprisingly, once I entered Canadian life, I became a most gregarious and convivial soul, continuously acquiring and only rarely relinquishing friends at all stages of my life. If I had a Rolodex it would be obese, bursting with entries of people with whom I had shared warm ties, sometimes briefly, sometimes for life.

Despite the primacy of the nuclear family, we were, of course, involved in a wider social circle. Most members were Baťa colleagues and their kin. The most popular recreational activity by far, was to drive to Kenskoff for a weekend — a tiny settlement enjoying an elevation of almost 1,500 meters. Since Port-au-Prince is only a few meters above sea level, the temperature at Kenskoff was considerably cooler and the air incomparably drier and fresher. The trip there passed through Pétionville, the posh residential quarter of Port-au-Prince, and then wound along a tortuous mountain road. Although a bit treacherous, the views were superb. A small, unpretentious and cozy hotel in Kenskoff, operated by a family of central European immigrants, was always our headquarters. It made a perfect base for walks and boasted a central European cuisine (*Küche*). I have a recollection of delectable schnitzels. One of the comic features of these excursions was that, on the night before our return to town, we left the car's trunk open. Once back home it was reopened, not only to retrieve our things, but also to enable us to sniff its stored coolness.

We occasionally entertained Otto Friedman, a Czech violinist and conductor of the local symphony orchestra. Pan Friedman lent me a violin and invited me to participate in rehearsals of his orchestra. I do not recall ever playing in a concert, either because of an eruption of my osteo, or more likely, because I was not good enough. Dr. Jalowec, who regularly came to the house to attend to my medical needs, also became a friend. But one person towers above all others: Guy Boulton.

He was a most cultured Englishman, seemingly of independent means, attached to the British Consulate or Embassy. We saw a great deal of him, and Rose ultimately became involved in some of his work. Although he was dressed and behaved like a civilian, it eventually became clear that he was in Haiti serving his country as an intelligence officer. The Battle of the Atlantic was a critical theatre of the war. Radio-equipped Axis sympathizers on land sometimes transmitted information about Allied ship movements to German subs; Mr. Boulton's task was to ensure that no assistance to the U-Boats was forthcoming from Haiti, Central America and the West Indies generally. He consequently tried to infiltrate the local European community and keep track of the activities and contacts of possible Nazi sympathizers.

Guy frequently visited our house and he and Rose played hilarious practical jokes on one another, and on others. After he learned of her little intrigues with Casablanca's chief of police involving Czech airmen, he decided to extend her cloak-and-dagger persona. He invented a promising trap to identify Latin American and Spanish diplomats and consular officials who might sympathize with the Axis, and persuaded Rose to provide private tutelage as a German teacher offering classes to individual pupils. He, as an amiable member of the diplomatic corps, steered potential clients her way, particularly from among the groups in whom he had a "professional" interest. The conversational component of the classes afforded lots of opportunities for broaching a wide range of topics, including current politics and the participants' ideas and friends. Mr. Boulton was informed if anything suspicious came to light and, thus, some Axis sympathizers were sniffed out and the intensity of their commitment was gauged.

The prevalence of crime was one aspect of life in Port-au-Prince that took some getting used to. But compared to the current and recent periods, it was considerably less malignant. In the downtown, middle-class areas of the capital, for instance, violence was relatively rare. We were able to walk or take taxis freely without fear of coming to harm. An attractive feature of this freedom was that it offered an opportunity to observe a cross-section of the local population. One striking aspect was the impeccable attire of so many people. The very poor, of course, dressed in ways that reflected their circumstances. But a surprisingly large number of the men in downtown Port-au-Prince wore pristine white tropical suits, washed, starched and ironed daily by the laundry women who worked in middle-class households.

Although violent crime was rare at that time in downtown Port-au-Prince, it may have been more evident elsewhere. And, not surprisingly in so poor a country, theft was ubiquitous. Virtually everything that was not screwed down disappeared fast. We became aware of this on the day after we moved into our house. Like everyone else, we spent most of the time outside on the porch where there usually was a breeze. Our first morning in residence we noticed that the outside light bulbs had disappeared overnight and were told by the maid that they had to be unscrewed and taken inside every evening. It speaks well for the resourcefulness and alertness of the thief to have observed that this precaution had not been followed that first night.

The high temperature assisted those who lived by their wits. It was unthinkable to sleep in closed rooms, so windows were always left open, preferably in a manner encouraging cross-currents of the (relatively) cooler night air. Malaria was a problem and obliged everyone to use mosquito nets. One evening Rose left her handbag on the night table next her bed and was shocked suddenly to see an arm reach into her room and take the bag. Before she could stop the theft, the arm and its prey vanished into the night. I was rather pleased with myself for having contrived an effective defence against uninvited guests. The sills on my two windows were quite wide and every night I hung by their heels a pair of shoes on the inside ledge. It made it difficult for an intruder to enter without making quite a racket by knocking them off. The clever stratagem was, partly to my disappointment, never tested.

The widespread petty thievery was annoying but also understandable. Jobs were scarce and wages puny. Given the prevailing circumstances, it was difficult to be unduly censorious about it. But more serious transgressions revealed other disturbing aspects of Haitian society. Soon after Tati took over the factory, lasts necessary for the production of footwear started to disappear, obviously being filched by some of the workers. The stolen items were of absolutely no value to anyone else, but essential to the company. No lasts, no shoes. Through anonymous intermediaries, they were subsequently offered to the company, for a price. The last-thieves were easily identified and eventually jailed, but were by no means dismayed by the experience. As soon as they were let out, a lawyer approached them and persuaded them to sue the company for wrongful dismissal or some such transgression. It cost much less to settle these cases out of court than to fight them. The lawyer and the petty criminal then divided the spoils. This kind of thing was routine. Clusters of less-than-prosperous-looking members of the bar were always seen hanging around the gates of the jail, waiting to pounce on potential new clients. They — the lawyers — also liked to eat.

Haitian history records innumerable acts of bestial brutality perpetrated by machete-wielding army and para-military units. *The Comedians* — Graham Greene's widely read depiction of the Tonton Macoute militia after the advent of Duvalier's dictatorship in the 1960s — well portrays this phenomenon. I have never been exposed to any of these manifestations of barbarity and find them in stark contrast to a contrary aspect of Haitian experience. In the demeanour of most people I found a certain quiet gentleness. There was also a soothing lilt to the local language. French was the official tongue, but the dominant local mode of communication was Creole. It is a kind of pidgin, based on French, but incorporating West African dialects. Since my Haiti days, it has attained literary respectability thanks to the efforts of some writers and intellectuals and is now one of the two official languages of the country. In the early 1940s, it was just a lowly dialect. Its version of "good night" is enchanting and nicely conveys why I find some features of Haitian life lamblike. It is "*dormi parfumé*," which means "have a fragrant sleep." People in the shops, restaurants, offices and on the street were always helpful, mostly kind and friendly and I never detected even the slightest hint of unusual aggressiveness or violence.

My acquaintance with the land was obviously limited and superficial. I realize that the national culture of Haiti, like that of everyone else, is made up of various, not always compatible traits. The violent and the gentle are both present, and both appear differently in diverse individuals and under varying circumstances. The Haitian experience may have started a process in me which ran its full course only after I went to Pickering College in Canada. It resulted in a complete revision of my attitude to nations and nationalities, originally developed when I lived in the highly nationalistic ambience of Masaryk's Czechoslovakia.

Our decision to opt for Haiti, among the alternatives offered by the Bat'a company, was wise. Some time in the second half of 1941, Tati was asked to come to Canada to head the export department of the Canadian company and its foreign branches. He accepted with alacrity and we were once again on the move. I do not know what the relationship was between Jan and the younger Thomas Bat'a at that time, but our relocation led to Tati moving from direct involvement with Jan to close collaboration with his nephew, Tom. His factory and headquarters were situated near Frankford, just north of Trenton, Ontario—a small town about 150 kilometres east of Toronto—and that is where we headed. More precisely, our destination was Batawa, a model company-town. In the course of its Canadianization, the Bat'a name fell by the wayside and was reduced to the simpler Bata.

Although the final lap in my meandering path to Canada was not nearly as tortuous as the trip from Casablanca to Haiti, it was not entirely straightforward either. The Japanese attack on Pearl Harbor occurred on December 7th, 1941, ensuring that the United States would at last become fully engaged in the world struggle. We left Haiti on New Year's Day, 1942. Appropriately for a Haitian departure, we travelled on a banana boat, the SS *Granada*, owned by the Standard Fruit Company. It ferried passengers as well as fruit, and conveyed us to Baltimore where we stayed a few days and saw a few Bata-linked Czechs from the company's nearby factory in Belcamp, Maryland.

Because of war-related restrictions, New York was out of bounds to us and the best way of reaching our destination was to take the train to Fort Erie where we were met by car and taken to Toronto. This is how I first entered what was to become my new homeland. We did not have a visa but were authorized to come here by a special Order-in-Council. The factory in Frankford not only made shoes but also operated machine shops. These were originally geared to support the manufacture of footwear, but were by then converted to produce parts for the gyroscopes and ammunition needed for waging war. To bring Tati to Canada, the company had to resort to a bit of a fib. It obtained permission from the government, which could only be granted by Order-in-Council, to bring him here as an essential cog in Bata's war work. It is possible that he was fetched to replace someone who had to be moved to war production. Once the parents were settled, Mami, like all available wives, did shifts in the factory performing manual work required for the production of ammunition. So if there was a grey zone, Mami made honest persons of everyone involved.

The immigration official who "processed us" at Fort Erie was, not surprisingly, unaware of the legal underpinning of our entry and had to get in touch with Ottawa to illumine the file. This took quite a while but eventually produced results. A rubber-stamped imprint in my passport, dated January 9th, 1942 allowed me to enter Canada. There are some mysterious, hand-written notations: "MC 75," "Duration," and "Ottawa file # 641570," which probably referred to the Order-in-Council. There are also the initials "J.R.S." under "Immigration Inspector."

I am not sure whether it was J.R.S. (Jolly Receptive Samaritan?) or another immigration officer we had to see later who made a profound impression on me and coloured my outlook on Canada. Upon arrival in virtually every one of the seven countries we traversed on the way from Morocco, the first question asked by the authorities was something like, "When are you leaving?" Not being nationals of the country in which we found ourselves was seen in a negative light and led to the often-impatient reminder that soon we would have to cease casting a shadow on its doorstep.

Canada was an exception: J.R.S. or a colleague did not want to know when (or if) we intended to leave. He asked me, a teenager determined to return to Czechoslovakia as soon as possible after the war, "What do you want to be when you become a Canadian?" This innocent, off-hand remark was a thunderbolt and left a deep, lasting impression. Its inclusive tone was in striking contrast to the exclusive queries posed by immigration agents in more chauvinistic and twitchy countries.

In Toronto we were put up at the Royal York Hotel, a luxury I was not able to repeat for many years afterwards, although eventually I did make it now and then. We went on to Trenton where the company had us stay at a cozy bed and breakfast, Firhurst Manor, while the wartime housing unit which was to be the parents' home in Batawa was being fixed up. The owners of Firhurst either were British or Canadian with strong ties to the mother country, as it surely was to them and to a great many other people at that time, at least in Ontario. All the sons were in the services, some overseas, some still here; the daughters did war work and ran the B & B. We

felt as if we had been spirited back to Britain. On our first evening
Tom Bata and two of Tati's Zlín colleagues, occupying key posts in
the Canadian company, Mr. Herz and Mr. Cekota, took us out for
dinner. Despite the war still raging, we felt that, while things were
still not well, for us they had taken a substantial turn for the better.

* * *

The warm, comfortable and comforting reception in Canada,
coming after experiencing the strong Anglophilia engendered by
John Grubb and Ottershaw, did not, however then lead me to see
Canada as my new permanent homeland, the country to which I
truly belonged. I was Czech and proud of it.

So how did the ardently patriotic Czech boy we knew in Zlín end
up wrapping himself in a maple leaf as a man? Was he a turncoat,
opportunist or brazen arriviste sensing on which side his bread
would be margarined?

To repudiate these allegations, I trace the transformation of the
Czech nationalist into a Canadian, which follows anything but a
straight or simple line. Unlike St. Paul on the way to Damascus, I was
not converted in a flash but gradually modified my former
attachment to become a committed internationalist. When this option
presented problems I drifted towards Canada out of necessity, quite
contentedly espousing my transatlantic refuge.

Czechoslovakia, to which I was sure I would return had, in 1948,
succumbed to a Communist coup. The Party members now in the
saddle completely followed the Moscow line, and my poor country
was no less under foreign control than as when the jack-booted
Germans were holding sway. The Czechoslovak passport became an
impediment rather than an aid to anyone wishing to participate in
the Western intellectual world. So, I admit, the principal motive for
altering my nationality was convenience. Only later, and gradually,
expediency gave way to emotional involvement and, ultimately, to a
powerful commitment to the idea and reality of my new country.

The nationalist transmutations, after the first flush of
socialization as a Czech patriot, I now realize, grew out of the
realization that people are not just individuals, but also members of
various collectivities. Nationality, the adhesion to a group linked by
numerous and varying factors—a shared language, history, country,
among others—is, with religion, the most powerful source of
collective attachments. I was sufficiently intrigued by this complex

notion to devote a large part of my M.A. thesis to it and repeatedly returned to it during my subsequent academic career, usually in relation to Quebec and French-English relations in Canada. Polonius's admonition, "to thine own self be true" is incomplete. One must also be true to one's country or nation, for it is an integral part of oneself. Without it, one is somehow not whole. This stress on the larger identity, indeed, the larger human family, was not an intellectual construct, but something I felt viscerally.

Later, when alerted by Joe McCulley to the destructive consequences of extreme nationalism, I reacted to the renewed enslavement of Czechoslovakia by questioning the very idea of belonging to a country. In 1948, the year I obtained my B.A., an American, Gary Davis, attracted a lot of attention by dramatically renouncing his American citizenship and declaring himself a citizen of the world. He advocated "one government for one world." His idea, like that of World Federalists, greatly appealed to me, although I knew it was utopian and quixotic. Nevertheless, I toyed with the notion that I would not replace my Czech nationality with the Canadian one, but become a world citizen.

Soon, however, I realized that the price of statelessness was huge and that without a passport I would encounter endless trouble travelling abroad. It seemed prudent to apply for Canadian citizenship. Since I liked Canada and almost all my friends were Canadians, this was no hardship. Canadian identity, for one thing, was an almost neutral, un-nationalist category, seemingly lacking any patriotic content. A great many Canadians thought of themselves still as primarily British subjects. To most of my many veteran friends, the idea of a Canadian fatherland would have been grotesque. Almost all of them had not fought the war for Canada, but to combat the German, Hitlerite madness, although some also harboured a lingering attachment to the Mother Country and the Commonwealth.

I applied for Canadian citizenship — a status which had only been created in 1946. I was quite happy to become the holder of one of those dark blue passports so ardently coveted by many people on the Continent. In truth, it was not any particular passion for Canada, although I liked the place well enough, but primarily a matter of convenience.

As I came to know the country and its people better, as I became immersed in its life and institutions and as I increasingly saw differences between Canadians and Americans, I developed a growing attachment to what I saw as the Canadian way. Then, when I observed how the branch plant economy beggared our research capacity, how so many Americans were subject to deep race prejudice and how imported American academics filled their Canadian students' minds with US lore and examples, and particularly when I saw how American media dominated the English-speaking Canadian landscape, I realized that Canadian culture was *sui generis* and in need of protection. From a Canadian of convenience, I became a Canadian of conviction — and affection.

PART II: Finding My Feet

IX

Pickering College

O n February 1st, 1942, less than a month after reaching Canada, I entered my second residential school. How this came about is quite a tale. While at Ottershaw, I did not brood much about my future career and had no particular desire to become this or that. My parents' earlier notions about hotel management or a business career were just that—notions. I probably even then possessed a trait which became pronounced later: a tendency to plan less and to respond more to arising situations. Virtually all major turns in my later life were taken in this ad hoc mode. Nevertheless, what I witnessed in Casablanca elicited a response out of keeping with this predisposition. I saw that the plight of many refugees resulted not only from German perfidy but also from economic realities. The professionals among them—lawyers, doctors, architects etc.—were trapped because their qualifications were worthless in any country other than that in which they were certified. Their professions were not portable. This really hit home and was related to another concern. I desperately hoped for an Allied victory, but had no illusions that it would be followed by any kind of panacea. An Axis defeat would not eradicate anti-Semitism. I feared, in fact, that even after the demise of Germany, I might at some future time be again obliged to flee and seek employment as a refugee.

So for what profession should I prepare myself? And what kind of school would be best? I mused a lot about the skills, goods or services needed everywhere on earth and eventually reached an irrefutable conclusion: food. Man is what he eats, as Ludwig Feuerbach famously asserted, although at that time I still ignored Feuerbach's existence and his ideas. Everyone belongs to what my future neighbour—a farmer—graphically referred to as "the eating public."

Eureka! Agriculture would become my thing. In particular, fruit farming seemed attractive. This sensible conclusion was followed by a tipsy but imaginative embroidery. When I became established in my orchard, I would develop a line of produce appealing to the rich and famous. I would devise a way of inducing nature to "imprint" into the skin of apples or pears the initials or crest of potential buyers who would commission these customized goodies, at an enormous price, of course. I thought that one might place some kind of stencil onto the fruit which would allow the sun to complete the art work. For reasons to emerge later, a change of plans occurred and I never turned agronomist. However, I gather that this kind of luxury produce is now being offered — in California, of course. So, I was only half as crazy as it may seem.

Very soon after our arrival in Batawa, Tati arranged for me to meet the head of the company's Personnel Department who had previously been a school principal and was familiar with Ontario's educational scene. I showed him the few school reports and certificates I had, and told him of my intention of becoming a fruit grower (but suppressed the impulse to mention the fancy scheme I had). His advice was clear: (1) I should enrol in the Ontario Agricultural College and (2) my academic background and motley collection of reports, while revealing an interesting past, made this impossible. They were woefully spotty and too flimsy to gain entrance to the highly esteemed agricultural academy in Guelph. I needed to earn an Ontario Junior Matriculation Certificate. But, he noted, it was too late in the academic year for any high school to enable me to complete the program by the beginning of next autumn's semester. Only one of the private schools would likely take me on and prepare me in time for entrance to Guelph. He suggested I try one of Albert College in Belleville, Pickering College in Newmarket, Trinity College Schools in Port Hope or Upper Canada College in Toronto.

It says a lot about the confidence my parents placed in me, their commitment to giving their children the best available education, and also their economic viability, that when I reported what had transpired they charged me with gathering the relevant information and with proposing which school I wished to attend. My inquiries produced prospectuses and letters from each, which made a good first impression. Further inquiries suggested that, academically, Albert College was not as strong as UCC and TCS, and Pickering was something of an unknown because, in its present guise, it was less well-established than the Toronto and Port Hope academies. It also had the reputation of specializing in "difficult boys." On the face of it, UCC and TCS seemed the most promising. But the accompanying letters made a difference. They were helpful but the one from Joe McCulley, Pickering's headmaster, struck a unique note.

"In view of the fact that you are in Canada under war conditions, you would be eligible for our special fees rate for refugees, evacuees, etc. Had you come in at the opening of this term, the fees for the winter and spring terms would have been $350. There will however, be a pro rata rate of approximately $20 a week reduction for each week of the current term that you had missed." This was indeed a telling point! The monetary aspect was important but not nearly so much as the letter's effect on my morale. As I noted, all the way-stations at which we alit after leaving Czechoslovakia made us feel suspect and unwanted. Pickering's attitude was in line with that of the immigration officer at Fort Erie who anticipated that I would become a Canadian. It reinforced the favourable impression of Canada I had gained upon entering and implied that I would be welcomed at Pickering as an equal. I arranged to visit the school at the earliest opportunity to meet the headmaster and to case the joint.

I cannot resist adding, although strictly speaking it is irrelevant, that compared to the few hundred dollars cost in 1942, the most recent Pickering prospectus in my hand lists the annual fee for a boarder as $ 37,800.

The follow-up examination of the school *was* a bit of a shock. I have never been very responsive to sartorial conventions but was amazed by the attire of the boys. They wore, even to classes, the most outlandishly sloppy clothes, including loud, thick letter- and number-bearing sweaters. These were part of their rugby uniforms, displaying their gridiron numbers and details about their teams. I learnt to decipher these markings later, of course. The raiments were a far cry from the subdued classroom wear of flannels, blazer and tie of Ottershaw, where sports clothes were confined to the groomed playing fields of England. I overcame the aesthetic onslaught and was taken by the palpable atmosphere of informality and camaraderie among both the boys and the staff. My impressions were sufficiently favourable to lead me to abandon scouting any of the other schools on the list. I returned at once to prepare for what I expected to become a happy life toiling in orchards.

Despite the striking difference between the garments worn by the school's pupils and those of my Ottershaw contemporaries, I unthinkingly assumed that Pickering would in most respects resemble the British school I knew from 1937 to 1939. The misconception was caused not only by my lack of experience but also by a certain naïveté which I have never quite succeeded in shedding. An early surprise concerned our sleeping arrangements. Instead of dormitories bearing the names of artists and musicians, we inhabited small rooms normally shared with only one other boy. My first roommate, Martin Shubik, became a lifelong friend, although physical propinquity has been replaced mostly by email bonds.

Soon after settling in, I noticed another less obvious but significant difference. At Ottershaw, as we made our way to breakfast in the morning, we never spoke to any one we passed along the way. The Pickering style was much more open and convivial. Cheerful wishes of "good morning" or some other salutation accompanied the descent of ravenous hordes into the basement dining room. I ascribed this variation to the cultural differences between Canada and Britain, reminiscent of the Albion's habit of not speaking to fellow travellers in those small, cozy train compartments.

One contrast had almost disastrous consequences. Mr. Hartley, the math master at Ottershaw, you will recall, allowed us to choose whichever subject we wished to work on at any particular time. I took this to be universal practice in Commonwealth boarding schools. Naïveté again? So when R.E.K. Rourke, Mr. Hartley's Pickering equivalent, who taught my algebra and geometry classes, assigned homework on each of my first days, I chose to concentrate on only one, leaving the other for later. At the beginning of next morning's class we were asked to report how many of the assigned problems we managed to solve—an inquiry repeated in the geometry class an hour later. On the first round, I allowed that I had done none but had overcome seven geometry puzzles. This truthful, polite and utterly innocent response provoked Mr. Rourke to explosive wrath. He mistakenly assumed that it was prompted by insolence and sloth. Endowed with a rich vocabulary and a sharp tongue, he delivered a dressing down which was particularly devastating because I had no idea what it was I had done wrong.

Daily chapel services, and the subsequent shoeshine parade, were also absent at Pickering, although the weekly assembly meetings were important and memorable. It was mandatory for boys on weekend leave to return on Sunday afternoons in time for them.

The values guiding life at the school were not forcibly drilled into us, but nevertheless tacitly permeated much of what went on. They were non-denominationally Christian, and strongly tinged with a Quaker flavour, bequeathed by the school's origins. The college was founded in the 1840s by the Society of Friends in Prince Edward County, but eventually moved to Pickering and then to Newmarket. The outbreak of the First World War led to the school's closing in 1916 and to the building's conversion into a military hospital. But it was re-opened in 1927 as a boys' boarding school, no longer controlled by the Society of Friends, whose tenets have, however, left their mark.

Joe McCulley, a Canadian University of Toronto graduate who had also studied at Oxford, was only in his mid-twenties when he was charged with developing the new school. He hoped to build a place whose philosophy fused the ethic of Quakerism with the educational philosophy of John Dewey. In guiding our comportment, it relied more on an inner code of conduct than on externally imposed discipline. Heavy emphasis was placed on the obligation of every boy to develop his potential and to contribute to society. Joe, as he was universally known, believed that virtually everyone had the capacity to become an effective, socially responsible person.

Extraordinarily young for someone re-inventing and running a boarding school, he likewise surrounded himself with a youthful team of colleagues. The average age of the staff, when Pickering re-opened, was twenty-six. Few, if any, of the masters had formal teacher training, and several of them eventually moved to other brilliant careers. Among them were Charles Ritchie (an outstanding diplomat and one of Canada's best diarists); John Holmes (another major star in the Department of External Affairs and, subsequently, a superb scholar and head of the Canadian Institute of International Affairs); Gerald Widdrington (an erudite Englishman who served with the YMCA and the RAF in the war and, later, with the Secretariat of the United Nations); Birnie (A.B.) Hodgetts (a legendary teacher and coach at TCS and an influential pioneer of Canadian citizenship education); and Ran Ide (a close friend and the founding genius of TV Ontario). Most of these had left by the time of my arrival, but they returned from time to time for pleasant visits, occasionally spoke at the chapel services, and added a distinct flavour to the school.

My goal was, as we saw, to obtain admission to OAC. A passing mark in eleven subjects constituted a Junior Matric and my program was constructed accordingly. No specialized vocational counsellors, no tests, and no shrinks were involved in mapping my course, only the advice of the headmaster. I was prescribed algebra, geometry, physics, chemistry, history, English, French, and German. The latter three subjects each required *two* examination papers, one in literature, the other in grammar. When the marks came in, my average was quite high, not least because, given my background, I aced the French and German exams. But I also obtained firsts in history and English, which led me to believe that I would survive in the Canadian educational system. While my marks in maths and science were only seconds, the overall average provided a sure passport to the agricultural school. But a complication arose.

When the Grade 12 results came out, Joe engaged me in a little conversation about my future. While tapping me encouragingly on the shoulder because of my results, he also raised the question of whether I should pursue the Upper School program leading to Senior Matriculation and, if I were interested, entrance to university. This would vastly enhance my future options, and who knows what I might wish to do in the long run? What if agriculture failed to satisfy me? I am sure, although not a word was breathed about this, that he thought that I was not cut out to be a farmer, and that a teaching, literary, political or academic career was more suitable. He was right. I likely would have botched the fruit project. Taking Joe's advice, I returned to Newmarket for another year.

Pickering offered the first stable and predictable environment I found since I left Czechoslovakia in 1937. That it afforded an opportunity for roots to sink, and thus a powerful antidote to the turbulence of the preceding years, was a compelling attraction. The effects of the upheavals went largely unnoticed while I lived through them, but I became aware of their impact and legacy later, when they began to recede into memory. I probably yearned for the warmth of a collective embrace, for a sense of belonging beyond that offered by family. When I left the school to enter university, I had come a long way towards becoming a secure and anchored young man with a sense that I was part of a loyal, warm community, which cared not only for me but also for all of humankind. Not a bad entrée into adulthood.

Several features of the Pickering experience combined to bring this about. The pages distributed at each Sunday service not only furnished an annotated agenda and lyrics for hymns but also contained poetry and prose items, quotations, writings of former students and striking aphorisms. The addresses were not always given by Joe; other masters and distinguished visitors sometimes addressed us. Very few of these were clergymen, although the Rabbi of Holy Blossom, Toronto's Reform Synagogue, occasionally spoke.

The boys on the School Committee, elected by the pupils, also took charge of a service each term.

Although a distinct religious, generically Christian whiff clung to these weekly spiritual sessions, the overwhelming thrust was not other-worldly but action-centred. The following extract, culled almost at random, received wide currency with chapel programs and was given a convinced and enthusiastic expression by us, as we recited it:

> We will never bring disgrace to this, our City, by any act of dishonesty or cowardice…We will fight for the ideals and sacred things of the City…We will revere and obey the City's laws and do our best to incite a like respect and reverence in those above us who are prone to annul or set them at nought; we will strive unceasingly to quicken the public's sense of civic duty. Thus, in all these ways, we will transmit this City not only, not less, but greater, better and more beautiful than it was transmitted to us.
> (*The Promise of Athenian Youth*)

These words, and others often repeated on Sundays, were mighty reinforcements of the gospel of a civic society which underlay the Quaker-inspired credo of the school. During a recent visit to Pickering, I was pleased to observe that current students still affirm the ancient oath.

Sundays were important for not only spiritual, but also aesthetic reasons. The famous Pickering Gilbert and Sullivan operettas, brilliantly directed by Bob Rourke, were one of the musical attractions of the school, but not the only one. The piano accompanist was the renowned John Newmark, who also gave Sunday concerts at Pickering, either as a soloist or as the accompanist to some of Toronto's fine singers. And Reginald Godden, our unusually gifted piano teacher, put his connections among Toronto's musical scene to good use, securing talented and sometimes celebrated soloists for our concerts. The Sunday performances were normal and enjoyable events rounding out our academic and sports-filled lives.

The ideas emanating from the chapel services challenged a most important component of my outlook, which, accordingly, underwent a titanic sea change. My visceral loathing of Germany and Germans gave way to a more tolerant view. The remarkable transformation was largely the work of Joe. There was never the slightest doubt about his engagement in the war and his vigorous support of the Allied cause, but he questioned my belief in the pervasiveness and immutability of national character. He understood why I detested anything Teutonic but rejected my lumping all Germans into one, despised bag. People had to be seen and judged as individuals, not only as members of a collectivity. Not all Germans were Nazis. This approach was hard for me to adopt, but in due course I was convinced. I initially accepted his position intellectually, rather than emotionally, but eventually I became a champion of the view that all members of any collectivity cannot accurately be portrayed with one brush. The foregoing notwithstanding, I believe that there is such a thing as "national character," but individuals vary enormously in the degree to which they reflect it.

I have no recollection of where or when Joe and I fought it out. We must have had several encounters before my final rout. Most of them likely occurred in his house which played an important role in the lives of senior students and junior staff. Joe was unmarried and there was no danger of our interfering with his family life. One of the school routines was that the Grade 13 gang gathered in his living room after dinner for coffee or tea (and smokes!). He was always present, usually accompanied by his sister, other masters and their wives. The kitchen was also available late in the evening, before lights-out, so we could pour ourselves a glass of milk and make toast. One of the rooms contained Joe's record collection and the music-lovers among us gathered there at various times to listen to some of his 78-rpm treasures.

Another room (likely the primary site of my lengthy conversions) must be counted among the principal locales of my education. It was Joe's study on the top floor. The walls were lined with books, there was a comfortable chair at a largish desk, occupied by the host, and benches and chairs nearby provided the perfect venue for far-ranging talk, often lasting well into the early hours of the morning. Those so inclined could help themselves to a drink or two. One unshakable and rigorously adhered to rule was that no matter how late one stayed up, and how one's tongue may have been lubricated, one's duties were performed punctually and smartly next morning. These informal seminars, for that is what they were, mostly attracted young staff. The masters on duty on any given day might drop in, before returning home, and when old boys or former faculty visited the school, they invariably attended. I never even heard of these séances before I returned to the school for my final year as a tutor.

No subject was taboo, but among recurring themes war news, political issues of the day, school events, and questions of pedagogy, philosophy and psychology tended to dominate. The application of Pickering's philosophical base to current problems or projects was always of interest. Joe was an assiduous reader of *The Nation*, the left-leaning American weekly, and some of its ideas occasionally fed the discourse. As more and more faculty enlisted and were posted all over the world, news of their whereabouts and activities, when available, were followed with avid interest.

Joe was physically and mentally a big man, self-confident and keen to imprint on his school and the world ideas he thought would improve them. He was also the host and headmaster. So his regular soirees inevitably became something of a podium for the McCulley philosophy. He had a passionate commitment to education and to the idea that virtually every human being was capable of growth, fulfillment and, if necessary, improvement. Only after serving as Canada's Deputy Commissioner of Penitentiaries was he forced to revise downward this lofty faith in human perfectability.

His was not the only influence affecting my development, although he did tower over everyone. Other masters and also a few fellow students assisted my growth and my acclimatization to Canada.

One of my earliest mentors was Harry Beer. Himself one of the first students of the re-opened school, he taught French and German and possessed a fabulous, but very quiet, sense of humour. His classes were laced with impassively straight-faced burbles of wit, so gently expressed that one had to be on one's toes not to miss them. It was this that made us follow even his grammar lessons with riveted attention.

Harry and his warm-hearted wife Betty occasionally invited me to their home and introduced me to a phenomenon which, to the best of my knowledge, was unknown at the time in Continental Europe: baby-sitting. Their twins, Charles and David, later to become strongly public-spirited graduates of the school, were well-behaved and no trouble to the novice sitter. They were so good, in fact, that during my first bout with them, my inexperience led me to commit a grievous baby-sitting faux pas. I became anxious over the silence ominously emanating from their room and so looked in. To see better I turned on the light. This woke them up, of course, but taught me the first lesson in the art of baby-sitting: let sleeping twins lie.

Barney (Berners W.) Jackson—also, like Harry, a Pickering alumnus—taught ancient and medieval history. He taught English as well, and his meticulously crafted chapel addresses were admired for their profundity and elegance. When I became a tutor, we shared corridor duty and I learnt a great deal from him about imposing discipline. He was never flustered, inhumanly patient, quick-witted. One of the things our collaboration taught me was that it is not only what one says, but also who does the talking, that determines how boys (only boys?) respond to suggestions and even commands. All Barney had to do when confronting a breach of discipline, or even a near-riot, was to appear on the scene. His mere presence restored order. When I – only recently graduated and distinctly wetter behind the ears – showed up, nothing happened. Occasionally, even masterful flights of hortatory oratory from me failed, while Barney's shadow would do the trick.

One of Barney's pastimes was collecting rejection slips from *The New Yorker*. This was one of the topics we covered regularly during post-mortems of our evening duty, when we gathered at the Jackson apartment and had a coffee with Maire, his spouse. Well, not the rejection slips exactly, which he did not really collect, but received. He admired the magazine and subjected its short stories to a rigorous analysis of their themes, settings, form, modes of expression and so on, with the view of devising a formula which, if followed, would guarantee acceptance of one of his many submissions. His motive was not primarily monetary, but literary. We hugely enjoyed the fun of analyzing the magazine's strategy and tactics vis-à-vis Barney's potential contribution. So the art of writing engaged us frequently.

Barney eventually became an English professor at McMaster. From there, in the 1960s he launched, and for years ran, the McMaster Stratford Festival seminars. For a relatively modest sum, the strictly limited number of subscribers received tickets to the best seats in the house, lectures from outstanding international and Canadian Shakespearean scholars, behind-the-scenes tours of the theatre's facilities, and admittance to seminars with the people who made the Festival, including many of its actors. Murie and I were enthusiastic participants for quite a few years, and helped Maire and Barney with numerous household chores and with the entertainment of both lecturers and, as Barney called them, "seminoles." We hobnobbed with visiting firemen and were exposed to the outward and inward front of Shakespeare scholarship. I even contemplated writing a book on politics in Shakespeare, a project which never left my drawing board but has since been tackled by several scholars, better qualified to do so than I.

My iconic English master was F.D.L. (Don) Stewart in Grade 12; after he joined the navy, Hy Mosey taught the Upper School class. Both were outstanding teachers but could not have been more different. To some extent, they typified the contrast between the private and public school systems. Don had no teacher training but a passion for the subject and for the educational process. Before teaching at Pickering Hy taught at a highly reputed public secondary school in Forest Hill. I do not know why he switched to Pickering but was glad that he did. He lacked Don's brio but was a most conscientious teacher, probably more focused on preparing us for the Matric exam than the more relaxed, urbane and free-wheeling Don. At Christmas time, during my Grade 13 year, I was amazed and delighted to receive a gift from Hy—a copy of *Roget's Thesaurus*—which, thereafter, never left my elbow and helped improve these pages.

Don Stewart had a wider and deeper influence on me. We saw quite a bit of one another after he was demobbed. His family was very much part of Toronto's upper crust and it was through our friendship that I obtained occasional glimpses into some of the folkways of Rosedale and summer life on Lake Joseph in Muskoka. His lively interest in the arts and literature strengthened and broadened my own inclinations along these lines. It was he, for instance, who first introduced me to *The New Yorker* and to many of Gotham's cultural jewels.

He also made me aware of the emergence of a new art form—the musical which, with *Oklahoma!*, entered our consciousness in 1943, my first full year at the school. His apartment was often filled with its catchy tunes. This path-breaking masterpiece—yes, I think that its energy and vivid, pleasing embodiment of important traits of American society justifies it being called that—received a good deal of our attention. In his English class, we read *Julius Caesar* and Don, an enthusiastic Shakespeare and theatre buff, wallowed in its exegesis. He brought a similar searching mind to the musical, although he did not allow this analytical approach to dull the immense sensual appeal of *Oklahoma!*

Don expanded my horizons in another direction, as well. He eventually left Pickering, married, and taught at an English school in Rome. He invited me to visit, and I managed a detour to the Eternal City while participating in a conference on the Continent. Don adored Rome and—by the time I appeared on the scene—knew it as well as the face that confronted him daily in his shaving mirror. He made a knowledgeable and sensitive cicerone to all the historical, architectural and scenic sights we had time for.

During our sorties, Don introduced me to what was to become my favourite church in all of Christendom — San Clemente (*Basilica di San Clemente al Laterano*). Its current, three-tiered edifice, dating from the 12th century, boasts a glorious apse and unforgettable frescoes and mosaics. Its most intriguing feature is that it sits on top of a 4th century structure which, in turn, is over an even earlier pagan temple. Archaeologists have made it possible to visit all these layers by means of an awful lot of stairs. Ngaio Marsh, in *When in Rome*, used this fantastic site as the venue for a gripping thriller.

San Clemente's magic has made me stumble briefly away from our story, but the detour was too good to miss. To return to the Stewarts, they fell completely into the relaxed, comfortable Italian lifestyle, thus enabling me to taste its appealing flavour. I have since returned a few times, to attend conferences or give lectures, but that first exposure was the most magical.

Two or three other adult friendships, and hence Meisel-moulders, deserve note, before I turn to some of my contemporary cronies — fellow students. Frederick Hagan, an indefatigably creative artist and one of Canada's leading lithographers, taught art and generally had a big hand in aesthetic decisions. He designed and built theatre and Gilbert and Sullivan sets, illustrated school publications and, with Rudy Renzius, a Swedish-Canadian wood carver and pewter worker, ensured that the visual ambience of the school was up to scratch.

I took no classes from Fred but we became friends, a friendship that grew into a threesome after he married Isobel — of course, another G & S enthusiast. His background was blue collar Toronto (Cabbagetown, I think), his father having been a cabinetmaker. Occasionally we visited his folks. This was how I obtained a view of Toronto quite different from that offered previously by the Stewarts. It was at least as impressive. Fred and Isobel's families were interesting, stimulating and clearly stellar embodiments of the virtues of the still faintly Victorian Toronto (the Good?) of the times.

Some of Fred's works reflected his rather sardonic criticism of prevailing social conditions. He knew his Marx, and he and Isobel called their first child Karl. I don't think that Fred ever flirted with "The Party" but, not surprisingly, had a more emotional sympathy with the working class than his more up-scale colleagues and friends at the school.

Fred and I shared two fantastic but starkly contrasting adventures. One was wonderfully constructive, the other horribly destructive. Let's get the latter out of the way first. He became very dissatisfied with many of his accumulated paintings and decided to clean house. So we set off to Toronto, where he had stored a great many of the discredited canvasses, and commenced destroying anything that could not be salvaged for future use. We burnt dozens of paintings in his mother's yard. One of them, which I rescued, still occupies a place of honour alongside some other of his works at Colimaison, the house Murie and I had built in the late 1960s. It is the principal home for my paintings. This incineration fell short of his cutting off an ear, and he always seemed eminently sane, but the spectre of Van Gogh was inescapable while we went about our business. Only one thing redeems this episode, but only a little. He was extremely prolific and when he died, at 85, he left behind—in addition to an enormous storehouse of work entrusted to galleries, private collectors, his dealer and his family—hundreds of devoted students to whom he taught printmaking. Some of these have become major artists in their own right.

Colimaison—my home and impromptu art gallery.

The much happier recollection arises from our collaboration on a little booklet with four woodcuts. He also bound it in impressive leather. The idea was mine and, I confess, inspired by my having been smitten by Kahlil Gibran's *The Prophet*. Most of my subsequent English profs would almost certainly have scoffed at what they might have seen as a shallow lapse of taste, but I and all my contemporaries found Gibran's perfumed poetry and accessible thoughts on big themes convincing and moving. So, as a Christmas present for Joe, and as a token of thanks for the many late evenings in his study, I composed a brazenly Gibranesque poem celebrating, no doubt in suffocating colour, the manner in which the great teacher led and enriched his young colleagues. There were, alas, trite images of the savant's tower and the arduous climb to his lair on a medieval-seeming, narrow staircase. Fred's illustrations were bold and not at all kitschy, and mitigated some of the youthful excess of my purple text.

During my two final years, *every* Saturday night was spent in the cozy apartment of the school's dietician. There, some of us seniors wallowed in the homey atmosphere provided by our gloriously friendly hostess, Irene, and the vocal artistry of Frank Sinatra. *Your Hit Parade*, the widely popular radio program, was ostensibly the main attraction of these never-to-be-missed séances, but Irene was equally important. She was Joe's younger sister, and the wife of Art Buckley, an army man, deployed overseas. Irene was hospitable and popular, and her home provided a weekly relief from the institutional ambience of a boys' school.

Although the camaraderie and setting of the Saturday evenings, and Irene's inventive snacks, copious cups of coffee and presence were strong magnets, the music was the main draw. I was generally attracted to classical fare, but the sensuous and accessible appeal of the tunes and words we listened to did not leave me indifferent. Remember that, because of my osteomyelitis, I had not learnt to traipse on a dance floor, so much of this genre of entertainment was terra incognita for me.

As a result, the Hit Parade was an educational exposure to North America, conducted and kibitzed upon by my mostly Canadian contemporaries. Although my memory normally resembles an old, badly moth-devoured sweater, it astonishingly provides a decent inventory of the songs we loved. Some were inspired by the war, of course, like *Comin' in on a Wing and a Prayer*, or *You'd Be so Nice to Come Home To*. Mostly love songs, they nevertheless covered a wide field and astonishingly almost all of them became classics. Here's a sampling: *People Will Say We're in Love, As Time Goes By, Don't Get Around Much Any More, Moonlight Becomes You, That Old Black Magic, Long Ago and Far Away.* Two items intrigued those of us interested in language use, because they reflected the delightfully relaxed approach to the spoken word characteristic of North America. The gibberish of *Mairzy Doats and Dozy Doats*, (Mares eat oats and does eat oats) delighted by its irreverence, as did the slightly ethnically tainted *Is You Is, or Is You Ain't, Ma Baby?*

I am struck by the gentleness, melodiousness and sociability of much of the music. Compare it to the raucous violence, crudeness, pelvic thrusts and other vulgarity of so much of what young folks frequently wallow in nowadays, as they move about in solitary splendour, ear plugs implanted into their heads, isolating them from the real world.

My first roommate and friend, Martin Shubik, had been at the school for a term or so before I arrived. He was very British, in every way, but his family had been Jewish immigrants to Britain from one of the Baltic States and he was actually born in New York. A tall, heavy-set lad, his outstanding prowess was cerebral, although he was an enthusiastic archer and, in his university days, something of a water polo star. It is impossible to rank people of outstanding intelligence on a finely calibrated scale—there are so many different kinds and manifestations—but amidst all the super-brains I have encountered, Martin places among the top two or three. He excelled in all subjects and wrote hilarious doggerel, some of which found its way into a rather left-leaning, never produced, operetta.

Martin was a congenial and compatible roommate who greatly helped me with my maths assignments. I had never found Bob Rourke's teaching of maths very accessible—despite his high repute in the field—and Martin managed to fill some of the gaps. We shared a lively interest in current affairs, history and social issues. Later we grew into university friends and, eventually, life-long pals.

I soon became part of a small group that chummed together. Its members shared many of the same extracurricular activities and quite spontaneously and unwittingly became something of a little power elite. Considering that the number of students in the whole school was less than 150, it was inevitable that even a tiny cluster of boys could form a critical mass in the school society and assume a leadership position.

We saw a lot of one another and occasionally visited our respective families on long weekends. Ward Cornell—Corky, as everyone called him—took leading roles in the school's theatrical and G & S performances. In due course, he acquired national fame as the regular commentator on the CBC's Hockey Night in Canada. Eventually he taught at Pickering and afterwards became a senior Ontario public servant acting, among other things, as the Province's Agent General in London for several years.

Jake Struthers was another very special favourite. He delighted in tinkering at the keyboard, and was a gifted lounge pianist. I liked visiting the Struthers very much, partly because I was very fond of Jake, and partly because his parents struck me as being quite English; visits to them in Port Dover, with their afternoon teas and all, reminded me of my days in Britain. Jake later joined the war effort, and was groomed for service in the East. He received intensive training in Japanese and, after the war, devoted his life to furthering Canadian-Japanese trade and cultural relations.

Our close friendship faltered for a while. He was engaged to the sister of a Pickering student a year or two behind us. For totally unfathomable reasons, given our close friendship, I was not invited to the wedding. I later learned that some members of the bride's family objected to my being Jewish, an impediment so very far from my consciousness that I never thought of it. I was Czech, remember—the Jewish part was incidental. All this was sorted out after a few years and Jake and I resumed our intimacy. He later died of bone cancer and his family asked me to deliver the eulogy. Nothing could have more eloquently annulled the wedding *contretemps* or shown that Canada was growing up.

Some of the school life centred on its clubs. These embraced drama, Gilbert and Sullivan, sports, crafts and arts areas, but two were more closely linked to the curriculum. Science- and maths-oriented boys became members of the "Root of Minus 1 Club" (a number which does not exist). "Rooters," under the leadership of Bob Rourke, weekly explored scientific and mathematical topics. The less hard-nosed among us, joined the "Polikon Club," devoted to equally regular explorations and debates of political, economic and social themes. Joe was its mentor.

Every session of the club was followed by a mini-feast which, in my case, became a major turning point in becoming a North American. Each club had its own gastronomical conventions. Following Bob Rourke's leadership, the Rooters prized Coca-Cola—

or was it Pepsi? but the Polikoners drank tea or cocoa, accompanied by a delicacy completely new to me—peanut butter and raspberry jam sandwiches. These were a fantastic discovery. They ranked, in my book, among the world's finest culinary triumphs, including Czech dumplings and gravy, pâté de foie gras, and well ahead of truffles. Although the raspberry jam is no longer *de rigeur*, I have a piece of toast with peanut butter every morning for breakfast, and enriched with sliced bananas, on other occasions. This is a far cry from how your average Czech of the 1930s begins his day or assuages a pang of hunger.

I continued to pursue photography and, in my tutor year, established a small "business" in partnership with a newly arrived master, George Ross. He hailed from the West and had a Ph.D. in English in the works at the University of Chicago. A few students were keen to have their portraits taken and, inspired by the currently famous Yousuf Karsh, we provided portraits of students for a risibly small fee. They shamelessly aped Karsh's famous chiaroscuro style and his habit of lighting the subject's hands. These likenesses were only sometimes successful, and the whole enterprise gave rise to considerable kidding and amusement.

Despite the original hurdle of my occasionally wobbly English, one of my principal "hobbies" was writing and editing. Joe, knowing that osteo prevented me from playing games, and noticing my love of words, asked me to edit the *Quaker Cracker,* the student paper. It usually appeared about five times during the academic year. When I returned to the school as a tutor, I was made the staff advisor to the *Cracker* and also the editor of *The Voyageur*, Pickering's yearbook. These early editorial responsibilities were precursors to similar stints I enjoyed as an undergraduate and, later, as an academic. It was at Pickering that I succumbed to both the contagion of printer's ink and the comraderie engendered by close collaboration among a small passel of enthusiasts.

Julian Tudor-Hart, a diminutive dynamo, equally at home in the sciences and humanities and with pen and brush, was a year or so behind me. An English war guest he was deeply into Marxism. He commanded a prodigiously vast vocabulary and a wicked sense of humour. Our working together on the *Quaker Cracker*, affinities in social outlook, and debating jousts in the Polikon Club laid the foundations for an enduring friendship. He returned to Britain, qualified as a doctor at Cambridge and then spent his life as both a general practitioner in a Welsh mining village, and an innovative, successful researcher and author.

Pickering enjoyed the services of a U of T psychologist who appeared from time to time as a vocational counsellor and giver of general advice. One of Dr. Karl Bernhardt's tools was "the other self-rating test": boys sat together in a class once a year while a master read out the name of each of the boys present; after each name, we were given time to write a short assessment of the identified classmate. His good and bad points were to be noted. The unsigned sheets eventually found their way into the hands of Mrs. Streeter, a very prim and proper school secretary, who transcribed the comments under the name of each boy. Most of us were very reticent about sharing our comments with others, but not Bob Young from California. He gleefully boasted to one and all that when the name of Peter S. — a rather brash, self-assured but not unlikeable boy — came up, he made this pithy comment: "A little bit of a shit, with sugar added." Our concern was how Mrs. Streeter would react to such gross language which was not in those days accepted in polite society.

Dr. Bernhardt then discussed his findings with each boy. During our interview, I discovered that, though I was well liked by my peers, one blemish came to light. Several boys observed that I had rather a lot of dandruff, something that had escaped my attention. In my man-to-man chat with Dr. B., he prescribed a simple solution: acquire a bottle of a preparation called "Booster" and apply it regularly to the scalp. I have never looked back. The scabrous scalp was a passing manifestation of adolescence.

The main focus of the Pickering experience was, of course, its academic impact, although Joe probably believed that enhancing our humanity was at least as important. I found the classes richly rewarding. That they were small had something to do with this, as did the cohesive atmosphere of the school in which the masters and boys formed a single, and rather single-minded, community. The staff was bright and fully engaged. I now realize that each one of them saw teaching as a mission rather than as a job. I was uneasy about my maths courses and did not develop anything like passion for physics and chemistry. But English and history did grab me. The jewel in the crown was Grade 13 modern history, offered by Joe.

There were twelve of us and not one left this class without being vitally affected by it. During the first session, Joe distributed the Ministry of Education's course syllabus and the recommended readings. Then he announced that in the final examination (set and marked by the province) we would be responsible for the prescribed topics and that it was up to us to acquire the knowledge and skills needed to obtain the necessary credit. He, in the meantime, would teach us some history. He did this by identifying key topics (there was, needless to say, much overlap between his and the Ministry's list), by assigning very frequent essay topics, and by discussing the papers in class. Although participation in these discussions was unfettered and vigorous, his own voice was dominant—not only because of its strength and his knowledge but also because of the fervour with which he held his views. Historical events were rarely left unrelated to current (1942–43) developments, and we were steered toward a tolerant internationalism compatible with the highest aspirations of the soon-to-be-created United Nations. No doubt was left that we, as individuals, had a role to play in the newly evolving world, and that it was up to us to seize the opportunities likely to present themselves after the armistice.

Nationalism, in his book, was at the root of most international conflict and had to be superseded by a higher view, one based on a shared humanity. This hope once led him to egregious error. He opened a class by announcing dramatically "nationalism is dead!" But, right or wrong, he managed to inspire a keen interest in, and concern for, the issues tearing the world apart, even though we were safely ensconced north of Toronto. He made us realize that any sense of comfort bestowed by our location was illusory. Whatever happened to our minds in the process of taking his class, the final examination results must have pleased him. In the days when excellence in scholastic matters was held in higher esteem than now, and the bell curve was largely seen as irrelevant, three of us received a first, three a second, three a third, and three a mere pass. And I, in due course, joined the United Nations Association and entered the University of Toronto intending to study modern history.

But my post-secondary career was delayed yet again, with Joe being the *deus ex machina*. My patriotic feelings and implacable hate of Nazism convinced me that, like so many other of my peers, I should join up to fight the war. That this was an unrealistic ambition emerged during my medical examination by the Czech army-in-exile. I was turned down flat, largely because of osteomyelitis but also because of imperfect sight. When I finished my matric, Joe suggested that I return to the school for another year, as a tutor. This would be my war service, since I would be doing the work otherwise performed by the masters who had joined up. I would receive bed and board and carry out such duties as would be assigned me. There were always one or two tutors about, helping with the coaching of a team, and completing their academic program. I did some teaching (Grade 10 Latin and Grade 13 German — to one student, the brilliant George McCowan), assumed corridor duties, undertook some editorial chores and generally supported the staff in some of their tasks. The duties were light and the year offered a marvellous opportunity to read widely, mature, learn from colleagues and students, and to embark on a self-taught typing course which did not, alas, break my too deeply ingrained habit of pecking away with two fingers, a technology still applied to the crafting of these memoirs.

The final touch to the contribution Joe made to my life was his advice about my future studies. The subject I would pursue was not an issue and evolved naturally from my interests and capabilities. I would embark on what, at the U of T, was the first year course in Social and Philosophical studies, the gateway to the humanities or social sciences. That I would go to Toronto was assumed as a matter of course, but to which college?

The U of T consisted of a number of professional faculties and four federated arts colleges, linked, except in one case, to the religious bodies which had founded them. Trinity was Anglican, St. Michael's, Catholic and Victoria, United Church. University College was non-denominational and, as such, was the preferred venue of Jewish students. Given my background, and non-attachment to any religious group, it would have been my natural home. But Joe thought that I would find Vic a more congenial place and suggested that I apply there. It was more residence-centred, had a larger proportion of students from outside Toronto, and was more of a community than UC. So when I landed in University, Vic became my physical and spiritual home.

X

Batawa

The Meisels' Canadian home, and hence where I spent the holidays, was not in your typical Ontario settlement, but a company town like no other. Thomas J. (Tom) Bata, the twenty-something son of the company's founder, launched an audacious project to save the Bata empire from the Germans. On the eve of the war's outbreak, he came to Canada with over a hundred Czech families to set up a factory on the Trent Severn waterway north of Trenton. This became the nucleus of Batawa, a replica in miniature of Zlín. At its height, almost 2,000 employees worked there. It was not quite as large when we arrived in 1942, but was a community involved in a shared purpose—the success of the Bata shoe company, which was by then also a producer of military hardware. The joint involvement in the war effort facilitated the harmonious co-existence of the tight-knit group of Czech immigrants and the surrounding sea of Canadians.

Batawa factory and wartime housing: comfy and secure from what Churchill called the "Nazi hordes."

Since I spent most of the year in Newmarket, I did not have any local school chums. Almost all of the Czechs were younger than my parents and there were no Czech kids of my age in Batawa. As a result, I fell in with Rose's circle of pals who, though a little older, were still within friendship range. Rose edited the factory's daily news bulletin and so knew a large number of people. This helped find congenial cronies of both sexes with whom she often shared such entertainment as was available locally or in nearby Trenton, and slightly more remote Belleville. She eventually moved to the RCAF station in Trenton where she also edited a daily newsletter and found additional friends. When I was around, I was welcome to tag along.

The parents' friends — most dating back to the good old Zlín days — were Czech and so my deep immersion into Canadiana at Pickering was complemented by a reminder of the old ways. Tati was sixty when we arrived in Canada and Mami forty-seven. They were remarkably adaptable and sensible. I did not hear either of them complain once of the tragic fate of some members of the family, the loss of their property in Europe or the reduction in standard of living. They knew, of course, how lucky we were to have escaped Hitler, to be together and to enjoy the security blanket provided by the Bata connection.

Some of the adjustments must nevertheless have exacted a huge price. I was not thinking about this at the time, but subsequently developed tremendous admiration for how they coped with the life changes imposed on them, particularly on Mami. She had always had at least one servant and other help but, once in Canada, was compelled to look alone after the house, the shopping and the kitchen. Working part-time in the factory was a big first for her; but making munitions was not unduly strenuous work, and she enjoyed the company of other Bata wives doing their patriotic thing. From my present vantage point in the twenty-first century, I blush in horror over the male-dominated conventions of the times. When at home, I did not even make my own bed in the morning and no one thought anything of it!

The parents became acquainted with their new homeland by exploring nearby sights. Even with gas rationing, it was possible to visit some of the little towns along the shore of Lake Ontario and the inland villages. They liked Belleville and were particularly taken by Cobourg, where we spent a glorious October weekend, overwhelmed by the gaudy autumn foliage. Prince Edward County was a favourite with its picturesque settlements and attractions like

Presquille Point, the Lake on the Mountain and the Sandbanks. Trenton, accessible by bus, was the nearest town, and thus the site of Mami's shopping. In some ways it was the least interesting. When furnishing our house, she found its furniture shops crammed with overstuffed monstrosities. It was only in Toronto that she found simpler pieces in the modern European, and particularly Scandinavian, design.

The family almost daily went on evening walks around Batawa, accompanied by Pepík, our cat, which betrayed feline decorum by always walking along with us, like a dog. Tati took part in some activities of local Czech organizations, but generally we stuck closely together and led a very quiet, family-oriented life.

My principal entertainment, other than swimming in the Trent River (and one whole summer, reading *War and Peace*) was, when my leg allowed, tennis. The Batawa club was made up more or less equally of Czechs and Canadians and was not bad, considering our size. We held internal tournaments and played other clubs in the region. One of these engagements, at a cement plant near St. Mary's, had an eye-opening follow-up. While still in Zlín, I was powerfully attracted to Coca-Cola (then quite unattainable in central Europe) entirely on the basis of the extremely handsome plastic containers in which it was advertised in Tati's *National Geographic*. I expected it to put all other beverages — including ambrosia — to shame. It was a shock, then, to discover, upon first trying a glass in North America, that I couldn't stand it. Its flavour and fizz put me off. The tournament in question was played on cement courts and on a tropically hot day. I played two singles and one double match and, towards the end, was hotter than I had ever been in tropical Haiti. Someone offered me a cool Coke and I, *faute de mieux*, gulped it down. What a delight! Nothing on earth could have been more refreshing. This reaction to the emblem of America's world supremacy was unique, never to be repeated.

The countryside around Batawa is pretty and I explored much of it on my bike. Normally I was alone but, on one memorable occasion, I was on my first date, sort of. Marion McKnight, one of Rose's friends, was a bit older than I, came from New Brunswick and had a university degree. Although a Maritimer, she seemed very British. Her manner was demure. All this greatly appealed to me. She owned a bike and occasionally we explored the surrounding countryside together. I particularly remember our first excursion to Stirling, about 15 km away, because I had never had an assignation, if that's the word, before—we had just agreed to undertake a little tour one Saturday afternoon. But because it was the first time I had ever been out alone with a girl and because the weather and scenery were so perfect, this outing over sixty years ago still vividly remains in my mind. Marion was extremely attractive and she triggered the first flutters of love in my breast. My bouts with osteomyelitis had limited the scope of my teenage experiences, and I was too shy to try embarking on a romantic adventure.

Batawa introduced me to the work world. In the summer of 1944, I obtained a job in the shipping department. My principal task was to go over orders for shoes from the numerous Bata shops throughout Canada, fill them from the spacious storerooms, and once their wooden cases were full, ensure that they reached their destinations. Most footwear in the 1940s was still made of leather, so there was a lot of heavy lifting and hefting. Women's shoes were lighter than men's and were easily manageable. But the men's, sixty boxed pairs to a case, weighed a ton, and could only be moved and conveyed by means of a sturdy handcart. This was hard work, particularly on hot days. Air conditioning was not in use in Batawa at the time. Oh, for a Coke!

One factor lightened our load significantly. Bata was among the world's most important manufacturers of "plimsoles"—rubber soled, canvas sportswear not unlike tennis shoes, but offered in many colours. All tennis garb, in those days, had to be pure white. The countless plimsoles passing through our hands weighed much less than leather goods, but there was a downside.

In addition to shipping shoes, one of my tasks was to check rejects—items returned by dissatisfied customers. Quite a few of these had rubber soles and, surprisingly, had been worn for lengthy periods. Some had also sat for a long time in sun-drenched, or otherwise steamy places. As a result those of us who verified the complaints performed a pungent, malodorous task, relieved only by the pleasure of gazing upon the pretty colours of the shoes' tops.

I enjoyed my first job; the work was interesting for a while and it provided a new set of experiences. Among my closest co-workers was a chap roughly of my age whose name, alas, has vanished. We often ate our lunch together and got along famously. I now wonder whether he thought that, though quite harmless, I was a bit odd. I was going through a Hamlet-loving phase at the time. Having memorized several of the passages and particularly some of the soliloquies, I tried to convince my pal of their subtlety, beauty and emotional force. I climbed to the top of one of the warehouse's scaffolds and, once there, declaimed to an imagined crowd below, cleaving the air with fancy speech. Already the inveterate teacher, I hoped to share with him the immense pleasure I derived from the bard's majestic tongue. It did not work.

We were on more common ground when, during lunch breaks, we stole together into the bushes along the Trent river to spy on our boss, a married Czech who, according to rumour, was having a dalliance with his single Canadian secretary. I do not remember whether we ever found our prey *in flagrante delicto,* but these clandestine sorties cemented our friendship.

A job later that summer was less remunerative but better related to career planning. I thought it useful, before going off to university in the fall, to find out whether I was suited to journalism. The closest paper was the *Trenton Courier Advocate,* about 10 kilometres away. I could bike to it quite easily. The crusty owner, a Mr. Moore, was not in the least interested, saying that they had all the help they needed. I surprised myself—not an even mildly pushy sort—by trying various ploys to change his mind, even volunteering to work for a pittance. I don't know whether it was my innocence, persistence, verbal facility, low sticker price or an unexpectedly soft heart under Mr. Moore's forbidding exterior that led him to offer a half-time job at $12 a week—a pittance so small that, even in 1944 dollars, it approached the vanishing point. The job was great and I did learn quite a bit about many things, but as an exposure to journalism it was a bust. Not only was a small-town weekly unrepresentative of the print media generally, but the *Courier Advocate* was an oddball paper.

Take Mr. Moore's approach to the sports page: while by far the widest interest in Trenton's summer sports was softball, he preferred hardball. He financed a hardball team which found only few adversaries, because Trenton's softball preference was shared by almost all nearby communities. One of our sparring partners was the Grimsby Peach Kings, whose location was far more distant than numerous nearby softball clubs. This gave me an opportunity to visit the Niagara Peninsula. What was passing strange was that our sports pages paid only the most scant attention to the softball games but contained column after column on hardball. These were, of course, penned by Mr. Moore. "Penned" is, however, not the right word.

Newspaper stories in those days were created on linotype machines with the aid of a keyboard. Expert compositors received the stories from the writers or editors, keyed them into lead slugs, and placed the slugs in frames, from which the pages were printed. Mr. Moore was so skillful that he wrote his stories and editorials straight into the linotype machine. The layout of each page was determined by the order and pattern in which the slugs were placed in their frames. This task, for the whole paper, was assumed by Mr. Moore. There were no proofs; he worked directly with the lead slugs, despite their being in a doubly reversed form, so everything was backwards.

There were a number of people in Trenton of whom he strongly disapproved. They were, as much as possible, kept out of the *Advocate*. When he went over my stories, he let me know which of the good citizens of Trenton were to be ignored. This posed a problem. One of my assignments was to write pieces about local events and happenings not covered by colleagues assigned to various specific files, like sports or local government. To do this, I developed a network of informants—the undertaker (who also owned local ambulances), people at the fire hall, some politicians and the like—who kindly helped me keep abreast of events. Some of individuals involved were on the blacklist, and when I mentioned them, the piece was usually dropped. Some items, however, were too important to be ignored. So, when he came across the name of a "prohibited" person, he reached for his pen-knife and cut the name off the slug—lead is soft and his knife was sharp. The story was preserved, but where the name appeared in the original, there was either a blank or a smudge.

Small independent newspapers confronted economic difficulties as long ago as the '40s, even, as was our case, when they were also in the printing business. The *Trenton Courier Advocate* was gobbled up, when I was still there, by the owners of the *Oshawa Times Gazette*. Like so many small organs, it fell into the hands of ever larger corporate entities and badly deteriorated. Although observing the beginnings of the take-over process was depressing, my daily routine remained unchanged.

My regular informants—a roaming and free-wheeling advisory board—introduced me to new and fascinating features of small-town Ontario life. One was the hunting decoy. There were no suitable lakes or rivers near Zlín able to support wild waterfowl and I had never heard of these beautifully carved and painted creatures. They may have been unknown in Czechoslovakia. The Trenton fire hall changed all that. The firemen hung around ready to respond to emergencies but had plenty of spare time in between calls, which they used to craft decoys.

I normally moved through Trenton on my bike, and was occasionally passed by the undertaker in his ambulance, hearse or car, whichever met the exigencies of the moment. He invariably loudly reminded me, with a huge grin and an amused glint in his eye, "No news is good news!" — an observation I have used often ever since.

The *Courier Advocate* introduced me to a literary genre of which I had heretofore been unaware: short weekly informal reports on the social life of small rural communities in the surrounding area, usually focusing on church-related activities, visits to and from friends and relatives, anniversaries, social events and instances of indifferent health. Their parochial quality gave them a distinct charm and mildly comic quality. I decided to write one about Batawa, but I was not sufficiently integrated in the community to chronicle its social highlights and was ignorant of church-related news. So, in addition to such conventional crumbs of gossip as I was able to pick up here and there, Rose's band of friends and I mischievously fabricated tales about ourselves, pushing their slightly scurrilous content as close to the limit as we dared. The pieces were harmless, and very likely less funny than we thought. If Mr. Moore was aware of what was going on, his straight, curmudgeonly face never betrayed him.

One of my duties had me baffled. On market days, I had to report the prices of the most commonly traded fruits and vegetables. Despite my one time ambition to become a farmer, there was no way I could do this. I did not know the name of a single item offered for sale. The words Ida Reds, Bartletts, Romaine or Pink Eye were worse than Greek to me, but the kindness of our compositor saved the day. I told him of my woes and he, a regular visitor to the market, offered to write the piece for me until such time as I mastered the language of Ontario crops. He was, apparently, a legendary figure among Ontario press folks because of his speed and accuracy. He had worked for a long time at the *Telegram*, one of Toronto's major dailies, but was an alcoholic and was eventually forced to leave. In my time at the paper, he never failed to perform in an exemplary manner, and found time to befriend and instruct a young ignoramus. His presence among us made me wonder whether Mr. Moore was quite as much of a hard-nosed misanthrope as he liked to make out. My acquaintance with the compositor also broadened my horizons. I learnt that the question of alcoholism was a complex one, and that those afflicted by it — often dismissed by the uninformed as drunks — may lead useful and productive lives. This is now widely accepted but was rarely perceived then, particularly by green persons like myself, still more than damp behind the ears.

Despite not being able, after Trenton, to decide whether journalism would suit me, I did gain some writing experience and strengthened my feeling that a career involving a typewriter might suit me. In addition to giving me the chance to do some sleuthing and writing, and affording the opportunity to learn a little about the production of a weekly paper in a small Ontario town — not to mention the names of Ontario fruits and vegetables — I learnt even more important things that summer. Some relate to the kindness of my voluntary, agricultural "assistant." His generous willingness to help and teach me grew primarily out of his personal make-up and reflected what sort of person he was. But his behaviour was also a particularly striking example of something that many others exhibited to various degrees. The environment at the *Courier Advocate*, and in the pleasant Bata shipping department, was convivial, tolerant and highly collegial. I was too young to have had workplace experience in Europe, but thought, probably on the basis of things I'd heard and read, that the relaxed openness and egalitarianism in Batawa and under Mr. Moore reflected something that was very Canadian. With Pickering College, the Batawa and Trenton episode revealed a most pleasing aspect of Canada.

The next step — university — followed, opening undreamt of new horizons.

XI

Varsity 1944–1948

University life started stressfully. I had obtained first class honours on seven of the nine papers in my senior matriculation, but an uneasy feeling gnawed inside me that this was a fluke. Four of those marks were on foreign language papers where I enjoyed a comparative advantage over less peripatetic examinees. That the "honestly" earned history and English marks were also high did not quite dispel the fear that I might not be good enough to glide over the much higher university hurdles. That similar concerns with respect to my Grade 12 marks were unfounded did not enhance my self-confidence, because I held the university in such exalted awe. Whatever the reasons, "apprehension" best describes the state of my mind in the fall of 1944.

The unease was heightened by a brief, unusual plunge into loneliness. Away from my family and no longer under Pickering's umbrella, I felt alone and isolated. I remember my first Sunday afternoon at Victoria College: lying on the bed of my room in North House, bereft of the ties that had become a necessary component of my person. A sense of anguish befell me, of a sort I had never experienced before, not even when I left Czechoslovakia for boarding school in Britain. Some profoundly gloomy moments must have darkened the early osteomyelitis days, but none left as indelible a memory as the loneliness that engulfed me that first Sunday at college. It may be that on previous like occasions, friends or family were near-at-hand, whereas during those first days in Toronto I was alone without links to anyone. I knew nobody.

A quite different factor sullied my college entry with unpleasantness: initiation. It now seems laughable that I reacted so strongly to it, but I did. Compared to what I have seen of this silly kind of rite at Queen's (particularly among the engineers), and heard of in other contexts, it was the mildest sort of tomfoolery. One prank featured college ties. We were all issued freshman ties, which had to be worn when we were out in public. They were allegedly gold but I saw them as sickly, slightly grubby pale yellow, exuding mediocrity. Any sophomore, approaching a freshman had the right to cut off bits of the symbolic cravat.

I saw this and similar indignities as a major onslaught on the individual, completely incompatible with my idea of a university. They struck me as infantile, vulgar, shocking and inexcusable violations of the dignity of the person. I obviously went overboard in my revulsion to what were little more than pranks, but still abhor any kind of hazing as an insufferable degradation of the human spirit.

But every cloud has, as they say, a silver lining. Sportive jousts, including a dodge ball encounter, were also an aspect of residence initiation. All the frosh domiciled at Vic were dragooned into the middle of a gym and surrounded by the resident sophomores. These sought to hit one of the greenhorns huddled in the centre with a volleyball. We were not waiting passively to be hit, of course, but tried to dodge the oncoming missile. Whoever was touched by the ball had to drop out. Astonishingly, I escaped elimination until only two of us were left. The final round became a lengthy, tense affair ending in my remaining "untouchable." I had never been a star competitive athlete but was fairly good at tennis and Ping-Pong. I suspect that it was nimble footwork, not to mention luck, which caused my triumph. Despite this momentary brush with stardom, I did not turn out for any of the college or varsity sports except tennis.

To obtain a degree in the arts or social sciences, one enrolled in a federated college and took courses offered both by university departments and a college. Some fields were taught by one, some by the other, and in certain areas both had jurisdiction. The rationale for this Byzantine arrangement lies in the accommodation reached by the university and the colleges in 1890, when the colleges affiliated into a federated university. The colleges provided some courses, libraries, residences, dining halls, clubs, sports programs and facilities, dramatic and literary activities and, with the exception of University College, religious fellowship and instruction. If your major field was a university subject, as in my case, and hence you took most of your courses outside your college, you were still obliged to obtain at least one annual credit on the home turf—your college. This option could be in a variety of disciplines, but was always referred to as the historically hallowed "RK option," the acronym standing for Religious Knowledge.

Vic was the epicentre of my universe at the beginning. In addition to feeding and housing me, the college consequently formed the crucible of my friendships. It was a comfortable, unostentatious place, proud of its history and still tinged by its earlier links with Upper Canadian Protestantism. By the time I arrived, it was non-denominational but retained close links with the United Church of Canada. The latter, building on its non-Conformist roots has been a force in Canada for a tolerant, caring and progressive social philosophy. Vic also engendered among its members and graduates a binding sense of community. Coming on the heels of Pickering, this was congenial to me and mitigated my early loneliness.

Apart from participating in residence life and taking several college courses, my involvement in Vic centred on debating, *Acta Victoriana* — the literary magazine — and, eventually, the Victoria College Union (VCU) — the student government.

Vic debates were conducted on parliamentary lines and scrupulously followed the guidelines laid down by the authoritative Sir John George Bourinot. They were much more formal than the shmooze-fests of the Polikon Club at Pickering. No peanut butter and jam sandwiches. The majestic manner and stentorian voice of the Speaker, Royce Frith, was awe-inspiring. He was in final year Law and subsequently became, among other things, a top Liberal insider and senator. Our paths crossed again on several later occasions, especially when he served as one of the members of the Royal Commission on Bilingualism and Biculturalism, for which I was a research supervisor.

I participated in the debates as soon as I arrived and eventually became a member of the Executive of the Victoria College Debating Parliament. This led to my getting to know Professor Eric Havelock, our honorary president, who participated fully in our deliberations. He was a leading classicist of the English-speaking world who, after he left Vic, assumed the headship of the classics departments at Harvard, and later Yale. He was also an outspoken activist on the political left, and was one of the founders of the League for Social Reconstruction, the intellectual precursor of the Co-operative Commonwealth Federation (CCF), of which he became a founding member. He was, of course, a controversial figure at U of T. As such, he was more than once threatened with sanctions by the University administration, which he invariably chose to ignore.

His deep immersion in ancient Greek culture and his concern for social issues led him to formulate path-breaking ideas about, among other things, the relation between the way societies communicated and the content of their thought. Reliance on writing, rather than merely speaking and listening, introduced rigidities which, over the years, changed prevailing ideas and social and political structures. Bureaucracies needed records, and clerks had to be able to read and write.

These views dovetailed with and influenced those being developed at the time by Harold Innis, Marshall McLuhan and Edmund Carpenter. These four have had enormous impact on the study of communications in the twentieth century. I took no courses from Havelock but found his mind so compelling that, although no classicist, I eventually read his translation and annotation of Aeschylus's *Prometheus Bound*, which appeared in 1950 under the catchy title *The Crucifixion of Intellectual Man*. Getting to know and interact with Havelock and other admired and admirable faculty members, even if one did not take courses from them, was an unexpected bonus of the university experience.

Another opportunity dropped into my lap as the result of the itch I had to write. I ran into Fred Hoeniger (he later preferred and used his other name, David), probably at one of Professor Cobourn's soirees which I will mention in a moment. He was editor of *Acta Victoriana* and had printed a couple of my short stories. He asked me to join the editorial board; I accepted and, in my final year, I became editor. Northrop Frye was the faculty advisor and, like Havelock, took his task conscientiously. This led to my getting to know him quite well. He was interested in Czech culture and always called me "Jan," the formal Czech name I used to sign my published pieces until I got tired of everyone mispronouncing it "djan," like the girl's name. I then adopted its English translation "John" which is what everyone called me anyway. Everyone except Professor Frye. He always pronounced it correctly, as if he were to the Moldava born. Frye was an accomplished pianist, keenly interested in contemporary Czech composers. He wondered whether my father might be able to obtain some of their published piano works, which Tati managed to do. I also, in fourth year, took (as my RK option) his celebrated course on "the Bible as Literature," an exciting, if daunting experience. He later asked me to serve on the editorial board of the *Canadian Forum* of which he was then editor.

Two other Vic instructors left an ineradicable mark. Cathleen Cobourn, the Coleridge scholar, offered a survey course on the English novel. In addition to giving particularly fascinating lectures on Virginia Woolf and E.M. Forster, she held a sort of mini-salon attended by a few colleagues, friends and students. I had the good fortune of being included on several occasions, offering the opportunity to meet and talk to a number of bright lights of Toronto's cultural scene. Jessie MacPherson, a philosopher and Dean of Women at Vic was among them, as well as Greta Kraus, the harpsichordist, and a fascinating psychiatrist whose name I have forgotten but among whose specialties was the mind of Emily Carr. And, as I mentioned, it was likely there that I first met Fred Hoeniger. My interest in the Bard of Avon prompted me to enrol in a Shakespeare course given by E.J. Pratt, whom Frye considered one of Canada's greatest poets. His lectures were not riveting but they enhanced my love of the English language and its most celebrated playwright. Pratt obviously adored both. It was his infectious enthusiasm, more than Shakespearian scholarship, which shone in his course.

"Ned" Pratt, as he was known, occasionally invited an undergraduate to his office for tea. I was chosen once and had an enlightening tête à tête with him, taken up largely with stories about his native Newfoundland and my tales about Bata. But the principal feature of the social hour was not his engaging charm, nor his conversation, but the truly monumental clutter of the ambience. This is a condition of which I am a connoisseur, indeed a pre-eminent practitioner. But the great bard's den surpassed anything I had ever seen or even imagined. It was so chock full of books, papers and bric-a-brac that the task of depositing a teacup seemed impossible. Still after much shuffling, piling and stacking a bare spot was found on which Professor Pratt deposited the pièce de résistance of our repast: a hard boiled egg still in its shell. This came as no surprise since it was common knowledge that this perfectly shaped nutriment always constituted the gastronomical centrepiece of Professor Pratt's hospitality.

My contacts with students were, of course, much more numerous than with professors; they were also highly educational. Some grew into lasting friendships and also professional associations. One of the most enjoyable and enduring of these was with Keith Davey, the famous Liberal apparatchik of the Pearson and Trudeau years. When the study of Canadian political parties and elections became one of my principal research interests, he proved to be a fabulous source of information and an invaluable sounding board and provider of introductions to politicians.

Burwash Hall, the faintly Oxbridgian, neo-Gothic edifice at the corner of University Avenue and Charles Street is among the principal architectural and communal sites of Victoria University. It comprises an imposing dining hall with a Senior Common Room as well as a number of residences which, up to World War II, served male students. Annsley Hall and Wymilwood, just across the street, catered to women students in like manner. During the war, however, so many men joined the armed forces that some of the male halls of residence would have remained empty had they not been made available to female students.

I occupied a second-story room in North House, overlooking the path linking Bowles House—one of the temporary female residences—with the Burwash dining hall. The girls had to pass my room coming and going twice a day. My window offered an unrivalled opportunity to observe and assess the behaviour, style and looks of the passing maidens and to chat them up. They were an uncommonly attractive lot, and a number of them became friends. Indeed, I made a list of several of them, intending to take them out more or less seriatim until I determined which one I liked best. I never exhausted it because I fell hopelessly in love with Number 4 and neglected the rest. Now comes the embarrassing bit: part of my motivation for making my overtures from above was low and mercenary.

I was still hooked on the filthy smoking habit acquired at Pickering and, when in residence, bought a package of twenty weeds a day. The daily ration often petered out mid-afternoon, compelling me to rustle up the craved, post-prandial fags. So, in an insufferably arrogant ploy, I leaned out of my window and graciously offered to accompany one of the Bowles House damsels on her short walk from supper, in return for a cigarette. While my need for a nicotine fix was real enough, the whole exercise was obviously a stratagem providing access to one or another of the remarkably attractive and interesting covey of girls. True, war conditions caused a paucity of men, but how could I have been so conceited and crass? I had neither the looks nor the talents of a Lothario. What arrogance to think that my company on the short walk home was valued or worth a cigarette! At the same time, I liked most people and sensed that this was often reciprocated. My Czech origin, foreign accent, and extensive travels cast an exotic hue which many found intriguing. I was different and, given that migration and travel were relatively rare phenomena at the time in North America, there was something slightly mysterious about me. I thought of none of this at the time, having always been quite unselfconscious.

I took out three of the girls, all of whom raved about one of their housemates, Murie Kelly, who also smoked and thus became part of my walk-home service. We eventually transmuted into what would, nowadays, be called "an item." She was a little older than the others, having gone to Normal School (teacher training) and taught for a year or so before entering university to study fine art. She was two years ahead of me and deeply involved in some aspects of Vic with which I was unfamiliar: Wymilwood, a women's residence and clubhouse, was one of them. Murie was regularly on desk duty there, as part of a bursary. One of her other tasks was to design and execute posters for the Wymilwood concerts which alternated with the Hart House Concerts as the principal musical series on campus. She also designed and helped construct sets for the productions of the Victoria College Dramatic Society. These, under the direction of Dora Mavor Moore, one of Canada's most celebrated theatre pioneers, were good enough to attract attention outside the college. She later also designed sets for Mrs. Moore's own Coach House Theatre, located at what was then the northern perimeter of the city.

In my fourth year I was elected one of the two Victoria College representatives on the university's student government, the Students' Administrative Council (SAC). This plunged me into university-wide politics and eventually led to summer jobs. During holidays I worked for, and eventually ran, the U of T Housing Service, which found accommodation for the swelling student body, including large numbers of newly married demobbed veterans, desperately requiring affordable housing.

Since all the components of the university were represented on the council, it offered the opportunity to get to know and work with a broader constituency than that of my course and college. I developed particularly close ties with Joan Thomas, my fellow member from Vic, and William Wadley, the University College representative, who was studying commerce. He and I shared views on most political and campus issues and often espoused the same causes. We also both intensively followed anything to do with contemporary media, about which he was better informed than I.

I was elected Communications Commissioner, responsible principally for the broad oversight of *The Varsity*, the student daily, and *Torontonensis*, the yearbook. One of the tasks of the Commissioner and his colleagues was to propose, to the whole

Council, a candidate for the post of Chief Editor of *The Varsity* — probably the most important officer of the council. We confronted a particularly difficult decision when two leading candidates for the editorship were Norman DePoe and Mark Harrison. Both were exceptionally strong candidates, as shown by their subsequent careers. Norm later became an iconic member of the CBC's news department. Mark held key reportorial positions with the *Toronto Star*, of which he later became editor, as he did subsequently of the *Montreal Gazette*. We settled on Mark, fearing that Norm's undoubted brilliance was accompanied by a certain risky unpredictability.

Bill Wadley and I were thrust into something of a *cause célèbre*, one that considerably diminished my respect for the quality of the non-academic leaders of the university. The issue was the price of student admissions to football games — a topic to which I attached a lower priority than to the fertility rate of one-eyed bison. But it was one of principle, that pesky enemy of bonhomie and notorious disturber of tranquility. The decision to impose a price, or raise it — I forget which — was made without student consultation or participation. We found this unacceptable and sought an audience with the University President, Sidney Smith. He was friendly but non-committal, and offered to arrange a meeting for us with some members of the Board of Governors' Athletic Committee, which included several Bay Street tycoons. Bill and I toiled mightily drafting a suitable presentation and consulted some of our constituents. It no doubt reflected our naïveté and penchant for over-kill, for it made some reference to Jean-Jacques Rousseau. We were set back when one of the mighty governors observed that he did not see what the views of some French Canadian had to do with the case.

Bill Wadley eventually qualified as a chartered accountant and worked for a Toronto firm owned by a Mr. Crawley. When first appearing on the doorstep of a new client, Bill — who had a sombre, almost cadaverous appearance — always introduced himself by saying "I am Wadley from Crawley."

Soon after I arrived at U of T, I saw a poster advertising a meeting of the Modern History Club and decided to attend. Since it was the initial session of the year, an election was held for the executive. Attendees from different years took turns standing up and then elected their representative. When the time for first year came, I rose and stood in solitary splendour, covered in embarrassment. The rest is history; I was acclaimed (by me?). The consequences were considerable. Not only did I become a regular participant in the meetings, but I also came to know quite a number of the denizens of Baldwin House, the home of the History Department, including many of the professors. I stood in awe of them—they were a formidable lot—but also noted that the Emperors were not always clad. A shared trait among them piqued my curiosity. Frequently snide comments were dropped about Bloor Street. This was a reference to 273 Bloor Street West, the site of the Department of Political Economy, sheltering not only political science and economics but also the brat discipline of sociology. Many of the eminent historians regarded the social sciences with petulant skepticism and some disdain.

This aroused my curiosity. I canvassed the opinions of friends taking courses in these upstart and inchoate disciplines, and eventually even talked to some professors. The result was that I gave up the idea of specializing in history and opted for the honours program in political economy with an emphasis on political science.

I did not turn my back on Baldwin House entirely, however, and continued taking history courses. In my two final years I faithfully attended the meetings of the History Club, ending up as its secretary. This august body had nothing to do with the plebeian Modern History Club into which I had stumbled in first year; it was linked to the History Department, whose professors attended the meetings and provided counsel and continuity. One did not join but had to be elected by existing members. The numbers were severely restricted, in part because the monthly meetings were held in the homes of various Toronto notables. A couple of papers by members were read at each session on a subject in the presenter's field. One of the great attractions was that members were selected from diverse disciplines in the humanities, sciences and social studies. They were supposed to be bright.

The club extended one's horizons by encouraging cross-disciplinary friendships and by dealing with issues arising in areas outside one own's specialty. The presence of history profs facilitated acquaintanceships with instructors at whose feet one did not sit in class. I missed taking Professor Frank Underhill's famous seminar on Liberalism, for instance, but managed to get to know him quite well, because he was always in attendance. During their refreshment phase, the meetings fostered extended conversations. But the club also raised the knotty issue of elitism. It was meant for top students and excluded many who would have liked to belong and who undoubtedly were talented enough to make a contribution. This was the first time, in so far as I am aware, that I noticed the inter-connection between excellence, elitism and exclusion.

University friendships usually are as important, if not more so, to post-secondary education, as are courses and extra-curricular pursuits. During my first academic year, I was totally immersed in university life. One of the earliest incentives for bonding arose out of the sharing of meals at Burwash Hall. Kindred spirits naturally gravitated to the same refectory tables and there continued the conversations and arguments growing out of their activities and preoccupations.

Most of the talk, on those occasions, was closer to the trivial than the profound, but one breakfast exchange, though seemingly comic, struck me as dead serious. Emmy Richards, a Welsh veteran of the RCAF who had briefly been at Pickering as a war guest prior to joining up, arrived for breakfast in a rare state of depression. He looked and acted despondent, although he said very little. When someone asked what was biting him, he told us that he was terrified by the previous night's dream: walking through an immense field, the only upright object between heaven and earth, a colossal finger pointed at him from high above and in an ominous voice said either "That's my boy Emmy," or "Emmy, you've had it!" He was tormented by his inability to remember which. We were aware that he was sometimes inclined towards a moody mysticism, possibly related to his Welsh background, and took his anxiety seriously.

My closest two friends were Alan Brown and Stefan Stykolt. The former was originally a farm boy who, though he won the Distinguished Flying Cross, had been perpetually terrified while in the air. He had hated the farm and the war. He was highly gifted. While still in high school, he had some poetry published in Ralph Gustafson's *Anthology of Canadian Poetry*, a Penguin book which was then about the only available volume of Canadian verse. With a great flair for foreign languages, he worked after graduation for the CBC in Europe, and eventually became an award-winning translator, primarily from the French. As a student he was erratically outstanding, rather than conscientious. His essays were often brilliant. One, on Edmund Spenser's *The Faerie Queen*, he wrote in imitation Spenserian stanzas; it fetched an astronomical mark. Northrop Frye once referred to him as "an intellectual beachcomber." He was fatally attracted to women and they to him.

Very musical, he played the violin and guitar and had a good voice. No wonder he was the centre of our gatherings, at which the singing of popular ballads, accompanied by inexpensive libations, was a principal component. His ease in handling diverse languages contributed much to the appeal of our parties. The playlist included items from all corners of the world and exhibited clashing ideologies. *Ochi chyornye* (*Oči černé* in Czech), *Volga Boatmen, Lili Marlene*, the *Internationale, Waltzing Matilda, The Marseillaise*, the *Horst Wessel Song, Mohr Soldaten* (the concentration camp song), and endless spirituals figured in our repertoire. I taught Alan some Czech and Slovak ditties as well, and *Kde Domov Můj?* (Where is my homeland?), the lyrical, gentle Czech national anthem, became a favourite. More! The songs of the currently fashionable Paris chansonniers received their due: Charles Trenet, Jean Sablon, Lucienne Boyer and, of course Edith Piaf. Among American balladeers, Burl Ives was big; a gathering rarely failed to include *The Foggy, Foggy Dew*, and we seldom neglected *I Know Where I'm Going*, and Hoagy Carmichael's *Buttermilk Sky*.

Alan's and my approaches to duty, authority, girls, our respective families, and the whole university experience could not have been more different. Yet, Brownie and I really hit it off, partly because of a shared, strong attraction to the literature and society of France. His command of the language was remarkable, considering his modest formal training; mine, backed less by talent than by the curriculum of my Haitian Lycée, was completely fluent. He usually called me "Mayzell," accenting the second syllable, the usual French pronunciation of Meisel, which amused him. We liked speaking French together and performed acrobatics with French words. He soaked up any lore about Czechoslovakia. We often sat together in his or my room, each scribbling or typing on our laps, working on an essay or a poem (Alan) or a short story (Mayzell). We worked together closely on *Acta Victoriana*, enhancing its quality and our fun. He was a fairly frequent visitor to my Toronto home, and my parents loved him.

Alan enriched me immeasurably by being such stimulating and amusing company, and by talking about his childhood and background. This showed me a feature of Canada—rural, farm Ontario—of which I had previously known nothing, despite my nodding acquaintance with the area around Batawa. He loathed farm life but, always the poet, succeeded in forcefully imparting what so bugged him about it and his family. His light-hearted, irreverent approach to rules, laws and regulations contrasted with my central European obedient and respectful view of the state. While not shaking my rigid sense of citizenship, he succeeded in modifying and humanizing it. Most importantly, he helped maintain my involvement with literature and writing at a time when most of my courses were in politics and economics.

Stefan Stykolt, my other close friend at university, was also a Vic student but did not live in residence. We met very early because, as a masterful logician and forceful speaker, he was a big wheel in the Debating Parliament. Although he was much more conservative than I and inclined to espouse economic liberalism, we were drawn to one another by many similarities. He was two years ahead of me in the honours course in Political Science and Economics, the same age as I almost to the day, also a refugee from a Nazi occupied country — Poland — and, as we discovered after becoming friends, the son of non-observant, assimilated Jewish parents. Like every Pole I ever met, he viscerally detested Germans — a sentiment you will recall I once shared and so understood. Before coming to Canada the Stykolts, who had always been well off, had lived in France, had relatives there, and were, again like many middle- and upper-class Poles, strongly tainted by French culture. Although powerfully engaged by his discipline of economics, Stefan also read widely, often in French, and it was he who seduced me into reading Marcel Proust's *Remembrance of Things Past*, the most explosive literary experience of my life. Since they were in the same year, he knew Murie before I did, and liked her — another bond. The three of us, along with his first wife, Heather, strengthened our friendship after the dispersal of our college-based gang, when we did graduate work in Britain.

What did Alan, Stefan and I do together? Everything. Meals, parties, guitar-accompanied evenings of song, films, plays, concerts, public lectures, gossip, but most of all, and enveloping it all, we talked, talked and talked. University courses, lectures, seminars, essays and events were naturally major topics, but so were public affairs, particularly the war and then its immediate aftermath, affairs of the heart, hopes for and fears of the future, our families and friends and anything that attracted the minds and funny bones of any one of us.

I was also close to other Vic residents, even though they were not part of our gang. Because Burwash Hall was closed for Sunday dinner we had to fend for ourselves elsewhere. I always did so with Noor Hassanali. Most Sunday evenings we joined the very proper old ladies who, in those days, inhabited and dined in the still unfashionable but ever so respectable nearby Windsor Arms Hotel. A Trinidadian law student, he had, at home, been befriended by a United Church missionary who directed him towards Victoria College and its residences. He became a friend and role model. His roots, in the dim past, were in India, and he abominated the presence there of the British. A gentle, kind person, possessed of a quiet but never remote sense of humour, he became angry, even violent, when talking of the Raj. He added much to my knowledge and emotional perceptions of the sub-continent and modified my generally exuberant anglophilia. I saw less of Noor after I left North House but remained in touch with him and, later, with his wonderful wife, and now widow, Zalay. He returned to Trinidad to practice law and became a judge on the Island's High Court, and eventually a universally respected and much-loved President of Trinidad and Tobago. He remained loyal and devoted to Victoria College and performed honorific functions in its governance until his death in 2006.

It was through student government that I encountered Murray Thomson. A Quaker sociology student a year ahead of me, and powerfully motivated by an acute and ever-active social conscience, he was an ardent and zealous member of the CCF, supported numerous progressive and peace-oriented causes, and never ceased mobilizing others to do likewise. We saw a fair amount of one another, and although I never joined the party — in fact any party — I responded to several of his projects for the betterment of humankind or the avoidance of nuclear war.

After we graduated, Murray occasionally recruited me for various good causes, particularly in the third world and in support of peace. He devoted his whole life to these ends, founding or co-founding several organizations to promote peace or social justice, including The Group of 78 and Project Ploughshares. In 1990, he was awarded the Pearson Peace Medal — Canada's equivalent to the Nobel Peace Prize. I have so much admiration for him and so trust his judgment that, to this day, when he seeks my moral or monetary support for one of his projects, which he still does from time to time, I do what I can, sometimes not even bothering to consult the supporting file. Lest you are now set to write me off as totally naive, I hasten to add that there was one occasion when I turned down his plea, though I no longer remember why.

Jim Eayrs is among a small number of relatively casual undergraduate friends with whom I developed much stronger bonds after we graduated, when our paths re-converged and criss-crossed in various ways. He was at Trinity, and obtained the highest mark in my course. Now retired, he still enjoys a stellar reputation as one of Canada's top scholars. A brilliant lecturer and teacher, he was also, for a while, a part-time newspaper columnist and CBC talking head. He was a member of the History Club, of course. The reason he occupies an indelible spot in my metaphorical undergraduate scrapbook, however, is not related to his powerful intellect but to an act of courage, for which he won my admiration as a human being. It grew out of his involvement with a fraternity, Lamda Chi Alpha, and occurred soon after the fraternity rejected a proposed member on racial grounds — he was of Chinese origin.

The world of fraternities is totally alien to me. As near as I recall, the US mother-house, like all such ornaments of American civilization at the time, excluded Jews and other non-Aryans, as Hitler might have put it, a practice to which some members of the Toronto chapter took exception. They resolved to defy the exclusivist ways of their American betters and open their doors to a candidate of Chinese origin. When it came to a vote, the initiative of the reformers was defeated; the Toronto chapter remained as untainted as its American counterparts. Jim resigned from his frat.

The story was relayed to me by another frat member, Michael Mackenzie, whom I'd met through a Pickering connection, and with whom I was then embarking on another lifelong friendship. Until Mike provided the background, I had no idea that fraternities were taken so very seriously by their members and that Jim's resignation ostracized him from a significant number of his friends. He chose, for the sake of principle, to espouse a course of action exacting a very considerable social and personal cost. We encounter Jim again in an upcoming chapter.

A few undergraduate contacts were less intimate and binding than the close friendships, but nevertheless left permanent marks. Ralph Hicklin was still in uniform when I first met him, but spent a lot of time in and around our residence. A connoisseur and lover of the arts, in my first year he wrote and directed "The Bob," the magnificent Vic annual theatrical review. He knew that I had been in Bob Rourke's highly touted G & S productions at Pickering and, as a result, greatly overestimated my vocal talents. The roles he assigned me kept shrinking, as my weaknesses surfaced, but I nevertheless retained more than a mere walk-on role. I can, as the result, boast that in my youth I gave a solo performance at Eaton Auditorium.

I had no sooner settled into my room in North House, than it developed into something of a meeting place, an entrepot, for the residence- and city-based members of our evolving group. I never locked my door and always had a coffee pot standing by. Friends were often hanging about when I returned from a class or a seminar. So, when Ralph wanted to leave a book for a pal living in the city, he arranged to have him pick it up on my dresser. It was S.J. Perelman's *Crazy Like a Fox*, and the recipient was Don Harron, an uncommonly versatile and gifted student taking double honours in English and Philosophy. Something of a theatrical celebrity on the campus, he played leading roles in Mrs. Moore's productions but had not yet created his alter ego, Charlie Farquharson. One of Don's now forgotten talents was his felicity as an inspired cartoonist. The editors of *Acta*, me included, exploited this. My *Acta* in many ways aped *The New Yorker*; in every issue, Don Harron had a full-page cartoon parodying the work of one of its currently famous graphic artists, but related to some aspect of the university. The draughtsmanship was indistinguishable from the work of people like James Thurber or Helen Hokinson. There were minor variations in the signatures. Although the appearance closely followed the originals, a George Price signature became George Priceless and a Mary Petty turned into Very Petty, but you had to look closely to notice. A Charles Addams imitation depicted a man-sized ape, with an undergraduate beanie on his head descending the steps of the Royal Ontario Museum, while chatting with a coed. The caption read, "I am an exchange student in Anthropology."

Ralph Hicklin's antecedents were strictly Chatham, Ontario, but he aspired to a lifestyle he thought was espoused by the glitterati of London and New York. Thus, with a few like-minded aesthetes, he subscribed to a box in Massey Hall for every concert of the Toronto Symphony Orchestra, and attended with his friends, all clad in tails, and brandishing canes. Years later, when I saw Granada TVs fabulous adaptation of *Brideshead Revisited*, I recognized Ralph in Nickolas Grace's flawless embodiment of Anthony Blanch—one of the more memorable characters in the TV adaptation of Waugh's novel. Ralph eventually became the mainstay of the *Toronto Star's* cultural pages and one of Canada's leading ballet critics.

I greatly admired his versatility and immense talents. He was outspoken, stimulating and very amusing. But he did not exactly ooze compassion; rather, he possessed a cruel streak and a rapier for a tongue. A single episode attests to this, as well as to the quickness and sharpness of his mind. It makes a blood-chilling but also highly comic story. In the short interval between lectures, when hordes of students were en route from one class to another, traffic flows in some corners of the campus were heavily overloaded. One of the most congested places was the rotunda of University College. Once, while navigating this jam-packed crossroads, Ralph inadvertently bumped into Professor McDougall, a senior and distinguished member of the History Department, known, among many things, for the minuscule size of the fuse controlling his temper. He took very badly indeed being jostled by someone, exploded, and tore a strip off his careless assailant. Ralph, who knew that Professor McDougall had been blinded in the First World War, responded, according to his account, by saying meekly, "I am terribly sorry, sir, but you see I am blind."

A total antithesis to Ralph's brashness was the tentative manner of another student, and later celebrity, the brilliant and many-faceted James Reanny. We shared Professor Flendlay's history seminar in first year and belonged to a loose group linked by its involvement in various publications and literary events. They included, among others, Robert Weaver, Ivon Owen, Colleen Thibodeau (Jamie's wife), David Knight, who occupied the room next to mine at North House, Alan Brown, Richard Stingle and David Hoeniger, all of whom attained some renown on the country's literary scene. Jamie was musical, had a facile brush, and was a prolific and versatile writer. He was highly regarded and admired by those who knew him, but was also viewed with scorn and ridicule by people guided principally by appearances. His ubiquitous, light-coloured raincoat was a riot of dark blotches. He did not favour fountain or ballpoint pens and, for some reason, as he traipsed from class to class, carried a bottle of ink in hand. My memory is that it was open, but this may be an embellishment wrought by time. When I wrote this, I was too embarrassed to phone him to find out and he has died since. There is no doubt that he stood out not only because of his literary and intellectual gifts but also because of his eccentric, bespattered appearance.

Another brush with someone later to achieve fame was highly concentrated, lasting only a short time and exposing me to an entertainment genre about which I knew little. For some reason I found myself collaborating with Norm Jewison on "The Bob," the Vic annual review which Ralph Hicklin had elevated to such a high art. I don't remember much about this exercise except that Norm's and my paths had never crossed before and I was not even sure whether he was at Vic. He had apparently been responsible for several successful shows in his Toronto secondary school. Since I remember so little about our collaboration, I surmise that my contribution was minuscule and vastly outshone by Jewison's far greater experience and panache. It was I, however, who came up with the corny title of the show. It was staged at the time when *The Jolson Story* was wildly popular on Toronto's screens. My title, *The Molson Tory*, was intended as a screamingly funny allusion to the film, but was merely a play on words only remotely connected to the contents. I have never come across this item among the long list of Jewison's theatrical and cinematographic credits even though he is, at the time of writing, the Chancellor of Victoria University. I have long admired his progressive outlook and his commitment to racial equality as well as the fact that, though hugely successful in the United States, he has, unlike so many others, maintained his Canadian roots and is making important contributions to our cultural life.

It probably says quite a bit about the nature of my undergraduate life that I have prattled on about it for so long without addressing its essence — the academic core. The trepidation I felt with respect to my ability to cope with the academic challenge led me to start as a model of conscientiousness. I attended every lecture, followed up every reading suggestion, and made careful notes of everything remotely connected to every one of my courses. The zeal paid off at the Christmas exams. I aced them, so much so that I wondered whether I had not been overdoing it. As time went on, I became more deeply involved in extracurricular activities and widening and multiplying circles of friends. I also began to discriminate between what I saw as important and what appeared to be ephemeral. Over the four undergraduate years, I slipped from the exemplary perch of a model student to the unpredictable path of a roller coaster. I did well in some areas and abysmally in others. My attendance at lectures varied with the appeal of the subject and its expositor. I went to some with Teutonic regularity and skipped others with Bohemian abandon. Whereas, early in the game, I would not dream of delivering an essay a second late, my subsequent observance of deadlines was scandalous. As the result of this descent into academic insouciance, my performance record was bizarre.

Students' marks were posted at the end of every term. We could, therefore, ascertain where we stood. After the admirable start, I coasted comfortably in the second class category, occasionally hitting a first, until I came to the end of the third year, when my average sank disastrously to third class honours, due in part to an uncongenial course and dull instructor in Money and Banking, and to a temporary incompatibility with statistics. A couple of osteo-caused sojourns in hospital may also have contributed, but I rather doubt it. The miserable third year result and the compelling nature of some fourth year courses led to my socks being pulled up in my final year. I stood I, 2 (one, two) at the end of it, meaning that I was second among those receiving first class honours. Since the standing in fourth year, rather than the average obtained in all courses ever taken, determined the mark assigned for the whole honours program, I graduated with a first class degree and, to boot, won the silver medal in political science. Because of a bout in hospital, I did not attend the graduating ceremonies at Victoria, but was told that the dean, Dr. Bennett, in awarding the medal in absentia, made some amusing comments about my astonishing leap to near the top of the class. My surprise was at least as great as the good dean's.

I was pleased particularly by having done well in courses led by Northrop Frye and Harold Innis, less so by a first in Industrial Relations — a bird course, in my view, no offense intended to our avian friends. Innis's offering was labelled "Economic History," but was really an exposition of his observations and theories on communications, which he was in the midst of developing at the time. Although one of Canada's most brilliant scholars, Innis was not a good lecturer. His delivery was less than dynamic, since he frequently chewed on the temples of his spectacles, and the degree to which he projected his voice left something to be desired. The impact of his analyses was also sometimes blunted by a tendency to leave out some essential steps in an argument. But his mind was so authoritative and his ideas so compelling that some of us went to extraordinary lengths to receive and decipher his thoughts. His formidable presence and awesome reputation no doubt added to our interest. His courses were compulsory for those in honours Political Science and Economics and in Commerce and Finance, and were therefore very large, for those days. A small group of us lined up at the door before the lecture hall disgorged its previous occupants, so we could make a frenzied dash to the first two or three front rows, from which we could hear him better. Then, after the lecture, half a dozen or so of us repaired across the street to the King Cole Room, a beer parlour in the Park Plaza Hotel, where we sought to deconstruct his lecture and, on the basis of our collective reading, fill in the missing parts.

To illustrate: while discussing the consequences of changes in newsprint technology, Innis noted that when rags started being used in the production of newsprint, to meet the ever more voracious demands of the media, there were implications for health. The death rate among London's population started declining. The question of how and why was left up in the air. When the knights sitting around the table in the King Cole Room considered these questions, the collectively arrived-at explanation, nourished by the shared acquaintance with Innis's papers, revealed the following. When rags began having an economic value, they were collected and removed from the dirty streets. This reduced the rat population. Rats were notorious carriers of disease. Fewer rats, fewer carriers of disease. Ergo, fewer maladies, fewer deaths. Simple! The attraction of the substance of Innis's material was immensely enhanced by the fun of our regular sessions working out the puzzles created by his hopscotch style. Not everyone cottoned to his oblique ways, but some of us — mostly better students — were fascinated by it and found Harold Innis's courses among the most challenging and enduring in our program.

Frye's lectures were less opaque, but they too required a great deal of thought and interpretation, and prompted subsequent discussion. There seems to be a pattern to the ways in which students respond to professors. In the early years they flock to orator-type lecturers who, while not necessarily glib, at least in part attract attention by verbal fireworks. In the later years, it is deep thinkers who become stars. One of our most popular lecturers in the two junior years was a controversial, *engagé* economic historian called Lorne T. Morgan. He was on the political left — an orientation which infused his lectures. His analyses of contemporary problems were amusing and scathing with respect to the prevailing order. He was more a propagandist than a scholar. His only publication, insofar as I remember, was a pamphlet entitled *Homo the Sap* — a droll but rather facile critique of the status quo. He was popular among freshmen and sophomores, but decidedly less so among advanced students.

It says something about the quality of our undergraduate program that, in the eyes of students in their final years, it was the Innises, the Fryes, as well as the Dawsons (Canadian politics), the Bradys (Commonwealth politics and modern political ideas) and the C.B. Macphersons (political thought, Marxism) who won our greatest admiration and eventually outstripped the Morgans and other early idols.

Ralph and his cronies, you remember, used to rent a box at Massey Hall to attend the Symphony concerts in dazzling style. I ignored this ostentatious extravagance but subscribed to an ordinary series subscription to the TSO concerts. One of these was scheduled for the evening of December 12th, 1944. The date won't mean anything to you unless you wallow in trivia or collect meteorological memorabilia. That day, Toronto was in the grip of a paralyzing snowstorm. Streets became impassable, no buses or trams operated and next day, the only of the city's dailies to appear was *The Varsity*. David Parsons, a South African friend, and I set out to wade down from the residence to Massey Hall, in hopes of attending our TSO subscription concert, if it was going to take place. The heavy snowfall continued and the city was embalmed in complete silence. No cars or plows were heard and the only sound intruding on this void was the crunch of snow under foot and such noises as we chose to make as we slowly trudged across Queen's Park and along University Avenue to Queen Street. It was eerie and magnificent.

As we approached Massey Hall, we saw a sparse trickle of bundled bodies make their way to the well-lit entrance curtained by a veil of gently falling snow. We took our seats in the half-filled auditorium and waited for the fun to start. Members of the orchestra were still straggling in, clad in wild assortments of winter garb. About three-quarters of the desks were filled by the time Sir Ernest MacMillan appeared, dressed *de rigeur* in evening clothes. He made a delightful speech, apologizing for the gaps in the ranks behind him and congratulating those of us who had ventured out into the deep snow and who actually succeeded in reaching our destination. There was a palpable feeling of triumph, shared camaraderie, and anticipation as Sir Ernest's baton descended to start the music. I have not the slightest recollection of what was played — and for once Google has let me down — but remember thinking that this was without doubt the most enjoyable concert I had ever attended. It was certainly the most memorable, for I still feel the warm glow with which the compositions were filtered as they reached our thawing ears. The absence of certain instruments was manifest, of course, but it was more than compensated for by the shared feeling that everyone in the hall was bound together by a genuine and intrepid love of music.

On rereading this chapter, I became increasingly uncomfortable. An apology, or at least an explanation is in order. There seems to be an awful lot of name-dropping—a despicable and demeaning practice. Often, when I mention someone who later gained public visibility, I refer to this, since I assume that recognition by the reader adds to the interest of the story. This is not intended to invite a pat on the back, but merely attests to the characters at U of T being an amazingly interesting and accomplished lot. An extraordinarily lucky convergence of the right place and the right time made the University of Toronto during my undergraduate years a place brimming with talent. The fact that so many of my classmates were veterans had something to do with it. The excitement and tensions associated with the war and its aftermath may also have been a factor. I was an unwitting but greatly blessed beneficiary of these circumstances.

XII

The Graduate 1948–1949

B ecoming an adult creeps up on one surreptitiously. When does it begin and when does it end? Several developments marked my way: graduating with the B.A. and embarking upon postgraduate studies, working at part-time jobs, becoming involved with the *Canadian Forum* and enjoying a significant turn in affairs of the heart.

The possibility of doing postgraduate work surfaced during my fourth year during a conversation with Harold Innis. He asked whether I had considered going on to an M.A. This was the first time anyone mentioned so bold a possibility—and in those days it *was* pretty daring: only a very small proportion of the population attended university at all, and only an infinitesimal fraction of it went on to graduate work. When I raised the issue with my parents, they did not discourage me but neither did they break out into unseemly huzzahs. Why the reticence? The family had not yet confronted the likelihood of our long-term future being somewhere other than in Czechoslovakia. The euphoria which followed Germany's collapse had not yet dissipated and the implications of the Prague Communist *coup d'etat* in the spring of 1948 had not yet sunk in. Tati and Mami probably thought that a Canadian M.A. would not be as useful to a returning young fella as more job-oriented, applied training. No one, including me, had given much thought to what this might be. Spending another year at U of T was very appealing: it offered further opportunities for reading, writing, and reflection, and promised to prolong the camaraderie of student life. It also postponed a decision about a specific career choice.

Since crafting a solid dissertation was the core requirement for an M.A., I pondered what would make a good topic. I had, in Zlín, idolized T.G. Masaryk and his democratic ideas, as you saw. After taking courses in political philosophy and starting to acquire critical faculties, I began to wonder whether my brain had been scrubbed a bit, both by the Czech educational system and by Tati. A cool-headed academic examination of Masaryk would test the foundations of my infatuation. To my surprise, he had not been subjected to serious academic study in Czechoslovakia, let alone abroad. Why not do a thesis on the social and political thought of Masaryk, and scrutinize how it affected his performance as President of Czechoslovakia? A return trip to Innis elicited his support for the project, provided I could scare up adequate documentation, much of which was not available in English. He added that if the question of research materials was met, I could go ahead under the supervision of Professor Karl Helleiner, an erudite Austrian scholar who, though an economist, was thoroughly familiar with the history and politics of central Europe.

Explorations of the university and college book holdings, Toronto's excellent Reference Library, and the potential of inter-library loans revealed that plenty of the relevant fodder was available, but that there were important gaps which would have to be filled by obtaining some items in Czechoslovakia, particularly Masaryk's works. That posed problems. After the German occupation and under the emerging communist clampdown on freedom of thought, many sources were unavailable. Important elements of life in the first republic had been eradicated by the Nazis and, later, by the Communists. Fortunately, a small, short-lived window of opportunity occurred between the departure of the first bad lot and arrival of the second. New editions of Masaryk's books appeared, which Tati secured through good, old-fashioned barter. Many necessities of "civilized" life in Czechoslovakia — cigarettes, silk or nylon stockings, virtually all delicacies and, more importantly, food items and medicines — were unavailable unless aid parcels were procured from abroad. The Communists, once in power, prevented virtually all foreign aid to enter the country. Under these conditions, private help from overseas was welcome and Tati managed to "pay" for my Czech books by sending food and other relief parcels.

Dr. Helleiner liked my topic and was a perfect mentor. His intimate knowledge of Austria-Hungary, and of central Europe generally, and an amazingly eclectic and erudite nose for relevant sources, were most immediately useful, but there was very much more. An exceedingly wise and thoughtful man, he taught me an enormous amount about life during our many, and always far-ranging, conversations. These occurred in his house on Cottingham Street, after the completion of every chapter and sometimes in between. Once I started submitting draft segments, Dr. Helleiner revealed that underneath his Austrian accent there dwelled a masterful command of the English language, and an acute ear for literary elegance. He was a meticulous editor who watched over and monitored every actual and potential comma. He was the first of the two or three of my writing coaches who impressed upon me the virtue of writing clearly and economically. Perhaps not quite the first. In my freshman year, I took a course in anthropology from a Professor Hart, who wrote in the margin of my first paper for him: "Words are tools, not missiles." I have, without acknowledgment, passed this advice on to innumerable students who, like me, occasionally went overboard when making a point.

Masaryk was by no means the sole presence in my conversations with Karl Helleiner. We regularly canvassed the current world scene, including the ever more disquieting geopolitical developments foreshadowing the Cold War, and the outlook for post-war economic adjustments. His disposition tended to be on the gloomy side. I was therefore surprised by his uncharacteristic optimism vis-à-vis the prospects for economic growth, despite the unwinding of war production. One of the reasons for his upbeat expectations arose from his circumstances. The Helleiners lived comfortably enough, but nevertheless found themselves on a short economic leash because of the parsimony applied by Innis — the head of the Political Economy Department — to his colleagues' salaries. No doubt prompted by his training as an economist, his rule was to pay them no more than what was absolutely necessary. The miserly strategy meant that scholars who, like Helleiner, were refugees and had few options for jobs elsewhere, were paid exceedingly little. Karl noted that his family lacked several of the common household labour-saving appliances which he would have happily acquired, if the means became available. He assumed that many others shared this yearning and that a promising, rich market was waiting to meet the needs of Canada's population which he expected to continue to grow and prosper. He was right.

Among the undergraduate courses I enjoyed most were those dealing with political ideas, particularly as taught by C.B. (Brough) Macpherson. If anyone had asked, as I started my M.A. year, which sub-field of political studies I fancied the most, I would have named political philosophy. The study of Masaryk fitted nicely and I also chose this field for my graduate seminars. One was offered by Macpherson and the other by Alexander Brady. The latter's course on modern political ideas was particularly pertinent. It placed considerable emphasis on the ideas of John Stuart Mill with whom —

I discovered with pleasure because I liked his thoughts—Masaryk had a great deal in common. In addition, I decided to take Russian, as an extra, because acquaintance with it would help in mining some of the sources required for the thesis. I also loved the great Russian novelists and playwrights and found the portraits of Russia they presented fascinating. But I never attained anything like fluency in Tolstoy's mother tongue and was teasingly accused by the instructor, a Professor Shore, of pronouncing it with a Czech accent—a natural enough failing under the circumstances.

It soon became evident that an overall probe of President Masaryk's life would be too vast an enterprise for a master's dissertation. I narrowed my essay by focusing on Masaryk's attitude to pan-Slavism, one of the many topics he had extensively expounded upon. He had also written *The Spirit of Russia*, a related two-volume magisterial study of Russian ideas and literature. He was intimately acquainted with pan-Slavism but had reservations about it; and consequently contributed to the new Czechoslovakia being firmly rooted in Western Europe. The thesis focus forced me to immerse myself in the literature on nationalism, much of which was in German. When I later became involved in studying Quebec politics and its place in Canada, the acquaintance with nationalist ideology and related -isms provided a useful context and reference point.

Brady's and Macpherson's seminars helped me find suitable philosophical settings for the thesis and also had larger implications. My continued acquaintance with Brough led to a subsequent friendship. Although I found his sympathetic introduction to Marxism helpful in identifying the sources of social problems, the solutions offered, while neat, were not quite convincing. Brady's emphasis on many British political thinkers, particularly the Fabians, was more relevant to the formation of my own political outlook.

I had three very part-time jobs in the M.A. year. Each in some unexpected and unforeseen manner provided contacts or training that would become useful in later life. Someone, I think Jessie MacPherson or Kay Cobourn, suggested that I take groups of school children on tours of the Greek gallery at the Royal Ontario Museum (ROM). I had taken Professor Moffat Woodside's college course in Ancient History, which embraced Greece, of course. My knowledge was rudimentary but I managed, with the assistance of a Miss Martin of the ROM's staff, to bone up on the background of the exhibits sufficiently to put together presentations on the artifacts in the display cases, which held the attention of the children. This was easier than teaching Grade 10 Latin—a challenge I met when a tutor at Pickering. This earlier experience as a tutor came in handy though. It taught me that one of the useful techniques of teaching is asking pupils questions. Plato and Socrates had this idea before me, of course. I also managed to deliver my information in a lively way. The job paid very little but it taught me a lot about Hellenic culture and about teaching. I loved it.

Another of my jobs was also in the ROM, but in the basement, and had no real connection with the Museum. Mrs. Moore, and when he was demobbed, her son Mavor, founded the first professional theatre in Toronto, maybe Canada, when they created the New Play Society (NPS), an outgrowth of Mrs. Moore's Village Players. The plays were presented in an auditorium below the main part of the museum. Likely on Murie's suggestion, I volunteered to be an usher for the Society's plays. This time, there was *no* remuneration but I had the chance to attend all productions for free. Thirty years later, when I was appointed chair of the CRTC, Mavor Moore sent me a warm letter of congratulations noting that my service with the NPS attested to my genuine and disinterested commitment to the cause of Canadian culture.

A much more challenging, also unpaid, extracurricular engagement was with the *Canadian Forum*. Although Northrop Frye, then editor, asked me to serve on the editorial board, I think that the idea was Ivon Owen's, a brilliant CCF-affiliated, Trinity College student who was part of the literary circle of friends in my orbit. I had various contacts with him and we both belonged to the History Club. He eventually worked for the Canadian Oxford University Press, and was, for many years, its head.

Although the *Forum* had no formal link with the CCF in my day, and sometimes criticized it, it was strongly committed to democratic socialism. The meetings were chaired by Frye, but the production, distribution and day-to-day conduct of all business, as well as the archiving of old issues, was in the hands of Lou Morris, the managing editor, and his wife, Kay. The *Forum*'s premises were in a former coach house on Huntley Street, shared with a radio repairman. The space was cramped because it also served as the Morris's home. They lived most modestly and they were totally committed to, and engaged in, the cause. But, unlike many dedicated militants, they also had a sense of humour.

Their daughter was called Rebel. I never found the nerve to ask whether her name reflected her parents' political aspirations for her, or her comportment in Kay's belly before she was born. When she reached school age, Kay inscribed her in the local public school, producing a *very* Canadian episode. She was asked what was the family's religion. The Morrises identified with no religious body. Consulting the principal on what to say solved the problem. He inquired after the parents' affiliation, and when Kay reported that her family had been Anglican, and Lou's Jewish, he shot back without hesitation, "No problem, just put down United Church."

We met once a month and some of us occasionally also came in to help with the mailing. Meetings opened with a wide-ranging discussion of recent developments at home and abroad. Those worthy of editorial comment were identified and discussed. If no obvious author for a projected editorial emerged, Frye asked someone to write it. The appointed scribe kept in mind the dominant ideas expressed around the table, but did write his or her piece. None of the editorials were signed. This worked well, largely because our progressive and internationalist outlook was compatible and because there were no ideological nitpickers among us. Sometimes we would request former *Forum* people like Frank Underhill or George Grube to do an editorial.

The *Forum* experience was as educational as taking graduate courses. Apart from the substantive light it shone on important questions of the day, it compelled one to receive and absorb diverse perspectives and weave these into a short piece, to be produced by an imminent deadline. In addition, not all present were academics; the involvement of highly intelligent and well-informed lay people, some of them linked to voluntary associations, including unions, was salutary. I resigned from the board when I left Toronto but continued writing editorials for it. The very first full-length substantive article I ever published outside a school or university context appeared in the *Forum*. It dealt with — guess what? — T.G. Masaryk.

In addition to its intellectual riches, my M.A. year also marked a profound emotional turnaround. My friendship with Murie imperceptibly deepened and we drifted into the awareness that we would spend our lives together. We went to plays, concerts, exhibitions and lectures, as well as on walks and visits to Toronto sights like the Island or High Park and, by no means least, we saw a lot of our respective, increasingly overlapping, circles of friends.

Murie shared, with a friend and fellow teacher, an apartment on Roxborough, where I was a frequent guest. I was delighted by Murie's unobtrusive but deep aesthetic sense which enveloped her entire life, whether it manifested itself in household furnishings and *décor*, the shape or texture of a sandwich, or the casual, but by no means unplanned, knot of a scarf.

She graduated two years ahead of me and gave a course for art teachers in the summer. Then she began a regular teaching stint in Leaside, a suburb of Toronto. An amazing stroke of luck put an end to it after only one year. Royal Dutch Shell conducted extensive oil explorations in Venezuela, where it employed a motley crew of nationals from around the world. Most had school-aged children. Shell needed two teachers qualified to offer instruction meeting the requirements of the Ontario Department of Education. Its prestige was high enough to ensure that the educational mobility of kids belonging to the international crowd of Shell employees was not impaired, once they left the exploration camp. On the recommendation of an inspector who had been impressed by her pedagogical prowess at Leaside, Murie was offered a teaching post in Venezuela near Los Conucos. She left towards the end of the summer for a two-year stint, thereby dramatically changing the modalities of our relationship.

One of the many attractions of the Venezuela offer was its high remuneration. She had incurred substantial debts from her two brothers, and sister who, while not starving, nevertheless had considerable financial responsibilities of their own. She was anxious to repay them, which was made possible by the savings from the Shell employment.

Our separation lasted only during her school term, because she came home for the summer holidays, again teaching summer school. But the absences were long enough to spawn an intense and voluminous correspondence. While we may not have been in Héloise and Abelard's class, our knowledge of one another was deepened immeasurably by our practice, two or three times a week, to put it all down on paper, never mind how much time and how many pages it took.

The likelihood of an impending marriage did not direct my thoughts towards the job market, but the choices were narrowing. A university career was not one of them. I realized that I was articulate and was slowly coming to think that I was reasonably bright. But I had much too high an opinion of what it takes to be an academic to think that I could qualify. Journalism was still a possibility, but the wonderful experience at Pickering also made teaching an attractive alternative. And I was enjoying graduate work a great deal, even contemplating the possibility of going on towards a doctorate — no matter what the ultimate vocation. As this idea started taking hold, I thought — likely under the spell of *The Slavonic and East European Review* — that regional studies, and particularly those related to the Slav world, would be fascinating. By the time I settled on going beyond the master's degree, it was too late to seek admission to one of the great schools in Britain or the US. To enter any of them I needed fellowships, the deadlines of which had passed by then.

A viable course, allowing for diverse future avenues, was to teach at Pickering, prepare for doctoral studies and perhaps also continue there. Joe McCulley had left and was succeeded as headmaster by Bob Rourke. Our relationship was not as close, but I inquired whether a position at the school would be possible. To my delight and, and slight surprise, he did offer me a job for at least a year, possibly longer.

Then a thunderbolt struck, in the form of Professor J.A. Corry, the highly respected political scientist at Queen's. He came to Toronto to see whether one of his former students, Rod Grey — then an assistant editor of *Saturday Night*, under the great B.K. Sandwell — would come to Queen's for a year to replace its public administration specialist, J.E. Hodgetts, who was going to Oxford on a Nuffield scholarship. Rod agreed and Corry then turned to a less weighty matter — the appointment of a junior person for one academic year to assist him with his famous introductory course on democratic government and to teach another course. Rod and I had met in Professor Brady's graduate seminar on Political Thought and had become friends. He mentioned me in sufficiently positive terms to induce Corry to check up on me with some of my profs. The upshot was that after a while I was invited to Queen's to discuss the possibility of a short-term appointment. All of this was unexpected and absolutely stunning.

The great man met me at the station when I arrived in Kingston to spend 48 hours with his family at their home near the campus. My visit had the double purpose of informing me about the nature of the possible appointment and, above all, of giving Queen's the chance of assessing whether I was worthy of an offer. I learnt that I would be teaching a course on American government (a field in which I had taken a half-course from R. McGregor Dawson) and that I would organize and keep an eye on the weekly tutorials accompanying Corry's big introductory course, take two tutorials myself and give the occasional lecture, when Corry had to be away. The appointment was for one academic session at a the rank of Instructor, a level below that of lecturer and so low, in fact, that it has since been allowed to vanish, like the smile of the Cheshire cat. The emolument was to be $2,000 which, even that long ago, was not lavish, but commensurate, I thought, with the duties expected of me and the fact that I had not yet quite obtained my M.A.

Although it seemed normal at the time, in retrospect a truly astounding feature of the exercise, apart from the fact that I had been found good enough to be the centre of it, was the care and time Queen's took for vetting so insignificant an appointment. I took up the whole of Corry's weekend, was shown the campus by him and, most astonishing of all, was interviewed on Saturday and Sunday morning, in their homes, by R.C. Wallace, the principal, and W.A. Mackintosh, the head of the joint economics and politics department, dean of Arts and vice-principal. Corry inquired what courses I had taken, and liked, and we talked quite a bit about my thesis, but I did not have to give a paper to the department. No search committee was involved. Not the slightest attention was paid to whether I was a male or female; black, white or *café au lait*; or Jewish or Christian — a matter which would have been of relevance a few years earlier. No one probed, as one would now, whether I was sufficiently in tune with anti-heterosexualism to pass muster with the appropriate campus watchdog, whether I could be trusted to be left alone with a student (of either sex) in my office with the door closed or whether I had a passionate commitment to campus diversity.

Alec Corry made an excellent first impression, although that was not the issue, of course. What counted was what impression *I* made on *him*. I was predisposed to think highly of him, in part because of his reputation and the admiring reports from his students, including Rod Grey. But his numerous outstanding qualities revealed themselves only gradually later on. One of his hallmark traits, however — being an unusually amusing, prolific and eclectic raconteur — surfaced during that first weekend. I vividly recall one of the stories with which he regaled his houseguest, possibly because I heard him retell it again several times later. It concerns a lady travelling on the Newfie Bullet, the (in)famous train running between St. John's and Port aux Basques, derided, among other things, for its snail-like progress. Some time after boarding at Port aux Basques, our heroine inquires from the conductor when they expect to arrive in St. John's. He tells her and goes on his business. Thereafter she asks at ever more frequent intervals. The conductor — a patient man — eventually no longer conceals his irritation, prompting this explanation: "You see, Mr. Conductor, I am expecting to give birth to a baby any time now." "Madam, you should not have boarded the train in that condition!" "I didn't," she replies. My version lacks the Newfoundland-Irish accents and the more craftily contrived tale from a champion raconteur, but *faute de mieux*...

Some time after my return home I received the anxiously awaited letter from Queen's: I had passed muster. I immediately phoned Bob Rourke to inquire whether change of plans on my part would inconvenience the school unduly. His reply was reassuring and heartening. There was still plenty of time to fill the position I was to occupy, and Bob was very pleased to hear of my good fortune. Congratulations! He was a loyal Queen's man.

The thesis was moving ahead, but at a pace reminiscent of the Newfie Bullet, making my self-imposed summer deadline problematic. The Queen's commitment ensured that I would not. Because of my original intention to concentrate on honours history, I did not take the gateway course, R. McGregor Dawson's introduction to Canadian Politics. This meant that I had never encountered the works of J.A. Corry, most notably his classic, *Democratic Government and Politics*, the core of the course I was to tutor. I had to make up for this neglect and could not resist casting about for reading material relevant to my upcoming teaching duties with the result that Masaryk suffered.

When the term was over, I returned to the SAC Housing Service while Murie, safely back from Venezuela, taught another summer course. We agreed to marry on August 6th in the chapel of Hart House. We opted for the simplest possible, stripped down service, in the presence only of our immediate families. When discussing the arrangements with the chaplain, who was a good acquaintance, he inquired, with a twinkle, whether this was a shotgun marriage.

For our honeymoon — we did have one, our otherwise minimalist approach notwithstanding — my parents suggested their small cottage in the Blue Mountains near Collingwood. We went there immediately after the wedding "reception" in the Park Plaza Hotel and spent a blissful month working our heads off. I prepared intensively for my teaching and Murie, in another small nearby cottage provided by Jozo Weider, the creator of the Blue Mountain

Resort, and a family friend, set up a silkscreen printing table on which she experimented with a new way of blending colours for her striking designs of greeting cards. Our two places of work were about twenty minutes apart on foot, through rolling meadows. The separation and proximity added a certain piquancy to our trysts which we held regularly in mid-morning and mid-afternoon. Sometimes we dropped in at an adjoining cottage — the temporary home and atelier of Walter Trier. As I mentioned in the Ottershaw chapter, he illustrated my favourite children's books by Erich Kästner and later designed the charming and amusing covers of all issues of *Lilliput*.

One of Murie's greeting card designs.

Murie took time out for a trip to Kingston where, with the help of the Corrys, she found us a small apartment at 135 Union Street, practically on the campus. In mid-September 1949, we set out for Kingston in my parents' car, for what we thought would be an eight-month stint, but in fact lasted two lifetimes.

XIII

Queen's: A Nibble

To portray my Queen's beginnings as exhilarating is a miserably inadequate understatement. I was drifting into a career and testing professorial waters, Murie and I began conjugal life, joining a university community, and we moved from a throbbing city to a mid-sized town in languid Eastern Ontario. I was immensely excited about being married and being a prof — and full of anticipation — but viewed the relocation to Kingston and Queen's with something like amusement.

This calls for a confession: I had unwittingly succumbed to a case of Trono-smugness and Varsity-vanity. There was nothing boastful about it, just a comfortable, vaguely formulated sense that Toronto and its university were the best in the land and hence more important than what I would be joining in Kingston. The comparison was not fully articulated, but I viewed my new destination as a sort of farm club to prepare one for the Big Leagues. A funny image to invoke, now that I think of it, for so non-jock a person as I. It was also a strange attitude since I had no idea whether I would be good enough for an academic career even in Podunk, and was still awestruck by the opportunity confronting me at Queen's.

There was also an ambiguity in our situation. We knew that we would be in Kingston only one academic year, but there was nothing temporary in the way Murie and I set out to establish our household. When I say "Murie and I," I fantasize; it was Murie who did it all. I concentrated entirely on my university job, as was then the custom in families — particularly European ones. In any event, I had no domestic skills, whereas Murie was superbly endowed with them and throughout her life ensured that we lived in an aesthetically pleasing ambience. I later realized that even so temporary an abode as a bed-sitter during a sabbatical would be subjected to beautification, endowing it with a touch of our personalities. I was delighted by this approach. So, while at one level we were aware of the provisional nature of our arrangements, we also began assembling the furniture we expected to accompany us "forever."

We did not have much money but all our acquisitions were well-designed and attractive, often because of our families' generosity and always because of Murie's good taste and manual skills.

We confronted a minor crisis at the start which ultimately led to a heart-warming experience. The apartment Murie found was ideally located, but it was partly furnished. The landlady, Miss Bailey, was willing to remove her appointments but not to lower the rent. Since Murie had the furniture from Toronto and found that Miss Bailey's pieces — mostly student cast-offs — jarred with ours, we decided to rent No. 2, 135 Union Street, even though we had to pay the semi-furnished rate. When we left eight months later, we were bowled over by Miss Bailey's *volte-face* on the rent front. When we said goodbye she pressed into Murie's hand an envelope containing the difference, for each month we were her tenants, between what we paid and what would have been the unfurnished rate. She knew that I was going off for doctoral studies and thought that the money would come in handy.

Another confession: I occasionally made a little fun of Miss Bailey. She was extremely forgetful, a condition with which I am — sixty years later — all too familiar, and find a whole lot less funny. On one occasion, when Murie and I came to her door about some trifle, she asked us in for a cup of tea. The phone rang; she answered it in an adjoining room and that was the last we saw of her that day. I was greatly amused, little suspecting that the day would arrive when this was the sort of thing I might do myself.

Her name also caused Rod Grey and me some amusement. He was, as planned, now at Queen's, and we saw a lot of one another. She reminded us of a quaint Maritime folk song, "The Unfortunate Miss Bailey."

> A captain bold from Halifax
> Once left his captain quarters,
> Seduced a maid who hanged herself
> One morning in her garters.
> His wicked conscience smitted him.
> He lost his stomach daily,
> He took to drinking turpentine
> And thought up on Miss Bailey.
> Oh! Miss Bailey, unfortunate Miss Bailey!

When we referred to *our* Miss Bailey, we invariably used the melancholy adjective.

The unorthodox arrangement affecting our furniture early attested to the collegial spirit animating the department. We did have one sofa but needed to order a set of twin beds. These took a while to arrive and in the meantime the great J.A. Corry came to the rescue.

"You'll need the departmental couch!" he announced. It seems that such a serviceable fixture had been circulating among the economists and political scientists at Queen's for some years. At different times, Professor Frank Knox, one of the outstanding teachers of his era, the W.A. Mackintoshes, and most recently the Corrys had the use of it. They no longer needed it and we became its custodians until it was passed on to the next colleague. The Corrys lived about half a dozen blocks from us and since the couch would not fit into the trunk of their car and we did not own one, Professor Corry (he was not Alec to me until later) proposed that we carry it over. A witness, luckily finding herself at the right place and at the right time, could have observed the distinguished Queen's senior political scientist, later to become the principal, and a gangly, awestruck, unknown young recruit proceed along Kensington Avenue and Union Street, and up a narrow staircase, lugging a couch which had offered repose to some of Canada's finest political and economic minds.

James Alexander Corry in his couch-carrying days.

A surprise on the first Sunday morning in the apartment enhanced our feeling of being welcome in Kingston. A noise could be heard outside the door and someone knocked, but by the time we opened, the visitor had vanished. On the threshold was a stash of breakfast goodies: fruit, cereal, muffins, and a jar of homemade jam. No note, no other sign of the benefactor's identity. It emerged subsequently that the good fairy was Blossom McDougall, spouse of Lorne — a professor of commerce and hence a departmental colleague — and aunt of my Pickering and Varsity friend, Mike Mackenzie. He had alerted her to my coming to Queen's, and she ferreted out my arrival dates and whereabouts. But she did not know that I was very newly married, and when she arrived bearing the goodies, was startled to hear a female voice within. In 1949, well brought-up bachelors did not entertain ladies in their apartments early in the morning. So she tactfully withdrew and later telephoned to provide an explanation. We soon discovered that she was a forthright, generous and colourful local personality, who became a fast friend.

As you can see, the earliest of our Kingston impressions were of a remarkably hospitable and friendly ambience. A soft landing was additionally ensured by our having been accompanied by a knowledgeable local guide. As I mentioned, Rod Grey — a Queen's grad — was also engaged to come to Kingston. He had previously established a close friendship with Helen Gatch, graduate student in psychology and a don in one of the Vic residences. She and Murie knew one another well and I too floated within her orbit. She was invited to teach psychology at Queen's at the same time as Rod and I joined the Department of Economics and Political Science. Helen, Rod, Murie and I — four love birds — landed in Kingston at the same time, and chummed together.

Our Vic past also facilitated rapid acclimatization. Vic people shared a social bond and we were almost immediately invited to spend evenings with several who had arrived before us. These visits often included some of the hosts' non-Vic colleagues and friends and thus were more than occasions for pleasantly recalling old haunts. They opened links to colleagues in other departments and to Kingston's modest cultural events. It seemed that almost all Victoria men in Kingston were married to highly musical ladies who sang in local choirs.

The most memorable person we encountered through the Vic circle was Gleb Krotkov. He was a Russian, Prague-educated biologist, enjoying an impressive reputation in plant physiology. (I almost said that he had an "international reputation" but quickly dropped this description when I recalled that it is now used indiscriminately in announcements of university appointments, nominations for membership in the Royal Society of Canada, and in citations of honorary degree recipients. Anyone who has received a parking ticket in Niagara Falls, NY, is nowadays so described, rendering the epithet meaningless.) But Gleb really was hot. He pioneered the use of isotopes for the study of the metabolism of plants and set up Canada's first radioisotope lab for biological research. He was a giant in his field and in life, exuding a colossal life force. A person of great charm, sweeping interests and insatiable curiosity, he was also quite unusually direct in his relations with people.

The very first time we met, he subjected me to a most searching and sometimes embarrassing cross-examination. I cannot reproduce the exchange exactly but the following conveys the drift of his questions: How old are you? What does your father do? How much does he earn? What is your religion? Are you practicing? What do you think of Queen's? Do you like Corry? Are your colleagues any good? What were your marks at Toronto? Which professor did you like least? Why? Where did you meet your wife? Did you sleep with her before you married? What are you working on right now? Why did you become interested in it? Where does it lead? How useful is it? The interrogation was conducted in the most amiable way, driven by the questioner's lively and friendly interest in everything around him. We were fortunate in later getting to know Gleb, and his highly intelligent and kind mathematician wife Valia, and greatly enjoyed their friendship.

Gleb's unselfconscious and forthright ways occasionally made one feel ill-at-ease. At the party where we first met, for instance, he joyfully described a series of observations which had been puzzling him and which led him to formulate some intriguing hypotheses. He had noticed that in an eddy at the point near the juncture of Kingston Harbour and the Cataraqui River, at the east end of the LaSalle Causeway, there occasionally floated a sizeable collection of condoms. Their accumulation at that spot led him to various scenarios about the recreational behaviour and sanitary practices of Royal Military College cadets, then only male, of course, who passed this place on their way to and from downtown Kingston and who, he surmised, were responsible for the observed phenomenon. I was still, I admit, a bit overly fussy and even prudish at that time — a failing I have since shed, I hope. But I am sure that others in the room — men and women who were for the most part active parishioners of the

United Church of Canada — also thought that the venue chosen by Gleb for the airing of his speculation could have been better chosen.

Beginning a completely shared life with Murie was a major innovation and dazzling experience, revolutionizing life, but the old Bať'a-inspired, Zlín-bred work ethic nevertheless resurfaced and started to take over. Despite a somewhat casual attitude to my studies while an undergraduate, a new set of priorities was emerging and taking hold. These priorities never left me. Work, the job, my vocation, these took precedence over everything else. I did enthusiastically pursue a wide range of other interests, but a strong commitment to being a professor was at the top of my priorities. And sometimes, I subsequently realized, the mild case of workaholism did lead to the neglect of other important matters.

The incomplete M.A. thesis dangled over my head but, at the beginning, teaching responsibilities blew everything else off the table. This was not merely because I was brought to Queen's for eight months solely to teach, but also because I adored the whole process: scouring the relevant literature; discussing it with colleagues generally and with reference to a particular course; identifying the salient facts and issues; and roughing out the architecture of the outline and then elaborating it into weekly segments of topics, themes for lectures, apposite readings, and issues to be addressed in essays or class discussion. I found the tasks of inventing, elaborating and teaching a new course among the most satisfying aspects of my career, as exciting as tumbling on a new insight, glimpsing a new vision or coining a striking phrase. But this was only a part of it. Enamoured of words, enjoying people, and being something of a performer combined to make the classroom experience immense fun. On top of all that, I was also greatly stimulated by my interaction with students.

My immediate academic home, the Department of Economics and Political Science, was one of the university's largest and most highly regarded. It embraced the two eponymous disciplines, a substantial offering in commerce, and a large correspondence program of courses in accounting and banking provided on behalf of the professional organizations in these fields. One of its professors also edited the *Canadian Banker*. The politics wing included the Institute of Local Government which likewise offered correspondence courses for municipal employees. The beehive of industry responsible for this extensive program of teaching, research and publication was housed in a grey brick edifice at 75 Union Street, a few yards from the corner of Union and Division streets. It had at one time been The Home for Friendless Women, i.e., single mothers. The nearby corner boasted the Queen's Tea Room where, under the benevolent gaze of George — the Greek proprietor who had a keen interest in our professional activities — we gathered daily for coffee, tea and extensive inter-disciplinary schmoozing. There was nothing friendless about our group, which comprised highly diverse and highly congenial colleagues. The Queen's Tea Room has long since vanished but its namesake has, Minerva-like, recently risen from its ashes on the same site, within an ecologically outstanding new building, Beamish-Munroe Hall, the administrative base of the Faculty of Applied Science. The current Queen's Tea Room, operated by students, is in every minutest detail, like its landlord, a model of environmental responsibility and innovation — a far cry from the smoke-infested den we frequented in the bad old days.

My principal academic tasks, you will recall, were to assist Professor Corry with his fabled introductory politics course and to teach United States Government. It was the practice that large courses consisted of two lectures a week, and a third period when groups of about fifteen to twenty students met to discuss issues related to the lectures. Helping Corry involved sitting in on, and co-ordinating tutorials for, his lectures, organizing and facilitating the smaller weekly gatherings, and marking some of the essays as well as some questions on the examinations.

Corry had a thoroughly collegial approach. Despite the monumental gap in our experience and rank, he did not merely deliver, prima donna-like, the lectures, but also did some of the evaluation and correction of essays and the marking of some of the questions on the final examination. This may in part have been a form of quality control; after all, his teammate was a rank novice. I learnt a great deal from him in the process and admired the high standards he applied when gauging the knowledge and reasoning skill of the students. He delivered virtually all the lectures, but occasionally when he had to be out of town, I held forth. My lectures went over well, largely I suspect, because I spent a lot more time preparing them. Corry, after all, taught three full courses and in our class had to perform twice, sometimes three times a week; I always had weeks to work up my one upcoming talk and so managed to research, polish and fine-tune it almost to excess.

A great many of the students in the tutorials were former servicemen on Department of Veterans' Affairs grants. Most brought a mature, purposeful attitude to their studies and related some of the course material to their wartime experiences. Many also refused to accept the word of a professor or a book, and delighted in challenging authorities. Quite a few of the "civilian" students were the children of Ottawa mandarins and therefore keenly interested in the course and also not entirely innocent of the goings-on in Ottawa's corridors of power. The tutorials were a joy, in part because of the lively interplay during our discussions between the returned service personnel and the younger, usually a bit more idealistic, members not scarred directly by the war.

My solo course on American government was offered to the third year. A couple of the students were Americans and far better grounded in the subject than I. On one occasion, I nevertheless caused excitement and astonishment by talking about a US president of whom no one had heard before. It was Martin Van Buren. Coming to him in my Czech mode, and probably never having *heard* his name spoken, I mispronounced it so egregiously that he appeared incognito, so to speak, until the confusion was cleared up. As I now recollect it, he was "Van Boooorennn" to me not "Van Byu-rn." Characteristically, everyone reacted to this boo-boo with amusement and kindness.

I had plenty of time to prepare my classes and, as we saw, devoted a good deal of my honeymoon to things American. In shaping the course and preparing the outline, I received help from Pauline Jewett who had taught it previously and, though no longer in Kingston, was most generous to her successor. We remained friends throughout her interesting life in universities, Parliament and good causes. I had not an inkling of how enormously kind she was until half a century later when I read a review of her biography by Judith McKenzie. She apparently felt betrayed by Corry, a long-time mentor and friend, when she was not appointed to the position I occupied at Queen's that year. I surmise that Corry thought that it was in her best interest to complete her Ph.D. without undue delay. Whatever her disappointment may have been, she lent me her notes for the course, gave me her outline and seemed happy to discuss it at length. She clearly harboured no rancour towards me, and I never sensed anything but warm affection between her and her former prof and boss. I did not adopt all of Pauline's suggestions, but followed a major one: I devoted the whole first term, before dealing with American *government* to the study of American *history*, about which most of the students knew little.

As a text on American politics, Corry and Jewett both recommended Pendleton Herring's *Politics of Democracy*. This book was something of a bible for those espousing an essentially pluralistic, rather than an ideological, view of governance in an open society. At the time there were two dominant schools of thought on the nature of parties. One favoured competition between ideologically based parties wedded to well-articulated political philosophies — liberal pluralism, Marxism, social democracy, left-wing and right-wing parties or what have you; let's call them ideological parties. The other preferred parties thin on specific, ideological lines, but devoted to mobilizing, under their banner, coalitions of diverse interests capable of co-existence under one partisan umbrella or, with luck, of winning elections. The essence of competition between them was not doctrinaire differences but whether they were in or out of office. They can be seen as essentially election-driven, pragmatic parties. When I left Toronto, influenced by my Continental European background, I strongly preferred the neat first type. The compromising, opportunistic style of the other model struck me as unprincipled and prone to encourage short-term solutions and even unethical political practices like patronage and corruption.

Pendleton Herring compelled me to confront an entirely different approach, one which, while not ignoring the messy aspects of pragmatic, decentralized parties, extolled their propensity to encourage moderation and compromise. It took me a while — several years in fact — but eventually I saw the advantages of the politics of compromise rather than of ideological strife. I now realize, although I was oblivious to it at the time, that a conciliatory style of politics was congenial to me because of my deeply ingrained aversion to strife. It was not so much that I found compromise congenial — on the contrary, I liked a highly principled pursuit of the public interest — but that I abhorred hostility and conflict. Some thirty years after my arrival at Queen's I was invited, along with some other political scientists throughout the world, to contribute an article to a special issue of *Government and Opposition*, focusing on our view of political science. I entitled it "The Fear of Conflict and Other Failings."

Exposure to Pendleton Herring, and to the supporting views of J.A. Corry, eventually strongly affected my political orientations, the manner in which I approached the political process, and the discipline of studying it. A related influence was Corry's commitment to liberal democratic ideals of government, which underlay his course and its textbook. These too "took" and became an integral component of my outlook. My first year of teaching at Queen's shaped the way in which my political values solidified. Lest what I have just said misleads you, please note that although Corry's approach to politics left a mark, we differed on some important issues: he was a Liberal and I, although free of formal party links, sympathized with the CCF. I am pretty sure that supporting it never crossed his mind.

The timing of my advent at Queen's was perfect. I just made it in the last moments of R.C. Wallace's tenure as principal (I am now on my tenth!) This gave me the opportunity to gain a glimpse of his style and to catch his pronounced Scottish burr, which some nasty-minded people said he put on with his Queen's principal's robes. More important, W.A. Mackintosh was still vice-principal and had not yet left the headship of the joint economics and politics department to succeed Wallace. This gave me the opportunity to get to know Mackintosh as a colleague and to watch him at close quarters.

He was the most prominent member of the department, with the younger Alec Corry coming up a close second. Mackintosh had spent virtually his whole adult life at Queen's, except for about seven wartime and postwar years in Ottawa as a senior public servant bearing major responsibility for economic policy. He was, with Harold Innis, one of Canada's foremost economists and with him, bore the major responsibility for developing the seminal staples approach to Canadian history. It placed as much emphasis, when accounting for a country's development, on the role of staples — the commodities which dominate the economy's exports — as on political factors. He was thus a scholar of the first rank as well as a devoted Queen's man. The latter meant that he placed heavy emphasis on good teaching and on providing students with a sound education. But he never abandoned a keen interest in public policy. These qualities resulted in his presiding over one of the best academic departments in Canada, over richly varied programs in long distance professional education, and over colleagues who were expected to pull their full weight in the classroom and in the students' lives. Mackintosh also continued the tradition, established by O.D. Skelton and Clifford Clark, of Queen's serving as an unofficial and informal "think tank" for Ottawa, before the term was invented.

Lest all this suggests that his shop was an austere, driven enterprise, rest assured that everyone was most relaxed, that we had

a great deal of fun, and that Mackintosh achieved results primarily
by setting a good example and by high qualities of leadership and
suasion. He was kind and humane and was seen by most of his
colleagues more as a friend than as a boss. The collegiality in the
department was palpable and, to my astonishment and gratification,
was immediately extended even to lowliest of the low on the totem
pole — me. I was made to feel very much at home and sensed that in
departmental meetings and seminars what I said was listened to and
assigned as much weight as the ideas of anyone else. The fact that I
had not even completed my M.A. at the time seemed to have made a
bigger impression on me than on my colleagues. While Mackintosh,
as head of the department, bore a good deal of responsibility for all
this, it was of course my immediate boss, Alec Corry, the Hardy
Professor of Political Science, who was my hands-on guide,
counsellor and interlocutor.

He, too, taught more by example than by exhortation. Arriving at
suitable criteria when assessing students provides a good example.
In his Politics 2, we made it a habit, i.e., he decided, that when either
of us assigned a "close" mark on the examination, one that might
affect the candidate's passing or rank, the other also read the answer.
At first, I was terrified when he reviewed my mark, not knowing
whether my standards were anywhere near his. It was a relief to see
that our criteria were quite similar.

The scholarly acid test came when I was asked to present a paper
to the department, as distinct from the Politics Club. The latter,
attended by the honours students, all politics faculty, and sometimes
visitors from other universities or from Ottawa, met from time to
time in professors' homes and was an integral part of the academic
program in politics. Departmental seminars, on the other hand,
included only profs and other professionals in any way connected
with the activities carried out at 75 Union Street. Those attending
were, therefore, not only political scientists and economists, but also
all the commerce instructors, local government experts, and
colleagues involved in the accounting and banking courses. No one,
ever, missed any of those meetings.

I offered a paper on T.G. Masaryk. Addressing this group was an
even bigger challenge than talking to the History Club at U of T. The
basic research was done, but how to cast my thoughts for so diverse
an audience? I spent an inordinate amount of time getting ready but
felt that it was worth it. The paper was well-received and I was
particularly pleased that Corry and Mackintosh liked it. I would not

be surprised if my eventual permanent job offer from Queen's was in part inspired by the favourable reception to my paper.

The larger Masaryk project had stalled, however, because I was so fully engaged in my teaching and in savouring the delights of Kingston. As the U of T deadline approached within which I would have to submit the thesis if I was to graduate in the current academic year, Professor Corry stepped in. He pointed out that I had already invested a great deal of time and effort in the thesis, was obviously on top of the subject, and that I MUST finish it NOW. That is NOW! To have it hanging over my head would only complicate future life and could interfere with my ability to tackle other looming challenges. I took the "advice" to heart and launched a Blitz putting the Nazi hordes in the Second World War to shame. For a couple of weeks, I got up at five and worked till the following dawn. Sometimes I stayed at the office overnight and caught forty winks on the couch of the ladies' washroom without my invasion being detected. I abandoned my former predilection for imitating the tortuous and hard-to-digest Innisian style which I had so adoringly espoused earlier. Murie ensured that a lifeline of basic victuals was maintained and, equally important, excised all remaining vestiges of jarring jargon. By the time Karl Helleiner received the penultimate draft, a pretty decent version emerged, to which he administered the final touches. Both Brough Macpherson and Alexander Brady were on my examining board; I knew them both to be fine scholars and kind men. At the defense, Karl Helleiner fed me some searching questions requiring erudition on my part, most of which had come up in our previous meetings, so he knew that the topic was one I had thought about earlier. I made it just before the deadline for graduation in 1949–50.

As my first year on the giving- rather than the receiving-end of university life unfolded, I knew that it was unlikely that I would find a career even remotely as congenial as serving on a university faculty. There were, however, very few openings at the time since the explosion in enrolment was still barely visible on the horizon and the era of launching new post-secondary institutions was yet to dawn. Although Ph.D.s were not quite as essential for a professor as they are now, I realized that my chances would be enhanced considerably if I became *Dr.* Meisel, a possibility that only a few years previously would have seemed madly utopian. I clearly had to engage in doctoral studies. But where? Rod Grey, Helen Gatch (they were in a similar boat) and Murie and I spent a lot of time musing over the possibilities and consulted various friends, including our Queen's colleagues. Although many of the great US schools beckoned, there was still a general tendency among many anglophone Canadian academics to do graduate work in the United Kingdom.

For Professor Brady's U of T course on political ideas, I had read and greatly appreciated two books by Harold Laski: one on British political theory, and another on communism. Then, when at Queen's I delved into US government, I read his study of the American Presidency. He was one of the stars at The London School of Political Science and Economics — the world renowned LSE — and was also an intellectual leader of the Fabian Society and the Labour Party. And although Oxbridge was obviously highly attractive, in the social sciences and at the graduate level, LSE was widely regarded as one of the world's very best. It offered programs in some of the newer disciplines, like sociology, for example, which were still viewed with suspicion by the older British universities. The idea of London appealed to Murie as well, and so I applied there. The fees were laughably low, compared to their current levels, and also to what they would have been in America. Only Toronto and McGill were viable Canadian alternatives but at that time they were simply not in the same league as the best British and US graduate schools. So, the reputation and character of LSE, London's beckoning cultural life, and the presence of Harold Laski combined to make us opt for LSE.

We were not, of course, spared the question confronting most graduate students: how to cover upcoming travel, tuition and living expenses? Bursaries, scholarships or fellowships were essential. I received a doctoral grant from the Social Science Research Council and my parents were able and happy to assist, Murie was assured by knowledgeable acquaintances that she would easily obtain a teaching job in London, thus taking care of our living expenses. At that time, before the otherwise salutary re-definition of the respective roles of men and women in society, virtually all married male graduate students were kept alive by their spouses. And Alec Corry also played a key role in reinforcing our coffers.

His *Democratic Government and Politics* was doing phenomenally well. No, he did not suggest that part of his royalties subsidize my studies, but indirectly perhaps they did. The American branch of Oxford University Press wanted to bring out an expanded version. The Canadian edition focused on the English-speaking, Atlantic democracies. Oxford asked Corry to add sections comparing these countries with the Soviet Union. He invited me to work with him on the revisions, primarily to research and draft the new sections on the Soviet Union. I thus fell into a summer job. The pay I received nicely augmented our kitty. In addition to the monetary benefits, discussing the issues with Corry and submitting drafts for his consideration and revision proved instructive. He was not only a searching analyst, forever seeking precision both in observation and expression, but also a writer, gifted with great imagination and elegance. An apprentice working with a seasoned master, I learnt a great deal from him about the careful sifting of evidence and about aiming at a lively style.

Another unexpected break arose, as has so often happened in my adult life, out of a chance encounter with a friend or an acquaintance. The faculty at Queen's being so small, and physically concentrated in the intimate heart of town, we knew almost everyone who shared our interests. In addition to my professional pursuits, Murie and I were ardent attendees and supporters of cultural events. There was then only one full-time faculty person in each of art and music— André Bieler and Graham George. We became friends with them and their families, deepening the relationships after our eventual return to Queen's. Through Graham, we met a German-born singer, Celia Bizony who, though she was based in London, was at the time attached to McGill. In 1950, she taught in the Queen's Summer School. We attended a couple of her concerts and had some interesting and pleasant conversations about ancient music, a field in which she was a pioneer, having founded and directed a group at McGill, *Musica Antica e Nuova*—probably the first Canadian ensemble specializing in early music. She eventually returned to Britain and a successful career as a musicologist and teacher. When, during one of our conversations, it transpired that we were off to London in the autumn, she mentioned that she would not be using her London flat next academic year. Would we be interested in renting it? It was centrally located, reasonably priced, and Mme. Bizony obviously was a person of taste; we liked her and rented it sight unseen. Thus, even before catching sight of the white cliffs of Dover, we found suitable accommodation.

With my acceptance as a research student at LSE, financial support cobbled together, and a convenient pad in London secured, we set off for London. You will recall that Helen, Rod, Murie and I were to go to Britain together. But fickle Cupid intervened. Helen met Malcolm Brown, a professor of internal medicine. They fell in love, thereby scuppering Helen's romance with Rod and our travel plans. One of the last things Murie and I did before leaving for Europe was to attend Helen and Malcolm's wedding in Toronto and it did not take too long before we became Aunt Murie and Uncle John to their children.

Our departure for London was preceded by a forced separation. Murie was again asked to teach a course for art teachers in Toronto, while I needed to be in Kingston to assist with Corry's book. We had vacated Miss Bailey's quarters at the end of term, and I teamed up with an economist colleague, M.C. Urquhart, to rent a top-story apartment on King Street. Mac, an Albertan, had worked with Bill Mackintosh in Ottawa and made so strong an impression on him that he was brought back to Queen's. He never finished his Ph.D., and his publication list never reached massive dimensions, but he was considered one of the finest economists in the country, apparently at ease in every sub-field of the discipline. An economists' economist, his advice was sought by colleagues nationally and internationally. He eventually made a gigantic contribution to Canadian historical statistics.

Neither of us were experienced housekeepers or cooks, but we managed to run our flat reasonably well, without spending excessive time on it or on our meals. Apart from a couple of hideously over-cooked steaks, the most memorable souvenir of our weeks on King Street was, however, not recollections of culinary invention or of deep talk about economics and politics. These received our attention, to be sure, but not as much as poetry. Dylan Thomas, to be exact. Murie and I had a couple of LP's on which he filled the air, in his sonorous, vibrant voice, with the verses of *Under Milkwood* and *A Child's Christmas in Wales*. Mac and I read and quoted Dylan's heady words to one another—a habit I considered a major triumph. He was a down-to-earth, hard-nosed guy, not given to flights of fancy. That I was able to entice him into poetry delighted me and revealed that under his ultra-rational approach, typical of many economists, there dwelt a feeling heart.

By the time we left Kingston my view of it and Queen's had undergone a substantial transformation. My supercilious and superior attitude to a small town and a small-town university vanished. We had found Kingston extremely pleasant and comfortable. Both the town and the campus exuded historic maturity and architectural charm. The confluence of the St. Lawrence and Cataraqui Rivers and Lake Ontario makes a visually striking setting for its parks and limestone treasures, enhanced by nearby islands and lakes. Friends, and particularly the Corrys, made sure that, though bereft of a car, we had occasion to view the splendour, by taking us to their cottages or other scenic gems. The camaraderie and relaxed fellowship within the university, and the presence of numerous excellent scholars and of an attractive student body all combined to endow the place with a seductive charm. A sense started to take hold in both of us that a more permanent engagement at Queen's would be extremely attractive and fulfilling.

This was, of course, a completely wild and improbable notion. The Queen's department had, in Corry, Crawford and Hodgetts, a core of permanent faculty whose courses for politics major and minor students were complemented by apposite offerings of the history and philosophy departments and by some economists. It was Hodgetts who offered a flicker of hope. We had not met him, since he spent the year at Oxford, but were well aware of his brilliance, popularity and impressive reputation. Maybe he would not come back, and thus provide an opening into which, with immense luck, I could slip. This was a utopian and unrealistic notion; I knew nothing about Hodgetts's principal specialty, public administration, there was not the slightest hint that he would be going anywhere else and, above all, who was I? I had only just completed my M.A. and was still uncertain whether I had the qualities needed in a university career. I was a cipher. These sobering aspects notwithstanding, we dared to dream, and admittedly with some amusement, to speculate about how we might contrive to come back. Despite these reveries, however, there was not the slightest likelihood that we would return to Queen's, certainly, in contemporary parlance, "any time soon."

XIV

Fishing for the PhuD

My quest for a doctorate was not linear and straightforward. The idea, you'll recall, was that I would study at LSE with Harold Laski, to emerge in two years as the proud possessor of a Ph.D. (Econ) from the University of London. Rod, Helen, Murie and I were to take the same boat overseas, transatlantic air travel not yet being an option in those days. But, in the oft-quoted words of Robbie Burns, "the best laid schemes o' mice an' men gang aft agley" — you can see that the Scots aura of Queen's had already taken hold! — Laski contracted pneumonia campaigning in the British General Election of 1950 and died shortly afterwards; Helen married her Malcolm and abandoned graduate studies; and my supervisor and my stupidity derailed my thesis project.

Laski's demise was a great blow. He was a truly stellar attraction and I could not think of anyone else at LSE to study with and so I simply allowed the system to produce a mentor.

The Ph.D., as I noted earlier, was a research degree. There were no course requirements, no general examinations in major or minor fields and no second language exams. To qualify one had to meet the two-year residence requirement and attend such lectures or seminars, if any, as the candidates or their supervisors thought germane to their dissertation. An acceptable thesis was everything. It passed muster if the examiners concluded that it was worthy of publication by a reputable publisher. One had, in other words, to produce an original piece of work of high quality. My doctorate came about in an even more complex manner. Here is how it went. After arriving in London I went to see the redoubtable Ann Bohm, LSE's graduate secretary. She was a powerhouse who more or less single-handedly administered the School's impressive graduate program and at the same time was the mother confessor and counsellor to us all. We discussed my dilemma caused by Professor Laski's death and my academic interests. I told her which courses and seminars interested me and conveyed my idea of comparing the

British and Canadian party systems. Eventually I was assigned a supervisor, H.R.G. Greaves.

This was a bizarre decision. He was a mid-level member of the faculty who later obtained a professorship—a rare distinction in those days—and was very highly regarded. His most recent book was on the British Civil Service. He cast an exceptionally wide net. In addition to public administration, he was an expert and respected author, then or later, on dissecting political theory, constitutional issues in Britain and elsewhere, and international affairs—particularly the League of Nations; rooted in the political Left, he had co-authored a little book supporting the government side in the Spanish civil war. The one area, however, which seemed to be of little or no academic interest to him was political parties and political behaviour. Because of this, the choice turned out a disaster. There was no congruence between his ideas about how to conduct political research and my plans for the thesis.

I saw him from time to time, usually in late afternoon. During the London winter his office was usually plunged in a fog-filled, gloomy darkness. He was pleasant and kindly, but aloof. We got along well enough and I developed considerable respect for his erudition. Our encounters were, however, marked by very long periods in which we sat not only in near darkness but also in interminably total silence. This was disconcerting. I heard that other students, including my good Toronto friend Jim Eayrs, who was also in London researching his Columbia thesis on the Fabians, shared these agonizing moments of quietude. When we addressed my thesis proposal we hit a roadblock. To test my hypothesis, it was essential to utilize opinion data gathered by polling firms like Gallup. Greaves had no use for polling, viewed sampling and interviewing with suspicion, and hence concluded that the subject I chose was impractical and the thesis undoable.

In these circumstances, I should have sought a third opinion and requested a different supervisor. I was too unsure of myself, too obedient and prone to accept prevailing rules and practices to contest or obviate his decision. Instead, I decided to take my topic to another, almost certainly American, university. British academe, including LSE, were too old-fashioned, not yet attuned to modern methods of social research. This was a stupid, cowardly, ill-informed conclusion—behavioural research was already being developed and applied in Britain, including at LSE, despite pockets of resistance. My problem was Greaves and the lack of fit between his academic culture and mine. So, twit that I was, I decided to seek my Ph.D. elsewhere. To organize that would take at least another year.

The first task was to secure a job that would support us while we put together the required finances for the next year. University hiring, such as it was then — and there was mighty little of it — was conducted entirely by word of mouth. There was no advertising, no publications listing jobs, no search committees. When an opening occurred, the people on the spot consulted their friends, usually at Toronto, and maybe McGill or more likely in the American or British graduate school where they had studied. Virtually all political science and economics appointments were in fact filled on the recommendation of the three or four most senior professors in the pre-eminent graduate school in Canada, Toronto. Innis and Dawson controlled almost all of the traffic, but Corry was also a crossing guard, highly regarded and well respected. He was very much part of the now so discredited and maligned old boys' network which ruled the roost. Since I knew him best in the Canadian political science pantheon, I turned to him as a matter of course. I wrote him from London, described my predicament and asked him to let me know if he heard of any suitable openings.

What happened next was stunning. Corry offered me what we now call a tenure-track position with a two-year probationary period. You could have knocked me over with a gnat's eyebrow. A series of unrelated developments created a favourable configuration of stars opening a job for me. The Engineering Faculty decided that its students should receive a politics course in their third year and someone had to teach it; the international relations course for politics students was taught by the History Department and Corry thought that a political scientist would fit better; and Rod Grey's and my pleas the previous year for a sociology course at Queen's were heard — my duties included an introductory course in sociology.

While ninety per cent at least was luck, a little was also earned. Corry must have seen me as a promising scholar and effective teacher, and my enthusiasm for Queen's surely helped. In his memoir *My Life and Work: A Happy Partnership*, Corry noted almost forty years later with respect to Ted Hodgetts and me, "I could not have wanted more congenial colleagues. Their views on matters political turned out to be close enough to mine to make us very harmonious in outlook," and then, characteristically, added "perhaps moreso [sic] than was good for our students" (p. 102). Anyway, he and Mackintosh must have concluded that apart from the academic contribution they expected of me, I would not detract from the pleasant collegial atmosphere in the department, a matter that was at the time openly and seriously considered when new members were being recruited.

It was enormously liberating to have been assured, for all intents and purposes, of an academic future. Although I abandoned the LSE doctorate before returning to Canada, I continued attending lectures and seminars there in 1950–51, partly in preparation for my upcoming courses. Without a thesis to worry about, I allowed my mind, reading and conversations to roam widely and to mine the human and academic riches offered by the intellectually seething, cosmopolitan ambience of the School.

Back at Queen's in the fall, I threw myself enthusiastically into my new job. It would be false modesty to deny that I was fairly good at it and that I was beginning to build a bit of a reputation. The students liked my classes and I published several articles, mostly in the *Canadian Forum, Queen's Quarterly* and the *International Journal*.

For a while the field of choice was international relations, but I soon veered towards scrutinies of elections and political parties. In the middle 1950s, with the aid of students and other friends, and modest funding from Queen's, I mounted a survey-based study of a federal and provincial election in the Kingston constituencies which led to my first paper to the annual meeting of the Canadian Political Science Association. In part because of its novelty, and because it combined several methodological approaches, the paper attracted a good deal of attention. Entitled "Religious Affiliation and Electoral Behaviour: A Case Study," it was accepted by the *Canadian Journal of Economics and Political Science*, which was highly regarded throughout the world. I had, in a small way, arrived. It was only a relatively short step to hatch a larger project: the examination of a national general election. Since I was ripe for a sabbatical year, I decided to undertake a study of the upcoming General Election of 1957.

You may well ask, "What about your doctorate?" Good question! It was shunted aside because my full daily routine crowded out all else. There may also have been a touch of hubris involved. The scandalous idea began taking shape at the back of my mind that I would not bother doing a doctorate. Most British academics managed admirably without the *PhuD*, as some of us young Turks derisively called the Ph.D., and I thought that I would pursue my vocation without it. My teaching was well received, my research flourishing and I was becoming moderately well-known in my professional circles.

The strong collegiality in our department and the minimal attention it paid to rank and status led to my meeting and establishing contact with a great many important scholars in our field and with leading figures in Canada's political and administrative milieu. Corry and Mackintosh had many friends and acquaintances in this world who, from time to time, visited them en route to and from Ottawa, Toronto or Montreal. They would break a rail journey to call on their Kingston friends, who often entertained them and local colleagues in their homes. I was invariably included.

Through my membership in the Canadian Institute of International Affairs, I also established contacts with some of the country's movers and shakers. In the 1950s, the CIIA — which consisted of a busy national secretariat — published the *International Journal* and maintained very active branches in major centres, at which learned and distinguished Canadian and international personalities from academe, public life, and the media presented papers. In pre-TV days, this was an important means for alert citizens to deepen their knowledge of world events and to discuss them with experts. I became the secretary of the Kingston branch (serving under the then president, the great historian A.R.M. Lower, whom I ultimately succeeded) and so developed a close relationship with the national office and some members of the board. Many of its pillars belonged to Canada's enlightened elite, people like Walter Gordon and Rolly Mitchener. I likewise forged personal ties with some of the visiting speakers.

These factors and my published articles made a growing number of people aware of my existence and brought further invitations to attend conferences, to present papers, and to engage in other writing and lecturing commissions. Here is a typical example: at a British, American and Canadian international conference held at Chateau Montebello, in which the CIIA acted for Canada, Corry asked me to join him as rapporteur. We crafted the appropriate summary document for the participants. An American I met there invited me to prepare a paper for an organization in which he was involved, which became a short monograph, *The United States and Canada: How Are They Governed?* published in 1956 by the American Council of Education.

My becoming absorbed by Canada's academic and intellectual mainstream allowed no time for introspection or for languishing doctoral studies. This unfinished business occasionally gnawed at my conscience and caused anxiety, but was soon dismissed.

Enter Clifford Curtis. C.A. Curtis, known to students as "Whispering Cliff," was an economist and, among other things, Mayor of Kingston. He succeeded Mackintosh as head of our joint department. While Corry was, as the senior political scientist, my immediate boss, formally it was Curtis. He called me into his office one day and asked when I intended to get my Ph.D. I was not a smart aleck but on this occasion, alas, my response momentarily put me into this odious category. "Never," I replied and sketched the reasoning behind this decision. Clifford did not argue with me but simply said that so long as he was head of the department, he would not recommend me for promotion or even a raise in salary, until I acquired a Ph.D. I took a dim view of his stance, but later greatly appreciated his being so tough, particularly, when as head of Politics at Queen's in the 1960s, I became deeply involved in the doctoral program, I was thankful that I had the formal qualifications for which we were preparing our students.

One way out of this crisis was to integrate my projected study of the 1957 election into a doctoral program. Could I reactivate my LSE file? A letter to Ann Bohm elicited the welcome response that if I returned to London I would be granted credit for the year I spent at LSE in 1950–51 and that my only remaining requirements would be to put in another year's residence and produce an acceptable thesis.

After examining masses of relevant documents, biographies of candidates, runs of several newspapers from all of Canada's regions, and the details recorded in the Report of the Chief Electoral Officer, I spent most of the summer in Ottawa scouring party files and interviewing political actors from the Liberal and Conservative Parties. I decided to focus only on the two main parties, leaving the CCF – the social democratic precursor of the NDP – for inclusion later, when I revised the dissertation for publication. This strategy almost got me into deep, deep trouble, as we shall see.

The election under my microscope was interesting for at least two reasons: it interrupted the Liberal hegemony, which dominated Canadian party politics until then during almost all of the twentieth century, and it became the testing ground for the recently emerged, Saskatchewan-based Conservative leader, John G. Diefenbaker – an infinitely more colourful politician than his predecessors during the King-St. Laurent era. Contrary to most expectations, the Chief, as Dief was widely known, led his party to more seats than St.

Laurent's. Although he fell short of a majority, he formed the next government, the first Conservative administration since 1935. The following year, in the 1958 election, he won a landslide.

My Vic friend, Keith Davey, the Liberal national organizer, was most helpful in talking to me for hours about the election, introducing me to Liberal colleagues in the capital and elsewhere, and producing virtually every party document I requested.

I was apprehensive about my reception by the Progressive Conservative leaders and the party's headquarters, where I had fewer friends and acquaintances. I need not have worried. The national organizer, Allister Grosart, was a skillful pol and, like Keith, he had a wide, curiosity-driven interest in electoral politics; he believed that everyone, including his party, would benefit from the public's greater knowledge of what goes on in politics. He was most helpful, like Keith, in opening doors and in allowing me to spend days and nights at party headquarters, making notes and copying prodigious amounts of material.

Davey, Grosart and I respectively reached an understanding that whenever I came across information in their files which could, if published, embarrass them, I would consult them and be guided by their wishes. I of course retained full freedom to write what I wanted, but thought it fair to protect the confidential information embedded in their offices. This arrangement worked smoothly and substantially enhanced the access and insight I gained to party affairs. I learnt to convey sensitive intelligence in an oblique and guarded manner, shedding light on what transpired without causing any harm. I also found that, having been alerted to some aspect of the campaign by confidential party papers, I would later stumble upon allusions to them in the press, enabling me to deal with them and cite the media source.

While ferreting out documents and insight at PC headquarters, I occasionally needed guidance from Allister's secretary, an amazingly competent, enthusiastic Cape Bretoner. She was Flora MacDonald who, with Dalton Camp and others, later played a key role in ushering in the leadership of Robert Stanfield, and eventually served in Joe Clark's and Brian Mulroney's cabinets. She became a close friend and rejoins us in an upcoming chapter.

By the time we set off for London, I had amassed so prodigious a quantity of material that it could not be contained by our luggage. In the end I placed the complete loot on the floor of our living room and engaged a carpenter to build a crate for it, in which it was dispatched overseas as freight. Considering that it was built to hold my hoard of data, it found a most appropriate end. After we unpacked, some boys from a nearby school noticed it on the street and asked whether they could have it as a residence for their hamsters, creatures well known for their capacity to amass and store vast quantities of supplies in their cheeks. Like researchers!

Despite my extensive preparatory digging in Canada, some gaps still had to be filled, but I soon settled down to drafting the manuscript. Immediately after our arrival, Ann Bohm arranged a supervisor sympathetic to my project. He was Reginald Bassett, an authority on British parties and democracy and a very close friend of Ann's. He claimed that he was an innocent in matters Canadian but assured me that he would happily be consulted on any topic of my choice. He requested to see one or more of the early chapters, and otherwise offered to stand by in case of need.

My first scholarly act at LSE was to renew my library credentials and check to see whether a sign outside the entrance was still in place. It had made a huge impression on me in 1950, for being so utterly British. "Umbrellas and other impedimenta," it read with a straight face, "must not be carried beyond this point." It was still there. Ever since, I have gleefully used "impedimenta" whenever an occasion arose. My second scholarly gambit was to secure a locker in one of the reading rooms, into which I subsequently deposited a carbon copy of each chapter as soon as it was completed, to ensure that a possible fire in our flat would not devour the fruits of my labour. Mr. Bassett reacted speedily and positively to my first chapters and confined himself to minor editorial suggestions.

My primary source was not the LSE library, but the reading room in Canada House on Trafalgar Square, then still the principal site of our diplomatic presence in London. It housed a rich collection of Canadian newspapers. The British Library Newspapers in Colindale, North London, also filled some gaps. But scenically and emotionally, the Reading Room of the British Museum, to which I procured a library card, was the most memorable. While it offered some important historical sources, I confess that my presence there was prompted largely by sentimental and aesthetic reasons. Its uplifting, lofty, imposing architecture and pleasing colour scheme made it a glorious place in which to work, and the knowledge that so many famous writers had preceded me, and possibly toiled at the very desk I was using, filled me with awe. It was possible that Karl Marx removed an unnecessary comma in the draft of *Das Kapital* while revising his magnum opus sitting in the very chair from which I babbled on about Diefenbaker. Such pleasant but idle speculation did not detain me unduly, however. Since I brought the bulk of my sources with me in the future hamster haven, I spent most of my time at home, pecking away on my trusted Olivetti.

By working steadfastly and, during most weekdays valiantly resisting almost all the seductive blandishments of London, I finished the first draft early in 1959. A lot of quantitative analysis was required and presented in innumerable tables. The computer age had not yet dawned, so this part of the work was almost as time-consuming as gathering the political material and writing the story. I engaged Winston Chambers, a former student of mine at Queen's who was also doing graduate work at LSE, to help. He welcomed the financial benefit this brought him and, being a conscientious and meticulous worker, was a great help. He had received a first class secondary education and was highly numerate, which was essential in the circumstances, and highly literate, which was nice. In due course I submitted the text to Mr. Bassett who, after proposing a few minor textual changes, concluded that we were ready for the oral board.

It, like so many other features of the LSE arrangements, surprised me by its informality. There were only two examiners, Reginald Bassett and R.B. McCallum. The latter, mind you, was likely the most highly qualified person on earth for the job. He, with Alison Readman, conducted the first Nuffield study of a British general election, called after the Oxford College which sponsored it. The studies, for many years associated with David Butler, continue to this day. In his first Nuffield study of the 1945 British election, McCallum coined the word "psephology," after the pebble *psephos* used in ancient Greece for balloting. The term is now widely used in Britain to describe the scientific study of elections. Although recognized by scholars in North America, it is less common here. McCallum was an excellent choice. Quite apart from his mastery of the subject, he was a greatly respected historian.

The examination took place in Bassett's office which was much brighter than anything I had ever encountered in the Greaves days. There were three of us, with Mr. Bassett acting as both chairman and examiner. We had a lengthy conversation about various aspects of my study in which, not surprisingly, the focus was essentially on eliciting my views and data. Things went well generally, but there was one sticking point which almost led to my becoming a cropper.

My decision to exclude the CCF from the thesis and leave it for the book upset Professor McCallum. He was a British Liberal and, as such, the supporter of a party which, in British terms played the same role electorally between Labour and Conservatives, as the CCF did in Canada between the Tories and the Grits. The role and performance of "third" parties greatly interested him and he was troubled by my neglect of the CCF. I should have entitled my study, "The Liberal and Conservative Parties in the 1957 Canadian General Election." We consequently debated my thesis design. There was much to be said for his view, of course, but I did my best to defend having placed the discourse into a two, main party, frame. In due course I was asked to sit outside and await the outcome of their deliberations. I waited, and waited, and waited. Eventually Bassett emerged and congratulated me on having passed. I learnt subsequently that he had quite a struggle persuading his guest that the thesis was okay. Later in the afternoon, Mr. Bassett, Ann Bohm and I went to a Lyons Corner House for a celebratory tea during which we conducted a post-mortem and chuckled a bit about Mr. McCallum's somewhat old-maidish ways.

I started revising the thesis at once and submitted the masterpiece to the University of Toronto Press. Its reader for this tome, Norman Ward — a rising star in the University of Saskatchewan and a friend — made a number of useful suggestions. Murie's artistic flair was mobilized to prepare fantastic maps, one of which, covering the whole country, was so large that it had to be folded several times and placed into an envelope attached to the inside of the back cover. The book appeared in 1962, as No. 13 in the Canadian Government Series — at the time the flagship collection on Canadian politics. I was thirty-nine years old, so it is fair to say that, after having made a very early start as an academic, I did not really obtain my formal qualifying papers until I entered middle age.

I enjoyed my lectures and seminars, the companionship with fellow students and, in particular, a special student-generated seminar in my first year in which Ralph Milliband and Harry Eckstein played leading roles. Both subsequently became widely admired ornaments of our profession in Europe and America. The seminar emerged spontaneously to make up for the absence of Laski and met regularly to explore the sort of problems we surmised Laski would have entertained. No faculty were present although I think that Milliband may already have been some sort of junior don.

Extraordinarily busy though he had been with his Labour Party and Fabian Society duties, not to mention his teaching, public lectures and prolific writing, Harold Laski had made it a practice occasionally to receive in his home colleagues, politicians and a few graduate students for an evening of conversation. Mrs. Laski — a distinguished intellectual in her own right — continued this practice after he died, and I was lucky enough to receive an invitation. The overriding impression it left on me was, to use an often invoked image, that a production of Hamlet without the presence of the Prince of Denmark does not work very well. One was constantly aware of the fact that the raison d'être for the gathering was missing. I did, however, meet and enjoy a longish conversation with Margharita Laski, the novelist daughter.

I was also struck by the complete absence of the snobbery and sense of superiority which we colonials occasionally encountered when in the company of English academics. I use "English" advisedly, for Scots never seemed to elicit this reaction in me and my friends. Indeed, during my second sojourn in London, when I became friendly with Donald McRae, a very bright sociology faculty member, he told me that he too had been condescended to by some English colleagues. We concluded, as we quaffed our pints in the George, a pub near LSE, that both Canadians and Scots were seen by some local colleagues as lesser breeds. Although this was vexing, the vast majority of our peers was mercifully free of this vestige of English insularity.

A related experience reminded me that the university was not the only site preserving traces of colonial mindsets. Our friend Elizabeth Eayrs obtained a job at Harrods, I think in the jewellery or perfume department. When she was serving a veddy, veddy British client he inquired whether she was American. The reply that she was Canadian triggered this retort, couched in the plummiest of plummy accents: "Well, that isn't *quite* as bad, is it?"

I met Donald McRae through Bob (R.T.) McKenzie, a Canadian mutual friend and lecturer at the school. The author of *British Political Parties,* he was one of the foremost specialists in the field. The BBC highlighted him as its principal commentator on telecasts of British elections, and he was thus a household name in the country. I attended his seminar and presented a paper to it.

Occasionally I sat in, with his permission, on Karl Popper's seminar on Logic and the Scientific Method. My motives were the intrinsic interest of the subject and Popper's fame as one of the century's leading philosophers of science, among other things. On one occasion the exchange between Popper and one of the students had a dramatic and shocking denouement. She was Russian—a great rarity in the West in the heat of the Cold War, if I may put it so. The issue was whether it was possible to behave rationally. Popper was skeptical; she, no doubt brimming with Marxist materialism, insisted that indeed it was. She chain-smoked throughout the long exchange, and in a manner then not uncommon among people trying to save money, cut her homemade cigarettes in half. This meant, of course, that for every cigarette, she was left with two butts instead of one. When Popper not too gently pointed to the economic consequences of this practice, she broke down in spasms of inconsolable tears.

Among the numerous other LSE academic luminaries who left a lasting impression on me was the wise sociologist Morris Ginsberg, the elegant economist Lionel Robbins, and the very cool W.A. Robson, one of the giants in the study of British public administration. But only Ann Bohm became a friend. For years, while stopping over in London, we had dinner together and took in a play and she never failed to visit us on her fairly regular visits to Canada, gathering support for the School. She continued these trips for years long after she formally retired.

While my quest for academic respectability was the raison d'être for the two London years, the dissertation and its emergence as a book were not the most memorable part of our stay. Although I liked LSE, it never provoked in me the strong emotional resonance created by Pickering College, U of T and particularly Vic, and eventually Queen's. LSE added a great deal to my evolution as an academic to be sure, but it was soaking up the magic of London that provided a critical component to our lives, particularly with respect to friendships, literature, and the arts. They etched into our beings an enduring intellectual and aesthetic legacy.

XV

London Kaleidoscope x 2:
1950–1951, 1958–1959

Spilling the beans (some of them, anyway) about how I trekked from a central European lad towards a Canadian prof led me to separate the academic dimensions of obtaining my Ph.D. from the social. Having dispatched the scholarly side, I now revisit a few memorable cultural and convivial features of the two London years. It is for the most part unnecessary to tell during which of them a specific event occurred, but when required I refer to *London I* (1950–51) and *London II* (1958–59). What could be clearer?

You may recall that we spent our first London year in Mrs. Bizony's apartment in Swiss Cottage. Eight years later, Glenloch Road in the nearby Belsize Park area was home. Both are at the edge of Hampstead, one of the city's most attractive areas with its Heath and other parklands, charming streets and pubs, innumerable plaques identifying former residences of famous British writers, musicians and artists, and above all, a population which seemed at the time mad keen on culture—like so much of middle class and lower middle class London. Musicians, painters, actors, mimes, sculptors, origamists, potters, puppeteers and their ilk were everywhere, some quite successful, others less so or still students, judging from the tentative squeaks and scrapings audible outside their windows.

Among Hampstead's treasures was The Everyman, a repertory cinema on whose screen, and in whose queues, we experienced innumerable consciousness-expanding moments (Bergman, Truffault, Godard, and earnest, as well as frivolous, exchanges with local cinephiles).

The Swiss Cottage neighbourhood was full of enchanting discoveries. The nearest shopping area introduced us to the local greengrocer, Boots chemists, the Sainsbury groceteria, and the inevitable tobacconists to whose Woodbine (i.e., cheap) cigarettes we were still addicted, although we had already gone through numerous phases of trying to shake the habit. A great many necessities were still rationed (*London I*) and one's general comfort level depended in part on the goodwill of local merchants. Many of these seemed to find our Canadian cousinhood/foreignness quite appealing. They joked a lot and did the best they could for us.

The good-humoured disposition of the merchants was manifested in a little comedy, regularly played out by the greengrocer and Murie when she inquired into the origins of certain items on the shelves. In our mighty effort to defeat apartheid in South Africa, we boycotted the country's produce. This called for inquiries into the provenance of the items she fancied. Her supplier, brimming with cockney savvy and humour, quickly tumbled onto what she was up to, and never admitted to any of his goods hailing from a region remotely tainted by racial oppression. Whenever an item she desired came from South Africa, her probe was met with a quick, "Empire produce, ma'am."

The world of London's green grocers also produced an incident of a different sort. After we acquired the adored Morris Minor during *London II*, we usually drove to plays and concerts. Parking then was nothing as gruesome as later, but it nevertheless presented challenges. On one occasion when going to a ballet at the Covent Garden opera house, we parked early on a rather somnambulant-appearing street not far away, almost entirely occupied by shuttered wholesale fruit and vegetable stalls typical of the district at that time. As usual, our arrival long before the opening of the show enabled us to find a parking spot easily and to nip into the Nag's Head, a rather ordinary pub at the corner of Floral and James streets, a stone's throw away from the theatre. Back at the car after the performance, the street was bustling with huge vehicles supplying its innumerable stalls. The Morris was hemmed in by huge lorries in front and behind; to inch back and forth into the traffic lane appeared impossible. I tried, but made only infinitesimal progress. My fruitless manoeuvres were watched with amusement by a handful of burly cockneys resting from their unloading toil. I was reminded of what they looked like some years later when I saw Stanley Holloway as Eliza's Doolittle father in *My Fair Lady*, singing, "Wiv a little bit of luck, wiv a little bit of luck." Noting our predicament, four of the observers stepped up and, without a word, picked up the car, its two seat-belted occupants securely buckled down inside, lifted it into the air, and moved it sideways into the street. The strain of their efforts made them look rather grim-faced but when the rescue was accomplished, they broke into broad grins, to the applause of their watching mates. When the startled surprise and shock wore off, we wondered whether our entrapment was accidental or part of a lark contrived by a few fun-loving porters wishing to relieve the tedium of their daily (nightly?) routine. Most of our weekends were devoted to exploring as many of the available entertainment goodies as we could cram in. We were usually joined during *London I* by our U of T friends, the Stykolts, who were on a sabbatical in Cambridge. Normally we started with a play Friday evening, followed by a matinee — perhaps a ballet — Saturday afternoon, and a play or possibly a concert on Saturday evening. Sundays usually included a visit to a nearby historic, horticultural or architectural site, a gallery, and perhaps a French or Swedish flick at the Everyman.

The opulence of our West End outings can best be conveyed by a drastically curtailed roll call of some of the giants who peopled them. For brevity's sake, and to avoid having to keep track of the chronological evolution of their fame, I omit their titles and numerous honours. These still linger in the mind: John Gielgud, Alec Guinness, Ralph Richardson, Robert Morley, Michael Redgrave, Peter Ustinov, Robert Helpmann, Lawrence Olivier, Edith Evans, Sybil Thorndike, Glynnis Johns, Margaret Rutherford, Anna Massey and Wendy Hillier. Myra Hess, Otto Klemperer, Mstislav Rostropovitch, Yehudi Menuhin, Thomas Beecham, Malcolm Sargent and William Primrose were among the musicians we enjoyed. Among the vast number of plays we saw, one in particular stood out despite its unostentatious venue. It was Pirandello's *Six Characters in Search of an Author*, directed by one of our most loved authors of detective fiction, Ngaio Marsh. Several reasons made this performance so special, apart from the high esteem enjoyed by the director. It introduced us to Pirandello, an intriguing playwright whose pervasive preoccupation with the elusive question of what is truth and reality fascinates me. Soon after we discovered him in London, we saw another of his works, a Paris production of *A chacun sa verité* (*To Each His Truth*) which, as the title indicates, pursues one of these themes. Pirandello is very much on my mind as I reconstruct the past in these pages. A distinct unease about the reliability of my perceptions and memory has never been far away, so much so that elsewhere in the book ("Reality Check: How True Is all This?") I explicitly address this pesky issue.

The London performance of *Six Characters* took place in 1951 when we were less experienced theatregoers than the veterans we grew into later. I also imagine that a great deal of innovation in presenting plays, characteristic of the modern era, had yet to occur. At any rate, the scene greeting us as we entered the theatre was surprising: the curtain was up but the set was still in process of being constructed. One has become accustomed to this sort of thing (*nothing* now surprises one in the theatre, except the absence of gimmicks) but at the time this welcome was quite startling.

During *London I*, as I mentioned, our most frequent companions to cultural events and to touristy sights were Heather and Stefan Stykolt. Their being in Cambridge meant that our encounters always had to be planned and programmed ahead of time. We also consorted with other friends. They included some locals, but the majority were Canadian, in most instances former Queen's people now working or studying in London, as well as some LSE colleagues living nearby. A third element in our circle were friends Murie made through her teaching or the courses she took in design, printing and pottery.

Among former students were Don and Helen Gordon. He was the rascal who once wrote a piece when he was a stringer for the *Toronto Telegram*, in which I was wrongly reported as having made some uncomplimentary references to the Queen. This bestowed on me, not one of Andy Warhol's fifteen minutes of fame, but one second of notoriety, because the sensation-seeking media found someone who allegedly referred to Her Majesty in less than adulatory terms. Surprisingly, this episode did not result in animosity between us; rather, it began a friendship involving not only Don but also our two families. While at Queen's he met a very bright medical student, Helen, whom he subsequently married. By *London II*, Don was the CBC's European correspondent, travelling widely but based in London. Helen, in the meantime, held the fort together in London, with the three boys. She was knocking out everyone because of her grace, good looks, and strength of character, and also because she worked as an anaesthetist. They lived in a ramshackle large house near us, and we visited often, even moving in for a Canadian Christmas house party. It included another former Queen's student, Charles Taylor, and Dee and Don Gollan. Don had produced some successful student variety shows at Queen's and was now toiling in Britain's nascent television industry. They were practically neighbours of ours and Murie designed and silkscreened curtains for their flat.

Charles Taylor was instrumental in exposing us to two quite contrasting theatrical experiences. The first was a Duke Ellington concert in a gigantic arena in Earl's Court. It was my first large-scale jazz spectacle, and Ellington's musical prowess and charm proved irresistible. This not withstanding, its effect on me was less telling than the other performance to which Charles took us. It was Bertolt Brecht's *Mother Courage and Her Children* which, at that point, was new to me. Brecht's raw, misanthropic realism got to me and aroused an enduring interest in his work, including the shows he crafted in collaboration with Kurt Weill.

Charles brought not only Ellington and Brecht into our orbit, but also the Harcourts. I met Peter, who was doing undergraduate work at Cambridge, at the Ellington concert, and we saw a lot of one another for several years. Before meeting him, I had thought of film as little more than entertainment. Just about that time, the Bergman movies were beginning to gain attention. *The Seventh Seal*, at the Everyman, of course, blew my mind away. Peter, who would go on to run the British Film Institute, was one of the earliest serious students of Bergman's films and, in addition to introducing me to the cinema as a full-fledged, legitimate art, guided me to a fuller enjoyment of the works of the brilliant Swedish director. I eventually had a hand in helping bring Peter to Queen's, where he founded and created its excellent film department. Some time after the Ellington concert we were invited to the Harcourts for dinner where we met Joan, Peter's then wife, later to become a highly regarded Canadian editor. She and I subsequently worked together in a variety of ways and places and she, Murie and I became the closest of friends.

The Gordons were friends of the Harrower-Leeches, to whom they introduced us, and who added much to our enjoyment of London. Leonard had served in the Foreign Office, and headed up the British Information Office in New York during part of the war. Sylvia came from a distinguished Yorkshire political family. We had dinner in their Mayfair apartment early in the game and occasionally later on. Their principal residence, as the tax people like to say, was a villa in Italy and their grand, antique-filled Mayfair flat had been reduced to being a pied-à-terre. They wondered whether we would like to rent it while in London. Murie, while impressed by the contrast between it and our modest bed-sitter, nevertheless decided that even if we had been able to afford it (which we could not, despite the ridiculously low rent they offered for so splendid a place), she had no intention of spending our year abroad in a state of jitters over the possibility of accidentally smashing a Ming vase.

Despite our refusal of what was a most generous offer, we became friends.

We clicked during our first dinner with them. They had no servants in England and Sylvia, a fabulous cook, constructed the meal around a yummy coq-au-vin. Now, while I like meat and fowl, what really disarms my palate is bread and gravy. Sorry about that. Good manners forced me to confine the bread to the side plate and not to exploit the gravy's full potential. This self-denial was torture. But after we were launched into our main course, Sylvia excused herself and reappeared with a tray bearing a plateful of steaming coq refills, a basket heaped with sliced baguettes *and* a huge gravy boat. She heralded her re-entry with a cheerful, "In this house we dunk!"

As our relationship matured, and we accumulated mounds of evidence that there was no side to them at all, Murie hatched a truly audacious idea. We invited them for dinner to our minuscule bed-sitting room. They likely had never before graced so constrained and cramped quarters. Murie, who was a meticulous and inspired hostess and no slouch in the kitchen herself, planned the repast. The centrepiece was a *boeuf-bourguignon* — a dish which she had over the years perfected to cordon bleu heights. The real challenge was the wine. We did not have the means to buy the sort of rare vintages our guests were used to or which matched the quality of Murie's masterpiece. What to do?

The infinite resources and charm of London saved the day. I visited our local hooch supplier from whom I regularly acquired an almost undrinkable cheap Cypriot, so-called sherry. I conveyed to him the full context and circumstances of our predicament and he thought of a possible solution. One of his customers on a trip to France came across an extraordinarily fine wine at a risibly low price. It was a 1939 *Chateau Calon Ségur* which, according to some connoisseurs, was just beginning to be past it. But they were wrong; he thought that it was remarkably good and bought the few remaining cases which he brought home and placed into the care, under the appropriate conditions, of our mutual vintner. Whenever he required a few bottles he picked them up. The temporary keeper of these treasures assumed that, for the sake of Commonwealth amity etc., and because the owner was an awfully decent chap, he might be willing to relinquish a couple of bottles for the price he paid. The merchant guessed correctly and we acquired two bottles of his precious hoard.

The evening started swimmingly. Leonard and Sylvia were charmed by the setting, warmed by a perfectly chilled *Tio Pepe*, and relaxed by the chatter. The aroma of the *boeuf* had already aroused expectations when it came time for me to pour the wine. I concealed its identity by wrapping the bottle in a linen serviette, poured a bit into my glass, and then filled the round. When Leonard took the first sip, indeed when he explored its nose, his expressive eyebrows shot up and he allowed himself what must have been a grievous lapse in British upper lip and upper class form by exclaiming "What is *this*?" I let him dangle for a while but then relented and told all.

Our London social life was also enriched by acquaintances and friends made by Murie through her involvement in teaching. Although her first London employment was with the Royal Mail, as an auxiliary postie during the Christmas rush, her principal jobs during both of our London stints were as an art teacher in local schools. At the same time, she availed herself of some of the ubiquitous opportunities London provided for courses in pottery, design and printmaking.

The most dramatic, but also most trivial, recollection of her experiences is the possibility that she crossed paths with Christine Keeler, the denizen of the demimonde whose role in the Profumo affair destroyed the career of the Secretary of War, John Profumo, a promising cabinet minister. When, in the early 1960s, we read about the crisis which followed the sordid revelations, Murie thought it likely that the femme fatale in the case was the same Christine Keeler she knew as the extremely attractive but unruly pupil she had to contend with while teaching in Richmond.

Two of Murie's friendships remain unforgettable. One, though vivid, is rather slight; the other added a new dimension to our lives.

Before we went to London the first time, Murie obtained letters of introduction from a couple of progressive art educators to like-minded British colleagues. Among them was a London art teacher, Mrs. Zabel, who helped Murie find her professional way in London. She invited us for dinner soon after our arrival. Mrs. Zabel lived with her ancient father or, more likely, he lived with her. At the time, Mr. Chambers seemed something of a Methuselah, but from my present octogenarian perch, I suspect that I was guilty of ageist myopia, he was likely only a mere youngster in his seventies. Whatever his age, he was indisputably a white-haired and white-bearded gentleman exuding dignity and a calm authority.

The pièce de résistance of the evening was not the meal, the details of which have long ago been forgotten, but what followed. We repaired to the living room where, following some pleasant chat, Mr. Chambers erected a screen and regaled us with an illustrated lecture inspired by his passion: the diverse small islands surrounding the main ones comprising Great Britain. In pursuit of his hobby he had during his life visited all 6,000 of them. The talk consisted of witty, richly illustrated series of sketches of about half a dozen of the isles, each representative of a particular kind and region. Intriguing historical morsels, personal anecdotes, scenic gems, stories of eccentric personalities, political and economic points, and literary scraps were neatly woven into an amusing travelogue presented in a diffident, charming manner.

Mr. Chambers came to represent, in our minds, a type of person we encountered more often in the United Kingdom than in Canada. Their defining character was that, in addition to their normal preoccupations arising from daily life, they intensively pursued some topic or interest about which they acquired almost professional erudition.

The phenomenon is not unique to the United Kingdom, of course. History buffs, philatelists, walking encyclopedias of baseball trivia, builders of model airplanes or boats, connoisseurs of particular writers, painters or composers, green-thumbed gardeners, amateur musicians and Sunday painters mercifully exist everywhere. What is unique in Britain is the tremendous variety of the fields involved, their sometimes exceedingly esoteric nature, and the extent of this kind of professional amateurism, to give it a name. I assume that the relative prosperity of the middle class in the country which first developed the industrial revolution has encouraged its development. I became aware of it after I left the relatively poorer Czechoslovakia to attend school in England. The contrast with Canada, on the other hand, may be related in part to the immense attachment of Canadians to outdoor activities and to their widespread cottage culture. Whatever the comparative context, the professional amateurism of many people we encountered, as epitomized by Mr. Chambers, stood out as an impressive feature of "our" London.

Another of Murie's friendships had a more profound and personal impact. At one of the courses she took at a nearby pottery she met, and struck up a friendship, with Lotte Dorner. She and her husband, Heino, came to Britain as central European refugees before the war and lived in the Hampstead Garden Suburb, a delightful area north of Hampstead. A prosperous middle class neighbourhood, it was home to many artists and musicians, some of who had also emigrated from central Europe to escape Nazi madness. Gerard Hoffnung, the famous tuba-playing musician-humorist and cartoonist lived near the Dorners and was an acquaintance, as were a great many other artsy-craftsy types. Near the geographic centre of the district stood an imposing building called "The Institute." It offered an astonishingly varied number of academic and applied courses. It was (and, the UK being the UK, likely still is) an educational institution catering primarily to adults, offering courses in all manner of domains, but with a heavy emphasis on arts and crafts.

Lotte told Murie of some offerings she intended to take at the Institute and they enrolled together in pottery, design and silkscreen printing courses. The habit evolved of their having lunch together at the Dorner's house, a stone's throw away from the Institute. In due course, the friendship also embraced Heino and me. We hobnobbed with one another, including the Dorner's gifted and very engaging daughter Jane (now an outstanding glass artist), and enjoyed numerous concerts, exhibitions and plays together. After we returned home from London, we remained in touch, making a point of visiting and staying with one another when transatlantic trips made it possible.

We were so close that when Heino died in the late '70s while I held a short visiting post in Glasgow, Lotte asked me to deliver the eulogy. I knew no one there other than the immediate family, but was delighted to meet Dame Janet Baker at the reception. She and the Dorners were friends. I had long enjoyed and admired her magnificent voice and musicianship and was not surprised to find her an unassuming, warm and congenial person.

Three other couples linger in the memory of our student friendships in London. All were Canadians. Is this revealing? Without consciously making choices on the basis of nationality or any criteria other than empathy, we consorted a lot more with compatriots than with locals. Bruce and Connie MacFarland lived quite close by, and we occasionally spent an evening together for a chat. A Montrealer, he studied sociology at LSE, and greatly impressed me then, and later, when he became a leading member of the sociology program at Carleton. He was an uncommonly wise, balanced and perceptive scholar, as well as a thoroughly decent and warm-hearted person. That he was of African descent was an exceedingly rare phenomenon in Canadian academe at the time. Connie, his wife, was a very appealing, intelligent person, with whom I shared a professional interest since she worked in a polling firm. I bumped into Bruce at innumerable professional meetings and conferences for many years, and on these occasions was always struck by his transparent decency.

The Bartletts — Dave and Betty — were old friends. Dave, on leave from a government post, was studying at LSE during *London I*. He and I had been classmates at U of T and later saw one another from time to time in Kingston where his dad was the head of the Queen's Physical Education program. Murie and I became very good friends with the senior Bartletts and, whenever Dave and Betty visited them, we got together. In England, Dave and Betty were considerably more enterprising than Murie and I in exploring the interesting historical and scenic corners of the land and thus spent many weekends away from London. But we had a lot in common and gathered fairly frequently to chat about Canadian issues, LSE and Queen's. Dave eventually became one of Canada's top cultural mandarins, as Secretary of the Canada Council and Secretary-General of the Canadian Commission for UNESCO. He was also deeply involved in local politics and conservation, and became the mayor of Manotick near Ottawa. He had a park named after him.

We did not share many of London's cultural gems with Jim and Elizabeth Eayrs but visited one another occasionally. They are both extraordinarily intelligent and articulate and possess a hilarious and slightly wicked sense of humour. Our encounters led not only to serious discourse but also, and invariably, to amusing probes into some of the seemingly eccentric British folkways, good-natured gossip or comments about our Canadian friends and colleagues studying in Britain, or about the instructors Jim and I encountered at the University of London. These sessions were more amusing because of the Eayrs's wit than of ours.

Jim and I shared, indeed perpetrated, one of those embarrassing moments that haunt us forever. The graduate student society at LSE occasionally organized a session at which some worthy visitor presented a learned paper. The meetings were informal and took place in a large graduate common room. One such séance caused considerable buzz because the speaker was Laski's recently appointed successor. After the great man's demise, speculation had been rampant about who would occupy his hard-to-fill shoes. The choice fell on Michael Oakeshott, an undisputed biggie in the field of political philosophy. He had for years been one of the leading lights at Cambridge but had just moved to Nuffield College in Oxford before accepting the LSE post, which was among the choicest of plums in political studies.

Oakeshott's coming to our common room was a major event leading, on the appointed hour, to its walls nearly bursting with overcrowding and anticipation. Jim and I found room on a three-seater couch where we were soon joined by a chap unknown to us, but who appeared to be a senior graduate student. This being England, we did nothing to acknowledge his presence and merrily continued our light-hearted banter consisting of an—in our minds—amusing game of guessing who, in the room, might be Oakeshott. In rejecting some and considering others as possibilities, we referred to what we knew about him—his awesome pre-eminence as one of the world's foremost conservative thinkers, his authorship of *A Guide to the Classics, or How to Pick the Derby Winner*, a guide to successful betting, and rumours about a slightly eccentric lifestyle: he lived on a houseboat. The session started late, and our game went on for quite a while, becoming increasingly boisterous and outrageous.

You guessed correctly! When the chairman ("man" had not yet become "person" in the 1950s) introduced our distinguished visitor and called upon him to share his thoughts, our couch companion took the floor. He had, all the while, been a stony-faced witness to our delayed undergraduate cheek.

Murie's and my social life, particularly during *London II*, also included family. Gert and Thesi were cousins who lived in London. They were the children of Tati's brother Polda, whom I mentioned in passing in a previous chapter and who makes an appearance again a little later in this one. We visited one another from time to time, although not frequently. While we got along well enough, our interests and respective networks of friends diverged quite a bit, particularly with those of Thesi and her husband Peter, in whose universe central Europe played a much larger role than in ours. Gert was an intellectual and, had the Nazis not interfered, might well have become an academic.

We shared a wonderful two weeks with Gert and Herta when the four of us drove to the Lake District for a walking holiday. A lovely bed and breakfast in Grasmere was our base, near St. Oswald's, the church where Wordsworth is buried. We drove and walked our hearts out, visiting the usual Wordsworth sights and the magnificent

countryside. Windermere, Ambleside, Rydal Water, Easdale Tarn
and Tintern Abbey stand out as quite unforgettable visual delights.

In the chapter on my struggle with osteomyelitis in Weybridge, I
mentioned Walter Marmorek's near life-saving kindness to me and
Mami. Over twenty years later, Walter had become a very successful
architect and from time to time invited Murie and me to a play or a
meal. It was he who gave us tickets to *Idomeneo* at Glyndebourne.
Although still displaying his Viennese accent and charm, Walter was
deeply immersed in, and knowledgeable about, Britain. Completely
outside the normal circle of our friends and acquaintances, he was a
fascinating and hugely instructive companion. Amazingly well read,
he retained his photographic memory well into his nineties. His
conversation invariably ended with a perfectly apposite, witty
quotation. He was married to a magnificent very, very British lady,
Rita. During my student days in London, it was they who, from time
to time, exposed us to a little bit of luxury which was normally
beyond our reach.

We rarely escaped the powerful pull of London, particularly
during our first year there when we did not have a car, but we
occasionally visited Cambridge, to see Heather and Stefan and their
friends, Harry and Liz Johnson, and also to visit Uncle Polda and
Aunt Trudka, Gert and Thesi's parents. After escaping the Nazis,
Polda re-established himself in Britain where all his legal work, and
his income so far as I knew, related to the Bat'as. Trudka, his
diminutive dynamo of a wife, came from Valašské Mezeříčí, a
Moravian town not far from Zlín. They eventually lived in London,
but previously spent several years in Trumpington near Cambridge.
Stefan was amazed and delighted upon first meeting my uncle
because, to my immense surprise, Polda was something of a figure of
mystery in the eyes of some Cantabrigians.

Like Trudka, Uncle Polda was tiny. He had a proportionately
very high forehead adorned by a small but noticeable bump—a
feature shared by many Meisel males—a genetic trait which
fortunately skipped Tati and me. He also sported a rather tame
goatee which enhanced his distinguished, scholarly appearance. He
did not have an office in Trumpington but, drawing heavily on its
holdings, worked in the Cambridge University library, apparently
always occupying the same table or carrel. He was a library fixture.
Stefan and his pals noticed him there, not only because of his gnome-
like appearance but also because they observed that when some of
the university's legal luminaries walked past him, they invariably

nodded respectfully and occasionally stopped for a short, hushed chat. Who could this learned-looking, dwarfish person be? By introducing Stefan to him I dispelled the mystery, in part at least. But why he should have been recognized and spoken to by some of the passing local celebrities remained a mystery.

I knew Harry Johnson slightly before coming to Britain in 1950. Considered one of Canada's most brilliant and promising economists, he almost rivalled Innis in fame. He was a wunderkind, although his ample size made it hard to see him as a "kind." He was Fellow of King's College during *London I*. It was he who introduced us to a time-honoured Cambridge pastime — punting up and down the river Cam in stately fashion, preferably on a glorious sunny day. Harry's introduction was one with a difference, however. When we came, along with Stefan, for an outing one Sunday, Harry was in full command and great form. Ever intent on excelling at everything he touched, and being an extremely competitive sort, he had no use for just gracefully propelling us towards Granchester in a leisurely manner, as was the custom, but was intent on propelling, if that's the word, our craft forward as fast as he only could. We thus hurtled up the river at high speed, while the other punters watched in wonder and shock as we whizzed by. At one spot, some boys clustered on the shore and looked longingly at a soccer ball which had strayed into the river. As we approached, Stefan, helpfully but naively, reached for it and then threw it energetically towards the bank. Challenging the pull of gravity, as he clung to the ball before releasing it, he disastrously followed it, fully clad, into the water. The scene played out to the accompaniment of the boys' raucous laughter and gleeful cry: "There goes another one!"

Harry invited us for sherry before lunch one day in his wonderfully appointed rooms in King's. Murie was not in these impressive surroundings long before being captivated by a smallish sculpture occupying a position of prominence on the mantelpiece. It was constructed in wood, abstract and very pleasing to the eye. She admired it for some time, all the while telling Harry which of its features particularly appealed to her aesthetic sense. She expressed great satisfaction over Harry extending his well-known wood-carving repertoire from whittling small shapes while conducting tutorials to the creation of larger sculptures. He seemed pleased with her encomium but told her that the piece she had so admired was no work of abstract art, but a three-dimensional graph he created to represent an economic relationship on which he was currently working.

His wooden shapes and figures were quite famous. When, some years earlier, he left a chair he held at Manchester University, a local bookshop organized an exhibition and sale of his work which was favourably reviewed in the *Guardian*.

He eventually moved to the University of Chicago but his brilliant career was cut short when he died of cancer in 1977 at 54. Some years earlier, we found ourselves on the same boat returning to Canada from Europe and spent much time together, not only during meals and in the bar, but also lounging or just strolling on the boat's deck. It was always easy to locate Harry because throughout the trip, when he was not holding a glass in his hand, he whittled and whittled, strewing around him chips and shavings of wood. When one came across a mere sliver somewhere, one could follow the trail and find Harry at the end of it carving, cutting, shaving, sanding or oiling some intriguing shape.

Harry's beastie.

As a memento of the trip, he gave me a little piglet he had created almost entirely while I was along. It is about ten centimetres long and instead of a stubby tail, as is the wont of the species, has a long one starting just above its butt and then creating a double helix — an intertwined true pigtail. In its nose there is a loose, movable ring. All of this splendour is carved from a single piece of pine. At dinner the day he finished it, he rubbed it thoroughly with salad oil, after which we offered to it a series of flowery, Russian-style toasts, not one of which I still remember. But the little critter occupies a place of honour in my collection of pottery, turned wood, carvings and other *objets d'art* and *objets de mémoire*, treasured for what they are and for what they evoke.

A major experience of the London years arose out of my close association with the CIIA. Edgar McInnis, the U of T historian who was its executive director, also provided a flimsy secretarial backup for the Canadian branch of Atlantic Treaty Association (ATA). It was — and still is — a "friends of NATO" outfit, providing information about the alliance, linking it to other citizen groups, and seeking to enhance its public support. Canada, being a member, was represented on its governing councils and was expected to be visible at its meetings and functions. Professor McInnis knew that I was going to spend 1958–59 in London and asked me to serve as the Canada man at the ATA while there. This involved little more than attending a few meetings, packing my dinner jacket (which I knew would be *de rigueur* at the occasional feast in a military mess). There was, however, one quite big and totally unforgettable event. The ATA's annual meeting, that year was held in Berlin, then a western enclave surrounded by a Communist sea. Remember J.F. Kennedy's later memorable affirmation, "Ich bin ein Berliner" ("I am a Berliner")?

I hesitated slightly before accepting McInnis's invitation because of an ideological concern. I had no illusions about Stalin's military and foreign policy tastes and knew quite a bit about the oppressive, malevolent and idiotic behaviour of the Communists in Czechoslovakia, but I was not an out-and-out Cold Warrior. I thought that the Western powers, and particularly the USA, were sometimes needlessly provocative, and half-hearted in pursuing détente. With respect to NATO, I strongly supported Lester Pearson's emphasis on the social and economic dimensions, as envisioned in Article II, which I thought NATO governments sadly neglected. But I did believe that NATO, or something like it, was necessary, and agreed to represent Canada at ATA while in Europe.

Becoming involved in its London activities introduced me to layers of British society of which I had heretofore seen very little, and also deepened my awareness of the intricacies of Cold War diplomatic and military issues. The Berlin meetings were particularly instructive in this context, because they were attended by high-ranking and knowledgeable diplomatic and military people who spoke frankly about how they perceived the international situation. I had dealt with NATO in one of my courses and had written some articles about the Alliance, but being on the spot, and talking about it with delegates and officials from diverse countries, directly involved in its policies and activities, richly complemented the "academic knowledge" on which I had heretofore relied for the needed background. My association with the ATA and particularly the Berlin conference paid two other, rich rewards. It introduced me to Berlin and to the Berliner Ensemble.

I had never *seen* Berlin before. In 1938, on our last pre-war visit to Czechoslovakia, we stopped at its railway station while in transit from Holland. But it was dark and, the Nazis being in power, we did not even poke our noses out of the railway carriage. I spent every second there in mortal fear. The ATA provided my first encounter with the city. The relatively sparkling West Berlin contrasted dramatically with grimy, grim and gloomy East Berlin—a difference the ATA made sure nobody missed. The charged political climate, engendered by the Cold War and West Berlin's exposed status between the West and the East, was of immense interest to me as a political scientist. I had, over the years, worked on communism and on the Soviet system, but had never had a face-to-face encounter with a communist state or community.

The truly fantastic part of the Berlin trip came about entirely by accident. As sometimes happens at conferences, a fairly intense friendship developed between three of the delegates, because they shared certain viewpoints and biases. In this instance, it was the Norwegian, Icelander and Canadian who bonded. The Nordic aspect may have had a little to do with it, and that we all came from small countries, at least insofar as population went, but the main reason for our empathy, and staying a little more aloof from others, was that we shared my apprehension about NATO, sketched above. We were doves, not hawks and, as is well known, birds of a feather...

Our Icelandic pal, whose name I have forgotten but whom I shall call Lars, was the editor of one of the country's leading newspapers. He also had a great interest in the theatre and translated some of Bertolt Brecht's plays into Icelandic. In the process he got to know both Brecht and his famous first lady and wife, Helene Weigel. She was, by then, a widow now but still one of the mainstays of the Berliner Ensemble, the world-famous Brecht home theatre and shrine in Berlin. She was in fact appearing in the title role of *Mother Courage and Her Children* at the time of our visit. The international renown of the theatre, its small size and Weigel's infrequent performances caused the show to sell out quickly. Lars nevertheless decided to get us in and wrote a letter to Helene Weigel soliciting her aid. This sounds easy here and now, but was anything but in Berlin. Communications between the two parts of the city were rigorously controlled and made as difficult as possible. Only two options were available: send a letter with a taxi driver (they could traverse both zones), or deliver personally, travelling on the U Bahn, the underground.

In his note, Lars told the diva that he was in West Berlin briefly and that he and two friends were desperately anxious to see her Mother Courage. Contrary to all odds, a reply—also conveyed by taxi—arrived, confirming that all performances were sold out—but telling us that if we came the following evening we would be seated. She added that in the basement there was a lounge where people gathered after the performance for a drink and a bit to eat. We were to go there. If she was not too exhausted, she would come down and say "hello."

When we appeared at the box office someone led us into the theatre and to our seats in the centre aisle: standing one behind the other, were three wooden kitchen chairs which offered an excellent view of the stage. If East Berlin had a fire marshal who worried about such things, he was nowhere to be seen.

We waited for Helene Weigel in the subterranean lounge after the performance, but in vain, which was hardly surprising. The role of Mother Courage is excruciatingly demanding. She may also have had more urgent things to attend to than seeing Lars and his friends. We eventually left the basement, reconciled to Weigel not turning up, and went back the same way we came, by the U Bahn.

Of the many theatrical experiences I have had while studying in London and during shorter expeditions to the West End at other times, attending plays in Stratford, UK and Stratford, Ontario, the Shaw Festival in Niagara-on-the-Lake, the Long Wharf Theatre in New Haven, and innumerable other theatres on several continents, and even while attending subsequent plays by the Berliner Ensemble, none even remotely equalled the impact of this truly dramatic outing. It provides an appropriate closing curtain to my kaleidoscopic glance at some of the non-academic features of our two years in London.

"And herewith ends the lesson," to recall the language of our chapel services at Ottershaw. Not really the lesson, but the chronological part of our tale.

From now on we see an adult, professionally emerging and gradually being established, JM doing his thing.

Henceforth, I throw caution to the wind, and we adopt perspectives of my work under what the social scientist in me is deplorably tempted to call its functional aspects. I thought that I had left jargon behind. But happily I resist the temptation and merely say that we shall forthwith tackle thematic topics — teaching, research, university and professional duties, and so on, some of which lead me to the policy arena.

Part III begins with teaching, in a real sense the alpha and omega of a healthy university career.

PART III: The Queen's Years

XVI

A Noble Profession: Teaching

T he cockle-warming spirit of collegiality — a hallmark of my first immersion in the Department of Economics and Political Science at Queen's — greeted us again on our return. My duties, like those of many others bitten by the university bug, sprawled over four overlapping but distinct areas: enlightening students; researching and writing; busying myself in university and professional affairs; and making occasional descents — or were they ascents? — into the larger world of Canadian public policy.

The emphasis placed on each varied over the years. Teaching by far out-weighed everything at first but, while never vanishing altogether, attenuated as a core preoccupation because other activities crowded in. Nevertheless, I never lost the conviction that the raison d'être of universities is to educate students and that their other functions, of critical importance though they are, must not be allowed to weaken pedagogy. Education in this context always meant more to me than teaching a subject and the skills of critical thinking: it involved encouraging the fullest possible development of the student's potential as an intelligent and decent human being, who appreciates the aesthetic potential of life.

The preferred teaching mode varied with the size of classes and the level of the students' knowledge, but two aspects were ever present: the desire to heighten the student's awareness of, and sensitivity to, unthought of and as yet undiscovered realities and insights; and the exhilaration of participating with others in one's expanding mental universe.

The vignettes which follow convey, in no particular order, a sense of what the teaching panorama was like.

The Quebec Seminar

The first coming to mind arose out of my work, in the 1960s, with The Royal Commission on Bilingualism and Biculturalism — the B & B Commission. It led to my immersing myself in the important and complex issues of French-English relations in Canada. I linked the research- and policy-focused preoccupations of the Commission to my own métier as professor, and decided that political science students in a national university like Queen's, the vast majority of whom were anglophone, should know something about the Quebec phenomenon and how it affected the rest of the country. I consequently continued researching issues related to Quebec and its relations to Canada, and began to *teach* students in this domain. With the help of Peter M. Leslie, then one of my doctoral students and subsequently a highly esteemed colleague and friend, I designed and offered a new seminar on "Society and Politics in French Canada."

Our new offering was a year-long course in which the students immersed themselves, during the first semester, in the relevant literature which was then pretty meagre. Half of the sessions in the second term consisted of weekly visits from Québécois academics, community leaders, activists in voluntary associations, politicians and others who presented seminars on their particular area of expertise. Contacts I made while with the Commission helped immensely in finding suitable speakers. I was also greatly helped by my Laval friend, Léon Dion, ably assisted by Vincent Lemieux. Because of their standing in Quebec and also the excellent reputation our students won among our visitors, which spread rapidly in the closed and small world of Quebec intellectuals, we attracted highly informative and experienced experts, some of whom were stellar Quebec personalities. I scrounged some money from the *Toronto Star* to cover the travel expenses of our visitors and was able to pay a mini, mini honorarium of $25. Even then this was closer to an insult than to a fair emolument. Our guests came because of the reputation of Queen's, friendship, and increasingly because the seminar made such a good impression on Quebecers.

Nevertheless, some knowledgeable and strategically placed speakers—mostly politicians, mandarins and technocrats—simply could not take the time to travel to Kingston from Quebec City. Remembering the old adage that "If the mountain will not come to Mohammed, Mohammed will go to the mountain," we resorted to a delightful stratagem. Like most Canadian universities, Queen's has a "reading week" in February (called "skiing week" by the students) in which there are no classes. By a stroke of luck this week always coincided with the Quebec Winter Carnival—a joyous and festive affair of street dances and parties engulfing a wide range of celebrants. This was a bonus educational feature acquainting our students with a non-political but significant side of La Belle Province. We took our class of about fifteen students to Quebec City, put up in *la petite maison blanche* — a *very* cheap lodging house, and arranged encounters with key players in Quebec's Quiet Revolution. Over the few years in which we offered the course, we had the good fortune of sharing open and frank seminars with three different Quebec prime ministers, several ministers, deputy ministers, heads of specialized agencies, journalists and other intellectuals, and various luminaries.

One such encounter was stunning. The Premier of Quebec was, during our first trip, Jean Lesage, formerly a leading federal Liberal minister who switched to provincial politics and became the Liberal premier. In this role, he more or less presided over the Quiet Revolution, the process through which Quebec transformed itself from a province stagnating under backward regimes into a highly efficient modern polity. A serious encounter with him would give my students (and me) a marvellous, rare chance to peer into the inner workings of the Quebec government. I knew Lesage's *chef du cabinet* fairly well and phoned him to see whether his boss might give us half an hour. Having had a lot of experience with politicians, however, I realized that a merely ceremonial encounter would prove sterile and so suggested to my pal that if the tone was to be of politesse alone, it would be a waste of Lesage's time and, though less so, ours as well. He got the point and said he would inquire. In a couple of days he called back to say that M. Lesage would be happy to meet us and to engage in serious conversation. And so it came to pass.

After we arrived at the majestic *Assemblée nationale* building, which then housed the premier's suite of offices, we were herded to the antechamber of the cabinet room from whence we were admitted to the inner sanctum itself. We uneasily plonked ourselves into the seats normally occupied by Lesage's ministers; soon after, the premier walked in and launched a florid praise of Kingston, Queen's and, somewhat oddly, the Royal Military College. I was dismayed: he either failed to take in my not so subtle hint about politesse or decided to ignore it. But after the lengthy and vacuous opening interlude, he suddenly stopped and said, "Okay, what would you like me to talk about?" A student suggested that M. Lesage share with us the considerations which had led to the formulation and adoption of the new, contentious agricultural policy. The topic triggered an amazingly frank, detailed and even indiscreet account of the complex forces affecting a critical component of Quebec's economy and society, and how Lesage's government dealt with them. He freely and frankly responded to our further queries and comments, seemingly impervious to the clicking of the clock and whatever other duties were waiting. The time allotted to our audience had long ago elapsed. After repeated, whispered prompts from an agitated clerk, Lesage saw us out and bid us adieu. The antechamber of his office was filled with scowling, clearly annoyed men — ministers — cooling their heels before the beginning of the delayed cabinet meeting.

Lesage's astonishingly revealing tour through an important *tranche de la vie Québécoise* — a slice of Quebec life — was by no means our only exposure to the critical and highest leadership of the Quiet Revolution. We received briefings from several ministers and senior officials, the so-called technocrats and mandarins who were replacing the Catholic clergy as the driving force of Quebec's governing class. A significant number of the architects of the new Quebec were leaders of the various *groupes intermédiaires* – voluntary or professional associations situated somewhere between government and the private sphere of the individual and groups. We heard from many of them.

Both as guests in Quebec and as hosts to her experts and activists, we were exposed to a remarkably varied cross-section of Quebec interests: labour and municipal associations, nationalistic and cultural voices, promoters of educational reforms, not to mention newly emerging economic and political interests.

The two Union Nationale Premiers who succeeded Lesage — Daniel Johnson and Jean-Jacques Bertrand — also met our class, but the magic had somehow diminished. Among the most exciting *vedettes* — stars — who addressed us was René Lévesque, then a Liberal minister but later the first head of the independentist Parti Québécois government. He addressed a joint session, contrived by Vincent Lemieux, of Laval and Queen's students. The lecture was held on the Laval campus, some distance from downtown Quebec City, where we'd just had a session with a government official. We were running a bit late, but I blithely assured everyone that there was no need to panic since René L. was notoriously late for everything and would on no account arrive at Laval on time. I was wrong. When we reached the assigned classroom some minutes after the appointed hour there was not only the assembled Laval gang but also a fuming (he was a constant smoker anyway) René Lévesque, awaiting our arrival.

I do not remember much about the lecture, except that although the subject was not particularly gripping, Lévesque's attractive personality, strikingly informal style and transparent frankness won us over and conveyed the feeling that we had been in the presence of a truly remarkable and exceptionally charming man.

Our course offered an unmatched opportunity to obtain otherwise inaccessible insight into the remarkable transformation of Quebec. Furthermore, encounters with many important agents of Quebec modernization enabled us to plumb the situation there, and to get a *feeling* for the cross-currents sweeping the province. Several factors combined to add various unanticipated layers to the seminar, making it unique and unforgettable: the coincidence of our visit and the *Carneval*, the small number of well-acquainted students, compressed for a few days with their dons in a Spartan B & B in Canada's most beautiful city; and the occasional joint sessions and partying with Laval students and professors. The mix, and the highly congenial relations among the participants, resulted in our enjoying a teaching experience rarely attained by a university course.

Because it was so special, it had ramifications far beyond the students and professors directly involved. Several participants went on to become university lecturers and some of them subsequently offered a similar or related course. George Anderson, one of our lot, became Deputy Minister of Intergovernmental Relations in Ottawa and later the chief honcho of the Forum of Federations, an important international think tank promoting the effectiveness of the governance of heterogeneous polities. Another of our class, John Rae, in addition to serving as a leading and most trusted member of Jean Chrétien's entourage, played a key role in the Liberal Party's efforts to retain Quebec's ties to the rest of the country. My interaction with both of them during their student days laid the foundations for close, enduring friendships. Peter Milliken, a local boy who later became the MP for Kingston and the Islands, and then the longest serving Speaker of the House of Commons, was likewise in the class. He, too, is now a friend. To our amusement, a Quebec visitor occasionally addressed me as "mon cher collègue," and so Peter, George and I to this day address one another jocularly by this somewhat stilted French appellation. Less dramatically, many of our students attained responsible positions in various Canadian public and private enterprises, where they managed to put to good use the lessons the Quebec seminar taught them.

As we saw, during the second term we invited Québécois experts to meet the class in Kingston. They usually caught a train back to Montreal in early evening, a process preceded by a small gathering at our house on Albert Street including, in addition to the speaker, a rotating smattering of course members. Sherry and niblets were the usual fare, the latter always beautifully arranged by Murie's artistry and the former unfailingly being very dry. One of our guests was Jacques-Yvan Morin, a prominent legal scholar and eventually a Parti Québécois minister. In looks, style and language, he was an exceptionally elegant man, his refined speech never betraying the slightest hint of *joual*, the dialect frequently associated with less educated Quebecers. Everything he said was always precise and its sound highly pleasing. When he finished his glass, I inquired whether he would care for a refill. His reply, after a quick glance at his watch, was the poetic "Une larme, s'il vous plait" — only a teardrop, please. Henceforth, this formulation in Murie's and my vocabulary outclassed the no doubt Queen's-inspired "only a wee dram," and became a permanent feature of our marital vocabulary.

The pre-train interludes following our seminars offered informal, unguarded and pleasant moments with a variety of interesting Quebecers active in politics, administration and the voluntary sector, ranging from the firebrand, radical separatist Pierre Bourgault, to "the Cardinal" Claude Ryan, so dubbed because of his august eminence among Quebec intellectuals, and his deep, ever thoughtful editorials in *Le Devoir*, of which he was editor before he became the leader of the provincial Liberal Party.

Marlene

Sometimes my teaching experience poignantly centred on an individual, not a whole class. Here is what happened in my introductory Sociology 1. It consisted, in the early 1950s, of about sixty to eighty students which allowed a fair amount of discussion. The wide-ranging subject, and varied academic background of the students taking it, ensured that the Socratic feature of my offering richly complemented the lectures and constituted an important element of the course. Early in the year I noticed that one girl, always sitting in the first or second row, placidly took in the proceedings but, while making copious notes, nary uttered a sound. I assumed that she was a bit of a sponge, did not have much to say, and would turn out to be a marginal, merely passing student. This dreary premise was excitingly shattered by her first essay. It displayed a secure knowledge of her subject and intelligent insight. When I discussed the paper with her, I sought an explanation for her class apathy. I had just begun teaching at the time and was still not sufficiently immersed in all the nooks and crannies of Canada to recognize a clue staring me in the face. The lethargic student's name was Marlene *Brant*. I failed to recognize Brant as an Aboriginal name, and so had no idea that Marlene's passive behaviour might have been caused by her cultural context.

In response to my inquiry whether she never had the urge to jump into the class discussions, she told me that she was a Mohawk who grew up on the Tyendinaga reservation near Desoronto, and that before arriving at Queen's she had never lived off the reservation. The new "outside" world was overwhelming and, while she had thoughts about what was going on in class, she did not feel sufficiently at ease or confident to voice it. Thereafter, needless to say, I made a point of bringing her into discussions and of facilitating her active participation. Much later she told me that this had been of the greatest importance to her growing self-confidence and later career. She obtained high marks, of course, and eventually a doctorate, and became a leading Canadian scholar in Aboriginal studies based at Trent University. In the 1990s, as President of the Royal Society of Canada, I established an advisory committee of some eminent folk to help us better connect with the larger community; Marlene agreed to serve and made some original suggestions emanating from her Aboriginal experiences.

Sociology 1

When I was brought back to Queen's in 1951 with sociology on my menu, I had no formal training in it, but had been impressed by several works of Max Weber, particularly his *The Protestant Ethic and the Spirit of Capitalism* and his observations on bureaucracy. I had also gained much insight from the work of Durkheim, notably his book on suicide which I found striking — an impression strengthened by its effect on Masaryk's booklet on the same theme. And at LSE, even before I knew that I would be teaching Sociology, I attended lectures by such greats in the field as Morris Ginsberg, and T.H. Marshall.

The points of departure were the library and colleagues in the field at U of T and McGill. In days ante-dating computer accessible databases, books and journals were the most opulent sources of intelligence. One started with the card catalogue but then, once in the stacks in pursuit of one's sources, an unsuspected, enticing title would leap to the eye. Most of the time I arrived at the check-out desk, my arms bearing the works found in the catalogue and a few accidental discoveries providing the spice. The process had a flavour and aroma not matched by the indisputably superb efficiency of current information systems.

Access to knowledgeable and seasoned colleagues was easy because of my being at Queen's. Our department, run by respected scholars, provided an effective base from which to merge with the larger discipline beyond. I was encouraged to become active in the Canadian Political Science Association (CPSA) which then consisted of economists, political scientists, students of commerce and finance, as well as social anthropologists and sociologists. At the annual meetings of the CPSA and on other occasions, the Queen's senior professors—usually J.A. Corry, in my case—made sure that the younger members of their department met colleagues in the then few other universities. And when committees performing various professional tasks were struck, or related tasks assigned, the senior professors were quick to put forward the names of their junior stable mates. I noticed that I was much better connected, and better known, than many former classmates with similar backgrounds, holding comparable junior positions, either in larger universities like Toronto and McGill, or lodged in one- or two-man departments in smaller centres. Being a Toronto grad also helped. I knew and became friendly with a number of senior Varsity profs from several fields, who in turn were aware of my existence.

I placed great emphasis on the lectures, essays and class discussion but also thought that a good, solid textbook was an essential component of a large introductory course. If one was found, many key elements of the offering could safely be left to the author(s) of the central, shared and compulsory reading. In the lectures and by means of essays and tutorial topics I could then deal with difficult points and what I considered the most interesting and important ideas and analytical tools. When settling on the textbook, I mined both the resources of the Douglas Library, particularly book reviews in journals, and the advice of battle-scarred colleagues. S.D. Clark, the head of Sociology at U of T suggested Kingsley Davis's *Human Society*. It appealed to us both for its avoidance of extravagant methodological gimmickry, a straightforward literary style free of jargon and its avoidance of ideological hang-ups. Davis was a demographer who, among other things, coined and made current the term "zero population growth," but his text was a well-rounded, thoughtful and humane lead-in to a field all too often encumbered by pretentious theoretical claptrap and impenetrable language. The students liked it and I stuck with it for a few years after which I turned to the somewhat more exacting *Sociology: A Systematic Introduction* by Harry M. Johnson. Its content was a little more advanced and it gave the course greater rigor.

When reflecting on my teaching I am struck, and a little shame-faced, by the realization that personal, as well as professional biases impinged on some of the classroom emphases, particularly in Sociology and in International Politics. I was a peacenik and anti-nuke-nik, and ambivalent about the virtues of social strife. Perhaps the personal and the disciplinary can never be kept quite apart. In Sociology 1, when dealing with marriage as a social institution, I emphatically conveyed that it was a good thing. I also selected as one assignment a book review from the sociological perspective, of a novel or a play. The idea was to teach students to distinguish between dealing with the human condition from the viewpoint of a social scientist and that of a creative literary or dramatic writer. My premise was that both are valid and rewarding but that it is necessary to differentiate between the respective relevance, strength and usefulness of each. A piece of social science had to withstand being falsified by a critic, whereas the validity of fiction accrued from quite different criteria. I also delighted in steering my students towards belles lettres, despite their more mundane registration in a social science course. One of the benefits of this assignment was that the marking of the essays was fun and fascinating, telling me a lot about each author's persona. They were people, not numbers, and in some instances the insights I gained in the process improved my capacity to write a good letter of reference, if and when the need arose.

Another intermingling of personal and professional considerations was manifested in my choice of Everett C. Hughes's *French Canada in Transition* as one of the compulsory readings. This was done in the early 1950s, long before I became involved with the B & B Commission and before I developed close links with colleagues at Laval. But I have, since arriving in Canada, been intensely interested in the ethnic and linguistic nature of the country and thought that it was important for my anglophone students to learn something about it. Hughes's work also commended itself for its imaginative design and methodology. An American sociologist who had close ties with McGill, he examined English-French relations in Drummondville — wittily transformed into Cantonville in the book — thereby writing one of the earliest and most illuminating studies of Canadian duality. Its subject matter, the openness of the approach, and its imaginative methodology suited me just fine, and I expected it to enlarge the students' awareness of a critical aspect of being Canadian.

One topic I chose for my course was likely a mistake, although by no means a total loss. I just handled it clumsily, failing to reduce it to the modest proportions it merited. I introduced my crowd to the celebrated Hawthorne experiments, particularly to the Bank Wiring Observation Room, conducted in the 1920s and '30s at the Western Electric Plant near Chicago, in which workers were studied while putting together telephone switching equipment. Researchers traced how changing physical conditions in the workplace, like better lighting, affected productivity. Every improvement led to increased output. So far, so good. Then working conditions were progressively *worsened*—lower and lower lights—with the astonishing result that performance still kept improving. The explanation was in the psychological realm. Work went better when workers saw their personal conditions and reactions mattered. The mere act of observing the workers implied, to them, that they were cared about and, thus, skewed the results. This exploration of unanticipated effects impressed by its imaginative, thorough methodology and by the manner in which it showed that strict analytical methods and procedures—the scientific method, in fact—can in significant ways augment and even alter insights suggested by mere common sense.

The students put up with my lengthy exposition of the Hawthorne studies, and those who kept up with the literature at least had the consolation of seeing that the Hawthorne phenomenon received massive learned attention for generations, arousing prolonged and vigorous methodological scrutiny and criticism, even the accusation by one team of Marxist scholars that the experiments were a capitalist plot. From my point of view, the focus on unanticipated consequences prepared me for a later series of insights prompted by functional analysis to which I return in a moment.

Teaching sociology was great fun, partly because of the eclectic nature of the subject, but also because the course was prescribed for programs other than the usual honours concentration in the politics, economics and history cluster. Among its clients, for instance, were students in what was then dubbed sensibly Physical and Health Education but which, in currently more pretentious times, inflated into Kinesiology. This, my dictionary says, is "the study of the mechanics of human body movements." Sociology was popular among those taking various concentrations and so-called "Pass Arts" students, those less specialized than the honours candidates and working on a somewhat lighter, three-year program. Furthermore, by venturing into the realm of Comte, Durkheim, Weber and S.D. Clark, in addition to my political science involvement, I entered the sociology fraternity and benefited from participating in many of its activities. This dovetailed nicely with what later became my central preoccupations with elections, electoral behaviour and political parties, the understanding of which is enriched by political sociology — a field I added to my academic armoury.

Sociology 1 taught me many things, including a precious lesson about the prevailing media culture and how to cope with it. Part of the course dealt with crowd behaviour (if that's the term). I happened to be waxing eloquent on this topic when Princess Elizabeth visited Canada, including Kingston, in 1951, shortly after I launched my course. I asked the class to observe, describe and analyze the way large audiences were responding to the royal presence.

One of the students, Donald Gordon, worked part-time as a stringer for the *Toronto Telegram* and sent in a piece on my assignment, in which he mentioned mass hysteria, one of the forms of crowd reactions I had described. This was somehow linked to the visit and all hell broke loose. Virtually all press references to the visit had been highly adulatory and an item seemingly critical attracted widespread attention, including mention in the *New York Times*.

I thought that my goose was cooked and that my link to Queen's would be terminated as soon as possible. Illustrious scholars like Eugene Forsey and Frank Underhill had been threatened at McGill and U of T for their radical views; what would befall a nobody just beginning to reach for the academic ladder?

I phoned Corry to tell him what had happened. His reaction surprised and delighted me. He chuckled wryly, as was his wont, and assured me that this was not the last time I was going to be misquoted by the press. Then he advised me in the strongest terms not to correct or deny the reports but to let them die. Any peep out of me would simply prolong the farce.

This wise counsel served me well then, and on several subsequent occasions when it diffused potentially threatening issues before they caught fire.

The Main Fare

Although sociology absorbed some of my time for a period, it was never more than a hobby. There was clearly a keen and widespread interest in the subject among students, and we soon recruited an "honest," i.e., full-time, sociologist, Martin Robin and established the Department of Sociology. I was its first head, in addition to my other duties, but only for a short while; I soon returned full time to my spiritual home, political science. There, although my writing was naturally confined to a few areas of special concentration, I taught a wide range of courses, as was the practice before the discipline became more specialized and the number of experts in the diverse sub-fields of politics grew. But in the 1950s, '60s, and even the '70s, it was expected of instructors to teach courses in several areas of the discipline, even if they were far removed from their previous studies or research interests. I began, as we saw, with teaching American History and Politics, and with his Introduction to Democratic Government and Politics. Later, I offered the first International Politics course at Queen's (as distinct from International Relations, offered by History) and at one time or another taught Comparative Politics (Europe), the History of Political Thought, the French Canada Seminar, another survey course on Canadian Politics for mostly second year students, and several courses on Political Parties and Elections. After my stewardship of the CRTC, I returned to teach the Politics of Regulation, Political Communication, and Cultural Policy.

The eclecticism emerged from several circumstances. The social sciences were less highly developed, rigorous and data-filled than they would later become; less empirical knowledge was available, and powerful theoretical frameworks were few and far between. Secondly, undergraduate, rather than graduate teaching was emphasized and was, in addition to building solid knowledge in one field, linked to some notion of a general education. Our four years Honours B.A. in Political Science demanded a heavy concentration in that field and also a reasonably decent concentration in a minor field. Furthermore, two general examinations in political science had to be passed, and each candidate had to write a short dissertation, the preparation of which was expected to take roughly the same amount of time as a full, year-long course, although it was usually more demanding than that.

Some of our graduates went on to do M.A.s and Ph.D.s, but there were not very many and a high proportion of our graduates found berths in the public service and the voluntary sector. A few invariably drifted into law.

Supervising theses occasionally led to remote and esoteric fields. I recall, for instance, that one of my early students, John Crosbie, wrote a dissertation on local government in Newfoundland. I knew nothing about it and discovered that I was not the only one; the subject had heretofore been completely neglected. Newfoundland's local politics differed from comparable experience elsewhere in Canada, because the ubiquitous presence of settlements along the coast meant that municipalities were only marginally preoccupied with streets and roads. Harbours were the thing, but they were mostly a federal responsibility. John, who was to become a major Newfoundland and Canadian political personage, broke the ice and produced so original, revealing and excellent a study that we sent it to the *Canadian Journal of Economics and Political Science* which published a shortened version of it. This was, to my knowledge, the very first time an undergraduate dissertation found its way into that distinguished, juried journal.

Another interesting and out-of-the way topic for those days was a study of the political philosophy of Arthur Koestler, as revealed in his novels; the author was Peter Hancock, who subsequently pursued a successful diplomatic career. I have long been interested in Koestler and read most of his books — a pleasure which even brought a tangible reward. Queen's bestowed an honorary degree on him in 1968 and I was asked to be his academic host. This meant that I saw a fair amount of him and had the opportunity to further probe his mind. Oddly enough, I found his writings more engaging than his conversation.

The Challenge of Large Courses

University teaching is not, of course, all of a piece. To design a large lecture course, construct the reading list, prepare the lectures, identify essay topics, devise interesting and searching examination papers and conduct the classes for 250 students differs dramatically from running a seminar for a dozen students emanating from one's research. All my really large classes (never exceeding 300 souls) over the years were overviews of Canadian politics in which I gave two lectures a week, supplemented by a third hour of tutorials. This allowed specified topics to be discussed by about fifteen or twenty students under the guidance of senior undergraduate or graduate students.

There was always a senior tutor—a virtual colleague and eventually almost always a friend—who was normally a doctoral candidate, not necessarily under my supervision. The senior tutor ensured that the tutorials were run well, regularly meeting with the tutors to plan the upcoming sessions. He or she also marked the essays and part of the examination papers. But I always set one compulsory question on the final examination which I marked myself. This facilitated the equitable final ranking of the top students—important for fellowship applications and for writing reference letters—and it also offered additional insight into the minds of individual students. When, in 2002, exaggerated and misplaced zeal for alleged fairness led to student names on exam papers being replaced by numbers, much was lost and little gained. I believe that I was able to assess an examination better when I placed it into the context of all I knew about the student and his or her work. Numbers on the exam papers do not facilitate this.

On rare occasions, like when I received an honorary degree, I actually wore a tie.

Being a tutor was a form of apprenticeship in which potential academics learnt some of the tricks of the teaching trade, and in which others acquired insight into group dynamics and, with luck, into clear exposition. Tutors often learnt as much from performing their duties as the students did from the tutorials. The currently rampant corporatization of universities—and the related hankering for collective agreements covering everyone in sight, from academics, teaching assistants, to students—has been largely successful. Tutors are seen by some as providing cheap labour, not as persons undergoing training, and they are sometimes indefensibly exploited. The issues are complex, but I betray my age and generation, and my utter commitment to teaching as a sacred trust, not a contractual duty, when I assert that unionization of academic staff at Queen's has been harmful to the academic and teaching enterprise. Without adding much fairness it has changed the prevailing collegial climate, bureaucratized human interactions, diminished university teaching as a service vocation and debased the currency.

These comments about the unionization of the university cause me acute distress. Historically, labour unions have played a vital and salutary role in improving the lot of the exploited, downtrodden and underprivileged. Times change, however, and nowadays, in Canada at least, it is largely the public sector unions who champion a constituency of the privileged, sometimes by actions which come close to blackmailing the less favoured taxpayer whose generosity supports them.

The degree to which the senior tutor lightened the prof's tasks depended largely on the younger partner's commitment and competence. Occasionally, a particular skill, interest or experience of the senior tutor offered serendipitous enrichment. Many of them linger in memory: Patrick Faffard, now at the University of Ottawa, for instance was a francophone from the West (!!!) — clearly a catch; Keith Brownsey, a keen pedagogue obviously destined for the academy, found a berth in Calgary; Margaret Little stood out as a smart feminist and untiring champion of the underdog. She also played the piano, which I liked. Peter Gary Smith (or was it Gary Peter Smith?) likewise became an academic and inspired us all by his wisdom, kindness and probing mind. He unfortunately died a few years ago.

Many of my senior tutors became friends. Most of them were impressive helpers. I have enjoyed the collaboration of many ingenious and *engagé* assistants who made quite substantial contributions to my courses, and who added not only to my familiarity with particular traits and idiosyncrasies of members of my large classes, but also some levity. We frequently shared humorous episodes arising in the lectures or tutorials, prompted by the good-humoured cheerfulness of so many of our students, or by the orneriness of the more sullen ones.

It helped, when teaching large classes, to be something of a performer, as I mentioned before. My own style evolved spontaneously over the years. I never, as some lecturers do, used prepared anecdotes or humorous incidents to lighten the proceedings and to recapture the attention of wandering minds. But, having luckily been blessed with an irrepressible funny bone, I always relied on the spontaneous popping into the mind of some funny example or turn of phrase. Other than the intrinsic interest of the subject of a lecture, an element of surprise and anticipation held the attention of the mass of listeners crowded, more often than not, into an overheated hall. I likewise learnt that the attention of the listeners was enhanced when what was said was expressed now and then in an unexpected form. This did not mean that I searched for esoteric or obscure ways of presenting the material but that I tried to present it in a manner different from what would normally have been expected. Most of the targets of this strategy were likely quite unaware of what I was trying to achieve by the particular phrasing of my presentation. But I know, from the expression on their faces, and the occasional chuckles, that many of the listeners responded positively to my style and artifice.

XVII

Research: Growth of a Cottage Industry

W hen I no longer needed to submit annual reports to the dean describing my "output," (this was always done one breath before the expiration of the deadline), I lost track of what exactly I had written and published, although in my study there are two long shelves which have, over the years, become filled with books I have written, edited, contributed to, alone or in collaboration with others. Since I am well past salary increments and promotions, for which the research confessions were intended, it would be a waste of time to compile a precise tabulation now. Always an eager and busy beaver, I have more than half a dozen books to my credit and, I guess, well over one hundred papers, articles, chapters and the like. Some of these are straight-laced, utterly solid articles on extensive and intensive research, others primarily essays arising from reflection and the perusal of other people's writings. "When you steal from one author," as the wag, Wilson Mizner, said in an oft-quoted quip, "it is plagiarism; if you steal from many, it's research."

How best to convey the scope, essence and flavour of all this toil and fun? There is no point for our purpose in resorting to the usual panoply of academic scribbles: bibliographies, citations, footnotes or endnotes, tables and appendices. In the unlikely event that any one is interested, libraries and the Internet stand by with a surfeit of Meiseliana.

In accounting for my research, I resort to a stratagem employed previously—the use of "chunks"—a literary device suggested by Charley Gordon, my memoir guru, when I earlier succumbed to a touch of writer's block. "Just produce relevant chunks," he said, "if you don't mind my calling them that, they'll fall into place as needed." I took the advice and immediately managed to sail full steam ahead. Only, ever striving for elegance, I think of them not as chunks but as morsels of my life. So here is a quilt of episodes, anecdotes and reflections about my research. They differ considerably in length and the type of subject they evoke but, I hope, show what Canadian social science research was like—or at least provide some examples of what one researcher experienced during his years as what was termed a "productive scholar." The "morsels" section is followed by a review of my research taken as a whole, which I grandly entitle "Panorama," and afterwards I have the temerity to attempt, in "A Big Shortcoming," an assessment of the whole ball of wax.

Grinning before the Meiseliana shelves—my writings from 1950 to 2012.

PART ONE: MORSELS

My Diefenbaker Interlude (with apologies to Peter Regenstreif)[1]

When examining the 1957 election for my Ph.D. thesis and my first book, I needed to discover how party programs were devised, how the parties were organized, candidates recruited and trained, and how the election plans were constructed and executed. Party

---

[1] Peter Regenstreif's 1965 pioneering study of voting and parties was entitled *The Diefenbaker Interlude.* I could not resist pinching and adapting his title.

finance—always a ticklish issue—also had to be explored. The only sources for this information were lengthy and frank exchanges with party warriors—generals as well as foot soldiers—and, to some extent at least, access to party documents. I can't claim that I was given permission to dig up *every* document in party files relevant to the election, but by and large most of the data in the federal headquarters of the Conservatives and Liberals were, surprisingly, made available for my inspection. I was allowed to work in the offices day and night and make notes and copies of everything I needed.

The magic wand, on the Liberal side, was wielded by Keith Davey, my old Victoria College friend. He was the Liberal campaign manager who opened doors, filing cabinets and avenues of thought which proved of inestimable value. But, as we've discussed, I had no close, or even remote acquaintances, among the Tories. This handicap was overcome early because the Tory headquarters was run by two quite unusual and rare individuals. The Conservative campaign manager—their Keith Davey—was Allister Grosart, a former advertising executive, and his secretary and right-hand "man," Flora MacDonald.

Both were of inestimable help. Allister Grosart's motives were no doubt mixed, but at least two elements were critical. He was convinced that the political process would benefit from people knowing more about it—a rare outlook among professional politicos—and that there was an enormous amount of unnecessary secrecy about how parties operated, which gave them a bad name. In addition, being an old advertising pro, he assumed that his party would benefit from being favourably portrayed in an academic study; so he ever so subtly tried to win me over and was always very nice to me.

On one occasion, when we were floating lazily during a swim in the lake near his Gatineau cottage, he inquired how the research was going and whether I had any questions. I did. On what grounds, I wondered, was he constantly insisting that the party under John Diefenbaker differed substantially from its predecessor led by George Drew? I acknowledged that the current leader's Western base added a new element, but otherwise it was pretty much *plus ça change, plus c'est la même chose*. I detected no transformation great enough to justify his favourite and oft-noted reference to the "Diefenbaker Revolution." "Ah," he exclaimed, "You must talk to 'the Chief,' and you'll see." I had a lot of reservations about the new

Tory leader and wondered whether I would gain much insight from meeting him, but was, of course, pleased that I would gain a face-to-face impression if him. And there was a question I hoped he would answer, about why a resolution adopted at the leadership Convention was left out of the party platform. He had the reputation of being extremely vain and touchy, so I stayed up almost the whole night prior to our interview, trying to formulate the lead-up to and wording of a question about it as inoffensively as possible.

On the appointed day I was ushered into the prime ministerial office, lined with beautifully bound volumes of statutes and Hansard — the record of parliamentary debates — and set out to ask the carefully prepared and neatly structured series of questions. But I had not counted on his sly, foxy ways. Allister had obviously briefed him about my concerns and before I could even pop the first question, he launched into a magnificent discourse about his vision of Canada. It was a class performance. He rose from time to time, reached for one of the tomes on a shelf near him and quoted parts of a speech he had delivered in the House of Commons previously. The oratorical tour de force lasted so long that there never was any time for my inquiries. Though disappointed, I was spellbound and deeply regretted my strategy of not taking notes during the interview, lest this should put him off. As soon as I was dismissed, I hot-footed it to the Parliamentary Library where I jotted down every single thing he said that I could remember. But I could have saved myself the trouble.

A few days later when I presented myself for an appointment with one of his cabinet ministers — I think it was Davie Fulton — I was told that our meeting would have to be slightly delayed. The prime minister was introducing his Canadian Bill of Rights in the House, and insisted that the cabinet be present during his speech. Why don't I go to the Visitors' Gallery, listen to Mr. Diefenbaker and, when he is finished, return to see my minister, who would be back by then?

When entering the House I heard familiar words. The prime minister was repeating more or less verbatim the oratory he had directed at me during our private séance. I never found out which came first. Did Mr. Diefenbaker like the substance of what he told me so well that he thought it would nicely serve a double duty, or had he already had his parliamentary speech in hand before we met, and decided to adapt it for my benefit? Neither I, nor history, will ever know.

A Quirk of the Subconscious

While reconstructing my past for this chronicle, I have been aware of the extreme fragility of one's memory. Here is an example of how the mind plays tricks on one, whether writing memoirs or doing research. In one of my earliest surveys I inserted a few queries into my questionnaire, testing the reliability of the respondents' answers. In one of these, I listed a number of fairly well-known names and asked whether the respondent knew who they were. I was not only interested in the political ken of my subjects but also in the truthfulness of their responses. Consequently, one of the names on the list was a fictitious one — a person I called Small. This seemed a neutral, non-committal name unlikely to arouse the respondents' liking or ire.

Consider my surprise when we found that several people thought they knew of Mr. Small and said things like "he's gone," or "he vanished." It turns out that in my mind's search for a name that was in no way "loaded," I hit on one which had entered Canadian consciousness because of a mysterious scandal years before. After the end of the First World War, a successful Toronto impresario, Ambrose Small, disappeared without a trace, and was never heard of again. There were rumours of foul play, and the episode inspired several literary accounts in Canadian fiction. When choosing a non-person for my questionnaire, my subconscious produced the surname of a real person who had ceased to exist. This coincidence was unnerving.

The Lodger Hypothesis

For an election study in the 1960s, it was necessary to identify the economic status of voters residing in small sections of their constituencies. In the absence of polling data, we were able to do this by superimposing census data, broken down into small units known as "census tracts" into the appropriate area of the voting districts. This made it possible to increase our insight into the relationship between the income level of people and their political choice. But there was a hitch: the main census, examining income, was conducted only every ten years and we feared that the time lag between when income was measured and the voting decision was too long. But we also knew that a smaller, more selective census took place every five years, in our case very close to the election we were examining. Unfortunately, however, the mini probe did not ask for the income data we needed. It did, however, show how many people in any given area lived in rented rooms. So we developed what we called the "Lodger Hypothesis." It assumed that the larger the proportion of lodgers in an area, the lower the income. In this roundabout way (and one which did not overwhelm with its scientific rigour), we managed to get a reading on the comparative income levels in the districts we examined.

We tested the accuracy of our ingenious stratagem in various ways and found that it worked better in some localities than others, but we stuck with it, and although we did not take the matter too seriously, we were pleased with the ingenuity of our solution. Gilles Paquet and I later wrote a paper for a conference on statistics organized by the Canadian Political Science Association, reporting, *inter alia* on the L Hypothesis.

Footing the Bills

Twenty-first century Canadian scholars must be baffled by how, with only minimal funding, my generation was able to do any serious research. I speak only of the humanities and social sciences here. The Canada Council, the Social Sciences and Humanities Research Council, and any of the other public and private granting bodies and programs now assisting research had not yet been heard of when I embarked on my voyages of discovery.

My first steps towards the systematic scrutiny and analysis of national elections, starting with modest local surveys and culminating in large national probes, were financed by microscopic grants from the Queen's Arts Research Committee; its subventions rarely attained the stratospheric heights of a four digit sum. We—my "apprentices" and occasional other helpers—formed a threadbare cottage industry. All the kind folks—mostly but not always students —who conducted the person-to-person interviews volunteered, their only compensation being the fun and intrinsic interest of the work. There was also a social benefit, I suppose. We met every evening in our living room to discuss the day's experiences, well sustained by the coffee, cookies and sandwiches from Murie's kitchen, not to mention her interested conversation.

I digress slightly to make a critically important observation. In the discussion of research aid, the contribution of spouses cannot be exaggerated. In those early days, most wives did not have jobs outside their homes and considered their family responsibilities paramount. Many, in countless ways, directly or indirectly helped their husbands do their work. There were hardly any instances of female colleagues until several decades later, where male mates could have reciprocated, even on the doubtful assumption that many might have been so inclined. Whatever the merits of this sort of arrangement, many of us benefited enormously from the help we received at home. Murie, for example, not only contributed in a major way to how I interacted with students, but she also produced charts, maps and graphs for my books and papers and even designed and executed the cover of my edited *Papers on the 1962 Election*, published by the University of Toronto Press. Wisely, she refused to learn to type, since the acquisition of this skill would inevitably have led to my exploiting her even more shamelessly.

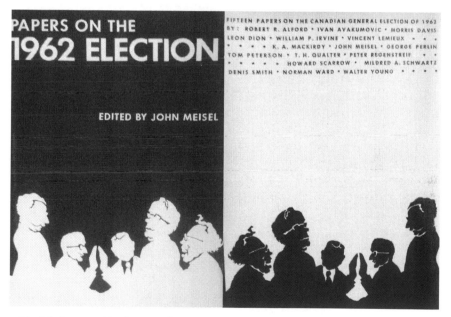

Murie's front and back covers for one of my books. The cutout portraits are of the five party leaders.

When, in the early 1960s, I thought of mounting a full-scale study of public attitudes during a Canadian general election, of the kind that the University of Michigan had made famous, and which, at the time, set the international platinum standard for such inquiries, the question of funding presented a colossal challenge. I figured that I'd need somewhere around \$50,000 or \$60,000 — a sum far exceeding the cost of any research heretofore undertaken in Canadian social science. I asked the Canada Council for \$25,000 but it had never made anything like so large a grant before and my request caused much navel-gazing, serious discussion and a near crisis in the Council. I was not privy to everything that went on, but found out that the council at first turned down the request, not because of the money alone, but because opinion surveys were seen by some members as lacking sufficient rigour. Shades of H.R.G. Greaves in 1951, my putative thesis supervisor in London, as you may recall! The whole Council apparently had a couple of long debates in which this issue was discussed. Finally, by a narrow margin, they decided that it was appropriate to support surveys, and they approved our application.

But another twenty or thirty thousand dollars was needed. Fortunately, the House of Commons had just established the Barbeau Committee on Election Expenses, with Khayam Paltiel, a Carleton colleague, as its Research Director. He agreed with my suggestion that the committee would benefit from learning how the public viewed some of the issues it was examining and accepted my offer to attach, for \$10,000, up to twelve relevant questions to my questionnaire. My principal research assistant, Rick Van Loon, and I also agreed to produce a report for the committee on our findings. So we had another \$10,000. I then approached a number of foundations and, with the help of Alec Corry, managed to obtain \$5,000 from the Laidlaw Foundation. Finally, Phil Converse, a stellar expert from the University of Michigan, whom I had previously recruited as the only non-Canadian member of my five member research team, managed to extract \$5,000 from his university. By this time the kitty held \$45,000 and Queen's put up the rest. To raise the needed funds from that many sources was extremely time-consuming. In addition to the successful sorties for money there were also failed ones, of course. Things are a lot easier now but the amount of paperwork required to fund research is immeasurably more onerous.

Things were different on the next round, when I undertook to do a follow-up survey of the 1968 election. This time I went alone (but with Rick Van Loon's very able aid), and I managed to finance the whole enterprise from a wonderful Killam Award of almost \$400,000 which not only offered five years' research time on Canadian political parties, but also covered all the expenses associated with the study of the 1968 national contest. (This sum was so staggering at the time, that its magnitude shocked me into wiping out the detail although it must have been I, of course, who specified the amount when I drafted the grant application.)

The Psephologium

By the time I launched the 1965 national election study and then, with the Killam Award in 1968, the scale of my inquiries leaped from the comfortable little cottage industry towards a large research enterprise involving numerous collaborators, including countless student research assistants. It was inefficient to have all these busy bees humming in their scattered respective homes, studies and offices, so I created a shared work space where we could all be within easy distance from one another, and where the accumulated questionnaires, tabulations, (no one heard of spread sheets then), punch cards, statistical collections, posters, journals, newspaper clippings, campaign buttons and all the other paraphernalia could be safely stored and accessible to whoever needed to consult them. Queen's had always been most accommodating in supporting my work and offered the use of the two bottom stories of a red brick, typical downtown Kingston house on Clergy Street, about five minutes from the Politics Department.

We called it the "Psephologium," playing on "psephology," the name occasionally bestowed on the study of elections. It served us well and enhanced the quality of what we did by providing an ambience in which a good deal of camaraderie developed among some of the research team.

A quixotic brainwave produced the idea that we could become a sort of egalitarian commune, adoringly beavering away in pursuit of the truth. I am not sure where this wildly romantic and unrealistic impulse came from, but it was doomed to failure. Although we got along famously and worked effectively at our respective tasks, we never even remotely resembled a Kibbutz. In my mind, we were all equals and ready to help one another, quite independently of our respective rank, station or main task on the project. One day when it began to rain I asked a female member to bring in my bicycle from outside. For some reason it was inconvenient for me to do so. It was a very heavy, old-fashioned working-man's bike (see the cover of this book), vastly different from today's elegant and feather-weight models, which cost as much as a Ferrari. She was not a robust person and took umbrage at this request.

I was disappointed and even shocked at first, but the incident made me look realistically at my romantic scenario for an ideal research infrastructure. Several things revealed that I had been dreaming in technicolour. While I expected others to pitch in wherever their help was needed, *I* only did *my* thing and never performed any clerical, secretarial or statistical chores. Nor did I rescue anyone's bike, but then I was never invited to do so. Another aspect should have been obvious to me: the wide interchangeability of tasks I had expected to develop was unrealistic because of our respective slots in the scheme of things. I was a full-time academic — my colleagues were clerical or otherwise non-academic employees, grad students and even near-beginners, bereft of even a B.A. Furthermore, it was inefficient for people who had acquired expertise in one area to fiddle about in another one about which they knew little. I was forced to conclude that my dream had been dumb and also something worse: self-centred.

Inexperience also contributed to the failure of my experiment. I did not take the trouble and time to present and explain my idea. Some people had no inkling of what was in my mind. Had I brought us all together and held a full discussion, everyone would have been much better informed and able to assess my scheme. Several people, I am sure, would have identified some of the difficulties and would likely have persuaded me to forget all about it.

I have given this minor episode so much space because it dramatically taught me an invaluable lesson: it is ever so easy to be thoughtlessly selfish and to ignore the full dimension and implications of one's actions. My bike not only assisted me in gadding about Kingston but also, in this instance, in acquiring experience in how to be more thoughtful, self aware and sensitive when dealing with others. Although I was over thirty when I tackled large research projects, I still had a lot to learn; one lesson was that the *way* research is organized and managed is as important as its theoretical, methodological and scientific side.

Learning How to Do It

One starts acquiring the skills needed for research as early as kindergarten. Inquisitiveness, imagination, orderly thought, diligence — these essential qualities are part of the mental equipment imparted to potential scholars through the normal process of socialization. The more specialized skills develop in school, when writing essays (or nowadays, doing projects), and are then fine-honed at university and, particularly, in graduate school while one sweats over a thesis. My M.A. dissertation under the meticulous supervision of Karl Helleiner and with the editorial care of Murie, was what taught me how to design, execute and report a substantial intellectual inquiry. Writing editorials for the *Canadian Forum*, although less weighty, helped develop writing skills which were facilitated by the experiences garnered even so far back as editing and writing for the *Quaker Cracker* at Pickering and *Acta Victoriana* at U of T.

Over and above these obvious and basic skills are the methodological issues which vary from research task to research task. These are normally first addressed by consulting similar studies, articles in the journals and proceedings of relevant conferences and colloquia. My convivial ways also led me to rely on consultations with knowledgeable colleagues. This usually paid off handsomely but there were occasional set-backs. When I started my first local election survey in Kingston, I consulted Professor Edgett — a highly regarded statistician the students fondly called Fidget Edgett. How large a sample did I need to obtain valid results? After some reflection he suggested fifteen or twenty. He had obviously failed to grasp my problem but I did not wish to offend him by pursuing the matter further and beat a hasty retreat. I then turned to Harold Poole, a colleague in the days when politics was still lumped into one department with economics and commerce. He taught business courses and had vast experience doing surveys for business firms. He guided me through statistics handbooks to a realistic number but also suggested that I contact Alan Saunders, the head of the Canadian Institute of Public Opinion, this country's Gallup Poll organization. We used his firm to conduct some later large surveys.

An important rung in my climb from a cottage industry to a large enterprise was the Inter-university Consortium for Political and Social Research at the University of Michigan in Ann Arbor. It was established in the early 1960s and has by now become the largest archive of digital social science data in the world. When I decided that Queen's should join, early after its founding, it too was a small cottage industry; it held annual meetings at which methodological issues affecting the collection, interpretation and archiving of data were discussed. I was put on the council, probably because it was thought useful to have someone from Canada. Although I did not take any of the courses it offered, I learnt an enormous amount just from being around, reading, and listening to papers, and, not least, getting to know some of the leading practitioners in the field of social and political surveys in the United States and Western Europe. I enlarge on the consortium experience in a later chapter.

My visits to Ann Arbor directed my thoughts towards the need for a survey-based Canadian national election study. When in 1965 the acorn grew into an oak, I decided to ask Phil Converse, one of Michigan's stars, to join my team of researchers.

My practice to seek out knowledgeable sleuths and practitioners before setting out on my own was not confined to psephology. When I embarked on explorations of the relation between culture and politics, for instance, I sought out Paul Schafer in Toronto. Although not a political scientist, he stood out in this country as an independent scholar, a beacon shedding light on its cultural soul. I will shortly report on how I became involved in this area.

Similarly, when I dipped into an exploration of science policy in Canada, one of the first sources I sought out (other than a scathing review of it by the auditor general) was Dr. Tom Brzustovski, a former academic and the president of the Natural Science and Engineering Research Council of Canada. He knew the ins and outs of this territory better than anyone and saved me hours of library time. Furthermore, his hands-on familiarity with the field helped me set it into a realistic context.

I suspect that when embarking on new explorations, I supplemented the usual strategies and tactics a lot more than many other researchers, by drawing on friends and acquaintances who had trod this ground already. They always gladly lent a hand, fortifying my enjoyment of the collaborative spirit animating academic life.

Gaining Notoriety

In the social sciences, research reports sometimes leak out of their academic trough (lectures, articles, conferences and books) and trickle into the popular media. This is so particularly when the subject relates to current problems and events, like issues of national unity or political parties and elections, both of which were in my intellectual bailiwick. When this happens, there is a danger of the scholar being seduced — by public visibility, popularity and sometimes even money — into deviating from academic propriety and playing to the gallery. Punditry has its cost. This was never a problem for me, despite my doing increasingly more work for both the English and French networks of the CBC, related to national political issues. While I greatly enjoyed these diversions, particularly when they involved Quebecers, I never allowed them to take precedence over academic work. My ability to withstand the blandishments of fame was not caused by decorous modesty but by the fact that I never was a superstar, just a reasonably competent expert in demand from time to time; I was never swept off my feet by an adoring crowd or clique.

One of my academic papers, however, caused a widespread and significant reaction. In the early and middle 1960s, when the Social Credit Party gained unprecedented support, I became convinced that our traditional so-called two-party system was undergoing profound change. The CCF/NDP had long challenged it and the strength of Social Credit created a new disequilibrium. I concluded that it would be increasingly difficult for any party to win permanent Parliamentary majorities, as had been the case in most of the past, and that we were entering a phase of alternating periods of majority and minority governments. In 1962 I published an article in the *Queen's Quarterly* developing these notions and examining their implications. Then, three years later, in a paper in *Cahiers de la société canadienne de science politique*, I deepened the analysis and in a foolhardy moment of chutzpah, predicted, two days before the new Canadian election, that again no party would obtain a majority. The gamble paid off.

I sent the *Quarterly* piece to Richard Gwyn, the editor of the Canadian edition of *Time*. Its meagre four pages devoted to Canada were, before the maturing of *Maclean's*, the closest we had to a weekly news magazine. I knew Richard slightly, our paths had likely crossed at a conference or a party event. To my surprise and delight, he did not merely refer to my analysis in one of his commentaries, but devoted a two column, boxed article, photograph and all, to a report on my piece. I was amazed at the number of people who saw and mentioned this exposure and who congratulated me on it and on "having made *Time*." Although news magazines were scoffed at as being superficial, in my circle there must have been a lot of closet readers.

Sensing some congruence between Gwyn's outlook and mine, I sent Richard my *Société* piece before I presented it. This time the photograph was dreadful, but my analysis was the centrepiece of the four column lead article, entitled "The Realm—a New Normalcy?" Again, the reaction was widespread and complimentary. I was pleased by these positive fallouts from media exposure, as I was by favourable comments garnered by my CBC gigs, but I was also troubled. I gained the impression that the quality and importance of my *academic* work was somehow being overshadowed by media exposure. The latter was welcome, but secondary. I feared that this fallout from the professor's life might overshadow the core of scholarship. The issue caused me some anxiety although, I confess, no loss of sleep.

The anxiety was heightened by the impression that some of the job offers I was receiving from other universities were prompted as much by media exposure as by basic scholarship. Some colleagues, less visible in the media, whose academic work was exemplary, were not being courted as assiduously as I was. I hasten to add, lest you think that my head had swelled insufferably, that we are talking here of an era when Canadian academics in the social sciences were in short supply, and many universities, particularly new ones springing up everywhere, were desperately looking for new recruits.

Why Culture?

Motives for undertaking research in a particular field are usually complex, even mysterious. They can arise from deep-seated personal traits and experiences a well as from casual, even trivial incidents. My becoming involved in the study of the relation between politics and culture—the arts—is a good example.

In 1974, as president of the Canadian Political Science Association (CPSA), I confronted the prospect of delivering the obligatory presidential address at the annual meeting. This is quite an event, attended by a very large number of members. The theme chosen by the orator usually takes one of three forms: the summation of what the president has learnt from his or her principal research interest, imparting the wisdom the president has acquired in a long, devoted scholarly career, or a rumination about the state of the discipline of political science. I thought it refreshing to avoid all three and tackled something quite unexpected. The French have a lovely phrase—*épater le bourgeois*—to shake or shock middle class or mainstream attitudes, and this is what I hoped to do. So I surprised my colleagues with a paper entitled "Political Culture and the Politics of Culture." It mapped the relationship between values, including political values, and arts and culture, and urged my brothers and sisters to subject this phenomenon to scholarly analysis as part of political studies.

I did not know what I had wrought. Before long, I started receiving invitations to present papers on this topic at conferences all over the world. I had unwittingly entered a new research area. In fairness I confess that I was in part responsible for this development. Soon after my presidential address I organized a roundtable in Cracow for the International Political Science Association, on my new interest, and I also devised a colloquium on it in Quebec City for the Royal Society of Canada. As time went on I wrote quite a bit about it and for many years annually taught a seminar entitled "Cultural Policy in Canada."

PART TWO: PANORAMA

I have been called a hummingbird and a butterfly — sometimes even by myself — not because of any lightness of touch but because my interests tend to flit from one subject to another, without seeking to gain a monolithic command of a single field.

Sometimes, impatiently drawn to collecting and interpreting data, I paid less attention than I might have to the existing relevant articles or books, and dove headlong into the research pool without doing all the warm-up exercises recommended by the best academic coaches. While this may have, on occasion, deprived me of useful knowledge and theoretical finesse, it saved me from being chained to the dominant conventions of the discipline and from entrapment by prevailing fashion.

In keeping with my non-planning, unselfconscious, and somewhat unreflective nature, before preparing the outline for this chapter, I had never stopped to consider the overall shape and scope of my research. I pursued each subject or problem one at a time, moving from topic to topic and from year to year, either because the questions it raised intrigued me or addressed current political problems, or because some male or female siren conned me into addressing it. Surprisingly, a clear pattern is nevertheless discernible.

I cultivated three major areas in considerable depth: parties and elections; Canadian unity and French-English relations; and cultural and communications policy. In addition, a number of topics attracted my intensive attention for shorter stretches of time. Science policy, government regulation, and the performance of Canadian bureaucracy constituted some of these detours. And — confirming at least in part the hummingbird and butterfly charge—there were numerous single shot excursions where the preparation of an occasional paper or lecture involved a concentrated and fairly deep exploration of a subject—a form of short-term, high-voltage research. These one-night stands usually called for quite extensive preparation and were prompted by invitations to participate in a symposium, deliver a special lecture or contribute to a Festschrift.

Three principal factors account for my having yielded to blandishments for papers, chapters or talks. One is sheer curiosity. I have always found it difficult not to pursue some novel and intriguing issue when being urged to tackle it. Another is what my friend Ted Hodgetts famously referred to as an incurable disability he characterized as ITSNO—Inability To Say NO! I confess to the third in my *c.v.* which reads, in part, "An enthusiastic teacher, lecturer and paper giver, he is incapable of resisting invitations to contribute to conferences or symposia if they are held in (to him) exotic places."

My first published work, other than editorials in the *Canadian Forum*, grew, as was to be expected, out of my thesis on Tomáš Masaryk. Although it appeared in the *Forum*, a monthly, it was a solid, fairly long piece on a subject virtually unknown in the English-speaking world. Once I started to teach, Slavic studies fell by the wayside and gave way to international relations. I offered the department's only course, at the time, and became an active member of the Canadian Institute of International Affairs. It was its *International Journal*—a respected academic organ—and the *Queen's Quarterly*—that provided the outlets for most of my early academic articles. I sporadically produced papers on world politics, so long as I taught the subject, but these dwindled into a mere trickle.

For a couple of decades after the late 1950s, elections and parties dominated my research agenda. They are so important in democratic politics that analyses of them were irresistible and Canadian, United States and West European demands for new papers on them never dried up.

In 1963 my Queen's colleague, Hugh Thorburn, brought out a slim collection of original papers and reprints, *Party Politics in Canada*, which became a favourite text book and went through seven editions, the last of which weighed in at 643 pages. When it first appeared, I deplored that so important a subject was brought out by a Canadian affiliate of an American publisher—Prentice-Hall. Labour was spelt labor, etc. But eventually I overcame my churlish scruples and over the years contributed four of my papers to Hugh's bonanza. One of them, "The Decline of Party in Canada," being rather provocative, was widely reprinted in other collections. It demonstrated how the role and effectiveness of parties were being diminished by, among other factors, the growing sway of executive and bureaucratic power; the replacement, in strategic decisions, of politicians by pollsters, spin-doctors and advertising firms; and by the growing emphasis in the media on the leaders at the expense of MPs and ordinary party members. When this piece reached retirement age, Hugh recruited a younger colleague, Matthew Mendelsohn, with whom I produced a spruced-up and somewhat modified version, "Meteor, Phoenix, Chameleon? The Decline and Transformation of Party in Canada." Hugh also disseminated my final word on the subject, "The Dysfunctions of Canadian Parties," which first appeared in a Festschrift honouring Khayam Paltiel.

Even the Americans joined the Canadian electoral study industry. The American Enterprise Institute, of all things, the right wing think tank, included us in its (excellent) two "At the Polls" studies published in 1975 and 1981. I contributed to both of them, and incidentally provoked the wrath of Iza Laponce, the creator of the online Canadian Bibliography of Political Science. I did not think of her when calling my piece—the 35-page opening paper—"Introduction." She rightly berated me for using a title that would be utterly unenlightening in a bibliography.

Many of my former students played key roles in the study of elections and parties. I had no direct involvement in the work of some after they flew from the nest, but kept in scholarly touch with many. Bill Irvine and George Perlin at Queen's, Ken Carty at UBC, and Jon Pammett and Alan Frizell (Carleton) spring to mind.

Although elections and parties occupied centre stage, they did not monopolize it. Indirectly, the interest aroused in nationalism by my master's thesis lingered on and transformed into a preoccupation with what holds or fails to hold Canada together. Questions relating to national unity (which were not unrelated to the performance of political parties), to language use, and to processes of accommodation kept preoccupying me and opened up a new research territory. I hereafter refer to it as the "national unity file." The primary impetus arose from the increasingly menacing tension between Quebec and what came to be known as ROC—the rest of Canada—which threatened to topple our lovely state.

Several developments in the middle and late 1960s powerfully contributed to my involvement in this area. The Pearson government created the Royal Commission on Bilingualism and Biculturalism (B & B Commission) in 1963, of which I became one of the research supervisors. Then, two years later, Queen's launched its Institute of Intergovernmental Relations (IIGR), focusing on Canadian federalism. I was party to the discussions leading to its birth and, in various ways, have had a little finger and sometimes even an arm in its doings ever since. And in 1965 I was asked by Premier Robarts to sit on his Advisory Committee on Confederation, whose purpose was to help him develop and implement policies guiding Ontario in its relations with Ottawa and with other provinces. These bodies, as well as Canada's national unity crisis, deflected my attention from the heretofore dominant area of election and party studies and led to new challenges and opportunities.

The national unity issue was fascinating from the political science perspective and also claimed my attention and concern because, as an emerging Canadian nationalist, I did not wish to see the country smashed. That I spoke French and found Quebecers *très sympathique* and had many close friends among them, likewise drew me towards explorations of French-English relations and their political role.

Virtually everything I published on national cohesion and language was derived not from the construction of an experiment or special field work, but from observation of current developments, perusal of literature and reflection. These are activities which some may not consider "research" but which, by shedding light on a problem, accomplish what research is intended to do. They are research just as much as conducting experiments in the lab.

One major venture into the new pasture arose directly from, and was an extension of, my 1968 national survey. I was invited to present a paper to the 1970 World Congress of Sociology, held in Varna, Bulgaria — a venue qualifying as "an exotic site." My piece, "Values, Language and Politics in Canada," relied almost entirely on my survey data and showed how language is related in Canada to innumerable social and political issues and alignments. I published it in my *Working Papers on Canadian Politics* and was later delighted to have it included in Joshua Fishman's monumental *Advances in the Study of Societal Multilingualism*. I cannot omit a slightly bawdy story about this article. The piece contained an enormous amount of detail about the attitudes of five language users — pure English, partial English, mixed, partial French and pure French. To graphically express this, I used a circle, or ball, to represent each of the five groups, within which percentages showing the attitudes of the group were provided, by age group, education, and religion. Some friends, smirking slightly, hereafter referred to this nifty pictorial crutch as "Meisel's balls."

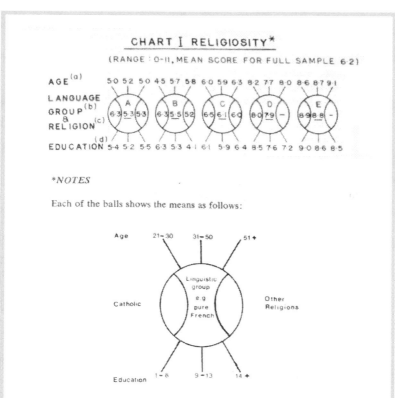

CHART I RELIGIOSITY*

(RANGE : 0-11, MEAN SCORE FOR FULL SAMPLE 6.2)

NOTES

Each of the balls shows the means as follows:

(a) *Age* The three categories for each of the language groups correspond to those in Table I. The score of the 21 to 30 year group is on the left, that of the 31 to 50 cohort in the middle and of the 51 and over group on the right.

(b) *Language* Group Pure English A; Partial English B; Mixed C; Partial French D; Pure French E. The score is underlined.

(c) *Religion* The score of the Catholics is in the left inset, that of all others in the right inset. The sample was divided into only two groups: Catholics and all others. The mean score of each of the language groups does not always correspond to that computed for the whole sample because 96 cases, whose religious affiliation is not known, had to be excluded. This explains the differences in the mean scores of Catholics and of the whole language group in D and E.

(d) *Education* The scores of those who have had up to eight years of schooling are at the left, those with 9 to 13 years of schooling in the middle, and of those with 14 years or more on the right.

Meisel's balls

In addition to being a research supervisor of the B & B Commission I also undertook, with my Laval friend, Vincent Lemieux, a full-scale study for it, of the manner in which French and English were used in certain Canadian professional and other organizations. *Ethnic Relations in Canadian Voluntary Associations* was published by the commission as one of its Documents series. Among the surprising findings was that, under certain circumstances, the relations between the two language groups were better and more productive when they acted separately but maintained viable collaborative mechanisms. Appearance notwithstanding, this was not a crutch for the independentist cause.

Vincent and I were tickled pink when over thirty years later David Cameron and Richard Simeon organized a follow-up study, *Language Matters: How Canadian Voluntary Associations Manage French and English* (2010), inspired by our work and leading to extensive comparisons between now and then.

In the late 1960s, Ontario's former premier, Leslie Frost, became greatly concerned that Quebec's voices expressing dissatisfaction with Canada's constitutional arrangements were heard everywhere, but that the other side was largely mute. Mr. Frost raised the matter with John Deutsch, Queen's principal at the time, wondering whether the Queen's IIGR might help fill the gap. A group of us met with Mr. Frost to discuss the possibilities and eventually Ron Burns, the Institute's director, edited *One Country or Two?* in which twelve anglophone academics dealt with the country's travail. Despite Mr. Frost having put the bee in our bonnet, we naturally preserved complete freedom in the views we expressed. My piece, "'Cancel Out and Pass On': A View of Canada's Present Options," early stated the axiom which underlay everything I ever said or wrote about our situation: "...when two or more groups of people have it in their power to survive within independent political entities, the only workable basis on which they can build political arrangements between them is compromise." Most of what I thought or wrote about with respect to the national unity file explored the resulting options. The title of my piece for the Burns book was inspired by Strindberg's *The Dance of Death* in which, as in Albee's *Who's Afraid of Virginia Woolf?* a married couple undergoing excruciating tensions and hostilities realizes that they have become so dependent on one another that they cannot live separately. Strindberg's couple agrees, in the end, to "cancel out and pass on."

The unity file came to absorb increasingly more time and energy. I became deeply immersed in the B & B Commission. The Robarts Committee also took its toll. Not only did it meet regularly, but it also promoted seminars, organized the huge 1967 Confederation of Tomorrow Conference and sponsored policy papers. Some of these projects were undertaken with the IIGR. It, acting alone, also produced important publications and held critical meetings, bringing together scholars and practitioners from Canada's diverse constituent communities. When, in 1977, the Pépin-Robarts Task Force on Canadian Unity was established, I served as one of its advisors; Léon Dion, Ted (E.W.) McWhinney and myself comprised its so-called "three wise men." Teaching my "Quebec Seminar" and giving innumerable public talks and media commentaries likewise added to the ever-higher mountain of goodies on my plate, cutting into the old potatoes and gravy of elections and party studies. Furthermore, the line between digging for data, armchair cogitation and manning the barricades became blurred.

With few exceptions, what I considered to be my informed and reasonable analyses met with more or less open minds, comprehension and sympathy. One of these few exceptions occurred at the sixtieth anniversary banquet of the Canadian Legion's branch in Sharbot Lake, near my home, where my speech provoked vigorous No! No! Nos! (and some subsequent discreetly delivered thanks from some folks glancing quickly to the left and right as they were uttering them).

One of my papers made an unexpected and treasured contribution to my wardrobe. "*J'ai le goût du Québec* but I Like Canada: Reflections of an Ambivalent Man" appeared in a 1977 collection continuing the discourse opened up in *One Country or Two?*. Edited by Richard Simeon, the new Director of the IIGR, it bore an equally sombre title, *Must Canada Fail?*. The heading of my piece borrowed a campaign slogan of the Parti Québécois, "I have a Taste for Quebec," but added an affirmation of my affection for Canada. The obvious point was that both these sentiments could happily flourish in a single breast — or country.

Some time after the book was published, a parcel arrived from the office of the Premier of New Brunswick, Richard Hatfield, whom I knew well. Our paths had crossed fairly often at various venues for constitutional debates, including IIGR events. Richard was an enlightened federalist. While travelling in Quebec he came across a

T- shirt proclaiming *J'ai le goût du Québec*, bought it and sent it along, with a note supporting the argument of my article.

My third major research area—Canadian aspects of culture, cultural policy, broadcasting policy and communications—is in many ways related to the national unity file. The extent to which a will exists in the country, and among its constituent sub-populations, to hold together and engage in a common enterprise is affected by the prevailing values. These values, in turn, emerge from, and respond to, the overall cultural context, including the arts. In the Canadian case, this context likewise affects our ability to withstand the colossal influence of our mighty neighbour. The study of these matters, while not forcing me to abandon previous research fields, nevertheless reshaped my agenda and, in part, caused my eventual, temporary absence from Queen's.

Although both sides of the equation between culture and politics attracted my attention, the primary focus was on what governments did or did not do for the arts, including broadcasting, and why. I was not the first to explore these questions. Frye, Atwood, Schafer, Crean and a few others were there before me, but none of them troubled much about the political context. This neglect called for redress.

My opening salvo, "Political Culture and the Politics of Culture," was followed by numerous essays and studies in the area I was hoping to graft onto political science. Among the most important and path-breaking of these was "Cultivating the Bushgarden: Cultural Policy in Canada," which I wrote with Jean Van Loon for *The Patron State: Government and the Arts in Europe North America and Japan*.

A subsequent study, published in the *How Ottawa Spends* series of annual volumes produced by Carleton University, sought to map the manner in which Canadian cultural policy comes into being and is executed. Flora MacDonald, who was at this time the minister responsible for communications and culture, facilitated my obtaining both data and insight. I entitled the paper "Flora and Fauna on the Rideau." She was again an invaluable source when, the following year, I worked on a case study for the same Carleton series, "Near Hit: The Parturition of a Broadcasting Policy." It dealt with the complex and politically fraught process of the delayed revision of the Broadcasting Act. Of all the articles I have ever written, this one most fully combined academic research of documents with my personal, hands-on experience as a broadcast regulator.

Sometimes, as I noted, a particular problem captured my attention but merely led to a single probe or short-lived research excursions. Delving into science policy was prompted by my friend Agnes Herzberg's conferences on Statistics, Science and Public Policy held in the Queen's International Studies Centre at Herstmonceux Castle in Sussex. I was a regular attendee during the first few years and was led to stray from cultural policy into looking at what the Canadian government did for science. "Caesar and the Savants: Some Socio-Political Contexts of Science and Technology in Canada" was the weightiest of the half-dozen or so contributions I made to these annual science-oriented gab fests.

And then there were these lovely one-night stands! An ongoing interest in George Orwell found focus in "Newspeak in the Information Society," when, in 1984 (!), I was asked to deliver the Dunning Trust Lecture at Queen's. Rather oddly, it found its way into *Archivaria*, the journal of the Canadian Association of Archivists. "Archives in Cyberspace etc..." an exploration of how the new information technology was transforming archives, also carried by this journal, was prompted by an invitation to present the annual lecture sponsored by the Queen's archives. The question would never have entered my mind had this lecture not come up.

I wrote and lectured quite a bit on various aspects of governance, regulation, and the bureaucratic phenomenon. "Bureaucrats and Reformers: A Remediable Dissonance?" is probably the piece of that genre I most enjoyed composing and presenting. The subject was suggested by the context. It was the Alan B. Plaunt Lecture at Carleton University in 1983. Plaunt had been the activist who, with Graham Spry, created the Canadian Broadcasting League which, under their leadership, brought about the creation of the CBC. Each of them was both a dreamer and a doer and their work on behalf of public broadcasting epitomized the need for vision and good management in public affairs. Both are badly needed in Ottawa and so this was a useful theme for a lecture there.

Being asked to give lectures or contribute papers to a conference now and then led me to look at new questions and societal challenges. A few years ago, for instance, the invitation to deliver the Hagey lecture at the University of Waterloo provoked me to seize on a topic to which I had never before given sustained thought. The result was a paper, "The Curse and Potential of Greed: Social and Political Issues Arising from Acquisitiveness." Its preparation drew me into heretofore unknown and unexamined philosophical and even theological territory. Weighing the positive and negative aspects of acquisitiveness also raised the question of whether universities ought to instill in their students a concern for these kinds of ethical questions. This was, after all, a public lecture at one of our better universities. To my surprise, this theme dominated the strongly sympathetic post-lecture question period which lasted over an hour. Subsequent efforts, made with some kindred spirits, to incite Queen's to assume some responsibility in this area, regrettably fizzled.

PART THREE: A BIG SHORTCOMING

It may strike you ludicrous that I should attempt to subject my research to critical review; others are much better placed to do so, were they so inclined. I don't see them lining up, however, which is probably just as well. But having, in the preparation of this tome, taken the pains to examine the profuse array of books and articles gathering dust on the aforementioned Meiseliana shelves, I confess a major weakness has been troubling me, for which I have sought an explanation. It says something about the delicacy of my political science colleagues that not one of them has ever whispered a word to me about it, although many must have been all too aware of it.

It is the absence of a major book arising from my massive national surveys. The point to note at the starting line is that I have never run a mile, let alone the marathon and have always been, academically speaking, a hundred yard man. I wrote a book on the 1957 election, arising from my thesis; my *Working Papers* which debuted with 220 pages in its first edition, have fattened to 290 in its last version. And there are, of course, many short monographs, and edited volumes, as well as lots of articles and contributions to various volumes on particular elections. But there is no sign of a definitive volume uttering the final word on any one election or on Canadian elections generally. This is the tragic flaw in my *oeuvre*.

How did it happen? The roots are likely in my character and the deepest recesses of my mind, concealed from view, happily even to myself. But a few explanations seem plausible. No single cause quite suffices to account for my copious but somewhat capricious research inventory. Superficially, the attributes confessed to at the opening of the Panorama section above are a factor: my affinity to hummingbirds and butterflies; the ITSNO affliction diagnosed by Hodgetts; and a bit of wanderlust have all played a part. But this yen to travel applied not only to a variety of *places* but also to a variety of *ideas*. A seemingly inexhaustible number of fields, problems and conundrums — or is it conundra? — engaged my attention and called for investigation.

One result was that, although I was interested enough in the subjects I was probing at any given time, there were always other puzzles in the background and at the margins, threatening to invade the currently central field of battle. Kindly unscramble the metaphor. My interest in the dominant topic to be examined at any given time, the study of elections, for instance, was not allowed to flag, but it was not pursued at the exclusion of everything else. I never came even near being *obsessed* by what I was doing and so was susceptible to distraction and to straying from the straight and narrow path leading to two covers of a fat book. Shorter pieces, sometimes consisting of a research report addressing some current problem, tended to dominate the agenda rather than the crafting of a single, definitive tome arising from many years of unrelentingly single-minded research and thought. One of the consequences of this pattern may be that my work makes a stronger claim to breadth than it does to depth and that in some respects I occasionally strayed from the uncompromisingly academic course to one approaching advocacy and even journalism.

One of the reasons for veering towards topicality, although by no means the only one, was that the national unity file was of much more than academic interest. Not everyone agreed, but I was convinced, even before my B & B immersion, that the country was in great peril of falling apart, a possibility I abhorred. This area of research came close to eliciting the passion not quite present elsewhere, and absorbed my intellectual as well as emotional being. Studies, investigations and analyses here were of more than bookish appeal, and led me to enter the area of policy advice and personal recommendation. No wonder, then, that the scholarly dimension was leavened by the wish to affect practical outcomes — a goal more readily achieved, in my situation, by making shortish contributions to committees, conferences and public gatherings than by writing books.

Another idiosyncrasy is relevant. I adored doing research. Few things in the academy offered as much satisfaction as formulating what, during my grad years, we rather mockingly called "researchable propositions," and then engaging in the thrilling process of undertaking all the diverse tasks required to test some of them. Working alone and with others on a project provided immense intellectual satisfaction and even social rewards arising from team work. This was quite a bonus for a gregarious type. I have also always loved writing and took pains to do so as clearly and pleasantly as I could. This made me a slow writer. Deadlines set by journal or book editors, conference conveners or lecture gigs were a necessary threat ensuring that I did not dawdle forever over completing a project. Though often excruciating, they also added a rather pleasant sense of excitement as one raced towards the finish line. I foolishly never set a deadline for the book-length wrapping-up of our big surveys, with a predictable result.

As I leave the confessional, I must add that though a *mea culpa* is in order, it would be unreasonable to go overboard in detracting from the value and scope of my work. My book on the 1957 election and the innumerable papers I published—some of which I mentioned above—made useful contributions to the understanding of various features of electoral behaviour and of the relations between voting, parties, and the democratic process in Canada. They provide a baseline for all subsequent such Canadian surveys, the data are deposited in the major archives in Canada, Europe and America, and they have been used in hundreds, if not thousands, of studies that could not have been done, had we not provided the raw material. Our efforts in this domain bore ample fruit and are still relevant. And last but by no means least, chickens do come home to roost. I was gratified to note, in 2011, that *Dynasties and Interludes*, an imaginative study of Canadian electoral history by Leduc, Pammett, McKenzie and Turcotte, which distinguishes between election results leading to enduring regimes and those which are a mere flash in the pan, is not only dedicated to the team I assembled to conduct the 1965 national study, but also draws on books and papers I published before and after the 1965 contest.

Without unbecoming false modesty, I conclude that my work on parties and elections and other probes have contributed to the understanding of Canada. I am pleased with some of my work despite being all too painfully aware of its shortcomings.

Three additional matters deserve mention. I have been itching to raise the first throughout this chapter. While almost all of my research was originated, planned and written up by me, it depended on the dedicated and sometimes heroic help from countless research assistants. Virtually all of them were students, but there were also others who were just "hired help," giving the lie to this sometimes derogatory term by the high quality of their work. More often than any reasonable person could expect, they made my cause their own, and became as identified with it as I was. Their number is far too great to be included here. But I would be remiss if I failed to mention the senior research supervisors who almost came close enough to becoming co-authors: Rick Van Loon, Patti Peppin and Dorothy Lele.

Secondly, research activities were often closely linked to teaching, because many students were involved and because the findings and problems encountered in the "laboratory" provided material informing and illustrating my lectures and seminars. Each was the complement of the other and together they made university life.

Finally, the title of this chapter suggests that my research activities grew from a library carrel to very small potatoes at the cottage industry level and, finally, to a large and complex enterprise. This is true enough, but the story does not end there. After my retirement from teaching, creating new knowledge continued unabated for a while but eventually diminished. The emphasis shifted from searching to reflecting. In the last few years, I almost ceased reporting on what was going on out there and increasingly came up with reflective essays pondering the implications of my own and of other people's findings. The piece on greed, noted earlier, is an example.

Someone asked me a while ago what I was currently researching. In an insufferably arrogant (and misleading to boot) crack, I replied, "'I beg to report,' as the good soldier Švejk (Schweik) liked to say, ironically more often than not, that I no longer do research; I now think." Like Oscar Wilde, but with only a pinch of his wit and talent, I can't resist a bon mot.

XVIII

The Third Pillar

A cademic work, as I noted, is a colossally wide and varied ant heap of activities affecting one's university, one's profession and the world beyond. I guess that close to a third of my academic and quasi-academic working time was devoted to non-teaching and non-research activities, to which I refer as the "third pillar."

"Working time" calls for elaboration. The routine was to rise at 6:00 a.m. and be at the desk no later than 7:00. All my writing was done at home in my study. For mysterious reasons, only partly related to my having become a tooth-flossing fanatic, it took me a lot less time in those days to shave and perform my ablutions. I am possibly more pristine now. Until the 1970s, when we moved to the country, I almost always came home for lunch on my trusted bike, which only took a few minutes. Bedtime was 10:00 p.m. Then I read for an hour, mostly novels, and *never* anything directly to do with work. Lights went out at 11:00 p.m. sharp.

Murie and I almost always took our time over dinner and went to a concert, play or movie when the occasion arose. Once or twice a week we visited or received friends, and there were, of course, occasional other distractions, but the rest of the day and particularly evenings were as a rule given over to work. Saturdays and Sundays were like any other day, except that we sometimes explored attractions offered by the scenic delights in and near Kingston. Tennis, playing the fiddle and birding also took their toll. A priceless benefit of academic life was that if anything worthwhile, a movie matinee for instance, came up during the day, we took it in unless there was a conflict with a class or meeting. Murie not working outside the house made this possible.

I have no idea how many hours were absorbed by work, but I exceeded the then hallowed forty-hour week by at least another half again. This was no hardship at all. In terms of enjoyment, I found little to choose from between work and entertainment. I loved both equally, with only a few exceptions like marking examinations or hearing the dreary drone of a garrulous colleague boring an interminable meeting. No sooner had the equation between work and entertainment wiggled off my fingertips, than I recalled J.A. Corry's memoirs, *My Life & Work*, to which he attached this tell-tale subtitle: *A Happy Partnership*. Amen.

More! I rarely complained about and actually liked performing many of the third pillar "chores," although I occasionally joined the chorus of groans because it was the thing to do. Participating in the work of professional associations was often challenging and time-consuming, but provided enormous fun. It presented many intriguing and important problems, ensured that one met and worked with greatly varied groups of colleagues, and offered opportunities to travel widely in Canada and throughout the world. Involvement in diverse, local, cultural organizations, offered opportunities to escape the cloistered university atmosphere and to enter the wider community.

In recalling some of the highlights of my third pillar, I start with a no-no—a cliché—the picture of a pebble dropped into a glassy pool, causing ever-widening ripples. Although a bit soggy, the allegory is very pleasing and accurate. My pebble was the Department of Economics and Political Science and its successor, the Department of Political Studies. There I was plonked into university waters and from there radiated most of my other relationships. I noted in an earlier chapter that the atmosphere was exceptionally collegial; my better-established colleagues greatly facilitated Murie's and my fitting into Queen's and into Kingston, as well as my immersion in the professional milieu outside Queen's.

The entire administration of the university and faculties was handled by academics who gave some of their time to running the ship. There was only one dean per faculty, one vice-principal, no assistant or associate this or that. So-called professional administrators were not even heard of, nor any specialists in human behaviour or misbehaviour, who now seem to outnumber teaching faculty. The one exception was "the Padre," Marshall Laverty, a United Church minister whose original role was to assist veterans but who, for many students, became an all around crisis manager and helper. No one dreamt of skipping gatherings of one's Faculty or of committees. The place was so small that we came to know almost all our colleagues. Since I taught a politics course in the Engineering Faculty I knew most of its profs, and being friends with the Browns led to our meeting many of Malcolm's colleagues in medicine.

In the absence of the overwhelming contingent of non-professorial types now dominating university life, academics performed administrative duties, and saw students on non-academic matters. And once universities started to expand, there was the colossal task of debating and deciding on the creation of new, needed structures like graduate schools, new programs and research institutes. These third pillar areas took up a lot of time, but also established wide-ranging associations and friendships, cutting across disciplines and contributing to the sense of social cohesion which characterized the university community.

I was profoundly concerned about everything affecting our department and took it for granted that time had to be allocated to nursing it along. We all did. Attending meetings and seminars; performing little, large and huge administrative chores; participating in ongoing discussions about policy and administrative decisions; identifying and hiring new colleagues; attending outside meetings whose outcomes might affect us; facilitating and organizing university-wide events like special lectures and concerts—all these tasks were deemed legitimate claimants on our time. At the beginning, the number of people involved was small, enabling many decisions to be made informally, almost unwittingly, at coffee breaks. As the programs offered and our numbers and student enrolment grew, committees addressing various aspects of the undergraduate and graduate programs emerged and assumed the tasks previously handled by the whole group. My involvement in all these things diminished gradually as the years rolled by and, when I returned from the CRTC in 1985, the department had ceased being the centre of the universe.

During four years in the 1960s, however, I devoted virtually my whole being to Political Studies, because I was its head. When Alec Corry—our *paterfamilias* within the joint politics-economics household—ascended to the principalship, he was replaced by Ted Hodgetts, the natural and most eminently suitable successor. It was he who presided over our gang—the politics group—moving out. He became the first head of the autonomous Department of Political Studies until he left in the mid-1960s for the U of T, his alma mater. I succeeded him.

Despite being small, compared to U of T, McGill, UBC or the University of Montreal, the Queen's Economics and Politics Department acquired an extremely high reputation, and not only because its members had been so instrumental in developing a competent national public service. The politics group shared in the lustre. With Corry and Hodgetts teaching there, Crawford's Institute of Local Government, Don Smiley for a while and then Ron Watts, Hugh Thorburn, Ned Franks, George Perlin, Khalid Sayeed, Jack Grove, Jayant Lele, Stewart Fyfe and my own work, we too showed muscle. In Jock Gunn, we recruited a peerless scholar whose extensive command of the literature and commitment to a lofty ideal of a university added a significant dimension to what we had to offer. Later, new recruits in several sub-disciplines generated further strength. My task as head of the still young department was greatly eased by its reputation which facilitated attracting able staff, despite new universities springing up like mushrooms after rain, and fiercely competing for faculty.

When I assumed the headship there was, relatively speaking, quite a bit of money available for hiring, but Ph.D.s in political science were exceedingly scarce and those graduating from Canadian universities could hardly be counted on the fingers of a ski mitt. This led to a massive influx of Americans which, in many programs, badly skewed what was being offered students and also what and how social problems were studied by scholars. Departments in some new institutions were overwhelmingly American.

We managed to avoid this situation at Queen's, and for many years we were the most un-American politics department in Ontario. The major reason was that I, and those who followed me in the chair, went out of our way to find Canadian recruits, whenever possible. We avoided becoming stultifyingly parochial and insular by attracting a wide selection of British, other European, Asian and Middle East nationals, and even adopted some Americans. But the overall flavour remained distinctly Canadian.

Our Kingston location helped, but also posed obstacles. Many young potential colleagues were leery of a small town and preferred the larger cities like Toronto, Montreal or Vancouver. In one instance, a very promising Canadian, finishing his Ph.D. at Yale, turned us down after lengthy deliberation for a slightly astonishing reason. He hoped to meet the right girl, and knowing that he was exceedingly bright, and wishing to hook a similarly cerebrally endowed damsel, feared that a small burgh like Kingston would be able to produce only the tiniest cohort of eligibles. He went to Toronto where he found a suitable bride; they eventually divorced.

In seeking to lure potential colleagues, I casually paraded a number of our strong points, and pounced when one or another of them aroused a flicker of interest. I used, as bait, the quality of our students, the congenial, strong department, the pleasant campus, the scenic appeal of Kingston, and the easy lifestyle there, our situation more or less midpoint between Toronto, Montreal, Ottawa and the Syracuse airport, and, as modestly as I could, our reputation. Conditions for sailing are ideal in Kingston, a point I never missed noting whenever my quarry seemed to possess sea legs.

Whenever possible, I took every job seeker we liked on an evening car spin around Kingston, ending at Fort Henry. It was built during the war of 1812 on a high point overlooking the St. Lawrence and the Kingston Harbour. This was, remember, in the days before Kingston's enlightened city fathers permitted its waterfront to be ravaged by hotels, condos and apartment buildings obstructing the downtown's view of the water. The skyline was still unspoilt and looked very much the way it did in the nineteenth century. The courtyard in front of the fort offered a stunning view. Immediately below were the magnificent buildings of the Royal Military College, surrounded by water shimmering in the moonlight (when available) and, farther away, the majestic Kingston City Hall with the highly pleasing edifices nearby. Taking in this imposing view, I sighed and said, slightly exaggerating my central European accent, "This reminds me of Budapest." It so happened that I had never been to the Hungarian capital at this point, and it was really *pictures* of Budapest I knew. Upon subsequently visiting the city, I was pleased to observe that my parallel was only a slight distortion.

Since there were many more jobs going than high-class Canadian candidates, it was necessary to resort to certain other stratagems. Two proved fairly successful. I wrote to the heads of the best American and British departments favoured by Canadian doctoral candidates, asking them to bring our openings to the attention of their Canadian graduate students. And I also figured that, since there was still, at many places, a certain reluctance to hire women, we should make a special effort to ensnare bright distaff candidates.

I would like to be able to say that I was so prescient as to foresee the impending wave of women's studies but, alas, am compelled to admit that my efforts to enlarge the pool of possible recruits was entirely opportunistic. I had absolutely no preference for either male or female colleagues, assuming that both groups included some top material, but thought that since elsewhere there was then still a lower demand for women, we might catch some gems among them which others were too blinkered to accept. At one point we had engaged two thirds of all Egyptian women in the world with a Ph.D. in Political Science, Nazli Choucri and Nadia Khalaf. There were only three altogether! Nazli eventually pursued a distinguished career at MIT and Nadia, a fine teacher, remained with us until she retired.

Those familiar with current universities will find it difficult to visualize our modus operandi during the formative years of our departments and for some time after. The hiring routine was still partly dominated by the old boys' network. When openings occurred, the principal means of finding people was to consult one's colleagues at other universities, although advertisements were beginning to be used. There were no special committees established to vet candidates. Each applicant, deemed creditable by the head, was discussed by the whole department; the two or three most promising candidates were invited to come to visit and present a paper at a departmental seminar. The department subsequently discussed the applicants. Only the departmental faculty was involved—no student or special interest representatives, no human rights, equity, or diversity watchdogs. No vote was taken after the full, and usually lengthy departmental discussion. The head was trusted to read the group's collective mind and to recommend to the dean whatever decision he considered appropriate. I need hardly add that there was no collective agreement with a union to consider.

A principal reason for the growing complexity and specialization within universities in the 1960s was their growth. As more and more students arrived, greater financial dependence on the provincial government required that detailed records be kept and an avalanche of forms called for completion. At the same time, academic disciplines themselves became more elaborate and sophisticated. Among the results was that paperwork underpinning the academic game grew exponentially. When I became Head of Politics, the administrative burden in the departments was much heavier than in the Corry and Hodgetts days, obliging the chair to devote a great deal of time to bureaucratic pursuits. They could have been carried out at least as well, if not better, by someone without years of specialized academic training, and with lower salary expectations. All this was floating in the mind in a rather ill-digested manner, when I received a phone call from Flora MacDonald. You remember her as the super-efficient secretary of Allister Grosart at PC headquarters, who had been most helpful in providing documentation I needed for my research. Her abilities led to her receiving successive promotions and assuming ever more responsible posts. But, under Mr. Diefenbaker's leadership, divisions developed in the party which put her at odds with the Chief.

Her phone call announced that she was going to be fired, and did I recall a conversation we had a year or so previously? I had suggested that there was a dearth of people with her skills in the universities and that, should she ever need a job, why not try Queen's? Had I really meant it? I assured her that I did but that I was hardly in a position to do anything about it just like that. But leave it with me. I went to see Principal Corry and suggested that we try an experiment. I was kept away from things I should have been doing by the growing administrative work, and why not engage Flora as a departmental administrator? Leave it with me. The upshot was that she came to Queen's in 1966 as the administrative officer of the Department of Political Studies and stayed until 1972 when she contested the local parliamentary seat and became the second MacDonald to sit for Kingston. Sir John A. was the first.

She set up an efficient administrative and financial structure in the department, became a tutor in a Canadian politics course and — with great élan — looked after existing and new faculty and graduate students. She found them housing, met them at the train upon arrival and succeeded in integrating them into our family. A mother or sister confessor to students, particularly post grads, she contributed much to our cohesion and harmony. Her previous office experience and outgoing personality ensured that our secretarial team was among the best and happiest in the faculty.

Flora was single, a workaholic who seemingly needed very little sleep, and totally committed to her job. She was on call night and day, seven days a week. But she was anything but a drudge. Here's one example of the imaginative manner in which she enriched us: it is 1967, the year of Canada's sensational Expo in Montreal. Her friends, Egan and Gretta Chambers — distinguished political, academic and intellectual players on the Montreal scene — have a fine large house in Westmount which they usually abandon in summer while they live in the country. Flora persuades them that with so many people looking for accommodation in Montreal, it is too bad to leave their house stand empty. Why not rent it to the Queen's Politics Department which will make rooms in it available to departmental and other local Expo-goers so they can have a reasonably priced place to stay? She invented the whole operation, ran it, did not lose any money, and ensured that her "tenants" left the place in good condition. Countless Kingstonians, including Murie and me, found their enjoyment of Expo greatly enhanced by the opportunity to put down at so lovely a home. We also enjoyed dipping into the Chambers' many books.

Some time after she arrived in Kingston, the folks at Ma Bell called her to inquire whether something was wrong with their billing mechanisms, for the long distance charges she was accumulating on her home phone were astronomical. Not at all, she assured them, she had done a good deal of phoning. "A good deal" was the understatement of the century and the explanation simple. Dissatisfaction with Mr. Diefenbaker's leadership had gained momentum and a campaign was under way to replace him with Mr. Stanfield. Flora, working closely with Dalton Camp, was in the thick of the palace revolution. She spent hours every night talking to party members throughout the country, mobilizing the "Dump Dief" vote at the upcoming leadership review. The rebels, as the history books show, were successful. The demands on her time, however, were such that even she—the indestructible dynamo—showed signs of extreme fatigue.

Having Flora nearby, and working with her closely, cemented our friendship which endures to this day.

Flora was not the only import to Queen's for whom I bear some responsibility. David Easton was another. A Canadian, he did his graduate work at Harvard, where he later taught before becoming one of the stars of Chicago's political science department. He ranked among the top four or five most outstanding and influential political scientists in the English-speaking world. Michael Oliver, the research director of the B & B Commission brought him to Ottawa as a special advisor. He participated extensively in the research of the commission, as I did, and we became friends. Although he was by this time thoroughly immersed in the United States, he had not relinquished all his links with Canada and regularly summered at a place he had in Muskoka. Keen as ever to retrieve expat scholars, I broached the possibility of his coming to Queen's with David and, subsequently, with John Deutsch, the principal. I argued that Easton would add substantially to the intellectual resources of the department and that his presence would signal to potential graduate students and academic recruits that Queen's politics department was aiming for the top. Deutsch was a bold and imaginative sort and liked the idea.

About this time, Queen's received a lavish bequest enabling it to create two well-endowed chairs, one in economics, the other in political science. After complex and tricky negotiations, Easton came to Kingston as the first Sir Edward Peacock Professor of Political Science.

The arrangement was not a marriage made in heaven. It was understood, when Dave arrived, that he would be given a certain time in which to disengage himself from his Chicago commitments, but that he would ultimately relinquish his ties there to assume full membership at Queen's. He found this difficult, however, and never quite felt at home. He was with us from 1971 to 1980, when he returned to Chicago. If you Google him, you'll be hard pressed to find any reference to Queen's. The experiment was, nevertheless, worth making. At a critical time, we sent a signal to the world about the level of work we were aspiring to, and while he was with us he did, of course, enrich the colleagues' and graduate students' lives.

Among the non-routine projects adding zest to the life of the department, like organizing an occasional conference or arranging and hosting visiting scholars, one development made an important contribution to Canada's self-knowledge and turned into one of my most enjoyable Queen's memories. It was the Skelton-Clark Fellowship, an unsung jewel which has contributed much to the university's strength in public affairs. The fellowship, in its heyday, brought some extraordinary Canadian scholars and political and administrative practitioners into our midst, usually for a year. In the beginning, it was *de rigeur* for each fellow to work on a book — a high requirement which has declined with the purchasing power of the fund.

Aside from my friend Jim Eayrs, who came to work on his defence policy studies, the most enjoyable and stimulating early holder of the honour, from my point of view, was Senator C.G. (Chubby) Power. A remarkably engaging person, he was one of the best-liked Quebec politicians. Fred Gibson (History) and I had interviewed him for our researches and had been impressed by his extensive knowledge, deep insight and openness. When the occasion arose, we succeeded in persuading both the university and Power that he'd make a fine Skelton-Clark Fellow; the rest is history or, more precisely, *A Party Politician: the Memoirs of Chubby Power*.

A charming, courtly and complex man, he was wise, impish and unusually frank when discussing party doings. The son of a Quebec anglophone, Irish Canadian, mini-lumber baron and parliamentarian, he studied law at Laval—an experience which made him into a bilingual Quebec patriot. Like his dad, he entered federal politics and—despite occasional lapses into too close and sustained an acquaintance with the bottle—managed to hold several cabinet posts in straight-laced Mackenzie King's cabinets, most famously as Minister of Defence for Air. He resigned from the King cabinet in 1944, but did not cross the floor of the House and continued to serve as one of the Liberal Party's leading Quebec organizers.

When Chubby and his wife, Rosemary, arrived at Queen's, we set them up in a rather palatial penthouse apartment atop one of the residences and established him in an office fully equipped with inviting pads of paper and a huge supply of sharply honed pencils. Since he was my baby, so to speak, I visited him frequently and sought to ease the metamorphosis from politician into writer. Fred and I took him by the hand and led him towards a manuscript. That proved quite a challenge. Although he was an amazing mine of information and insight when talking, he dried up when left alone. So I ordered a fancy recording device and left him to it. But this, too, was too sterile a set-up, even after Fred and I gave him a list of topics and questions we suggested he might tackle. Heroic action was called for and implemented when we resolved to take turns sitting with him in his office, ply him with questions and record every word

he uttered in response. Fred, Ted Hodgetts and I henceforth became his foils and elicited from him hundreds of pages of text. The enormous mass of material needed to be subdued, shortened and shaped into a book. We persuaded Norman Ward at the University of Saskatchewan, one of Canada's leading experts on Parlia-ment, and a celebrated humorist (*Mice in the Beer*), to trim and edit the cornucopia, which he did admirably. The complete transcript is in the Queen's Archives. Some time after the book came out, the *Canadian*

Chubby at his beloved Saint-Pacôme.

Encyclopedia described the memoir as "one of the best written by a Canadian politician."

My friendship with Chubby grew out of our shared interest in Canadian politics and my close involvement with the memoirs, but was also nourished by my curiosity about Quebec. On one occasion, he invited me to join him on a visit to his friend, Jules Brillant, an entrepreneur and philanthropist who was a major player in the economy of the lower St. Lawrence region. He was also a generous and mighty supporter of educational institutions and of the Liberal Party. We were met by his driver in Rimouski and taken to a colossal estate containing numerous large lakes, streams and ample hunting areas. The drive from the gate to the "lodge" seemed to take longer than traversing Prince Edward Island. The lodge was nothing of the sort, but a surprisingly small and simple cottage, clearly the hideaway of someone who had no need to impress by ostentation. Not a word of English was spoken during our entire visit, but our conversation centred on Quebec's culture and interests, and the obstacles these encountered in the face of Anglo-Canadian haughtiness and prejudice. Jules and Chubby were strong federalists; the idea of Quebec's separation would have been utterly unthinkable to them. But there was a sense of grievance smouldering in Jules, picked up in strongly felt sympathetic vibrations by Chubby.

One incident recalled by Jules truly shocked me. When it became known that Price Brothers, one of Quebec's major lumber and paper concerns, was looking for a new owner, he called on the bank handling the sale to express his interest, only to be told not to bother, for they would never sell to a francophone!

When talking about "us" and "them"—francophones and anglophones—Chubby surprised me by including himself among "nous autres," i.e., "us," for I had always thought of him as an Anglo-Canadian, which is really what he was. Nevertheless, he had resigned from the King cabinet, out of solidarity with other Quebec ministers, over the prime minister's reneging on a promise not to introduce conscription for overseas service.

Murie and I visited the Powers a couple of times in their summer home at Saint-Pacôme on the South shore of the St. Lawrence. Their place was a miniature and intimate version of the old Seigneury Club at Montebello east of Ottawa. The centrepiece was a living and dining space under an imposing cathedral ceiling, with a balcony leading to the bedrooms circling it. As at Chateau Montebello, everything was made of wood. A favourite destination from the house was a bench affording a dramatic view of the rapidly descending land down to a gorge flanking the Ouelle, the local stream. Murie made a sketch of this "picture book scene" and later put it to an inspired use. The Powers loved jigsaw puzzles and always had one going on a large table under the dome of the living area. When we returned to Kingston from one of our visits, Murie made a painting from her sketch and pasted it on plywood. Then Ted Hodgetts, who owned a jig saw, cut it all up into a jigsaw puzzle which we dispatched to the Powers with our thank-you note. It delighted them.

Chubby's presence on the campus was a huge success; the students loved him, and found in him a generous and knowledgeable source of otherwise unattainable lore about Canadian politics. And those of us who worked with him could not have wished for a more co-operative, convivial and dedicated colleague. He did, however, cause one disappointment. Never able to resist the lure of a pun, I suggested that he entitle his book *Power Politics*. His normally ebullient sense of humour notwithstanding, he turned me down flat. So did Norm Ward, the part-time humorist. Pity.

An important part of one's university service was to sit on various committees. These dealt with every conceivable and inconceivable aspect of life, and some were a bit of a pain. One quite minor incident associated with these sessions sticks in the mind because it recalls the generous spirit of a senior colleague. I served on three or four committees chaired by the austere and formidable Rollo Earl, Dean of the Faculty of Arts and Science. At that very time, after being rather heavily addicted to the filthy weed ever since the permissive Pickering days, I finally shook the habit.

For some bizarre reason, I seemed to take a scunner to Dean Earl while he chaired our sessions and was, quite uncharacteristically, aggressive in persistently opposing his views. I was obviously undergoing some sort of momentary personality change causing me to focus my withdrawal symptoms to focus on the hapless dean. I was thoroughly ashamed of myself and felt the need to explain my misbehaviour. After one of the meetings I stayed on and apologized. Dr. Earl, whom I always found a dry stick, to my surprise congratulated me on my resolve to kick the habit, and assured me that so long as I did not fall by the wayside, he did not mind how I treated him. He even smiled a little when he offered his absolution. A very small thing, but to me it was the sign of dealing with a big man.

Reviewing the faculty- and university-wide committees on which I served over the years and the tasks I undertook shows the extent to which, like the profusely sprawling roots of sumac, I infiltrated every nook and cranny of the whole garden.

Chores lying outside my department ranged from aspects of the residences, campus planning and the construction of new buildings, and emerging research institutes or centres, to cultural activities like CFRC, the campus radio station, selection of a new head of drama or the director of the gallery, the Richardson Fund supporting cultural and other arts activities, campus lecture series and debates. And there were numerous one shot events like eating at High Table in one of the residences or sitting in on "French" dinners, where guests practiced Canada's other official language. Some occasions were unique but very labour and time intensive, like the farewell celebration for retiring Principal Mackintosh. I was a member of the committee chaired by John Orr, a bacteriologist and superb organizer of festive occasions. When Alec Corry's term as principal came to the end, I chaired the committee overseeing his Grant Hall farewell. It went off beautifully, largely because I enlisted the aid of Stan Swain, the visiting English head of the Agnes Etherington Gallery. His imagination, energy, resourcefulness and know-how about audio visual aids made this the party of the year.

Then there were the campus financial campaigns. They were quite infrequent and modest in the beginning but gained a full head of steam towards the end. I confess that on the first round I declined chipping in because I thought that we drones were already doing more than enough for the university. I later saw the error of my ways and became strongly involved. When the very first approach was made, however, I delivered myself of a quip of which I was inordinately proud and which very quickly made the rounds of the campus. "Why," says I, "this is feeding the hand that bites you." Imagine my surprise when, many years later, I discovered the same wisecrack attributed to Henry Fairlie, the British essayist who, in the middle 1950s, used it in the *Spectator*. I don't know who was there first. After my retirement, I was asked to co-chair, with Joyce Zakos, the part of the Fund Raising Campaign beamed at retired staff and faculty. This later evolved into key roles for the two of us in the soon-to-be-formed Retirees Association of Queen's.

A number of responsibilities arose from other than academic matters. Some dealt with cultural issues and others even approximated social work, like the Community Welfare Council, the

World University Service, and our efforts to help refugees fleeing Czechoslovakia after the 1968 Russian takeover. At various times I served on the boards of such organizations as Theatre 5, the Kingston Symphony, the Kingston Art Collection Society and Grand Theatre Board.

For many months in the early 1960s, the restoration of the Grand Theatre claimed a colossal amount of time. It was built about a hundred years earlier as an opera house and legitimate theatre. In 1898 it burned down and was rebuilt by none other than Ambrose Small, the man whose surname, you may recall, many years later popped into my mind from nowhere when I invented a fictitious person for a list to be identified by respondents in an opinion survey. Like many of its sisters, the Grand Theatre was eventually converted into a Famous Players movie house. Then, in 1961 it was bought by a syndicate planning to tear it down to make room for a parking lot. A group of citizens under the leadership of Jim McDonald, a professor of Spanish, resolved to save it and return it to its original purpose.

The salvage operation turned into a monumental effort, engaging a great many of the cultural community — our crowd. The city fathers, a pretty philistine lot for the most part, and almost certainly in some cases in the pockets of developers, were at first opposed; they had to be converted to the idea that Kingston needed a publicly owned community theatre. Money had to be raised, architectural drawings and building estimates procured, public opinion mobilized and channelled, and the ears of influential citizens bent. Virtually all our friends were on side, as were some non-university folks whom we had not met previously. Michael Davies, the publisher of the *Kingston Whig-Standard*, became an indispensable and decisive champion of the cause. He and his wife Elaine subsequently turned into most imaginative and generous supporters of the arts in Kingston, literally changing its cultural face.

Even as we worked to save the theatre, a huge mobile wrecking device was dispatched from Toronto to destroy it. The Grand narrowly escaped the machine's massive, lethal ball when, at the very last minute, City Council narrowly voted to buy the building and make it into a municipal theatre.

I do not recall occupying any formal position in the campaign, but was involved not merely up to my neck, but well above my balding pate. Jim McDonald and I talked on the phone nightly to review progress and plan ploys, and spent a lot of time inciting others. Had he not been so deeply involved, the Grand would have been demolished.

When we returned to Kingston in the early '50s, we acquired Murie's family upright Heintzman piano, which she played, although not as often as both of us would have liked. I resumed my acquaintance with the violin, which had lapsed after we left Haiti. On the advice of Dr. Tracy, the musically all-knowing head of the Classics department, I contacted a local violin teacher, Jim Rini. He had originally moved from Italy to Kingston to work as a silent film accompanist in one of the local cinemas. Jim welcomed me with open arms (when he was not fiddling away) and did his very best to tune and fine hone the rusty instrument I had become. My shaky skill notwithstanding (I did not practice nearly enough and, alas, lacked talent), he invited me to join him in the Kingston Symphony Orchestra, where he occupied the first desk in the second violin section. I sat with him and he did his utmost to carry me along. The orchestra itself was amateurish, but struggled along under the baton of Edouard Bartlett and gave, from time to time, a reasonably tolerable concert.

Despite my shortcomings, playing in the orchestra was of tremendous importance. I hope that my recollections so far portrayed a reasonably relaxed and easy-going chap, but when engaged in an enterprise of moment, I became quite intent and focused on what I was about. When I started teaching, the preparation and giving of lectures and my involvement in university affairs absorbed just about every nanogram of my being; it was difficult to take my mind off them. The only escape was the orchestra. There, reading the music, counting time and following the conductor wiped everything else off the table or, more precisely, the music stand. Music was an escape into another world.

Being part of an orchestra also exposed me to the culture of an "in group" with its own rules and priorities, which excluded outsiders. The only other time I experienced a similar sense of intimacy and belonging was when, much later, I stayed overnight in a mountain hut in the Alps, and listened, over free-flowing schnapps, to all the talk about equipment, trails, guides, maps and, above all, weather, which are so critical to hikers and mountaineers. Many avocational groups bestow a strong sense of belonging on their members and possess similar group-defining traits, but the high level of concentration and co-operation required of an orchestra member exclude everything extraneous, in the end, even people outside one's own boat.

When I went on sabbatical leave in 1958, I withdrew from the orchestra, knowing full well that I would eventually be fired, because the Kingston Symphony was being spruced up into a high-class ensemble under Alexander Brott.

Another involvement in the local music scene fell more directly into my third pillar rubric. It was the University Concert series which, although beamed at the whole community, was strictly a Queen's enterprise. It brought artists to the campus for concerts in Grant Hall.

Graham George, the university's resident musician, should have provided the leadership required to make a success of the series, but this was not his thing. He was an impressively intelligent man and a marvellous musician as well as a fine writer, but an organizer he was not. He was notorious for convening choral or orchestral rehearsals but failing to turn up, or turning up on time, but arriving without the music or other accoutrements required for the job at hand. Under his leadership, the concerts committee was losing money; and, worse, by the time I hove on the scene, only about two hundred people attended and almost no students.

The committee responsible considered discontinuing the concerts. My friend, Malcolm Brown, one of its members, however, proposed that one more effort be made to restore them to their former glory. He thought that I might be able to do the trick and proposed that I be asked to chair a rejuvenated concerts committee. Victim of Hodgetts's ITSNO (Inability To Say No), I agreed and added a new string to my bow.

As usual, and as elsewhere, there was an amazingly dedicated and capable toiler behind the committee's work, who not only assembled the necessary material for its decisions but also put most of these decisions into action. She was Miss Healy, the secretary of the university's then pivotal Extension Department. Kay's work had been impeccable; the recent failure of the program lay elsewhere. She supplied us with the names offered by the various concert agencies and provided the necessary continuity between the old and new team. We added a student co-chair, Edo ten Boek, because we thought that student involvement and concert attendance were preconditions of a turnaround. Ken Russell, a British-born professor of chemistry, was my sidekick on the committee. His wife Esther and Murie also added depth when it came to looking after our performers. On one occasion, Esther saved our bacon when Glenn Gould's piano arrived from Toronto too late to acclimatize itself to the Grant Hall temperature. Gould, with remarkable equanimity, used Esther's hair dryer to hasten the critical adjustment. The committee worked effectively and achieved the unthinkable: our first season, and those that followed, were sold out, all 1,220 seats of them! Our success resulted from teamwork, but some of my friends nevertheless tweaked my non-existent beard by calling me Sol Hurok — the name of the then leading American concert impresario.

Sheer luck had a lot to do with our triumph. During our first two seasons, in 1966–67 and 1967–68 we managed to bring, among others, Lois Marshall, Glenn Gould, the Buffalo Philharmonic conducted by Josef Krips, the Duo di Roma, the Hart House Glee Club under Boyd Neel, and the Detroit Symphony under Paul Paray. Kingston's location enabled us to attract some of these "acts" when they could fit us in on a "free" night between performances in Toronto, Ottawa or Montreal.

Dame Fortune did not just smile at us, but offered a roaring laugh when we snagged Glenn Gould. He was an up-and-coming virtuoso when we approached Columbia Artists management about engaging him, but nothing like the superstar he became later. His fee was $ 1,500 which was a steep price but small potatoes in relation to what occurred soon after. Between our signing the contract, and the opening of our season, he gave his celebrated New York performance of Bach's Goldberg Variations which propelled his fame (and fee) into the stratosphere. Impressively, despite his lofty status, he was unassuming, friendly, most approachable and generous, particularly with students. His performance was a smash hit, including the eccentric mannerisms — sitting on a very low stool, softly muttering an accompaniment and wearing those decapitated gloves.

The practice of consulting knowledgeable experts, first employed when embarking on new research, also helped us bring rare gems to Grant Hall. When dealing with the Toronto Symphony Orchestra, I became friendly with its manager, Ezra Schabbas. He was most helpful in establishing our contacts with some artists and in opening otherwise forbiddingly closed doors.

A magnificent interlude of my Sol Hurok days occurred in 1962, at the opening of the Agnes Etherington Art Centre, one of many benefactions the Richardson family of Winnipeg and Kingston bestowed on Queen's. We decided to mark its formal opening with a major musical event. Ken Russell and I managed to bring the New

York Pro Musica to Queen's, not just for one concert but for a festival of three. They were one of the earliest modern ensembles specializing in Baroque and Renaissance music performed on original instruments, and they were outstanding.

Mention of the Richardson family irresistibly imposes a short detour, quite unrelated to the price of eggs and my Hurok career. Dorothy Richardson of the Kingston branch, by then a widow, visited a niece's home and helped her set the table prior to the arrival of dinner guests. The niece fussed irritatingly over matching the guests' interests and the conventional alternation between men and women, until Dorothy's patience wore out. Drawing herself up to her full height, she exclaimed, "They come to dine, not to mate!"

A more academic experience than the concerts was also highly satisfying, but disappointing. Four idealists tried to devise a super undergraduate course destined for really good students. Very elitist! The dreamers consisted of Ted Hodgetts (politics), Syd Wise (history), Ron Watts (philosophy and politics) and JM. They went to a retreat one weekend to the Queen's Biological Station on Lake Opinicon, north of Kingston to break down some of the barriers hampering the social sciences, and to map how students can bridge academic work and the cruel world out there. Our dream program would work like this: all students in the program would be supported by fellowships and would commit each of three full calendar years to the program, leading to an honours degree embracing our three disciplines; during summers they would work in government or private organizations engaged in areas relevant to their courses, and the summer experience would dovetail with their academic program.

We were exhilarated by our plans, confident that we broke new ground both in inter-disciplinary co-operation and in post-secondary pedagogy. When we sought to persuade the powers that be and our colleagues that our program was well worth pursuing, at least on an experimental basis, we met conventional minds and feet of clay. All of us, except perhaps Ted, were relatively young and fairly low on the academic ladder but were not fly-by-nights. Our quartet included two distinguished future university heads (Watts at Queen's and Hodgetts at Victoria University in Toronto), and Syd Wise, who rose to become Dean of Graduate Studies and Research at Carleton. I was the only academic pleb who never got beyond being head of a department. Subsequently, programs echoing our dream were successfully employed at, among other places King's in Halifax and Waterloo University. We were merely ahead of our time.

In addition to matters cultural and utopian, myriad professional chores competed for my time. One was the writing of letters of reference for students in search of berths in graduate schools or fellowships, and for colleagues applying for grants, being considered for promotion or tenure, or meriting a prize or award. Even more time consuming was evaluating research proposals and manuscripts for journal editors or publishers, assessing academic programs at one's own or other schools, and also assisting potential employers in evaluating job applications. Most of these tasks usually do not amount to much but together they absorb a considerable amount of thought and time.

During the early years, most of these reviews fell into the category of one's teaching portfolio, but as I aged, became better known and inescapably donned the mantle of a senior scholar and worthy citizen, the focus changed. Nominating, suggesting, pushing, judging, promoting and applauding colleagues and others for honours, prizes, memberships and distinctions multiplied until they became quite a burden. Once I was elected—first as a fellow, then as president—to the Royal Society of Canada (RSC), and inducted into the Order of Canada, the requests for such services occupied a portion of almost every working day. Writing prefaces, forewords, and conclusions for conference proceedings and the like also whiled away the time.

A minor, but quaint, activity was to assist the Prince of Wales in drafting HRH's address when he received an honourary doctorate from Queen's in 1991. Before the royal visit, one of the Westons—of biscuit and other fame—approached Tom Symons of Trent University to help prepare the pearls of wisdom. Tom, ever meticulous and thorough, did not, à la Abraham Lincoln, scribble his thoughts hastily on an envelope and dispatch them. He established a speech industry. I forget how many people were consulted, but there were an awful lot of us. We were asked to send in ideas which were collated; this led to a meeting in Toronto at which the mass of suggestions was winnowed and channelled into the royal oration. I did not take the trouble to journey to the meeting, but submitted half a dozen mildly amusing suggestions. To my delight, when I sat in Grant Hall to participate in the ceremony, gazed at the Royal couple on the dais (and admired Princess Di's shapely legs), I found that at least one of my suggestions had wandered into the princely mouth.

It was an American magazine's claim, that one could tell Americans from Canadians by the latter's polite habit, upon completing a transaction with a bank machine, of invariably saying "Thank you."

R.K. Merton (*Social Theory and Social Structure*) famously distinguished between two types of group members, including academics: parochials and cosmopolitans. The primary focus of the first, the locals, is on their campus — teaching, students, campus issues and nearby colleagues. The second group, the cosmopolitans, is rather ecumenical, more concerned with professional, disciplinary affairs spilling beyond the confines of their own school. Most professors exhibit traits of both categories, but the balance between them varies enormously from individual to individual and varies over time. At some stage, one of the models may predominate; at a different stage, the other may fit the bill.

So far, in describing my third pillar, I have dwelt on the local side but have also espoused the other. Most of my stories have dredged up experiences occurring long ago. One of the reasons is that the emphasis in my optic underwent change, and as I progressed in my career, I became more deeply involved in professional and other issues outside Queen's. The cosmopolitan stream increasingly fitted better and at times led into waters far from the confluence of Lake Ontario and the St. Lawrence.

My professional development coincided with the emergence and maturing of the social sciences, including politics, as autonomous disciplines. This involved the creation of organizations, networks, publications, and structures enabling para-academic bodies to assist universities and research centres perform their tasks. Many of the services and institutions had to be built from scratch. This meant that members of our profession who were interested in the growth and well being of their field spent quite a bit of time nurturing this aspect of academic life, despite it often being quite far removed from teaching or research.

For many years, my principal extracurricular playing field was the Canadian Political Science Association (CPSA). This was particularly the case after we separated from the economists, who founded their own solo association. Although it helped that a joint national body existed before we were born, we had to devise a new constitution and create new structures required to service the discipline. These tasks were undertaken at a period of considerable uncertainty and upheaval. A real danger existed that francophones would create their own unilingual association and desert the CPSA.

Deep theoretical and methodological divisions (behaviouralists vs. institutionalists; Marxists vs. pluralists; "scientists" vs. "artists," "pure" scholars vs. social activists, etc.) threatened to split the discipline and its organizations into fragments, each pursuing its own ideological and sub-disciplinary objectives; the first stirrings of the feminist movement in the academy also exerted fissiparous effects.

These features bestowed on national professional organizations a super-charged atmosphere in which decisions had to be contrived with the greatest delicacy and tact. The nationalist and linguistic challenge was particularly threatening. The CPSA strove manfully (at first) and superhumanly (after the rise of feminism) to become equally hospitable to anglophones and francophones and to accommodate both pan-Canadian and Québécois interests.

As is so often the case, events were shaped by the commitment and effort of a small number of particularly concerned and dedicated individuals. There were many, but my close friendship and collaboration with Léon Dion, Jean Laponce and John Trent were indubitably also a factor in the success with which the CPSA met its formidable challenges. Incidentally, the same quartet subsequently played a creative role in the affairs of the International Political Science Association.

One concrete manifestation of the linguistic challenge the CPSA faced emerged in connection with the editing of its political science journal. In 1967, I was asked to become the founding co-editor of the CPSA's *Canadian Journal of Political Science/Revue canadienne de science politique*, generally referred to in English as the CJPS. The title "co-editor" is significant. The new association explicitly adopted both French and English as its languages, and the editorship of its journal has always been in the hands of a duo—one member primarily anglophone, the other francophone. Gérard Bergeron was my first co-editor, and Léon Dion, his successor. Both were from Laval and both, friends. We created structures and policies designed to be equally hospitable to scholars from both language communities. Because of their disparate sizes, and the greater interest of anglophones than francophones in the pan-Canadian association and journal, the anglo editorial team (JM and my side kick, Ed Black, also from Queen's) bore a disproportionately heavy load in creating a respectable organ for Canadian political science. A purely francophone journal was eventually founded by the Société Québécoise de science politique, with the CPSA's blessing. The CJPS still flourishes as a joint project of French- and English-speaking political scientists, co-existing happily in the pan-Canadian association.

Editing the CJPS took a considerable amount of time and energy. Importantly, it also afforded me access to the nerve centre of the association even before I served the inevitable years on the executive committee. Many academics assume responsibilities in their professional associations and some sit on the executive as secretary, treasurer, committee chair or president — a stint that usually involves several years, for the normal pattern is to become president-elect, then president, before sinking into a glorious sunset as past president. It would be nice to be able to say that this cycle is followed by oblivion, repose or a return to making an honest living as a teacher and researcher, but this, alas, is not always the case. There are several academic associations to which one belongs and which cry out for attention and elbow grease. So no sooner is liberation achieved from one, than the noose is tightened by another body.

I went through the whole cycle not only in the CPSA, but also in the Social Science Research Council of Canada (then not a granting body but an association of associations) and the Royal Society of Canada. In addition, often by virtue of working on these and other bodies, I assumed tasks and offices for various periods of time in the Canadian Sociological and Anthropological Association, the Canadian International Studies Council, the Canadian Institute of International Affairs, the Canadian Commission for UNESCO, the Institute for Research on Public Policy, the Canadian Communications Association, the Order of Canada Advisory Committee and innumerable others whose identities are now forgotten.

A group of totally absorbing third pillar commitments, related to what I call the national unity file, were mentioned briefly earlier. They are the Royal Commission on Bilingualism and Biculturalism, the Queen's Institute of Intergovernmental Relations, and the Ontario Advisory Committee on Confederation. In addition, I worked for shorter terms on committees pursuing special tasks established by government departments (External Affairs, Heritage, Defence, etc.) or agencies like the Canada Council, the Social Sciences and Humanities Research Council, the Canadian Conference of the Arts, and countless other worthy bodies doing good. These were in addition to projects affecting university governance and other issues, initiated by one's own or other universities. Some extra-territorial commitments are described in an upcoming chapter entitled "Foreign Affairs."

Having spewed forth even this partial list has left *me* breathless and *you* probably bored, for which please accept my apologies. I do not know how otherwise to share with you a glimpse of the profusion of extra-curricular activities and engagements making claims on a professor's time, at least one professor's time. While not every academic of my generation has quite as lavish a list, almost all of my friends could, if they were so foolish as to attempt it, come up with a similar catalogue. Some would be longer!

And sitting on committees, boards and executives is only part of the story, of course. To flesh out this assertion, I'll return to the CPSA. In addition to producing a major journal, it also regularly published a bulletin for its members, reporting on current activities and relevant public issues. It organized annual national conferences, meetings of heads of departments, sponsored some regional activities, and maintained contact with related organizations at home and abroad. Further, the CPSA created extremely valuable national and provincial legislative internship programs for young politics graduates and established various prizes and awards to recognize excellence; recipients of which had to be selected by committee. The executive kept an eye on all this, but the real slogging was undertaken by numerous members, including myself. After I completed my years on the executive, I served for a long time, for instance, as one of the CPSA members active in IPSA, so much so that IPSA became the principal focus of my associational involvement, as shown in Chapter 20.

The foregoing spillovers from the teaching and research work at Queen's were all related to membership in various organizations. Others arose as professional or benevolent engagements lying elsewhere. One that played a particularly big role in my life consisted of talks, formal lectures, broadcasts and the area of publications.

In addition to offering classes and seminars as part of my regular teaching, I also gave lectures at other universities, research centres, and conferences all over Canada and abroad. I also spoke a lot in less structured settings. Alumni groups, service clubs, organizations interested in political, social and cultural issues or international affairs are forever in search of someone to enlighten and/or entertain them, and professors are fair game. So, like many of my colleagues, I spent a fair amount of time on the road or at airports and in diverse church basements, lecture halls, club rooms and hotels. For the most part, I enjoyed these sorties a lot because one usually encountered interesting and pleasant people. A process of self-selection is at work:

those attending such events tend to be interested and hence interesting. And, like conferences in different parts of the country, lecture gigs took one to many places, large and small, to which one would not otherwise stray. Former students frequently showed up and even engineered some engagements, or parents of students, thus linking these excursions to one's own constituency and home turf.

Although some of these orations took me farther afield from the narrow academic last than was probably desirable, they contributed to the university's visibility and were, in a small way, a public service. And, not to be sneezed at, I did, as I noted, enjoy them. One of their drawbacks was that they eventually presented an inventory crisis. In many instances, my visit led, towards the end, to a small token of esteem being extended the speaker which, when added to earlier booty, posed a storage problem. What to do with all these pewter beer mugs, plaques, crested bookends and other bric-a-brac? It was far too risky to give them to some charity yard sale, for one of the donors might chance across them. I did succeed in finding a home for some items, however, but discretion prevents me from saying any more. And several of the presents, Canadian pottery or what was then called "Eskimo" sculpture, for instance, still adorn my home and continue to provide pleasure and happy memories.

A related activity, broadcasting, offered an avenue for reaching a wider public than was possible in face-to-face encounters. CBC Radio in the '50s, '60s and '70s mounted by far the most effective platform for the discussion of public issues. One of its series in this genre was a late Sunday afternoon talk on international affairs, "Weekend Review." The same speaker appeared every three weeks which ensured that there was both variety of views and continuity. This was the program on which I cut my teeth as a radio performer. I had done numerous interviews and talks on both local and university radio, and had been interviewed often by the CBC, but this was the big time, requiring a more sustained and polished performance.

My first show was not an unqualified success. The content seemed okay but the packaging was somewhat lacking. My talk was delivered in a studio of the Kingston CBC affiliate, CKWS, and relayed to Toronto from there. There was no production supervision or advice, and it showed. In writing my script, I had trouble squeezing my deep insights into the allotted fourteen minutes and, even after practically cutting my text by half, still did not quite make it fit. So, I emulated a then fashionable American airwaves pundit. His name now escapes me, but his style was unforgettable. He raced through his texts with break-tongue speed, breathlessly producing Cassandra-like oracles, as if the world was about to come to an end. One or two of my friends who heard my talk liked it, but even they did say they could hardly recognize who was speaking; everyone else kindly suggested that in future I might slow down a bit. This was decidedly the CBC's view as well, and for my next program they invited me to Toronto, where I received proper coaching and spoke at a measured pace, surrounded by a pack of technicians fiddling with the studio equipment. The chaps in the Kremlin, as the CBC's Toronto headquarters were popularly called, allowed me to do subsequent programs from Kingston.

Media organizations tend to have their favourites, on whom they call a lot. These do not stay *en vogue* forever and are eventually replaced by new sages. In part, no doubt, because my research dwelt on parties and elections and on national unity questions, I was for a time called upon quite often to respond to questions posed by radio analysts; since I also managed French, and studied Quebec politics, I was often recruited by what we called the French network, later to become Radio-Canada. There were, in fact, so relatively few anglophone "experts" willing to be interviewed in French that, for a while, I almost became the voice of English Canada on French CBC current affairs radio reports. This was fun and enabled me to keep my linguistic versatility up to scratch.

In the television era, on the evenings when ballots were counted or when leadership conventions were held, I was often summoned to Toronto, Ottawa or Montreal where I joined the panels commenting on the emerging results. Journalists and academics were always represented at these sessions, providing a welcome opportunity to get to know, and work with, some of our best press and electronic media people. Although I have been critical of the manner in which public affairs are treated in print and on airwaves — too much like horse races — I was invariably impressed by the very high quality of many popular scribes.

In 1958, I participated in *Fighting Words*, a radio — and later, television — series presided over by Nathan Cohen, the drama critic and stormy petrel of Canada's English cultural community. Cohen presented a quotation to the show's four panellists, asking that they both identify the quote and discuss the issues it raised. To describe my partners, *definitely* e*x*cluding *me*, as the intellectual *crème de la crème*, is a pale understatement. I was flummoxed by having been included but was content to count my blessings and leave it at that.

The other panellists were Hannah Arendt, political theorist and author of the classic *The Origin of Totalitarianism*; Karl Polanyi (*The Great Transformation* — a really BIG book in my life); and Irving Howe, leading American anti-totalitarian socialist and editor of *Dissent*. JM had not yet obtained a doctorate and had only a few piddling articles to his name. We failed to identify the quotation which was by George Orwell. Two little teasers were put before us for debate: "*1984* is not a rational attempt to imagine a probable future," and "In times of passion the duty of the intellectual is to remain silent because in such times one has to lie and the intellectual has no right to lie." The atmosphere was heated and the debate tense but we agreed on one point, that in *1984* Orwell's target was wider than just authoritarian regimes; even democracies were in peril.

I was, naturally, overwhelmed by the company of the giants and likely made only a slight contribution to it all. Hannah Arendt astonished me. Her body language conveyed a state of the greatest tension. I feared that she might collapse or explode. She looked, in fact, the way I felt. I think that she was shaking and wondered whether she always behaved like this when she debated knotty problems or whether something was deeply upsetting her at the time. Some of her writings do convey high tension. I was prepared to like her, having been impressed by her book on totalitarianism, but found her so forbidding that I felt somehow estranged. The other two guests — whose writings I had also admired, particularly Polanyi's *The Great Transformation* — and our host, were very smart, pleasant and exhibited no prima donna traits, as is usually the case with *truly* top people.

John Polanyi, one of Canada's most brilliant chemists (Nobel Prize, 1986) and a leading advocate of nuclear disarmament and other important causes, was in the studios after the show to spirit his uncle Karl away. This was the first time I met him and although we said little more than "Hello," I was impressed by him. He exuded quiet authority. Our next encounter was at the selection committee for the Killam Awards, for which I had applied. He (the committee?) made the right decision.

In addition to editing two hefty political science journals, one Canadian, the other international, I also served on various editorial advisory committees of journals, duties which tend to be pro forma and involve little work. A different encounter in the Guttenberg domain, however, arose from changes affecting Canada's granting agencies in the arts and social sciences.

Prior to the creation of the Canada Council in 1957, the Social Science Research Council (SSRC) — then consisting of learned societies — made small but valuable grants to graduate students, researchers and academic book publishing. The emergence of the new granting council threatened to put SSRC out of business. Its leaders believed that all eggs should not be left in one, government-dependent, basket, and that non-governmental agencies, like theirs, should survive. So they searched for new missions. One of them was to free promising, still impecunious scholars, whose economic circumstances compelled them to earn extra income, from distractions keeping them away from writing.

It was Del Clark at U of T who carried the banner here, and he liked to cite the case of a brilliant, emerging scholar (I think it was John Porter) who could not afford to have his house painted and so intended to spend the summer doing it himself, away from his book. Why not launch a program making such unscholarly diversions from the typewriter unnecessary?

The Council obtained funds, ironically from the Canada Council, to launch a new interdisciplinary book series which would help alleviate this problem and asked me to become the general editor. My series "Studies in the Structure of Power: Decision-making in Canada," published by the U of T Press, first appeared in the early '60s. I edited seven volumes representing several disciplines. They included works by young scholars which were destined to become classics: Eayrs's *In Defence of Canada*, Porter's *The Vertical Mosaic*, Hodgetts's *The Canadian Public Service, 1867–1970*, Simeon's *Federal-Provincial Diplomacy* and others. I relinquished the editorship when I went to the CRTC in 1980 and the series, by then under the auspices of the Press itself, was nicely continued by my Queen's colleague, Jack Grove.

When I chose the pillar image in this chapter's title, I used the word "third" in part as a ranking in importance. This was wrong. The professor's work as citizen, academic and, dare I use the much abused term, public intellectual? is a major feature of his or her vocation.

At the opening of my teaching chapter — "A Noble Profession" — I said that in addition to teaching, research and writing, and looking after professional affairs — the third pillar — my professorial duties also involved "occasional descents — or were they ascents? — into the larger world of Canadian public policy." One such temptation threatened to reroute my whole career and hence calls for its own chapter. Read on!

XIX

CRTC: The Human Side of Czardom

The CRTC episode began in 1979, my 56th year. In October or November, I received a call from Lowell Murray, one of Prime Minister Joe Clark's closest advisors. A few years previously, he took a break from politics and public service to enrol in a Master of Public Administration program at Queen's, where he took my Cultural Policy course. We knew one another well and I was not surprised to hear from him. But the purpose of the call knocked me off my pins. Would I come to Ottawa to head up the CRTC?

I was blissfully happy being a prof and had never given even a nanosecond of thought to abandoning academe. Nor was I at all sure that I had the skills needed for the job. So, at the end of a pleasant talk, I thanked Lowell and his colleagues for the confidence and honour they showed me and said, "No." But the threat to my idyllic status quo did not fade away. A few days later David MacDonald, the Minister of Communications, joined the fray. MacDonald was the conduit through which the Canadian Radio-Television and Telecommunications Commission (CRTC) reported to Parliament, as well as the minister most closely concerned with appointing the Commission chair. I knew him as well and greatly respected his progressive outlook. When I again failed to assent, the really heavy artillery was mounted by an old friend, Bernard Ostry, who happened to be the Deputy Minister of Communications, and hence MacDonald's right hand man.

Bernie, as he was to his friends, shifted the balance. His letter succinctly delineated the appointment's context and made a telling point: although my tenure was to be for seven years, I did not need to stay the full stretch and could return to university earlier. He also sent a hefty package containing official documents describing and defining the chairman's job. Its covering letter is a masterful effort of persuasion. The inclusion in memoirs of correspondence, press reports, theatre and concert programs and the like almost always clutters the narrative and makes eyelids droop. That is why so far I have been assiduous in avoiding them. Such heroic self-denial calls for a reward, however, and podium time is now! Here is a shortened version:

> I would be surprised if [the enclosed] material affected your decision...because it doesn't at all tell you why *you* should take this job. My purpose...is to provide what the attachments do not—a sense of how important the CRTC chairmanship is to the future of the country.
>
> Like all developed nations, Canada stands poised at the brink of a fundamental transformation..."the information revolution"...which will affect...our economy, culture, social relationships and polity. The Chairman of the CRTC will be one of the key players to determine...whether the host of developments that parade under this umbrella spell the end of Canada as a sovereign nation or the renewal of a people whose national will has certainly become bowed, if not broken.
>
> In the short run, the major challenges will be in the broadcasting area. The Chairman will...have to deal with the twin issues of pay-television and satellite services. These issues are archetypes, the current incarnations of a cultural dilemma that is as old as Canadian broadcasting. Faced with a massive invasion of cultural programming, our cultural survival hinges to a very great extent on our ability to define our distinct nature and to construct an institutional framework which will express it...
>
> The telecommunications issues which the Commission will have to face are perhaps even more important to the future of our country. In our own history...cultural subservience has gone hand in hand with economic dependence, and whatever efforts we make to strengthen our Canadian culture through broadcasting will be in vain unless we take parallel measures in the control of the information sector of our economy...
>
> The telecommunications carriers are the key players in this sector and the largest of them all respond to the CRTC...
>
> It is important...that the CRTC Chairman be known and respected across the country and in the broadcasting

industry, be sensitive to federal-provincial relations, but above all else...it is essential that the Chairman see his role for what it is—a position which is almost without parallel in public life for the influence it has on the fate of the Canadian identity. It is not a comfortable position; but it is a challenging and exciting one and the watershed is now. It would be easy to refuse, but you, of all people should be prepared—for a while at least—to get your boots dirty in the public arena...The country needs you—come.

This was strong stuff. But although my moorings loosened, I still saw some obstacles. David MacDonald suggested that I talk to the PM. I had known him for a long time because of my research into political parties. Joe Clark's response to one of my questions went a long way towards finally tilting the balance. I mentioned that I was aware of the cabinet's power to overrule CRTC decisions, and that I knew that my outlook was somewhat to the left of that of the mainstream of his party. Could he give me some assurance that "my" decisions would not be struck down by his government?

His reply, in addition to assuaging some anxiety, also conveyed an appealing honesty and realism. No one could offer such a sweeping guarantee, he said, but he and his colleagues knew where I stood on related policy issues and would not have asked me had they found my stance unacceptable. This sounded convincing, since Lowell Murray, David MacDonald and the other MacDonald—Flora—who must have been one of the instigators of my appointment, certainly knew my general outlook.

A factor unknown to the Clark folks helped determine my decision. It arose from my guilty conscience over not having served in the Second World War, as did so many of my contemporaries. I had wanted to join up, as I mentioned, but my osteomyelitis and nearsightedness stood in the way. The CRTC appointment would atone for this neglect and provide an opportunity to serve my adopted country in another way. Four years later, when I announced my resignation from the Commission before my seven years were up, I referred to having done my "war service," a quip widely picked up by the media who, however, assumed that I was referring to the numerous skirmishes in which the CRTC inevitably becomes embroiled as it stands on regulatory guard.

As soon as I agreed to become what some media referred to as Canada's Communications Czar, I informed Queen's and made arrangements about the completion of my teaching. Murie, who had of course been in close consultation throughout my dithering (she rather thought that I should go) found us an apartment in Ottawa's Sandy Hill area. While I needed to work the Ottawa social scene and to some extent did, I resolved to spend as many weekends at Colimaison as possible and not be sidetracked by diplomatic and bureaucratic partying which, while occasionally useful and even enjoyable, takes up a lot of time. Beating a hasty retreat on Friday evenings, loaded with three huge government briefcases containing urgent reading, provided a credible excuse for turning down invitations.

Headquarters was at Les Terrasses de la Chaudière in Hull (now Gatineau), on the Quebec side of the national capital. Because of its insalubrious atmosphere, which made some of the staff ill, my anglophone helpers referred to it as "Terrace de shoddy air." I never succumbed to the noxious fumes but noted when I first laid eyes on the place that its elegance was several notches above that of my eminently adequate, but essentially utilitarian university digs. I received an early warning of the fantastic difference between Queen's and Ottawa's cultures when one of my senior staff asked how I wanted my quarters redone. The CRTC chair, although not part of the regular civil service structure, has deputy minister rank, and it was common for officials at that level to have their offices redone when newly settling into their mandarin chairs. I expressed complete satisfaction with the status quo but requested an outside umbrella so, when weather allowed, I could comfortably transact business on my balcony overlooking the Ottawa River. Once or twice I observed a peregrine falcon while sitting there that had chosen us as its habitat.

I also embellished my office with a regular supply of flowers, some of which—the hyacinths, tulips and daffodils—I forced at Colimaison. I also borrowed a lovely collection of Canadian paintings from the National Gallery's Art Bank, a perk available to government offices. Adjusting to the new quarters was a breeze. By contrast, accepting the habits and conventions of the public service, and the culture of the CRTC, was another matter.

Physical access to government offices was controlled. One could not wander freely from place to place, as at Queen's; the credentials of everyone seeking admission were scrutinized at all entrances and exits by commissionaires. No one was allowed to proceed until telephonic approval was granted by the person the visitor wished to see. Since I usually arrived very early, and left late—times of little traffic—I chatted and became friendly with our guardians. Weather permitting, I bicycled to and from work on my old, beat-up bike. The commissionaires, virtually all bilingual francophones, referred to my beloved conveyance as "le Cadillac du président."

The CRTC sends out a huge number of letters every day, many of which are signed by the chair, although written and vetted by a hierarchy of officers. During my first month in the job, I made a point of reading every piece of mail requiring my John Henry. So, late into the night, I sifted through reams of correspondence which, serendipitously, familiarized me with important areas of our work. I found many of "my" missives quite unacceptable. The letters to which we replied were always attached and I was shocked to note that many of the responses failed to address and answer the issues raised. Worse, the meaning of some of our replies escaped me. It dawned on me that some were carefully constructed so as to give the impression of dealing with the matter raised but in fact revealing nothing. They were smokescreens protecting the Commission's and its staff's bottoms. I sent many letters back to their writers with requests to come clean, but they found it hard. The security surrounding our building went deeper and permeated their minds, begetting a "What they don't know won't hurt them (or, more exactly, won't hurt us)" mentality. All of this, on top of the deplorable fact that most of what I was asked to sign was expressed in execrable bureaucratese—language no sane person would think of using in daily conversation. Shades of *Yes Minister*.

After numerous attempts to remedy the situation failed, I established a correspondence unit which was responsible for clarifying our outgoing messages and putting them into plain English. I brought my trusted friend and editor, Joan Harcourt, from Kingston to run this search for clarity, candour and beauty, which she did admirably. She drafted most of my own letters, infusing them with personal allusions and references, and conveying information in lucid, straightforward and attractive form. She furthered my ambition to give the CRTC a human face.

Two episodes stand out as the most eye-opening of my early CRTC experiences: one concerned the behaviour of one of my fellow commissioners; the other the ethics of the management regime within the commission.

In my time, the Commission consisted of nine full-time members, who constituted the executive committee, and a number of part-timers. Together we made all its major substantive decisions. The executive committee met at least once a week to discuss and decide the myriad issues confronting us and to approve decisions growing out of our public hearings, whether dealing with the results of licence applications or broader policy matters affecting broadcasting or telephony. All formal decisions were made collectively and were reached by vote. One of the chair's tasks was to run the shop, ensuring the effective functioning of the commission, and presiding over the executive committee and full commission meetings. An equally important task, to my mind, was to steer decisions towards goals he espoused. The commissioners had to be melded into, and sustained, as a harmonious and effective team. This was the kind of co-operative and collegial spirit I knew at the university and expected at the CRTC. A few days after my arrival, I discovered, however, in a most dramatic way, that my expectations were unrealistic. Most of my colleagues were straight shooters and team players, but not all.

Before my precipitous departure from Queen's, I had to ensure that my teaching duties and other commitments were covered until permanent arrangements could be made. This was one of the matters I discussed with Joe Clark before saying yea or nay to his invitation to make the change. He agreed to my phased withdrawal from the academy. My big introductory course in Canadian Politics was taken over by a colleague, but I went to Kingston every two weeks to give a couple of the lectures, and I completed some of my long-standing IPSA gigs. One of these was to give a paper in Paris on January 7th, only six days after my arrival in Ottawa.

When I returned, I was picked up at Mirabel airport by Claude Leblanc, my driver, accompanied by Eric Boyd, the senior administrative officer and Jean Guy Patenaude, the Commission secretary. The latter two briefed me on what transpired during my absence. After completing routine matters, they turned all grave and mentioned one other thing. Max Keeping, the host of a popular Ottawa CTV evening news show, reported that the new chairman of the CRTC continued teaching at Queen's and maintained his consulting business, and that—only a few days after his arrival—he went to Paris for a holiday. This was a completely misleading and malicious distortion of what transpired, and an invention to boot. I never did any consulting work and certainly had no consulting business.

Eric filled in the background: the story was fed Max Keeping by BM, one of the full-time commissioners. He is deceased, and I refrain from using his real name. BM are not his initials, but stand for Bad Man. He was a great admirer and loyal friend of Charles Dalfen, the Commission's vice-chair, and deeply resented my appointment. He sought to have me ousted and replaced by his pal. Eric Boyd also revealed that the commissioners' personal staff kept him abreast of their boss's activities, and that BM's secretary reported that, before the telecast, BM had initiated a long conversation with Keeping. Circumstantial evidence? Not bloody likely!

The chances of BM's ploy succeeding were remote but not entirely out of the question.

The reception to my appointment as CRTC chair was decidedly mixed. Most of the industry was leery of my lack of experience in their domain, of my background as an academic and a cultural nationalist. The pack-think world of journalism was aghast over a statement I made during the minister's press conference announcing my appointment and introducing me to the media. When asked which TV program I enjoyed most, I truthfully but idiotically replied that, as an academic, I worked at my typewriter evenings and that I did not watch television. Douglas Fisher, for example, the erudite *Ottawa Sun* columnist, with whom I had overlapped — and sparred — at Victoria College, argued that being a popular professor was an inadequate qualification for the job. The cultural community, on the other hand, was delighted, a few rosy-eyed, over-enthusiasts even claiming that my appointment was the best decision the short-lived Clark government had made. In light of the ambivalent reaction to my appointment, and since Pierre Trudeau had replaced Joe Clark as prime minister, it may not have been completely quixotic to try having me unseated. But, perhaps naively, I had not the slightest worry about being fired. I had known Pierre Trudeau, the new prime minister, as an academic colleague for many years, was on good terms with him and respected his integrity.

Still, Eric Boyd's revelations induced a state of shock. I cannot tell whether I was revolted more by the fact that a colleague had behaved so disgracefully or by my senior administrator encouraging secretaries to spy on their bosses. I was never before so scandalized by anything. I also realized, with a thud, that the agreeable, cozy, family-like atmosphere at Queen's was now replaced by a climate reflecting Thomas Hobbes's dark thought that "the condition of man …is a condition of war of everyone against everyone." I was shattered. But *la vie continue*, and next morning I opened the weekly commission meeting by turning to the routine agenda as if nothing untoward had occurred.

BM requested the floor before we tackled the agenda and, mock-horror filled, mentioned the Keeping report. He insisted that I call a press conference and issue a full rebuttal. I responded by correcting, for the sake of my colleagues, the inaccuracies of the telecast and told them that that was the end of the matter. Referring to lessons learnt in the past, I insisted that a denial would merely keep the issue alive. As expected, it sank into oblivion in no time and I left the CRTC at a moment of my own choosing four years later, having enjoyed a good ride along the way.

Not all the surprises I confronted in Ottawa were caused by what I found there; one was produced by myself. I had in the past been critical of politicians, and also of the CRTC, for not sticking steadfastly enough to their principles. In contrast, I had always thought of myself as a person of unwavering integrity. It was therefore jolting to find, only after my second or third executive committee meeting, that I was behaving as opportunistically as some of the parties of whom I had earlier disapproved. Decisions were taken by majority vote, as I mentioned, and as chair, I did all I could to bring about "the right" outcome. Some items before us were of critical importance in setting policy, while others dealt with minor matters. There were issues to which I was largely indifferent and others, like the welfare of public broadcasting, Canadian content or maximum access to telephone service, which I saw as being of primordial consequence.

After a couple of weeks on the job, I noticed that not all my voting decisions were taken exclusively on the basis of what I thought best, but also on how they might affect the outcomes of key votes, i.e., votes on issues that mattered most. When I needed the support of certain colleagues to ensure passage of a vital proposal, I refrained, when I did not care that much, from antagonizing them by opposing their pet causes, in hopes that they would return the favour in support of mine. If you scratch my back, I'll scratch yours. None of this was ever even mentioned and instances of log-rolling were rare, but they occurred and I was a party to them. I was not pleased when I became aware of what I had been up to, but believed that the process served the public good, as I saw it. Starting down a slippery slope?

Realizing what was happening brought home a lesson: theoretical knowledge is one thing, practice another. To read about politics does not bring quite the same understanding as doing it; one does not know what a process really is until one *feels* it by being part of it.

One of the fallouts from the Keeping episode was that I lost confidence in Eric Boyd's integrity and ethics and resolved to replace him as my senior officer. Not that he was inefficient or incapable of doing his job. On the contrary, he was an exceptionally able master of *all* the rules governing the public service and played the latter, virtuoso style, with true brilliance. He was able to finagle *any* project or deal and was, in his way, completely loyal to the CRTC and to me. I needed him for some time and soon learnt that the bureaucratic ethos and complexity made it virtually impossible to fire or even move anyone, let alone so consummate a stick-handler. Eventually I managed to shift him aside a little but not entirely. He continued to manage the mechanics of the shop and died at his desk some time after I left. But I needed a trusted lieutenant on the staff and in due course arranged, with Eric's reluctant assistance, to have Ken Wyman appointed Executive Director, Operations, at the same level as Eric. An extremely intelligent and knowledgeable telecom specialist, he had run our whole telecom operation and was a person of unassailable integrity. After his promotion and reassignment, he and Eric managed to reach a workable arrangement between them. But Ken failed me in one way.

Several CRTC officers were not, in my view, up to scratch and allowed the inordinate length it took to process applications for licences and reach timely decisions. I wanted these roadblocks removed and expected Ken to do the dirty work I could not face tackling myself. He turned out just as big a bleeding heart as I and we failed to clean house, commiserating with one another about our woes. What I should have done, but was at the time too inexperienced to attempt, was to bring in outside consultants who would have proposed a needed reorganization and, if asked, executed it. I have always been leery of consultants — so many fail to live up to expectations and turn into expensive distractions. On this occasion, had I found the right one, an outsider would have helped.

In all other respects, Ken worked out well. His appointment also strengthened us indirectly. He had to be replaced as the senior telecom officer, and we chose to elevate a young member of the legal branch, Hank Intven. He had come to the Commission from the

Consumers Association of Canada, which I thought a highly appropriate preparation for a regulator. He was an extremely well rounded and capable resource not only on telecom matters, but also on issues affecting pay television in Canada. He eventually became one of the country's leading communications lawyers.

The foregoing may convey the impression that the CRTC staff members were wanting. We did have problems, particularly delivering decisions in a timely manner, and the Commission did exhibit many of the foibles of all bureaucracies, but I was impressed by the quality, commitment and professionalism of most of the people around me. There were some weak sisters and brothers about, but my guess was that, proportionately, they were no more numerous than in many other organizations, including universities. Most were strongly committed to our cause.

As time went on, I built up a small praetorian guard of close collaborators, attached to the chair's office and reporting directly to me. Some of them had been my students who contacted me to offer their services and some I sought out. My three secretaries were routine employees of the Commission with whom I established an excellent relationship. It is possible that they prattled to Eric about my doings but, apart from the principle of the thing, this did not disturb me; I had little if anything to hide. As we fell into our routines, their loyalty to me became unquestioned.

I did, however, offend them deeply at one point. Although my French was more than adequate for the job, and I employed it constantly and made numerous French speeches off the cuff, my grammar had declined from the days when its rules were mercilessly drilled into the head by the Christian Brothers in Haiti. My written command of the language had fallen behind the oral and, even when speaking, though completely fluent, I made mistakes. I, therefore, engaged a French teacher who came into the office *very* early in the morning to give me lessons. Like a great many bilingual secretaries in the public service, my helpers came from the Outaouais region North of the capital, where the *lingua franca* is a regional patois constantly laced with English words. It sounded, and was, awful. I suggested that the Commission engage my teacher to give *them* some lessons as well. Unaware of how badly they spoke, they were mortified. After a while, however, they realized that the training was useful and appreciated the classes.

Various trade groups, cultural and other organizations expected the chair to address them, which required considerable preparation and careful drafting. These tasks made me aware of a significant difference between public institutions and universities. In the latter, much of what one does is essentially solitary. Teaching and working with research assistants are sociable tasks, but preparing lectures, researching documents, reading other scholars' work, thinking through a problem, and writing are best performed alone. They seldom involve committees. At the Commission, even deep cerebral toil was often co-operative and undertaken with others. Before I went there, my preparation of speaking notes and texts was always my own task. Now parts of my addresses were prepared by the specialists on the staff and had to be integrated into a harmonious whole in substance and tone. I did not always have time to prepare my addresses either, and met with helpers to whom I conveyed what I thought needed to be said, upon which they produced a first draft. In some cases, even the topics covered were proposed by staff who specialized in the relevant files. I was fussy about how I expressed my ideas and made sure that the final version "was me." Eventually I benefited from the help of Colette Trent as well as two former graduate students, Nick Sidor and Jean Van Loon. The latter was my executive assistant, and the former something close to it. Jean, on one occasion, played a critical role in what turned into one of the most successful addresses of my life.

In 1982 I was invited to speak at the Annual Telecommunications Policy Research Conference in Annapolis, Maryland. This huge gathering is attended by North American telecommunications scholars and practitioners, where Canadians constitute an insignificant minority. America, without a genuine national public broadcaster like the CBC, or the provincial educational channels, with few publicly owned telephone companies, a lesser involvement of the state in the construction and operation of broadcast satellites, and with a more market-oriented economy and outlook than Canada, was generally uninformed about and leery of the way we handled these issues. Remember how Canada's medicare system is pilloried in the USA? I anticipated that the reaction to my talk would be hostile and my position excoriated, for I made a strong plea for the need, in telecommunications and broadcasting, to ensure the dominance of the public interest over private gain. And, likewise, I showed how Canada's identity was threatened by the exuberant market expansionism of American cultural interests.

Jean and I discussed what I had in mind, whereupon she produced a superb draft requiring no major interventions on my part. Her role was so important (she even made an amusing and apposite reference to Ray Charles's *Georgia on My Mind*; I had never heard of Ray Charles before) that I invited her to join the CRTC team attending the Annapolis jamboree. I delivered my spiel entitled "Babies and Bathwater, or What Goes Down the Deregulatory Drain," to a colossal, attentive and seemingly unscandalized luncheon audience on the final day. The talk was greeted by applause the length and intensity of which I had rarely encountered before. When it finally quieted down, and the chair asked for comments or questions, the first voice from the audience inquired "Where were you when we needed you?" In the course of the subsequent discussion I was able to acknowledge Jean's role in the production of what was certainly *our* paper.

Parliament paying attention to the chair!

In addition to Colette, Jean and Nick, the secretaries Suzanne, Terry and Yolande, Claude my wonderful driver and Joan, the peerless correspondence head, two unconventional recruits complemented my team. One was Joanne Sarrazin, also primarily a writer. She gave a huge boost to my continuing involvement with the IPSR, and on one occasion facilitated a jolly innovation. I was disappointed that few paid much attention to our Annual Report to Parliament which was, admittedly, a soporific document. Joanne was given the task of making it more interesting. She had flair and was able to deliver an unexpected bonus. A friend of Terry Mosher, a.k.a. Aislin, one of Canada's best cartoonists, who spices up the pages of the *Montreal Gazette,* she persuaded him to accept a laughably modest commission for illustrating our report. It was more a *succès d'estime* than the making of a bestseller, but some kindred spirits enjoyed it, including a few MPs. The commissioners appeared in all the cartoons clad in heavy armour. The chairman smote all in sight, not with a sword, but a fly swatter.

My other special appointment, with whom I worked closely, was John Peter Lee Roberts, a former CBC Radio music executive. He undertook special tasks related to radio programming, and I saw him as our principal link to members of the cultural community, where he was highly regarded. The CRTC interacted more frequently with commercial broadcasters and telecommunications companies than with creators of programs and films, and I thought it desirable to maintain closer links with the latter, as well.

My relations with the other commissioners were every bit as critical as those with the Commission staff and my own bodyguard. They ranged from very friendly to courteous. I liked some of my colleagues a lot and established close friendships with a few of them, partly because the chemistry between us gelled and partly because of ideological affinities related to the Commission's mandate.

A word is in order about how BM and I managed to work together, after the disastrously rocky start. Oddly enough, we found a civilized and productive mode of interaction. What had been an inexcusable transgression in my eyes was never mentioned and I even developed a certain admiration and respect for him. He was a brilliant, wide-ranging intellectual who had made important contributions to Canada, both in broadcasting and in government. He knew many leading politicians of all parties, understood Ottawa's folkways and liked to share with some of us perceptive, illuminating and pithy quotations from his voluminous reading. I accepted, as a sort of peace offering, that I was among the recipients of these occasional gems, always boldly inked with a colourful felt-nibbed pen. I respected his intellect but had grave misgivings about his character.

Rosalie Gower and I were kindred spirits. A one-time nurse from British Columbia, she was a hard working, intelligent and consumer-friendly supporter of public broadcasting and Canadian culture. Always mindful of women's interests, she never let us overlook them. We were on the same side on virtually all issues. Although more mercurial and unpredictable than Rosalie, Réal Therrien, the Vice Chair, Broadcasting, also became a friend. He had served on the Commission for quite a long time, had been in the telephone business previously, and was predisposed to sympathize with the underdog. He was a vigorous defender of Canada's French fact and of the use of French within the Commission. Our paths had crossed before at some conference, and he knew that I liked French Canada which, I am sure, predisposed him in my favour. Like Rosalie, he was utterly fair dealing, and was offended by any manifestations of disloyalty. My third kindred spirit was Jean-Louis Gagnon, whom I knew from the days when he was a member of the Royal Commission on Bilingualism and Biculturalism, where I served as a research supervisor. He had enjoyed a glittering career as a Quebec journalist and public intellectual. We saw eye-to-eye on most things, although he was approaching crusty curmudgeonhood and harboured a visceral resentment of the CBC which, he thought, inadequately performed the functions of a public broadcaster. The rescheduling of the national news to accommodate hockey games drove him crazy. I shared some of his concerns, but nevertheless believed that the "mother corporation," as some called it, was an indispensable national resource—a faith he had lost and I still clung to for a few years until, I too, abandoned it.

John Lawrence and I also shared a similar outlook on broadcasting and telecom issues, and many other things as well. He had been on the Commission's legal staff in the 1970s and, after Charles Dalfen resigned, was sworn in as a commissioner and succeeded him as vice-chair, Telecom. We worked harmoniously and with ease. Chuck, I assumed—but was not certain—had not been in cahoots with BM's scheme to unseat me, but I thought that he could have been more vigorous in restraining his friend's perfidy. So although he, Réal and I made an effective leadership troika, in which the question of loyalties never came to the fore, I was never completely relaxed with him. This was not the case with John.

I saw much less of my part-time colleagues, but a few of them bequeathed lasting impressions. They lived in different parts of the country, which provided a healthy corrective to the Ottawa-centric perspective that often afflicts folks within hearing distance of the carillon chimes of the Peace Tower. Even I, though sensitive to this danger, and trying hard to escape it, occasionally surprised myself by losing sight of the countrywide context. The part-timers sat on the broadcast hearing panels, providing, among other things, local knowledge and a local voice to the regions affected by the outcomes. Although not part of the executive committee, they were, on broadcasting matters, voting members at meetings of the full commission. The respect I had for the CRTC, when it was first created, was in part earned by Northrop Frye, serving as one of its part-time members, although to my regret, he had left long before my time.

Jacques de la Chevrotière, whose appearance and speech were as elegant as his name, was a senior executive of a large, socially conscious insurance company in Quebec City. His business experience, Quebec domicile outside Montreal, and caring, humane approach were invaluable. In his splendid basement workshop he turned out marvellous wood creations. He made an old-fashioned candle holder for Murie and me—a replica of a kind traditionally used in Quebec before the advent of electricity, when the *habitants* toddled off to bed in their nightgowns and in candlelight. He travelled a lot, often in France, always well supplied with smallish bottles of Quebec maple syrup. These he distributed to guests at adjacent tables in the fine restaurants he liked to frequent, as an example of the rich culinary tradition of his province and country.

Our most famous part-timer was Jacques Hébert, one of Quebec's outstanding writers and journalists, who was associated with Pierre Elliott Trudeau in the founding of the periodical *Cité Libre*. One of PET's oldest friends, he had years previously travelled with him to China and then co-authored their *Two Innocents in Red China*. A passionate civil libertarian, he also founded and masterminded *Katimavik* and Canada World Youth, organizations promoting exchanges of young people and their involvement with good works in Canada and abroad. He had considerable charm which he once demonstrated when, during a full meeting of the Commission, he sent me a short note requesting that he be excused for part of the proceedings. Because of its pithy seductiveness, I filed it away, so effectively that I can't now find it. In rough translation, and allowing for my rotten memory, it read something like this. "In a moment of weakness I was so imprudent as to accept an invitation to lunch with the prime minister today. Please allow me to take French leave;[1] I shall not be long."

I was always intrigued by the circumstances that led to my colleagues' appointments. Positions on government boards and commissions are greatly sought after, particularly by those who believe that political parties owe them a patronage nod. Important jobs are sometimes involved and the qualities of the nominees cannot be ignored. While most of my mates had friendly relations with the government party that appointed them, I was impressed by how quickly and thoroughly the partisan tinge, if any, vanished. I recall only rare instances when decisions of commissioners were influenced by anything other than the substance of the cases before them. When, as occasionally happened, a conflict occurred between the Commission and the Minister of Communications, my colleagues' loyalties were unequivocally with the Commission, not their former party.

In a few instances, someone was given the nod who had had no trade or truck with the appointing government. John Grace, for instance, was made a full-time member of the Commission by Pierre Trudeau. He was a wise, even-handed, intelligent man, respected in Ottawa by all sides. A Conservative, he had been editor of the *Ottawa Journal*, a decidedly right-leaning daily paper which ceased publication. I guessed that he needed a job and some powerful voices succeeded in finding him this berth. A fair-minded gentleman, if ever there was one, he made a fine commissioner, although he was uncomfortable with the idea of any government regulation. Were I to refer to him using masking initials, I would choose GM, for Good Man.

Comparing my team with members of other boards and commissions, citizenship judges, for instance, where pretty weak sisters and brothers sometimes find a berth, the quality of both full-time and part-time members, as revealed by intelligence, devotion

---

[1] Jacques's use of the term "French leave" is amusing. Strictly speaking it means "absence without permission," so was not applicable in this situation. But this is not what caused my glee. It was that what in English is imputed to be a French transgression is considered by the French to be an English one. It is "filer à l'anglaise."

and independence, was impeccable. In their decisions, regional loyalties, rather than party ties were more evident.

Relations between the CRTC and the government are always delicate but were mostly straightforward and amicable during my watch. As an independent regulatory agency operating at arm's length from the government, the Commission enjoys considerable autonomy. Members are appointed by the Governor in Council (the cabinet) and hold office "during good behaviour" which means that they can only be removed "for cause," i.e., for having done something pretty execrable or having been grossly delinquent in performing their duties. The government has the power to set aside a decision granting, amending or reviewing a broadcasting licence or to ask the Commission to reconsider the matter, and it can vary, set aside or return for reconsideration any CRTC telecommunications decision. I remember only a solitary instance of this occurring while I was chair.

In many areas, the respective responsibilities of the Commission and the ministry touch and even overlap. For instance, frequencies used by radio and television broadcasters are assigned by the Department of Communications (DOC), but the content of what they carry falls under the CRTC. Therefore, contacts frequently occur between the staffs of the two bodies. But the principal link between the CRTC and the government is the relationship between the Minister of Communications and the Commission chair. Though the Commission reports to Parliament through the minister, he cannot tell it what to do.

David MacDonald and I had relatively little contact with one another, since our overlap in office was so short. We occasionally attended the same events, usually to participate in ceremonies or to deliver speeches. At the very first meeting of what was to become the annual Banff World Television Festival, in which we were both involved, he was asked why the Clark government had appointed a communications neophyte like me to head the CRTC. I listened to his response with rapt attention, needless to say. It ran very much along the lines of the Ostry letter I cited near the beginning of this chapter. He stressed particularly my interest in, and knowledge of, the dilemmas of Canadian unity.

After the fall of the Clark government, David was replaced as Minister of Communications by Francis Fox, a likewise highly intelligent and reasonable man. A leading Quebec member of the Liberal caucus, he was said to have the ear of the prime minister. We arrived at an easy, relaxed relationship and learnt not to step on one another's toes. But very soon after his arrival, he almost stumbled.

Pay television was popular in the United States, and numerous Canadian interests, expecting it to become a cash cow, agitated vigorously to have it introduced here. Cable companies in particular, led by the now defunct Canadian Cable Television Association, saw a potential bonanza over the horizon and, busily salivating, pressed all the buttons they could find or invent to get the Commission to set the scene and call for applications from possible service providers. Both the Commission and the minister were under relentless pressure to get moving. The responsibility, however, was entirely the Commission's, not Francis Fox's. Still a greenhorn in his job, he was unaware of this and made speeches about the matter, and calls to me, indicating that he wanted us to call for licence applications.

We also had a new Deputy Minister of Communications, Pierre Juneau, who replaced Bernard Ostry, who left Ottawa to continue his mandarin career in the service of Ontario. Both the Commission and the minister were lucky to benefit from the advice of the new deputy minister. Not that Bernard had been anything but a discreet, strong supporter. But Pierre, as founding chair of the CRTC, knew a great deal about it—much more than I, at this stage—and was an ardent champion of its goals. I met with him from time to time quite privately, usually for lunch at the *Au pied du cochon* in Hull, and learnt greatly from our conversations. A serendipitous benefit was that he persuaded me, by example, that if one's taste advised it, it was quite OK to drink red wine with fish.

Juneau was not only a connoisseur of wine, but also a seasoned traveller along the boundary between the DOC and the CRTC. He gently but firmly guided his boss toward an appropriate stance vis-à-vis the regulator. He informed Fox of the Commission's ongoing inquiry into the plight of Canadians who—despite the efforts of the Therrien Committee on Extension of Service to Northern and Remote Communities—still had *no* television services, and persuaded him to stay within his jurisdictionally correct enclave and let the Commission address pay-TV issues after it dealt with the needs of underserved areas, including the homeland of large numbers of Aboriginals.

Thereafter, my contacts with Francis were usually friendly, although from time to time differences of opinion did call for tact on both sides. I was startled, at one stage, by the receipt of a draft letter to which he requested my reaction. I had never encountered this courtesy before and found it rather endearing. The draft was of a letter that he was going to send *me* about something we had been discussing. But before it was actually dispatched, I was given the chance to comment on it and, presumably, influence its final substance and wording. This practice was repeated by both of us on subsequent occasions. I presume that the courtesy is common in the public service but at Queen's it would have triggered boundless mirth.

On another occasion, I was annoyed, as was my staff, when radio broadcasters informed us that the DOC was conducting an inquiry into new rules affecting FM broadcasting. Who, they wanted to know, is responsible, DOC or the CRTC? They were justifiably confused and objected to having to cope with two agencies. I wrote a moderate letter to Francis, expressing my concern, seeking clarification, and requesting that the DOC stay out of our cabbage patch. We successfully settled the issue on the phone, but a few days later I received an aggrieved call from Robert Rabinovitch, who had replaced Juneau as the DM. Why did I not raise the issue with him rather than the minister? I had made it a point, *never* formally to deal with the department which, in my view, did not have vertical ties with us and could not be allowed to be seen as an actor in areas of the CRTC's jurisdiction. The *only* legitimate contact, I held, between the regulator and the government was through the interaction of the minister and the chair. Bob disagreed, and asserted that since we were both Order-in-Council appointees, it would have been more appropriate for me to raise the issue with him before addressing the minister. To accept that view would have put me at the level of just another DM, not the head of an independent agency.

One issue which I frequently raised with the minister, although it was not directly my responsibility, was the filling of vacancies on the Commission. The government was slow in replacing departing colleagues, making it difficult for me to find breathing bodies to sit on our many hearing panels. The chair has no say whatsoever in the matter, but acutely suffers from being short-handed. So his squawking is understandable. I not only kept reminding Francis of my plight but also furnished names of suitable candidates. One of them, Alain Gourd, was particularly attractive. He was a philosophy instructor at Ottawa University before joining the family broadcasting company which he led most creatively and, from the CRTC's view, most responsibly. The minister knew him, welcomed my suggestion and would take it up with is cabinet colleagues.

That's where the matter stood for quite a while, when Francis, yet again in need of a new deputy minister, phoned me to tell me that he had appointed "my nominee" to this post. Not fair, but a good appointment.

The fundamental chart and compass of the Commission in the '80s were the Broadcasting and CRTC Acts and, on the telecom side, the Telecommunications Act and a number of other key pieces of legislation. No religious über-zealots have ever been more guided and controlled by their scriptures than the CRTC is by its legislative anchors. If, between 1980 and 1984, I heard, invoked or cited section 3 of the Broadcasting Act once, I did so 10,000 times, or so it seemed. The operative terms are clear and simple: "(a) broadcasting undertakings in Canada make use of radio frequencies that are public property...(b) the Canadian broadcasting system should be effectively owned and controlled by Canadians so as to safeguard, enrich, and strengthen the cultural, political, social and economic fabric of Canada." The means used to achieve these goals include establishing policies and regulations and granting, amending, renewing or revoking licences to broadcasters. On the telecommunications front, the Commission approves rates to be charged by telcos under federal jurisdiction and ensures that no unjust discrimination exists in the provision of services.

The critical point is that broadcasters do not own the frequencies they use but are allowed to make money from these publicly held treasures so long as they abide by the goals identified by Parliament and the CRTC. I leave it to you, the reader, to decide how effectively these ideals are met, but assure you, that whatever success or failure is achieved, results from a constant and titanic struggle between the industry and the regulator. In my time, I regret having to report, the gap between what was happening and what was intended in broadcasting was extremely wide, although no more than before.

It would take volumes to identify the causes of the dissonance, but the basic root is quite simple. The Canadian public is imbued with North American values. They share North American cultural tastes, generally prefer market forces to government intervention, and feel, compared with almost all other nations, a low level of nationalism. Some of these loose generalizations apply less in Quebec where, for instance, unlike in English Canada, locally produced TV programs attract large audiences. Canada's TV industry has on the whole been unable, and I assert, largely unwilling, to make the effort and pay the price of reversing this trend. In TV drama, for example, it is easier and very much cheaper to buy highly popular television programs from American networks than to create and popularize indigenous series. That is why the CRTC imposes Canadian content quotas, which many broadcasters circumvent or water down whenever they can. They love scheduling Canadian shows at the least watched hours, like when most people are asleep. The CRTC has been complicit in this game. Some sports are considered Canadian content, hockey for instance, in some cases even if both teams are American.

Laws, rules and regulations in a free society only work if substantial support exists for them. Thus, the CRTC, and the DOC discovered, in the 1980s, that the prohibition of unauthorized satellite dishes to receive American programs was ineffective and even led to threats of violence when the Mounties attempted to remove them. To deprive broadcasters of their licences is to silence them, and the CRTC is aware that in most situations this would be utterly unacceptable. It cannot, therefore, apply this option, even when it is called for. So, although the Broadcasting Act endows the CRTC with powerful sanctions, they cannot, in practice, be applied. This is a reality I learnt only on the job, when trying to live up to the goals of the Act.

A couple of years after I left the Commission, Herschel Hardin published *Closed Circuits*, an outraged critique of Canada's broadcasting regime and particularly of the Commission and all its chairmen. Its argument is encapsulated in the subtitle — "The Sellout of Canadian Television." I knew him as a Queen's student and admired his earlier *A Nation Unaware*, a perceptive examination of Canadian identity. Although his excoriation of the CRTC grew out of a thorough knowledge of the situation — a personal involvement in a British Columbia cable undertaking which failed to receive a CRTC licence — and a passionate concern for a socially responsible broadcasting scenario for Canada, it failed to bring redress. The principal reason was that although it was one of the few serious efforts to critically assess the status quo, its extreme, venomous and one-sided approach robbed it of realism and prevented it becoming a major factor in the national discourse on broadcasting policy.

While bemoaning in a heart-rending fashion the inadequacies of the private broadcasters, I happily acknowledge that some of them were exemplary citizens, individually and corporatively. Doug and Gordon Rawlinson in Alberta and Saskatchewan and Harvey Glatt (Chez FM) in Ottawa, an indefatigable music promoter and entrepreneur who strongly supported Canadian talent, were radio operators who willingly seemed to accept the logic of broadcast regulation in Canada, as did Wilbrod Bherer, a philanthropist and activist in La Malbaie, who owned Télé Capitale in Quebec. André Chagnon, a major Quebec cable operator, had no trouble accepting Canada's regulatory regime. There were other allies and exemplary licence holders, but they were a minority outweighed and out-yelled by the big guns. CTV led by Murray Chercover, Baton (the Bassetts and Eatons), Global Television and the Canadian Cable Television Association were not particularly helpful in enabling Canada even to approximate the goals Parliament specified in its section 3 of the Broadcasting Act.

One media personality intrigued me particularly — Ted Rogers. He was amazingly energetic and implacable in pursuing his objective of becoming Canada's dominant TV cable provider and ultimately, through the use of cable technology, a serious competitor of Bell's telephone interests in Eastern Canada. By contrast, on broadcasting issues he accepted legislative guidance and did not fight the CRTC tooth and nail, as did so much of the rest of the industry. I assumed that it was, in part, because of his influence that the cable industry responded well to the Commission's prodding to create effective community cable TV channels. Partly prompted by the Commission, but not only because of that, he and his company were also major players in the establishment and operation of the Cable Public Affairs Channel (CPAC). It carried parliamentary debates (after the CBC bowed out), proceedings of some parliamentary committees and other public affairs programs.

We met some years previously when Dalton Camp, as a Queen's Skelton-Clark Fellow, was writing *Gentlemen, Players and Politicians* (1970). He invited Murie and me to dinner with Ted at a Toronto club. The Rogers family had connections with Pickering College and I was interested in learning something about this link. I was also curious about his earlier relations with John Diefenbaker, of whom he had been an enthusiastic admirer.

He appeared before Commission hearings more than once in my time, invariably defending bold proposals and turning his presence into a somewhat bizarre and comic theatre. Although granite hard in pursuit of his aims, he treated the panel members to what was no doubt meant to be a touching family scene. Unlike most broadcasters, his large team always included a very proper and distinguished lawyer, John W. Graham, his stepfather. But there were also two or three of his children who, while not uttering a word, were paraded before us, looking rather bored. The strategy seemed to work. Before I arrived in Ottawa, Rogers had been denied the right to purchase Premier Cable, a large, Vancouver-based operator, but during my tenure he succeeded on a second try. The community services and other benefits this acquisition offered the subscribers were deemed by the Commission to justify this takeover. I agreed with the majority.

The Vancouver hearing where the issue was decided threw a new light on BM. On all other occasions, when Commission panels travelled to cities outside Ottawa, all members stayed at the same hotel. Arrangements were always made by staff, who set up the hearings. This time BM abandoned this practice and booked a room at the same hotel as the Rogers group. During the hearings he kept feeding them leading questions offering opportunities for the presentation of evidence making their acquisition of the western cable company look most attractive. After resigning from the Commission soon afterwards, he accepted a position with Rogers as its European manager. Heads shook and brows furrowed.

Complacent self-confidence was a noticeable characteristic of leaders in the communications industry. Occasionally it was even justified. Moses Znaimer, for example, was one who (like Rogers) bristled with imaginative and innovative skills. I came across his name before I went to Ottawa in an article in which he was quoted as asking something like, "Other than sex and money what is there"? I was appalled and clipped it for my "Quotations" file in which I collected ammunition for skirmishes in the culture wars. My opinion of him rose from the subterranean level, based at the start on this quotation, to admiration and respect for his innovative courage, imagination and originality as a broadcaster. As the genius behind Toronto's CITY TV—a service bringing the lightness and flexibility of radio to the TV screen—he was miles ahead of the industry and a delight to watch. His other innovations in the arts were similarly impressive but are irrelevant here.

Whatever failings Ted Rogers might have had did not include arrogance. One of his public personae was a somewhat awkward, shambling tall drink of water who, as the author of one of his obituaries observed, "would display the guileless innocence of an untrained puppy dog." He did, actually, often pose as another kind of canine, an underdog, particularly in his rivalry with Bell. This appearance of modesty contrasted sharply with the comportment of most other big players on the communications scene. Their haughtiness, occasionally tempered by a fawning desire to win favours, diverged sharply from what I had found even among prima donnas on campuses.

John Bassett was the first harbinger of the difference. He was a newspaper tycoon and co-owner, with some of the Eatons, of Baton Broadcasting. They had launched the first Canadian TV station, CFTO, which later became pivotal in the creation of the CTV network. Soon after I assumed office, he sent word that he would welcome a visit from me when I was in Toronto. I looked in on him soon afterwards, and a second after I entered his office, was greeted with "When are you going to resign?" I allowed that this was not something troubling my mind, but why did he ask? His reply, though not flattering, was at least frank. He said that I was bound to fail in the job and would be better off back in the university. Despite this reception, I came to like him and have since wondered whether the inquiry might have been sprinkled with a dust of kindness.

No such possible extenuating circumstance excused the snobbish effrontery of his Baton kinsman, one of the Eaton "boys." I think it was Fred, but am not sure, never having taken the trouble to sort out Timothy Eaton's grandsons. It may have been John Craig or George Ross. As sometimes happens to scions of very successful and affluent families, some of the young Eaton men were reputed to have been on the playboy side and not as devoted to minding the store as their granddad. The Eaton empire's later decline reflected the younger generation's neglect and lack of judgment. I encountered this young man at a huge reception at one of Toronto's clubs, held to honour Pierre Juneau. The young lion was seated on a couch and as soon as we were introduced launched an abusive harangue accusing the CRTC of incompetence, unwarranted interference with legitimate business and God knows what other misdemeanours. I was so taken aback by this outpouring of bile that I simply walked away, a most unusual strategy for one who enjoys a good argument.

The foregoing paragraphs recall the arrogance of some of the broadcasting and cable giants. Their sometimes disdainful and sneering behaviour looks like grovelling flattery compared to the treatment we occasionally encountered from Bell, and particularly its head, Jean de Grandpré. He and some, but—I stress—not all, of his colleagues saw their company as some sort of privileged principality towering over everything, including, even, the government of Canada. We were given to feel that if we went too far in interfering with their perfection, they had channels to the powers-that-be in Ottawa who would do their bidding. Jean de Grandpré reorganized his company during my tenure at the CRTC, so as to enable some of its holdings to escape the CRTC's regulatory hand. These manoeuvres ultimately failed to pay off and tarnished his former reputation as a corporate whiz kid. His condescending manner notwithstanding, I respected and even admired him. He had wide interests and rendered substantial services to a number of academic and cultural institutions.

Having whined a bit about some insulting behaviour from industry, it is only fair to add that, whether resignedly, joyfully, or grudgingly, the companies under our jurisdiction accepted the status quo and complied with what we demanded of them. They had no choice, of course, but some ensured that the process of regulation was civil and reasonably pleasant, whereas a minority failed to do so. The companies and their professional associations were generally anxious to maintain good relations and effective ways of communicating with us. We reciprocated in the latter and the CRTC chair always attended the annual meetings of the trade associations and delivered a major speech, setting out his current preoccupations. I welcomed these occasions and used them to create a climate in which, I hoped, the goals of the legislation would not only be adhered to, but willingly and positively espoused.

Keeping in touch was sometimes difficult. We adhered uncompromisingly to our policy of entering into no communication, outside of formal documents, with any firm or individual who had an application before us requiring a hearing and decision. To do otherwise would be like a judge consorting with a defendant before confronting him in court. Thus executives of a company like Rogers, which always had several cases on our agenda, found it difficult to gain access to the ear of any commissioner outside a formal hearing. During one of the rare occasions when nothing in the Rogers empire was before us, Ted Rogers invited me to dinner. I was delighted to discover, upon arrival, that this was a completely casual family affair at which I was the only guest. Although we did not sit around the kitchen table, the prevailing pleasant, family atmosphere made it feel as if we had.

I regarded the companies we regulated in a societal and national policy perspective, but my personal tastes and habits could not help but colour how I *felt* about them. I have never been a television person (though, while at the Commission, I tried hard to make up for that with the help of a Betamax player). I now watch a few programs, almost all on TVO or PBS. Radio was another story. Partly because of my keen interest in public affairs and my love of music and French Canada, I have been a CBC Radio junkie during most of my adult life. So, though I had no emotional attachment to the private broadcasters I did have a strong, and positive one to the CBC, until recently, when it forsook my generation and class of listeners.

Ever since its inception in 1936 it has been charged with programming of much greater diversity and higher quality than what is expected from private broadcasters. The terms of reference in the Broadcasting Act, its legislative anchor, are lofty indeed and, although technically in force have never all been met by the corporation. Among their requirements, in the words of the Act, is that "its programming should inform, enlighten and entertain...be predominantly and distinctively Canadian...be of equal quality in English and in French...contribute to the flow and exchange of cultural expression...reflect Canada and its region to national and regional audiences...[and] contribute to shared national consciousness and identity." The corporation in the 1980s sought to fulfill its mandate by providing complete radio and television services in French and English, programming for Canada's North, Radio Canada International—a shortwave service in numerous languages, and a Parliamentary Channel covering the House of Commons debates. It offered the first Canadian FM service and was always in the forefront of adopting new broadcast technologies.

Among the reasons the CBC fell far short of its assigned goals was that Parliament never provided sufficient funds and the CBC developed extremely expensive habits. It augmented its income by selling commercial time, first on both radio and TV, but later only on the latter. As the evolving difference in quality between the visual and aural services showed, the acceptance of commercials downgraded its programs to the point where CBC TV is now largely indistinguishable from the private broadcasters.

CBC Radio established a splendid record in providing Canadians in both cities and countryside with informative and useful programming and in offering unparalleled cultural shows. Its Citizens' Forum, farm programs, the Wednesday night Stage series, and Max Ferguson were, among others, popular and envied by radio connoisseurs internationally. By the time I arrived at the CRTC, however, television had become dominant. CBC fare was still somewhat better, and more Canadian, than what was offered by the private services, and what the CBC dished up subsequently. Only CBC 2 and one or two special talk programs on CBC 1 eventually lived up to the promise of a public network until most of them, too, succumbed to the vandals within the management. The CBC Radio audience was significant but not huge. Until the end of the first decade of this century, but no more, it was almost fanatical in its devotion to the public network.

When, in 1980, CBC applied for a licence to offer a new, high quality cultural service to be available on cable, it was expected that it would receive a warm welcome from us. The idea sounded promising and I was among those looking forward to its advent. When we received the licence application, and during the subsequent hearing, however, it became apparent that the proposal raised serious problems. They were related in part to the Corporation's repeated failure to provide its services to certain parts of the country, particularly in New Brunswick. These shortcomings had come to light at previous hearings, and the CBC more than once undertook to tackle them, without, however, doing anything of the sort. The excuse was always lack of funds. The Commission was astonished to find that money was available for this new service when there wasn't any for reaching the public broadcaster's obligation to better serve remote areas. Since the new service, promising though it was, would have been available only to cable subscribers, i.e., urban dwellers, it would have increased the gap separating how town and country folks could access the CBC.

The Commission was also seriously concerned about the budget provisions the CBC submitted for the new service. Our analysts found them to be wildly optimistic and certain to result in substantial overruns. How would this affect other programs? Would it further delay the corporation's meeting its obligations vis-à-vis areas bereft of its service? The panel hearing the application, and subsequently the whole Commission, considered these and other issues at great length and concluded that it had to turn the application down. I sided with the majority, notwithstanding my overall warm support of the CBC.

Our decision may have cost me an old friendship. Al Johnson, the CBC President, was one of Canada's most creative and distinguished public servants. He was also a bookish chap, and contributed to academic journals devoted to politics and public administration. Our paths had crossed on many occasions because of the Queen's-Ottawa nexus, and I was glad to publish a strong article of his in the first issue of the *Canadian Journal of Political Science* during my tenure as editor. I, therefore, derived satisfaction and comfort from knowing that I had an old pal in the CBC president. He deeply resented the CRTC's rejection of what he saw as an imaginative and promising application. Our relationship was never restored to the previous level, perhaps for other reasons as well. Our future paths diverged.

This hearing nicely illustrates an important discovery I made at the CRTC. After studying the underlying documents, I usually had a pretty good idea of where I stood on matters before us. But not always. There were times when the evidence presented at a hearing shed light I had not seen before. And sometimes the discussion by the panel afterwards caused a reversal of mind. Public hearings, I learnt — a procedure never used in academic inquiry — can be of inestimable value in reaching informed decisions.

The CBC hearing also brought the issue to the fore of the alleged dissonance between elitism and populism. Both the CBC and the CRTC were considered by some to be elitist and out of tune with public taste. Some industry members saw the CBC 2 initiative as a demonstration of the corporation's la-di-da proclivities — a view I rejected categorically. Though we had to turn the proposal down, I saw its plans as a means of providing programs that had been neglected and were a desirable "flow of cultural expression."

I confronted this dichotomy on more than one occasion, when private broadcasters threw the E-word at me. My unceasing insistence on the need to provide more Canadian content, particularly in quality drama, where it was so lacking, was considered by the industry as ignoring popular taste, which favoured American shows, and trying to cater to a small minority. This, they believed, was rank ELITISM. In my counter-arguments I reversed the tables. It is they, I asserted, who lacked confidence in the Canadian public's capacity to acquire a taste for good quality shows when given the chance, by flooding the market with American trash. The CRTC and I, on the other hand, believed that high-class programs would find Canadian audiences. I often invoked the arguments of Lord Reith, the first head of the BBC, who insisted that the role of the public broadcaster was to *elevate* the level of what the public wanted to hear and to enable them to develop a liking for higher-quality content. While private broadcasters, I said, need not go that far, they, too, have a responsibility for broadening the experience of their listeners and viewers by introducing them to challenging programs. They were elitists when underestimating the ability of audiences to display good taste.

The quality of programming was always on our minds, as was the puzzle of how to complement the tsunami of US programs with domestic offerings, but these issues became particularly acute when we tackled pay-TV. It was well established in the United States and attracted growing numbers of Canadians, who resorted to unauthorized satellite dishes. These seemingly unstoppable horrors, which were four to five times larger than the modest sized ones currently garlanding our homes, were spreading across the land faster than an outbreak of measles. Not surprisingly, no Canadian shows were included. We hoped that the introduction of pay television into Canada, under CRTC rules, would correct the imbalance, at least to some degree. After the Commission received the Therrien Report, it set about to specify what it expected from such Canadian services and called for licence applications from interested parties.

A semi-comic cyclone hit us even before we got fully under way. As so often occurs in such instances, it was of infinitesimal importance to the innovations we were about to introduce. Our call for licence applications, as I mentioned briefly in a previous chapter, brought a raft of news stories announcing that a Canadian version of the American Playboy Channel intended to bid for a licence. A torrent of outraged responses followed from hordes of Canadians of pure mind, a great many of them orchestrated by organized moral guardians. In my four years in Ottawa no topic elicited even a fraction of the number of letters I received on the subject, 99.99 per cent (plus or minus) of them opposed.

The public, little able to distinguish between the CRTC and the DOC, besieged the minister, whose mailbag also exploded. Worse, a number of questions were put to him in Parliament. Francis asked me what we proposed to do about the application and wondered how to respond to his het up interlocutors. I replied that until the CRTC actually received an application it could do nothing whatsoever, and no application was in our hands. Furthermore, MPs and everyone else had to realize that the decision about the applications was that of the Commission alone. The minister could do nothing until a licence was either granted or refused. All the brouhaha, though distracting, in the end saved us a lot of time, and possibly some deep soul-searching: the Playboy people decided that, given all the fuss, they would not submit a licence application.

The Playboy affair briefly earned me an uncharacteristic and unwanted title. The Canadian Cable Television Association, as part of its lobbying game, annually held a reception on Parliament Hill for MPs, ministers, mandarins and industry leaders. One of these bashes took place just as the pay-TV drama was unfolding. I happened to be standing near the entrance when Jeanne Sauvé, the Speaker of the House, arrived. I was the first person she saw. "Ah," she exclaimed in a loud voice, "the Porn King!" giving me a big wink. Her husband, Maurice, a Quebec Liberal Party stalwart, spoke to one of my French Canada seminars in Kingston, accompanied by his wife. The three of us clicked during the usual pre-train sherry party and, though not close, we became friends. Hence the little joke which she had likely not intended to share with the whole assembly.

A possible Playboy invasion?

Soon after my CRTC appointment was announced, the *Globe and Mail* cartoonist, Anthony Jenkins, had me stand in a ring appropriately clad for a bout, my arms and huge boxing gloves resting on the ropes. The caption read, "Meeting all comers." Eric Boyd bought the original from the artist and presented it to me from the Commission staff on the occasion of my birthday. Subsequently, whenever an amusing caricature of me appeared somewhere, I tried to acquire the original. These are always much larger than the small versions one sees in the papers and are fun on the wall. Many of my acquisitions adorn the bathroom at Colimaison. The Playboy story appealed to the imagination of several cartoonists and is represented in the throne room. Rusins of the *Ottawa Citizen* had a toothy and bosomy Playboy bunny pull on a hefty rope in a tug-o-war with Francis and me, clad as scantily as our adversary. The result seemed to be a draw.

The three-week-long pay-TV hearing in 1981 was televised, and received national attention. The general contours of the television landscape to be created were determined by our earlier call for licence applications. The fundamental issue we faced was to decide which of the applicants for the new services would be entitled to provide the pay-per-view or subscription services and channels. Was pay-TV to be in private hands, public or mixed? What kind of services should be given a chance to test the market—national, regional or both? Should we licence religious, multilingual, arts-centred services, and under what conditions and, specifically, how high could we set the bar for Canadian content?

Our deliberations took a long time and were on occasion acrimonious. But in March of the following year we delivered our baby, albeit not unanimously. The Commission staff, led by Hank Intven, was most helpful in mastering and winnowing the masses of evidence we unearthed during the hearings and in teasing Solomonic verdicts out of them. Six services were blessed (too many in the eyes of a minority of commissioners): a national general-interest broadcaster, First Choice/Premier Choix offering programs in both languages; three regional general-interest channels; one regional multilingual (strongly Chinese) service and a cultural (mainly performing arts) offering.

I was not delighted with our menu, but it seemed the best bet under the circumstances. Dilemmas abounded. The Commission had repeatedly grappled with defining "quality." What makes a television service good, bad or indifferent? We simply could not find a clear aesthetic definition. The best we came up with, and I found it inadequate, was that diversity was the key. So we settled on the notion that a package covering a wide swath of varied programs was as likely to include good shows as anything we could specify and impose on the broadcasters. We hoped that the mix we licensed would result in decent quality programming.

It will not surprise you that *ceteris paribus*, as economists used to say when Latin was still breathing, i.e., other things being equal, I would have preferred a public, rather than a private, system.

I did not have great confidence in the good will and civic responsibility of most commercial operators, but there was at least some hope, and the alternatives were even less promising. To set up a new public corporation for pay-TV would have been my first choice but, given the political realities, totally utopian. Successive governments had underfunded the CBC for years, forcing it to go partially commercial, and there was not a phantom of a chance that either a Liberal or Progressive Conservative government would provide the funds for a public organization handling pay-TV.

The other public avenue was the CBC, but it already had more than its hands full, and its failure to live up to commitments it had made demonstrated that it was deaf to the CRTC's hymn book. Much as I respected its avowed devotion to high-quality Canadian programming, I had no confidence that it would deliver what it promised. An equally strong reservation arose from my conviction that, largely because of the restrictions imposed by its union contracts, it would stratospherically drive up the cost. This fear resulted partly from my experience as an occasional CBC public affairs broadcaster. I noticed that whereas CTV or other lesser fry conducted interviews by deploying a minimum of staff, the CBC invariably relied on a small platoon of operatives. In a radio encounter, for instance, the interviewer holding a microphone could not plug his gear into an outlet, because only a member of a different union was allowed to do so under the prevailing collective agreements. The quality of CBC work was usually higher than that of the others, but at a substantial cost. I thus concluded, with some unease, and with the majority of my colleagues, that the private route was better.

The CBC was not the only body living too high off the hog. One application we received towered above all others in my opinion. It was from Lively Arts Market Builders (LAMB) for the C-Channel, intending to present high-quality performing arts. Three of Canada's cultural icons were behind this bold idea: Arthur Gelber, arts advocate, administrator and philanthropist, chair of the Ontario Arts Council; Lou Appelbaum, composer, animator, administrator and co-chair of the 1982 *Report of the Federal Cultural Policy Review Committee*, and Hamilton Southam, arts enthusiast, animator and founding director of the National Arts Centre in Ottawa. Ed Cowan, former editor of *Saturday Night*, as president, was the hands-on guy who piloted the licence application and ran the show. This great project, alas, ran out of money six months after its launch. There were many reasons, of course: overly optimistic expectations of the number of subscribers; an extremely expensive management style, reflected in, among other things, its lavish offices; and, perhaps, the exacting conditions the commission attached to its licence.

The C-Channel appealed to me and I was a strong supporter. It came as a shock, therefore, when months later in a casual encounter with Arthur Gelber, he berated me for having caused its collapse. When I subsequently sought some elucidation and sympathy from Lou Appelbaum, who was a friend, he confirmed Gelber's view: the LAMB group, including himself, thought that it was the CRTC 's too exacting imposition of Canadian content quotas that caused the company's collapse. I am certain that other factors contributed to it at least as much, but do wonder whether we might not also have misread the market for programs of such high quality, given the amount of capital available to our licensee.

Whatever the short-lived contribution the C-Channel may have made to Canada, it enriched my life more than almost any other CRTC experience. It introduced me to Hamilton Southam. As a student of Canada's cultural scene, and a subscriber to various series at the National Arts Centre, I was aware of his leadership in the arts, but we had never met. I saw a television interview Patrick Watson conducted with him for the CBC, which presented him as a fascinating, wisely philanthropic, admirable person. My support of the C-Channel was, of course, unrelated to my reaction to the TV interview, but grew out of a belief that such a service was highly desirable.

Empathy between us developed during the hearing process and when the issue was finally settled, we decided to meet for a drink in the Opera, then the splendid bar of the NAC. Subsequently we got together off and on, in Canada and Europe, in one of his residences or mine, but most often for lunch at "his" table in the corner of the Rideau Club's bar. Some years after we met, I organized a symposium in Quebec City for the Royal Society of Canada on cultural policy and invited him to present a paper on the role of elitism in the arts. He did a fine job, as I knew he would, one that few could have carried off.

His friendship was of such great importance to me partly because it came so late in our lives. Special school and college friendships usually last a lifetime and go so deeply that newer camaraderie tends to pale by comparison. There are exceptions and the bonds Hamilton and I developed were appreciated by both of us, in part for this reason. I have been most fortunate in receiving all sorts of honours. Either Monica Datta or Becky Holmes, two kind souls who reorganized my library, made me chuckle by labelling a container, "Honourary degrees, diplomas...accolades." The last is a fine word. One recognition I received was of a different kind. Hamilton asked for a signed photograph of me, to hang in his study. Since the room in no way resembled a national portrait gallery and contained only a few likenesses of family and friends, I was deeply touched by this gesture. This was, indeed, an accolade.

The pay-TV decisions were not the greatest moment in the CRTC's history. Several licensees in addition to the C-Channel developed difficulties, and our hope that the new regime would substantially extend the viewing of high quality and Canadian programs was not realized.

This sombre reflection invites an attempt to evaluate my CRTC years from a longer-term perspective. I therefore turn to what I see as my contribution to the Commission, an aspect probably better undertaken by others, and also to what I derived from my stepping out of the academy by, in Bernard Ostry's terms, getting "my boots dirty in the public arena." On this aspect I am the world's best-informed witness by far.

The benefits accruing to me from the Ottawa stint probably outweighed what I brought to it. I learnt an enormous amount, much of it during the apprenticeship of the first year. In the foregoing pages, I made a few harsh comments about some of my colleagues and the institutional culture enveloping me, but neglected to give credit where it was due. Most of my fellow commissioners, and the staff of the Commission at all levels, went all out to help me do my job, from Eric Boyd and, of course, Ken Wyman at the top, to those performing lesser tasks. They taught me, and broke me in, in the kindest way. In one sense, indeed, it was the Commission that directed me rather than the reverse. Like a huge ocean liner, it plied its well-established route, sometimes resisting the efforts I made to alter course. This did not always work, but was done with the best intentions and the public interest — as one saw it — in mind.

What were the principal lessons I learnt, apart from a lot of the nitty-gritty of government and other large-scale organizations? Two, mentioned briefly before, stand out, like sturdy dandelions in a newly seeded lawn: the enormous usefulness and merit of public hearings, and the revelation that to fully know and understand a situation, may sometimes require that one be emotionally implicated in it, dangerous though this may be.

The academic mode of a scholar — producing a finding, flying it by a few colleagues and then unleashing it for wider appreciation and review — is fine in the republic of ideas, but inadequate in the cauldron of policy-making. There, the widest, most open and heterogeneous process of testing the water is essential and should be applied to virtually every major legislative initiative and policy innovation. And one should always be mindful of the need, in some cases, of financially and otherwise assisting potential targets of a policy so they can effectively participate in a hearing.

The second lesson is more subtle and has wider implications. At one level it is obvious, but it dawned on me fully and viscerally only when, to achieve a higher objective, I found myself behaving in a manner I had previously abhorred in others and rejected for myself — abandoning principle. Academic, second-hand knowledge, so to speak, is essential, but can have limitations. Cerebral awareness may need to be accompanied by experiencing and *feeling*, the emotional dimension of a situation. Book-learning alone cannot do this. I first encountered this simple fact, as I noted, while observing that at Commission meetings I sometimes made compromises while seeking majority support for policies I deemed essential. The process has universal and alarming implications. Is it possible to judge another person fairly without being in his skin? Take a collaborator, like Quisling, or a Jew "collaborating" with the Nazis in an extermination camp. How can a person in other shoes judge them? The French saying, *tout comprendre est tout pardonner* — to understand all is to forgive all — neatly points to the problem, one which has preoccupied me much more after my CRTC years than before.

Something else I learnt was not quite a lesson but a deeper awareness of an important aspect of how governments work. It arises because, for reasons of efficiency, fairness and accountability, bureaucracies are highly stratified. Everyone fits in his niche, engraved on an organizational chart, and his conduct and freedom of action are circumscribed by those above him, and in some ways even by those below. An atmosphere of collegiality and even camaraderie, of sharing a common cause, is often evident, but also the sense that everyone occupies a slot, exacting duties and bestowing rights and privileges. All this is enhanced by the fact that the public service constitutes such a critical mass in the Ottawa cocoon and, thus, a distinct society with its own folkways. I have nowhere sensed a similar and so distinctive a subculture.

I had an inkling of this state of affairs before I arrived and subtly but forcibly made the point, as head of an independent regulatory agency and as an academic, that I was aloof from it. I never relinquished this pose and never tired of reminding everyone of it by speech, comportment and even dress. At a time when shirt and tie were still *de rigeur*, I wore a turtleneck under my jacket except on the most formal occasions. It became something of a trademark. In speeches I so often used the phrase "as a lifelong academic" that it became tiresome and a joke. But it worked.

On one occasion I fell victim to Ottawa's status conscious mindset. An issue arose which I wished to discuss with Michael Pitfield, the Clerk of the Privy Council—the highest-ranking public servant. I knew him and left a message asking him to call back. My requests remained fruitless. He was doing a teaching spell at the Kennedy School at the time and so maintained a residence nearby. I asked a friend at Harvard to give me Michael's Cambridge, Mass. phone number and called him there. Bereft of his Ottawa sentry, he answered himself. Why had he ignored my repeated requests for a call? His reply, as best as I recall, was "To remind you of who's on top." I was not sure whether he was being funny, but could not quite dispel the idea that he was not.

Before I switch from acknowledging some of the benefits I derived from the CRTC to the contribution I made, another priceless gain claims recognition. It looms large in my life. I have already noted my friendship with Hamilton. There were many others, less intense, but precious nevertheless. Two were with journalists. Jack Miller, the entertainment columnist for the *Toronto Star* was one of the media people I found most impressive. He was thorough, fair, diligent and deeply knowledgeable about his beat, including its regulatory dimension. And he was a thoroughly decent man. I thought so highly of him that I suggested to Francis that he might make an excellent commissioner. It never came to pass.

The other journalist was Lawrence Surtees, then the *Globe and Mail*'s telecom expert. Like Jack, he was not flashy or pushy, but had a command of his file far above that of almost anyone else I knew. We collaborated on writing a paper, "Space Invaders: Some Canadian and International Implications of Telematics," published at Queen's and then morphed into a revised version for the IPSR. In my mind, we were co-authors, but one's memory is a treacherous tool (see the postscript, "Reality Check"). It seems that he served as a research assistant rather than co-author; what I recollect is that he knew a lot more of the details of the subject than I. He was, to me, an insufficiently appreciated jewel of the fourth estate.

Bumping repeatedly into Rick Schultz in connection with telecommunications and other CRTC matters deepened an old friendship and laid the foundations for a close lifelong bond. He was a political scientist, co-editor of a book of readings on Canadian politics, one of our shared fields. He was also an expert on regulatory issues. Our paths crossed frequently while I was in Ottawa. Afterwards, he became an annual star visitor to my seminar on regulation and I gave lectures and participated in several conferences at McGill where he became the James McGill Professor and Head of Political Science. He was and is strongly market oriented which led to our being productive foils. We have shared our good-natured exchanges before and with countless students. Uncompromising, fearless and sharp, he is also one of the wittiest of my friends. With two daughters in Toronto, he drives there twice a year from Montreal burdened with bags of that city's peerless bagels, a dozen of which he always deposits, horizontally split in half, in my Kingston freezer. Then we go out to lunch. Although I did not share his outlook, his insights were, on innumerable occasions, of help when I grappled academically and in the field of battle with regulatory issues. I was fortunate to be able to draw on his advice while in Ottawa and happily, ever since.

The citation I received when, in 1989, I was made an Officer of the Order of Canada, referred to my academic role and went on to say "he was also a major force in the restructuring of important sectors of Canada's telecommunications industry as chairman of the CRTC." That, I fear, was a flattering exaggeration. I helped steer the Commission towards socially responsible directions in the public interest, but was not a "major force." On the telecom side, I trusted my colleagues and the excellent Commission staff and largely confined myself to making sure that the Commission functioned smoothly. I agreed with the prevailing sense that a competitive, rather than monopolistic, telecom scenario was in the public interest because it would facilitate technological innovation and reduce costs. The only issue on which I had strong feelings was a trivial one: whether Bell should be allowed to raise the cost of phone-box calls from ten to twenty five cents. Since I believed that it was mostly low-income people who used pay phones, I thought that their costs might well be subsidized by the better-heeled subscribers. I realized that re-distributing income was not part of our mandate, but also knew that regulatory decisions invariably have implications which surpass the statute books.

Broadcasting concerns absorbed about three quarters of my time. Here I was an ardent and vociferous defender of the view that frequencies bringing income to the broadcasters should primarily serve the public interest and not the bottom line of communications companies. Whenever and wherever I could, I championed Canadian content, particularly in drama, the arts, and high-quality programming in general. Motherhood, you may say, but a motherhood all too often neglected and always in need of a voice.

I saw the CRTC chairman's job slightly differently from my predecessors. All of us shared a total commitment to the regulatory process, of course, but probably because of my background in education, I had a slightly broader view. The cut-and-dried process of "policing" broadcasting and telecom had to be supplemented by efforts to convince our "charges" of the importance and value of the legislative goals. In addition to regulating behaviour, we should also influence minds. What might be called this quasi-regulatory, or value-added, role was likely shared by us, but I attached greater importance to it than the others. It may well have been utopian, but it was consistent with my past.

My encounters with what was sometimes called "the industry," my speeches, articles, and interviews with media, were driven — aside from the bread and butter issues appropriate for the moment — by this motivational strategy. I hoped to imbue Canadian leaders of the communications sector with a desire to ply their craft in a public-spirited manner and to awaken or reinforce their awareness of the need to foster Canadian culture.

Was it a delusion of grandeur to conceive the chair's role as a sort of public conscience with respect to broadcasting and telecommuni-cations? Perhaps. Some saw me as an idealistic, academic dreamer, too little concerned with their need to make money. On the other hand, I encouraged and strengthened the cultural community. The industries we regulated were not homogeneous and while my exhortations fell on deaf ears in some quarters, they met with a positive response in others. The impact I had was likely small, but I was sure that it was there. If nothing else, I encouraged and strengthened the resolve of most of those on our side.

One of my strongest convictions was that, to be effective and to truly serve the public interest, a regulatory agency had to be open, accessible and transparent. In one respect, I may have gone a little too far in giving in to this belief. I was aware, before coming to Ottawa, that officials and politicians are inclined to treat access of information legislation cavalierly. They are often ingenious and even devious in trying to conceal what was really going on. The CRTC was no exception. Our otherwise excellent legal branch went as far as they could in preventing information seeping out. They were animated, in my view, by excessive and unnecessary caution. On one or two rare occasions I did something which was totally improper; I leaked background information to a trusted journalist because I was convinced that to do so was in the public interest. These indiscretions were of such a minor nature that I cannot even recall the details, but I did spill the beans now and then with no baleful consequences and always slept well afterwards.

On less perilous ground, my efforts to make the Commission deal more effectively with the public, through such means as the correspondence unit, and my near obsession with clarity of expression, were part and parcel of the same wish for transparency.

In 2008 Liora Salter, an old friend and specialist in, among other things, the relationship of social science and technology, published, with a colleague, an 800-page tome about the Commission. *The CRTC and Broadcasting Regulation in Canada* is dedicated to four former chairs, and one of the first, prematurely deceased, commissioners. The dedication reads "To: Pierre Juneau *Who made it smart,* Harry Boyle *Who made it fun,* John Meisel *Who let the light in,* André Bureau *Who made it work,* Pat Pearce *Who made it all worthwhile.*"

Some will think that letting "the light in" does not amount to a hill of beans; I find it a pleasing epitaph on my regulatory career.

I left the Commission in mid-November 1983. I had never, as you know, intended to stay the seven years because I feared that so long an absence from the university would disqualify me from a return to academic life—I would have lost touch with the relevant literature. Murie and I took a holiday in Europe and, at the beginning of the next term, I returned to Queen's where Ron Watts, the principal, friend and former academic ally, invited me to become the Sir Edward Peacock Professor of Political Science.

Soon afterwards, I learnt that the paintings I had borrowed for the Commission from the Art Bank were returned by Eric Boyd within 24 hours of my departure. This disappointing news was offset, however, by another piece of intelligence. Suzanne, Terry and Yolande, the secretaries in my office suite who were at first indifferent, we might say, to the artwork I had chosen for our walls, now bemoaned its loss. They had come to love it. This confirmed my view that if the public is given the chance to see and hear high-quality programs for a while, it may well come to like them.

* * *

Although I resigned from Queen's when I went to Ottawa, my academic persona, as I noted, never quite atrophied. The CRTC years were simply a very special and longer than usual instance of the kind of extracurricular activity I described as the Third Pillar. So, while at the CRTC, I not only exploited the academic connection in my comportment and style, but also drew heavily on the skills in analysis, writing, and lecturing which Queen's had taught me. That those whom I had taught or encountered in my research had gone on to hold government posts also facilitated my work Doors opened, mandarins beckoned and information flowed as the result of my academic past. The classlessness of professors was an unmistakable asset in this process.

Gone!

And when I returned to what I had always seen as my home, the shoe was on the other foot. The content of what I taught and the new research paths reflected the Ottawa immersion. In addition to my traditional gig of Canadian politics, I now taught seminars on and wrote about Broadcasting Policy, Cultural Policy, and the Politics of Regulation. Political parties moved from the centre to the periphery and communications and the arts gained ascendency.

I had never quite abandoned IPSA and resumed my contacts there and some of the other activities abroad and overseas about which I have so far remained largely silent. Amends are made in the next chapter, "Foreign Affairs."

XX

Foreign Affairs: A Plain, A Mountain, and Seven Peaks

L ooking back on my activities abroad, I see an extensive plain stretching from present into the past, with a mountain and seven peaks rising above it. There are actually many more than just seven peaks, and the flatland boasts lots of enticing hillocks, but to make this tale manageable, I select a few joys which stand out. The dominant feature, the mountain, is the International Political Science Association (IPSA). This is where we'll start; when we descend from there we'll embark on the less strenuous climbs of the seven peaks.

The Mountain: IPSA

I attended the 1967 IPSA World Congress in Brussels, thereby beginning a relationship (as they say nowadays, meaning something else), lasting close to thirty years. The then triennial congresses were hosted by the main political science association of the member countries. IPSA's executive committee meets at least yearly and its gatherings also always involve a round table on a topic relevant to the discipline, so that there is at least one IPSA meeting somewhere in the world annually, and during a congress year, there are at least two. The world body of political scientists engages in a variety of activities enhancing the quality of their discipline, of which the congresses, the research committees and publications are the most important. The research committees convene regularly in a globe-trotting pattern. I participated primarily in the committees on Political Sociology, and on Language and Politics.

In the mid 1970s the CPSA elected me as its representative on the IPSA Council, a decision leading to two momentous developments: it started my annual, sometimes biannual, journeys to some place on the globe attending a gathering of colleagues, and it cemented my friendship with Jean Laponce. He was the IPSA man par excellence, even becoming president. We have since collaborated on innumerable projects linked to the CPSA, the IPSA, the RSC, and other causes. Our bonds of friendship continue, and although he lives in Vancouver, and I in Kingston, every first Tuesday of the month we spend about an hour on the phone, catching up with one another and our dear ones.

Laponce and Meisel: inseparable cronies at IPSA and elsewhere.

Jean became convinced during his presidency that IPSA should launch a genuinely international general political science journal, providing an overarching venue hospitable to all the theoretical, methodological and geographical chapels of political science. He would have been the ideal editor but, as president, could not take this on. Enter JM. I started the *International Political Science Review* (IPSR) in 1979 and edited it alone for six years (with Jean's informal advice and help) until he joined me and we became co-editors for several years. In 2011, more than thirty years after our debut, we were gratified to learn that IPSA was establishing a prize in our names for the best IPSR article published in the journal in the interval between congresses, to be awarded first in 2012 at the World Congress in Madrid, and at all subsequent congresses.

The IPSR editors were ex officio members of the IPSA executive committee, and thus I participated in the association's decision-making and management apparatus for about twenty years.

Compared to being a tourist, there is an enormous advantage in visiting faraway places as a guest of, and hobnobbing with, a local organizing committee. In IPSA's case, I had come to know many of these colleagues well in previous encounters. We always approached the local society — at least its academic camps — as guests of experienced and communicative locals who directed us to the really worthy sites, warned against tourist traps, and ensured that we plunged into the thick of current issues animating local society. The host committees, usually subsidized by governments, also made sure that we stayed and ate at pretty ritzy establishments.

The precise substance of what transpired and what intellectual puzzles engaged us is overshadowed by recollections of encounters and friendships with colleagues from everywhere, some famous architects, builders and leaders of the discipline, others obscure toilers in the vineyard. Both included fascinating types and a few excruciating bores. Many became friends.

As all conference goers know, it is almost always the "extracurricular activities" — the meals, parties, shared visits to historical or scenic sites and cultural events, and particularly evening and late night gatherings in cafés, taverns, bodegas, bistros or, often, in the home of a local savant — which make the deepest and most enduring impressions. The topics in these séances always included heavy loads of political science talk but also invariably strayed into considerations of currently hot political issues, academic politics, and comparisons of life in our respective homelands.

In this context, my incapacity to withhold candies and the delight this story causes me, compel me to recount an anecdote I picked up from an Irish colleague at one of our meetings. A Spaniard and Irishman compare their respective homelands over a Guinness. They note many similarities: both countries are strongly Catholic, situated at the fringe of where the major action is, long troubled by sectarian strife, and their populations tend to indulge themselves in a rather relaxed life style. At one point, the Spaniard asks whether Erse contains a term that has similar connotations as the wonderful Spanish mañana, meaning both "tomorrow" and "at some time in the future, maybe." After a long reflection, the Irishman replies that there are several such terms, but that none conveys anything like the same sense of urgency.

The places where these think-fests were held linger in the mind more forcibly than their formal themes. Lists are poison, but the best way to convey the breadth of my IPSA travels is to identify some of the places they took me to, in several cases more than once. Going about it more or less chronologically, they were Brussels, Munich,

Paris, Bellagio, Montreal, Jerusalem, Zurich, Dubrovnik, Zagreb, Edinburgh, Weimar, Moscow, Florence, Rio de Janeiro, Tokyo, Kyoto, Washington, Berlin (both East and West at different times), Chicago, Prague, Buenos Aires and, I suspect, a few others which have slipped my mind. Even Kingston, Ontario was the site of an international conference which I organized.

It would be criminal of me to withhold from you a minor incident associated with the last-named Kingston colloquium. My editor will complain that this interferes with the flow of the narrative, but, darn it, some stories insist on being told. During a break in our sessions, Jean Laponce and I went for a stroll in a nearby residential area, in the course of which we encountered two little boys playing in a front yard. They gazed at us, as we passed, with an inexplicably puzzled look on their faces. "Are you from *Mad* magazine?" one of them asked. When we denied the charge, the other urchin said, "Well, you must be professors."

The IPSA meetings occurred on both sides of the Iron Curtain despite the Cold War. Relations between East and West — then quite rare — were, in fact, one of the most fascinating features of the IPSA exercise. The Soviet Union — and hence the satellites as well — actively participated in and supported IPSA's activities. This was so largely because of one Georgii Shakhnazarov, an important member of the Institute of State and Law in Moscow, who was a very big man in the USSR. He held powerful positions in the Communist Party, spoke English (as well as several other tongues), played chess whenever the opportunity arose, authored numerous Marxist articles and books and a science fiction novel, possessed a remarkably open mind, and knew and understood the West. He was more of a pragmatist than an ideologue. Totally loyal to and correct vis-à-vis the Soviet state apparatus, he tried, as best he could, to encourage peaceful co-existence. He was very close to Gorbachev, was one of the architects of Perestroika and, after Gorbie's entry into private life, closely collaborated with him in the Gorbachev Foundation.

Like virtually all communist-country scholars attending conferences in the decadent and perfidious West, Georgii was always accompanied and assisted in everything by a sidekick. He was William Smirnov, the secretary of the Soviet political science association. We were never sure whether William's real function was to spy on his boss or just to help him. He, too, was an open-minded, very smart person, well versed in up-to-date methodologies, including the use of opinion surveys — a tool used rarely, if at all, by

Soviet-bloc scholars during my early IPSA days. He is now a political science bigwig in Russia.

The First Peak: Ann Arbor—Surveys and Ceramics

My fairly intensive association with the Inter-university Consortium for Political and Social Research in Ann Arbor, which I already mentioned, provided an early exposure to scholarship in "the States," and to life in America, which I found in many respects quite different from that of Canada. The "feel" of American cities and towns evoked slightly jarring sensations of familiarity and foreignness. Some aspects were off-putting, even menacing, particularly the ubiquitous manifestations of national pride—the stars and stripes were everywhere—and the American approach to law and order, particularly guns, bothered me. Once, while sitting in the passenger seat of Phil Converse's car, I looked warily at the glove compartment and asked whether Phil carried a gun. The guffaws elicited by this query left no doubt that I was widely off the mark. Later, after I had visited diverse regions of the country, I realized that to generalize about the United States is ridiculous. Like Canada, the place is so large and variously textured that it exhibits substantially diverse and widely divergent subcultures, although there are probably more shared traits across the land, including ubiquitous patriotism, than is the case in Canada. All my foreign visits also brought home that there is an academic culture which usually displaces differences occasioned by nationality and geography. The focus on ideas and professorial collegiality wipes out or diminishes much of the distinctiveness occasioned by diverse places of residence and passports.

The Ann Arbor encounters, which started in the early 1960s, exposed me first hand to the latest methodologies and technologies of data collection and analysis. The consortium was founded in 1962 and was still something of an infant when I persuaded Queen's to join a few years later. Its purpose was to enhance the quality and scope of social and political surveys, and the management and storage of their findings. The then state-of-the-art North American election studies were at the time being done by Michigan scholars who were closely associated with, and indeed the driving force behind, the consortium. Their authors, Campbell, Converse, Miller and Stokes, created models of the art which dominated the field and influenced similar probes in other countries. You may recall, from the earlier account of my research, that I recruited Phil Converse as a member of the team undertaking the first Canadian election study in 1965. An interest in comparative studies and in heightening comparability among explorations in various countries resulted in the Michigan consortium regularly attracting political scientists, historians and sociologists from Western Europe and, particularly, Scandinavian countries.

Occasionally, the Survey Research Center organized symposia around a particularly intriguing issue. One such event, in 1967, was called a "data confrontation conference." It was an exercise in comparative analysis matching and comparing data from diverse jurisdictions. Every paper offered was produced by at least two scholars, drawing on data from more than one country or research setting. I was invited to participate and teamed up with Georges Dupeux from Bordeaux in France and Phil Converse. The two were the pioneers of French election studies and had data from that country comparable to those generated by Michigan for the United States, and those Phil and I just produced with our collaborators in the 1965 Canadian survey. What emerged was "Continuities in Popular Political Culture: French and Anglo-Saxon Contrasts in Canada." The idea and execution were entirely Phil's, and I was embarrassed by the modesty of my contribution to it. I have never cited this paper among my works. At the time of the conference, the analysis of the Canadian survey was still far from complete, and I was very ill at ease in interpreting its findings. Phil had the very bright idea of using the French, Canadian and US data not to analyze the substance of the responses, but to compare how French Canadian and Anglo-Canadian responses differed. They varied in their reactions to identical or similar questions and to those from comparable French and American electors. The paper shed new light on differences between the two principal language groups in Canada, and between them and people in France and the United States.

Ann Arbor also led indirectly to one of my first returns to the Continent after the war. The brief visit to Berlin in the late '50s, for the NATO Association meeting mentioned earlier, does not count; except for our attending the Brecht theatre there was NO contact with the ordinary life of the city. Among the colleagues I came to know at some of the consortium affairs was Klaus Liepelt, a young, enterprising German who had done graduate work at Michigan and maintained close contact with his alma mater after his return home.

He ran a research institute in Bad Godesberg near Bonn and, in 1968, convened a workshop there attended by several of the Ann Arbor, as well as other American and European, experts. I was included and so had my first exposure to the German scientific community and, more memorably, to Bonn—then still the capital of West Germany—which I had only briefly passed through in 1959.

Despite the great academic and professional benefits of the Liepelt conference, it was the setting that left the deepest mark. I recall Bonn's town centre, with its cobblestone streets and a lovely square, pleasing ancient architecture (nothing so tall as to dwarf the human scale), absence of garish advertising and—a miracle—a large pedestrian area in the middle, free of cars. This great invention, not uncommon now although still too rare in North America, was then new to me and I welcomed it with all my being. Since the workshop schedule and the associated social events were demanding, I was able to visit this paradise only rarely, primarily to buy a few presents.

Murie's prize was a pottery, blue-carapaced, turtle whose head, loosely hung, moved pensively from left to right when the body was tipped ever so slightly into one or another direction. I am not sure why I am using the past tense, since the creature still graces my home and still wobbles. It sounds grossly kitschy, but is actually a lovely piece because the design, pottery, and glaze are so exquisite and the head's movement so unobtrusive. The line between kitsch and good taste is slender and personal, not always easy to draw, despite snobbish arguments to the contrary.

A more prosaic purchase—a gift for myself—provided a nostalgic return to pre-war Europe, the Europe I had left thirty years earlier. It was the practice, in those more formal, sports jacket-, blazer- or suit-filled days, to wear shirts calling for cufflinks. These were never huge, ostentatious, macho knuckle-dusters of the sort favoured more recently by *some* sort of men. Normally, they came in diverse colours and were made of elasticized string artfully tied at each end into a small ornamental knot which bound each side of the cuff. They looked like tiny, textile dumbbells. By the time I came across some black specimens in Bonn, I had long worn out my old ones and was absolutely delighted to be reunited with the genuine article after all these years of deprivation.

The consortium meetings always coincided with a large and magnificent ceramic exhibit held by an Ann Arbor guild of potters. I unfailingly managed to take it in and to buy Murie one or more pieces for our collection.

The precious presents for Murie, lovingly acquired here and there then unveiled soon after my return, were certainly intended for her — she was, after all, the family's No. 1 aesthete — but they offered me at least as much pleasure. It might have been better to select some piece of jewellery or a sartorial ornament. But bijouterie left her cold and she had a far superior taste in clothes than I, many of which she made herself. And anyway, I happily admit that we both derived a lot of pleasure from sharing the pieces of pottery I brought home.

The Second Peak: Bellagio—The Silk Route

Among the few places from which I brought Murie something just for herself (well, primarily for herself) was Bellagio. I was there in 1973 at a symposium also attended by Ghita Ionescu, a Rumanian, British-based, good friend. He had founded and edited *Government and Opposition* — a fine journal with which I enjoyed a long-standing association. Ghita reported that Italy was a magnificent source of fine silk. Valence, his wife, accompanied him and the three of us set out to see what enticing fabric we could find. I bought several metres of wonderful material for a long evening gown. The silk was so splendid that Murie engaged a professional dressmaker to design and make the gown.

Until some taste-deprived developers appropriated its name for an insanely expensive, ostentatious and garish Las Vegas hotel-palazzo-casino (it cost $1.6 billion US!!!, allegedly employs about 10,000 people, and permanently hosts the *Cirque du soleil*), Bellagio was known mainly as a quiet and idyllic small place in Lombardy on the Southern tip of Lake Como; academics were aware of it as the site of the Rockefeller Foundation Centre. The latter provides magnificent facilities for scholars in residence and for conferences, during which the conferees mingle with the longer-term residents, who are invariably interesting writers, artists and researchers. At least this was the case when I was there for a highly stimulating round table. Not only the company, but also the cuisine and cellar were outstanding.

The purpose of the gathering was to scrutinize A.O. Hirschman's, *Exit, Voice and Loyalty: Responses to Decline in Firms, Organizations and States*. This short, path-breaking book begins, as I remember it, with a discussion of a seemingly innocuous question:

what is a long-standing Cadillac owner disillusioned with his latest model to do when he is about to purchase a new car? Does he complain to the company about the shortcomings he has encountered (Voice)? Does he go to another brand (Exit)? Or does he give another Caddy a chance (Loyalty)? In an astonishing twist, the same set of choices is then presented to parents living in a neighbourhood with inadequate public schools. Do they become politically active to ameliorate the situation, send their kids to private schools or just do nothing? The socially responsible conclusion is obvious and has far-reaching implications for theories of economic behaviour. Although Hirschman does not push the analogy this far, it implicitly undermines the laissez-faire and market-dominated assumptions of many economists. His book thus raises a number of questions highly pertinent to social scientists. The round table, organized and led by Stein Rokkan under the auspices of IPSA and the International Social Science Council, spent a few fascinating days addressing and debating them.

I can't recall who were all the authorities present, but they were a high-powered lot of diverse national and disciplinary backgrounds.

Lake Como and the <u>real</u> Bellagio.

A.O. Hirschman himself was, of course, the Prince of Denmark. Elegant, gaunt and a bit austere, he was nevertheless approachable. Brian Barry was the rapporteur. The quintessential transatlantic scholar in that he held several distinguished academic posts at various times, both in the United Kingdom and the USA, he was at the time a Fellow of Nuffield College. One of the most pre-eminent political philosophers of his time, he had just published an influential book on John Rawls. He made sure that the discussion was deeply searching and tough. Another pretty vigorous and impressive participant was Samuel Huntington (Harvard) about whom I have more to say in a moment, when we clamber up the next peak.

You may wonder what I was doing among this august assembly of deep thinkers. I'd love to believe that I was invited because of my fame as a political scientist, but that, alas, was likely not the case. IPSA's next world congress was to take place later that year in Montreal and Stein, the then president, was anxious to settle a number of organizational issues with some of the executive committee, and particularly its two Canadians—Jean and I. So there we were, included in the *crème de la crème*, and even contributing to its intellectual repast.

The Third Peak: New York—Trilateral Woes

It was the Trilateral Commission which, a couple of years later, caused me to connect with Sam Huntington again. Founded by David Rockefeller, it sought to enhance co-operation among Europe, America and Japan and to improve economic conditions as well as democratic institutions. While undoubtedly conservative, it did not justify the onslaught unleashed on it later by conspiracy theorists on both extremes of the spectrum, from the John Birch Society and Barry Goldwater on the right to Noam Chomsky on the left. Its membership comprises, among others, corporate CEOs, academics and university heads, trade unionists and NGOs involved in international aid. Its director was Zbigniew Brzezinzki, the Polish-American wunderkind who eventually transmuted himself from a high-class academic into a major figure in foreign policy councils of US Democratic administrations. The Commission undertook a study of democracy in its three areas, which appeared in 1975 as *The Crisis of Democracy: On the Governability of Democracies*.

Ignoring the well-known quip that the camel is a horse designed by a committee this tome was not only the work of three authors, but also emerged from extensive consultations with diverse groups on three continents. I was invited to New York, in February 1975, for a small meeting at which the introductory chapter, and the three regional sections, were discussed with the authors, Michel Crozier (France), Samuel Huntington (USA) and Joji Watanuki (Japan). In addition to the authors and Brzezinzki, among those attending were S.M. Lipset (Harvard), James Cornford (Edinburgh), Erwin Scheuch (Cologne) and, to my great delight, Arthur M. Schlesinger (New York). He had not only been a close advisor, and historian of several of the Kennedy clan, but his progressive *The Vital Center* (1949) was one of the earliest works I reviewed (favourably) for the *Queen's Quarterly*. I also utilized his book on Andrew Jackson when I taught my course on American politics.

My encounter with the whole group, including Schlesinger was, however, a big disappointment. Despite being thoroughly well informed, erudite and well meaning, most of the little band seemed quite insensitive to what I considered to be a self-evident and sad feature of the status quo. There was a lot of talk about the dissonance between what people expected from government and what it was able to deliver. Currently fashionable buzzwords like "system overload" and "ungovernability" were bandied about and applied to portray what were considered dangerous impediments to stability and a climate fostering economic well-being. Decline in public trust was deplored, as were various means of expressing alienation from governments. I shared some of the latter concerns, and rejected the violence and street brawls which sometimes accompanied public protest. But I was all too conscious of the wide income disparities, extreme poverty, unemployment, inadequate social and health services, and of many other shortcomings of the "trilateral countries." I thought, in short, that there was a lot to be disaffected about. While I rejected some of the means used to express dissatisfaction, I thought it dangerous to brush shortcomings under the rug and remain deaf to complaints calling for redress. In expressing this reservation, I was supported by only one other person, an Englishman. Not even Arthur Schlesinger voiced my concern, which I found very strange. The almost arrogant self-confidence of Huntington and Brzezinski was chilling.

Some time after this fascinating consultation, it dawned on me that many of those present, and particularly Lipset and Scheuch, had during their lives undergone something of a conversion. Starting on the left, they had gradually moved to the right, until they flirted with conservatism and even reaction. Schlesinger did not follow this path, but his social philosophy, as revealed during our discussions, was now far from the position he took in *The Vital Center*.

To its credit, the Trilateral Commission took into account that there were important differences between Canada and the United States. One of the reasons may have been that Zbig came to Montreal from Poland as a child and grew up there. He knew Canada well and saw to it that *The Crisis of Democracy* contains a fairly lengthy appendix addressing the themes of the book in a Canadian context. This section is less pessimistic, apprehensive and skittish than the reports preceding it. Its principal inspiration was a Trilateral conference held in Montreal in May 1975, several months after the New York consultation.

It was not surprising that the larger Montreal gathering produced a more balanced document. The thirty or so people involved represented a Canadian academic, political, public service and journalistic elite, and included many who were in no way identified with the establishment and some who were known to hold progressive views. I won't list them all, but among those who will ring a bell were politicians Jean-Luc Pepin, Gordon Fairweather, Francis Fox, Jacques Lalonde, mandarins Geoffrey Pearson, Peter Dobell, Michael Kirby and Simon Riesman, academics Garth Stevenson, Robert Jackson, Stephen Clarkson and journalists Claude Ryan, Richard Gwyn and Doris Anderson. I knew most of them reasonably well but was particularly pleased by the presence of my friend and former collaborator, Vincent Lemieux from Laval. And it was at this gathering that I first met CRTC's founding chair Pierre Juneau, who later became a friend and counsellor. Brzezinski and Huntington, needless to say, also attended.

A remarkable incident, linked to the Trilateral session in New York, is etched ineradicably in my mind. Some of the details are fuzzy now, but the main action is as clear as if it were unfolding before my eyes as I write. We were put up at the Waldorf Astoria and the meetings were held at the Japan Trade Centre (which at the time housed a superb exhibition of Japanese packaging, which Murie would have adored). The two places were at some distance from one another, but I decided to walk to the first morning meeting. I unwittingly left the hotel at a truly ungodly hour, because I had no idea how long it would take me to get there on foot and because I had failed to notice that my travel alarm clock had not been adjusted to a recent time change.

It was a chilly day and the streets were still completely empty. I can't tell you where I was, but there were nice open spaces and some body of water with benches alongside. I noticed at one point that I was being followed. He eventually caught up with me and I saw a somewhat scruffy fellow who had a few teeth missing, but looked quite pleasant. He appeared to be sober. We fell into conversation and it emerged that he was anxious that I take him to wherever I lived. I was absolutely certain that there was not the slightest sexual context to this suggestion – this is something one can usually tell. But I did think that he might have wanted to steal some money and possibly other things as well. Was I about to be mugged? I started talking to him and suggested we sit down on one of the nearby benches. I imagined that as time passed, some other folks might come along. I talked incessantly, telling him that I came from Canada to a conference, that I was a professor and that this was my first ever visit to New York City. I also mentioned that originally I came from Czechoslovakia. He gradually became interested in my tale and reciprocated by talking about his own childhood, somewhere in the South, his older brother and his parents and his spotty education. He was African. His requests that I take him to my place (I mentioned that I did not have one but was at a hotel) became less frequent and insistent, and he eventually gave up. I mentioned that I had to go to my meeting, and we parted amicably. I may have been wrong, but felt pretty certain that I had talked myself out of some sort of attack. New York at the time was not all that safe a city. If so, I was lucky that my putative assailant was not an impulsive man and not crazed by drugs or dangerously deprived of them.

Later, when I reflected on this episode, I thought that there was a connection between the preoccupations of the Trilateral Commission and the presence of this man on that unidentified street or avenue. I suspect that, even had any of my colleagues around the Japan Trade Centre table been apprised of my little adventure (which they were not), they would most likely have been blind to the connection, or would have placed it very low on their list of policy priorities.

The Fourth Peak: Strathclyde—A Scottish Rhapsody

Richard Rose, whom I knew well from Ann Arbor, IPSA and other meetings, was for many years the head of politics at Strathclyde University in Glasgow. He was, and is, an astonishingly fertile and versatile writer, and an ingenious and effective promoter of numerous academic and pedagogic initiatives. In 1978, he contrived to get me invited to the UK by the British Council on a short-term visitorship with a fancy name. I can't quite remember exactly what it was, but the words "distinguished Commonwealth professor" or "visitor," greatly impressed Murie and me. The terms were amazing. We were given an apartment in Glasgow, and I was to present one colloquium, and make myself available to colleagues for consultation about their research, i.e., sit in my office and welcome whoever felt like dropping in. The visitorship also required that I be invited to give a seminar at four other UK universities. Aberdeen, Glasgow, Edinburgh and Cardiff became my brief but stimulating and generous hosts, and I also gave a lecture in London, under the aegis of Canada House.

Murie and I were excited about the prospect of spending some time in Scotland. We had adored London, as you may recall, but saw relatively little of the rest of the country. Glasgow seemed a little scary. We knew that the dock area along the Clyde, the Gorbels, was a pretty rough slum teeming with drunks. They gave the town a bad name. We were in for a surprise. The area was substantially cleaned up by the late '70s (although it went into another decline later) and Glasgow revealed itself as a lovely city. It had a rich cultural life — later (1990) being named by the European Community the cultural capital of Europe. It maintained a fine botanical garden, situated only a minute away from our flat, so we visited it often. The legacy of Charles Rennie Mackintosh, Scotland's greatest architect and *art nouveau* designer, was much in evidence, particularly at the Glasgow School of Art. And one of its small restaurants, which we visited occasionally, went under the delightful name "The Ubiquitous Chip." The weather that year was glorious, encouraging the bonny acres of rhododendrons to render us speechless, even me! They were particularly unbelievable at nearby Helensburgh, where the Roses lived, and where we occasionally visited.

The raison d'être for being there was not, of course, cultural or botanical, but academic. The standards of my colleagues were high and I learnt at least as much from chatting with them as they from me. The Scottish National Party (SNP), seeking Scotland's separation from the UK, had been in ascendancy in Britain, although it had suffered a significant setback in a Glasgow by-election just before we arrived. Given my interest in Canadian parties and in the viability of the Canadian state, I was fascinated by parallels with, and contrasts between, the two countries. I struck up a particularly pleasant and close relationship with one colleague, Jack Brand, one of Scotland's leading experts on Scottish nationalism. He was also an enthusiastic practitioner of the art. Very active in the party, he took me along on a day's campaigning on its behalf in a nearby by-election. "We" lost.

Although I found the SNP campaigners I met very engaging, I was ambivalent about their party's goals for two principal reasons. Breaking up a long-established country, *in the absence of really compelling reasons*, is likely to have, on balance, more negative than positive consequences. It benefits a small group of zealots associated with the revolt and does little, if anything, of lasting benefit for to the rest. I also feared that the party's electoral success would come at the expense of Labour and so split the anti-Conservative vote. This would strengthen Margaret Thatcher's chances of becoming PM. I thought her a menace and could not stand her. During numerous conversations with Jack, I not only deepened my knowledge of British politics and Scottish nationalism but also, because of the opportunities offered for making comparisons, gained new insights into national unity issues in Canada. Jack Brand was not the only "teacher" I found at Strathclyde. Richard Rose is an inexhaustible font of new and intriguing ideas and so being in his vicinity also bore rich intellectual fruit.

I greatly enjoyed the side trips imposed by the British Council; they provided an opportunity to discover new places and universities and to hear, from a wide mix of colleagues, views on some of the ideas which preoccupied me at the time. And, anyway, I always enjoyed giving talks and papers. The themes of my presentations were political parties in divided societies or the relationship between politics and leisure culture.

Aberdeen was particularly pleasant and attractive, as was Cardiff. In the former, as in other Scottish towns, I deepened my admiration of and fondness for malt whiskey, and in the latter I discovered a new meaning to an old word. In the staff club before lunch, someone inquired whether I would care for a schooner. My puzzled look was met with the explanation that in those parts sherry is served either in schooners or clippers. The usage was inspired by the sort of ships that brought the liquid gold from Spain. The clipper is the larger ship (and measure); needless to say, it was my choice.

On a less frivolous level, I note that, on these brief excursions to some of the smaller out-of-the-way places, I encountered one or two relatively little known scholars who were outstanding either because of their vast general knowledge or because of an uncommonly thorough and insightful command of their field. There is a tendency in the larger, dominant universities to assume that their less notorious sisters are bereft of stellar scholars. Not so. Innumerable factors attract and bind professors to a place and account for the fact that real treasures can sometimes be found in the most unexpected places. I hasten to add that this observation in no way reflects on the quality of my host institutions. They were highly reputable and led me to expect top talent. But both in Canada and abroad, there is a tendency to underestimate faculties in the less renowned places.

The Fifth Peak: New Haven—A Year Among the Yalies

Widely sharing one's assumptions, knowledge and insight is part of the academic game, linked to the verity that discussion, confrontation and argument test and improve knowledge. We professors therefore do a lot of guest lecturing, conferencing and visiting with one another. These interchanges assume many diverse forms. Strathclyde was one model; it lasted a few weeks and did not require the production of a specific publication. I partook in many such encounters of diverse lengths and formats in Europe, Canada and the States. Some lasted only an hour or so, others a day or two or maybe a week. My longest, and in some ways most exciting, venture of this sort took a whole academic year.

The visiting professorship at Yale came about indirectly because of the largesse of Canada's taxpayers. To mark the 200th anniversary of the founding of the USA, the government of Canada gave Yale University an imaginative gift. It funded five visiting professorships, each for a year at a time, enabling Yale to invite a Canadian scholar to offer courses and partake in the life of the university. The history department was chosen to invite the first guest and named Ramsay Cook (York), one of the country's most astute and articulate chroniclers of its national and dual identity. The following year, 1976, the political scientists won, and I was their choice.

When Joe LaPalombara, the head of the Yale department phoned me to make the offer, I was incredulous. His was probably the best political science department anywhere and I found the prospect of joining it for a year daunting and slightly terrifying. How would I make out? How would I be received? I wasn't in that league. The place was teeming with some of the giants of academe: Robert Dahl, Robert Lane, Juan Linz, James Fesler, David Apter, Charles

Lindblom, LaPalombara himself and many others whose work figured large in my and everyone else's reading lists.

I was to teach a course in comparative politics normally given by Juan Linz, who was to be on leave, and world of wonders, one on Canadian politics. This was not a heavy burden and, having just completed a heftyish piece of research and writing, I decided to use my year in New Haven as something of a sabbatical. Teaching, yes, but no serious research or writing, apart from finishing a couple of papers well along the path to completion. I would recharge my batteries by using the Stirling Library for widely flung general reading, unrelated to any particular research. This is a luxury seldom available to us hard-slogging academics.

After house hunting in June, Murie and I stuffed a recently acquired Saab to the gills and set out in early September for our apartment at 400 Whitney Avenue, New Haven, within easy walking distance to the university. The first sight of my office began to dispel my apprehension and sense of being an insignificant tadpole in a large, glorious pond. I had anticipated working in some shabby cubbyhole at the periphery of the action. Not at all. My home was a huge, luxurious chamber—the head's office, in fact—temporarily available while LaPalombara was off in Italy on his sabbatical. It was within a whisper's distance from where several leaders of our discipline penned their masterworks.

The hospitable message conveyed by my spatial reception was echoed in the demeanour of my new colleagues. Had they been more friendly, they would have been gushing. A seemingly unspoken practice in the department, and Yale generally, was that a visiting professor was to be made welcome and included in as many of the ongoing activities as possible. So, before I got to know everyone, around noon one or another of my neighbours or field-related colleagues dropped by on the way to a nearby cafeteria, to inquire whether I would care to join him and others for lunch. Even Robert Dahl, of whom I never ceased standing in immense awe, occasionally stopped by.

Many others in the department ensured we were not bereft of friends and invited us to their homes or to share some pleasant outing. Among them, the David Apters, Jim Scotts and David Camerons linger as particularly congenial. But is was Robert E. Lane, whom I had long admired for his *Political Man* and *Political Ideology* and whom I had met before, when my colleague Khalid Sayeed had the inspiration to invite him to give a seminar at Queen's, who outshone others in the manner in which he went out of his way to make us feel at home. He and his wife Helen, whose *nom de plume* as a novelist, was Helen Hudson, became friends. Bob from time to time suggested that we have lunch together and also facilitated my occasional participation in a marvellous informal faculty seminar presided over by the formidable Charles Lindblom. It was here that he and Robert Dahl, with others including Lane, fine-honed their analyses questioning the assumptions and prescriptions of market-centred theories, and in which they identified many failings of capitalism. Bob's socio-political orientation and his important contribution to political psychology find expression nicely in the title of one of his later books, *The Loss of Happiness in Market Democracies.* He also extended my familiarity with the folkways of the department by getting me involved in one of his Ph.D. supervisions: I sat on the board examining John Dingwall's thesis proposal. I was surprised that at Yale this preliminary hurdle on the road to the doctorate was at least as demanding as the final defence—a practice not followed at Queen's. John, who had been one of my Queen's students, was doing a fascinating thesis in which he likened Canadian parliamentary debates to certain forms of philosophical inquiry.

Being in New Haven also offered opportunities to rejoin my very old Pickering chum and roommate, Martin Shubik. A brilliant economist and games theorist, he was head of Yale's Cowles Foundation for Research in Economics. He had been at Yale since the '60s and knew New Haven and New England well. He and his wife, Julie, made sure that we came to know many attractive local and nearby sights and restaurants.

Yale has succeeded in providing its undergraduates with a vibrant residential college experience. Several colleges made it clear that they would have liked me to become one of their Fellows. I settled on Pierson, which proved a good choice, not only from my point of view, but also from Murie's. She took the opportunity provided by our New Haven year to take some courses in silkscreen printing and stained-glass making offered by the Creative Arts Workshop—a lively, community centre for crafts and art folks. When she discovered that Pierson had attracted a highly gifted Vietnamese batik artist who offered a course in his craft, she signed up for it. It was a resounding success and this, to her a new medium, considerably extended her enjoyment of printmaking.

Murie met Drika Purves in a couple of her classes. She worked in the Beinecke rare book library and her husband was a professor of architecture. Like the Shubiks, they enabled us to become acquainted with parts of Yale other than my home department. We saw quite a lot of them and occasionally went together to performances by the wonderful Yale Rep and the equally lustrous Long Wharf Theatre. The friendship survives. The Purveses have a cottage on Codfish Island, a little East of Kingston, which brings them to my neck of the woods every summer and offers Alec opportunities to do sketches for his delicate watercolours. Without fail, the Purveses and I and Hanna, my partner, get together in Kingston and attend performances at the Thousand Island Play House in Gananoque.

This thespian evocation reminds me of a truly memorable theatrical evening. The site was the Yale Rep, the director Roman Polanski, the play, I think, was *Tango*, by one of Polanski's compatriots, Sławomir Mrożek, and the leading lady a most gifted undergraduate actress called Meryl Streep.

Yale offered other opportunities for brushes with greatness or fame. One of the senior students I came to know well was Sue Halpern, now an exceptionally compassionate and insightful American writer. She was in the first batch of female Americans to win a Rhodes Scholarship. After she was chosen, she came to discuss whether, as one who strongly disapproved of some of Cecil Rhodes's imperialist views, it was ethical for her to accept the scholarship. Some time after I returned from Yale, one of her letters persuaded me, because of the impending world shortage of H_2O, to stop letting the cold water tap run while brushing my teeth.

Our sojourn in New Haven was also filled with opportunities to meet or see those who had already made it in a big way. At a concert we sat behind an elderly gent who, after the rendition of an Aaron Copland chamber music work, commented volubly on the performance, which he had every right to do—he was AC himself. Former President Gerald Ford came to give a seminar to the department. William F. Buckley, attended a dinner at Pierson—his former college—and brought with him some memorable wine. My Queen's colleague and fine economist, Doug Purvis, who was also spending a year at Yale, and whose children we occasionally baby sat, invited us with Trish, his wife, for dinner with James Tobin, who had recently won the Nobel Prize in economics. I had tea one day at Martin Shubik's when the other guest was his friend, Harold Lasswell, one of the world's top authorities on the relation between politics and communications. Fellow Canadian and Queen's grad, Alan Bromley, was head of the Physics department and, soon after our arrival, invited us to a party in his garden. One of America's leading physicists, he served as science advisor to American presidents and as a mandarin in several Republican administrations.

Although I viewed the year as something of a sabbatical, it was not all skittles and beer. I *did* have to finish a couple of papers, and I gave some seminars and took my teaching seriously. The enrolment in my Canadian politics course surprised me. There were about sixty keen faces confronting me when we first met. I asked every student to tell me why each chose the course. It turned out that about fifty were Canadian, a fairly large proportion of them on hockey scholarships. One girl's family owned land on Georgian Bay and thought that, in light of growing Canadian nationalism, it might be wise to have one family member become a Canadian. She was their choice. Another was an enthusiastic train buff, who wanted to know more about a country whose rail system he admired. A third and lone member without an ulterior motive, so to speak, was just interested in Canada. A most unusual American!

I was impressed by the extraordinary level of community spirit among the undergraduates and by their attachment to their college and university. The "Queen's spirit" was said to be unusually strong in Canada at the time, but seemed modest in comparison with the cohesion and loyalty at Yale. This was reflected in the manner in which graduates of the two universities, and the faculty as well, supported them financially.

The Sixth Peak:
Beijing—Playing Footsie Behind the Scenes in China

Because of long-standing missionary activity in China, Canada has enjoyed a presence there denied many others. Dr. Norman Bethune, a politically radical Canadian surgeon who died of an infection while operating in China in the late 1930s, captured the hearts of the Chinese nation. He became a popular hero, particularly after Mao Zedung's essay "In Memory of Norman Bethune" was made compulsory reading in Chinese public schools. Much goodwill was also generated when Canada established diplomatic relations with the communist Chinese government almost ten years before the USA. Even I—a scholar specializing in Canadian politics—had, in the early 1990s, a brush with Sino-Canadian relations. This engagement was so slight that its mere mention seems a pretentious, spuriously self-aggrandizing exaggeration. Still, there was a teensy whiff of an involvement which was fascinating and instructive. While a very small droplet in the sea of our relations with China, it was a memorable episode in my life.

I was elected president of the Royal Society of Canada (RSC) in 1992. We were subsequently approached by Charles Burton, a Sinologist successfully straddling two careers — academician and diplomat — who was attached to the Canadian embassy in Beijing. He reported that the Chinese Academy of Social Science (CASS) had launched a study of Canadian democratic institutions and practices and was looking for a Canadian partner. Would the RSC put together a team of scholars interested in working on this project with Chinese colleagues?

We agreed and eventually discovered that this initiative was not quite as purely scholarly and innocent as it first appeared. Some members of the Politburo of the Chinese Communist Party — the nerve centre of the country's political power — were of the view that, given the liberalization of the Chinese economy, the political regime would also, in due course, have to undergo adjustments, at least in part, endowing the political order with characteristics resembling those of democratic societies. Adherents to this school eventually garnered sufficient support enabling them to designate "The Canadian and Western Democracy Research" a priority research project of CASS. This feature of the project, of which we became aware only once we had established some intimacy with our new colleagues, endowed it with potentially far-reaching consequences exceeding its intellectual and scholarly appeal.

Several isolated encounters between Canadian and Chinese scholars had occurred before the RSC's formal participation, but the project was launched in earnest only when the Chinese and Canadian teams visited one another's countries and carefully explored certain features of prevailing political practices. Under the leadership of Chen Quineng, a respected historian and director of the Canadian Studies Centre at CASS, five scholars associated with CASS came to Canada in 1992 for five weeks to engage in fieldwork, conduct interviews, and prepare reports. For our part, we assembled a handful of seasoned Canadianists suited to guiding our colleagues to synthesize the essence of Canadian democratic experience. They were political scientists Alan Cairns (UBC), Peter Russell (U of T), Stéphane Dion (Montreal), Craig Brown (history, U of T) and me. A few others, mostly historians, also became involved at different times — Blair Neatby (Carleton), Ramsay Cook (York), David Bercuson

(Calgary) and several additional scholars who attended only one of our seminars. My colleagues insisted that I act as the leader of our group, no doubt because I was the current head of the RSC. But we were an utterly collegial team of equals. We went to China twice and received our Chinese friends in Canada on several occasions.

Despite the utter seriousness with which we tackled our work and the importance we attached to it, we did not completely neglect the famous sights afforded by our two immense countries. We hardly scratched the surface, of course, but the Canadians made sure that our visitors saw the Rockies and Ottawa, were splashed by droplets of Niagara Falls, and attended seminars at pleasant places like Lake Simcoe, Kingston, and Niagara-on-the-Lake. For our part, we admired the terra cotta armies at Xi'an, visited Shanghai and, of course, set foot on the Great Wall of China. Strictly speaking, although I visited this unforgettable sight, I did not quite set foot on it. I had developed a blister on one of my toes, and was carried to and along part of the wall on the back of a sturdy Chinese peasant whom CASS had hired for this important task.

Our first full-scale conference in Beijing was attended by about forty or fifty scholars who, we observed, were strikingly polite, even obsequious, toward their senior colleagues. We were making much of the fact that the effective functioning of democratic institutions required the presence of a healthy civil society. Here, many citizens participated in voluntary social relationships and in non-governmental organizations. In these, we maintained, people were steeped in the free give-and-take of consultive decision-making. It was desirable that every view be frankly aired and that people felt comfortable, in all circumstances, in voicing their opinions. Excessive respect for, and subservience to, authority inhibited truly free discussion. This point had to be made as vividly as possible. So, during one of the breaks, the Canucks convened to teach a lesson by example. At the first opportunity thereafter, and then from time to time, my compatriots vigorously and mercilessly questioned much of what I—the group's leader and president of the national academy—said and had written. The weight to be attached to any idea depended on its merit, not the rank or authority of its oracle. The changed tone of the Canadian discourse was immediately noticed and its significance taken in. Our hosts were very bright and very quick. It was hard to say who was more delighted with the outcome of our little stratagem, the Canadians who saw their pedagogy working, or the Chinese who enjoyed asserting themselves.

I am not sure whether the Chinese were surprised by our egalitarian demonstration, but on another occasion they astonished us. When visiting Kingston, I wished to take them to a local restaurant and inquired whether they liked French, Italian, Canadian or any other cuisine. Anything will be fine, they replied, except a Chinese meal. Having tasted what we locals called Chinese food, they found it at some variance with the diet they enjoyed at home and avoided it whenever possible while here.

During one of our joint meals in China I committed a social gaffe. As part of one of our Beijing conferences, the head of CASS hosted a formal banquet. It was a splendid and speech-filled affair which, however, had its uncomfortable aspects, quite apart from my uncouth behaviour. Throughout the looooong evening, we were seated on the floor around several very large Lazy Susans. Unused to this position and setting, our joints creaked and complained. The Lazy Susans were laden with prodigious numbers of porcelain dishes containing mysterious delicacies. At each cushion there were some chopsticks and a couple of empty bowls waiting to be filled. I was seated on our host's right and when it was time to start, he very kindly used his chopsticks to deftly place a few morsels into the empty vessel by my cushion. I thought that that was a charming gesture which I emulated from time to time during the dinner. After returning to the hotel that evening, I consulted my Chinese guide book and discovered to my dismay that it is the practice in China to begin formal dinners, not with the recitation of a grace or with a wish for "bon appétit," "Guten Appetit," or "dobrou chut'" but with the "ceremony" of transferring the first bite onto the guest of honour's plate. I subsequently apologized to the CASS president who laughed merrily and allowed that, as one who had done his Ph.D. in the States, he knew all along what was going on but did not wish to spoil my fun.

Although the titular head of the Canadian team when we were abroad or interacted with our Chinese counterparts at home, I was by no means the most critical actor, nor the driving force. Once we mobilized the appropriate scholars and launched the exercise, the management and ongoing leadership fell to other hands. I participated fully in all our intellectual and social activities and made sure that my principal interventions to the seminars were put in publishable form. A paper on regulatory practices was likely the most apposite and useful. Based on my experiences at the CRTC, it showed that the public interest could be effectively defended and promoted, in a market or mixed economy, by the establishment of a regulatory regime, headed by an independent agency operating at arm's length from the government. CASS published it, as well as another piece I wrote for our friends, based in part on personal experience and in part on the description and analysis of the co-existence in Canada of two official languages. "Living in a Bilingual Society" first appeared in Chinese in *Canadian Horizon,* a CASS publication edited by my counterpart on the Chinese side, and good friend by now, Chen Quineng.

The originator of the China-Canadian collaboration was Charles Burton who, still a relatively junior scholar and foreign-service officer, started the ball rolling and dribbled it successfully throughout the whole exercise. His knowledge of China, Mandarin, the intricacies of diplomatic relations, and by no means least, his excellent, relaxed personal relations with local scholars, were essential building blocks of our edifice. Almost from the start, and throughout, Craig Brown, the U of T historian, acted not only as a senior scholar but also as a caring, considerate leader and hospitable chaperone and facilitator. The overall direction was left to an advisory committee chaired by the RSC President, which was serviced by the Brock Centre for Canada and Pacific Studies under Burton, with the assistance of a Ph.D. student. In addition to the academics involved, Fred Bild, the Canadian Ambassador in Beijing, also made some valuable, experience-inspired contributions, and ensured that we had the full support of his embassy.

The official blessing was intrinsically invaluable, but it also demonstrated that a completely independent academic and intellectually engagé body, like the RSC, could informally and productively collaborate with a government agency in a matter which served Canada's (and China's) public interest. This aspect of our project was almost certainly not lost on the Chinese participants.

Our involvement was extremely enjoyable and highly instructive for all participants. There was no way of knowing, however, whether it led, or perhaps will lead in the future, to changes in Chinese society and politics affecting the well-being of the Chinese people.

The Seventh Peak: Vienna—A Balkan Challenge

This uncertainty about the outcome of our China project likewise clung to the events of the final peak I revisit in this chapter. It concerns the fraught relations between Serbs and Croats in the former Yugoslavia. My involvement was also linked indirectly to my presidency of the RCS. Its headquarters are in Ottawa and, while there, I became acquainted with Walther Lichem, the Austrian Ambassador. An outstanding diplomat who has made major contributions to Austro-Canadian cultural relations, he was an old UN hand and an accomplished activist and expert on, among other things, issues related to human rights, security and conflict resolution. One day, late in 1994, I received a call from Michael Platzer, a friend of Lichem's, who was at the time attached to the UN in New York, and deeply involved in efforts to diffuse the ethnic conflicts tormenting Yugoslavia. Platzer asked me to chair an upcoming conference in Vienna, at which a well mixed and carefully selected group of Yugoslav intellectuals would explore what might be done to find an acceptable modus vivendi among the major, deeply divided, contending parties. I was intrigued and puzzled. "Why me?" I asked, and indicated that my knowledge of the Balkans was only a minute fraction of infinitesimal. Never mind, he allowed. They were familiar with my work and career and thought I'd do fine. The agenda would be prepared by his team at the UN, and all I needed to do was facilitate and lubricate the talk, and ensure that the atmosphere was conducive to frankness and civility.

The UN organizers referred to the gathering as a "confidence building" exercise which was not expected to come up with new solutions. It was hoped, however, that it would clarify the divisive issues and the positions the key parties took towards them. A better understanding of what everyone thought and believed would contribute to an atmosphere encouraging compromise. The approaches of the intellectuals would bubble up into, and penetrate, the public discourse affecting the future of the country.

As soon as I acceded to Michael's request, I informed the appropriate people in the Department of Foreign Affairs and International Trade of my challenge and requested that I be briefed about the background of my "mission," the department's position on the outstanding issues and anything else they thought I should know. The response was fulsome and highly competent: a number of departmental officers at various levels of seniority met me and attended sessions in the Pearson Building, at which most of the outstanding problems were discussed by knowledgeable people who were not, by the way, always in agreement with one another.

After my arrival in Vienna in January 1995, it was Platzer and his staff who specified more precisely what they expected from the conference and they also provided invaluable background about some of the participants. The setting was imposing. We met in a huge tiered auditorium in Vienna's UN campus, closely resembling the meeting place of the General Assembly in New York, well known to television audiences. Sophisticated electronic trimmings, including complex translation services, were in place, enabling the participating Yugoslav teachers, academics, journalists, etc. to exchange their views on the topics identified by the agenda or which surfaced as the result of the discussions.

The areas covered were numerous and immense, touching on much of the history and nature of the major issues responsible for the ethnic strife in the former Yugoslavia and its successor states and principalities. Disagreements were profound, but the overall tone of the sessions was one of reasonableness, despite the strong convictions of the speakers. I tried to set the right tone in my introductory statement by sketching my personal background and Canada's experience in seeking to accommodate its racially mixed population. I mentioned Mackenzie King's famous observation that if some countries had too much history, Canada had too much geography, and that this makes it easier for us to live together than is the case in places like Serbia, Croatia, Bosnia-Herzegovina, Macedonia etc.

My approach seemed to suit the occasion, for, at the end of the conference, when it was decided that the talks had been fruitful enough to justify another encounter, I was asked to chair it as well. We met a few months later at a wonderful castle in Stadtschlaining in Burgenland, Austria's most easterly province, where the Austrian Study Center for Peace and Conflict Resolution has its headquarters and conference facilities in a storybook castle.

What looked like a positive outcome of our conferences, at least at the level of personal relationships, led me to suggest to DFAIT that we invite a group of Serbs and Croats to Canada to observe our inter-ethnic practices and talk to some knowledgeable people about them. I recruited Jean Laponce to become involved in a symposium we held in Ottawa, and he did much to make these visits worthwhile.

As I noted when we began the ascent onto this last of my seven peaks, it was impossible to tell whether the conference and its aftermath had any effects on how the post-Yugoslav world settled into its present tolerable state of accommodation. The outlook and approach of "our" Yugoslavs after the last meeting in Burg Schlaining was certainly not so belligerent as to block progress. Our discussions, the attractive setting of the meetings and the rather lavish hospitality of the UN and Austrian politicians and officials almost certainly encouraged a good-humoured and positive approach to the issues at hand. But, then, this group represented only a tiny segment of the populations involved, and though an articulate one, it was by no means decisive in reaching the agreements bringing stability into the region.

So, like the collaboration with Chinese scholars, the brief, shallow immersion in Balkan politics proved instructive and enjoyable to the Canadian side, consisting in this instance of only me. Whether it achieved its avowed objective is anyone's guess. Again, like the RSC/CASS collaboration, it showed that only time, and access to the relevant records, will enable posterity (if it cares) to decide whether the results justified the efforts made. But whatever the verdict, it was fascinating and encouraging in an unexpected way to see how well an academic life prepared one for making contributions to the wider society, surpassing mere disciplinary and scholarly bounds. It also underlined something which I first learnt very early after my arrival at Queen's: it is possible for students of politics, working in Canada, to derive enormous benefit, with no loss of freedom, from closely interacting with government departments.

Looking over the history of my far-flung foreign affairs, including many unreported here, evokes two concluding reflections. They entered my consciousness only when, pocket diaries at hand, I started to relive the past. In my early academic years, and for quite a long time, it seems that I stuck closely to Queen's and Canada, venturing abroad only rarely. The Ph.D. in London was an exception, but even then, because of my thesis topic, I was strongly focused on things Canadian. It was only in the 1960s, over ten years after my first steps at Queen's, that the paths I trod took me outside the country. This resulted in my academic roots and early socialization being solidly Canadian.

Secondly, academic trips outside Canada usually aroused extraordinarily strong reactions, particularly at the beginning. I loved foreign parts, colleagues from other cultures, and noting differences in the way our discipline varied in, but transcended, diverse contexts. But I had no desire to move to Britain, the Continent or the USA, and never suffered from *greener*-pastures envy. Rather, I was strongly drawn to, and fascinated by, *varied* pastures, whether greener or more arid. But much as I enjoyed being abroad and navigating in different languages, I was not in the least tempted to relocate from Canada, nor from Kingston, for that matter, on a permanent basis. If Queen's was my tribe, as I extravagantly sometimes thought, then Canada is my land.

Curtain Call:
A Life of Learning, a Life of Doing

When I taught what were then seen as gargantuan classes of two hundred or more students—nowadays groups that size seem like seminars—I tried to conclude each session with a pithy summary of the main points. After a 50-minute presentation, that was easy. But what do I do now? As the curtain falls, I need to encapsulate over eighty exciting years.

My happy childhood and cheerful genetic endowment bequeathed a legacy of *joie de vivre* and good humour. Indoctrination of Masaryk's democratic principles, and Tati's social democratic influence, fostered a social and political progressiveness, and my strong commitment to Czech nationalism slowly transformed itself into a grip-like attachment to my new home—Canada—and its cultural identities. Having lived in several countries and cultures gave me linguistic facility and an openness to diversity. Osteomyelitis taught me to accept the inevitable. Once in Canada, the Quaker- and John Dewy-inspired philosophy of Joe McCulley's Pickering College taught me tolerance. Victoria College and Murie and her family impressed on me the fundamental decency and wholesomeness of Ontario values.

This, in a nutshell, is what I brought with me when I started the life of a prof. Then J.A. Corry's enlightened but somewhat skeptical liberalism impressed on me the merit of liberal democratic political institutions, while my research revealed the volatile vagaries of popular opinion, and the Queen's-Ottawa affinity drove home the benefits of linking academic knowledge to policy decisions.

My adult values, arising from this base, grew out of the social sciences, studies of international politics and political parties, political sociology, cultural policy and, profoundly, the ethos of the university.

The American Council of Learned Societies, in its Haskins lectures, annually invites an outstanding scholar to address it on the subject "A Life of Learning." The orator is invited to reflect on a lifetime of work as a scholar and of performing the tasks I have dubbed "The Third Pillar." Since the lectureship goes back to the

1980s, the complete harvest, available on the Society's web site, conveys a wonderful image of what university life is about. A frequent theme evoked and illustrated in multifarious ways is, not surprisingly, that learning, discovering, finding out, and extending knowledge are the fulfilling essence of a university. Among its priceless gifts is that it compels its members not only to master facts and gain insight but also to organize and verbalize them for use by others. Research, reporting one's findings and teaching are the defining features of the academic experience and for some, including myself, endow it with a fatal attraction.

In addition, as the "CRTC" and "Foreign Affairs" chapters reveal, the university background and setting also led to the world outside and linked learning to practice. One reason I was asked to go to the CRTC was that my research, lecturing and writing explored aspects of French-English relations in Canada and issues of national cohesion. I also assume that my involvement with China and the Balkans, described earlier, would not have come about had I not been a university person.

The wonderful gratification I derived from the purely academic aspects of Queen's was enhanced substantially by their extension into the so-called real world. In addition to the instances I just cited, there were many others: involvement with the Institute of Intergovernmental Relations and Premier Robarts's Advisory Committee on Confederation, both of which influenced the evolution of Canadian federalism; advisory roles in Ontario and Quebec with respect to electoral reform; preparing the Centennial celebrations; consultations in the Pearson Building in Ottawa on foreign policy issues; conundrums related to governance and performance of the public service; presiding over the Royal Society of Canada; and deliberating about who should be inducted in the Order of Canada. These and many others, at different times, claimed my time. Some such exercises were quite minor, others substantial. They all extended my classroom and "lab" commitments to the outside world and provided a link between academic work and public policy.

During the first two decades at Queen's, teaching, writing and lecturing were completely dominant. Then gradually they were complemented by involvement in the outside world and the application of knowledge. Mr. Chips also became a public intellectual and a dabbler in policy. R.K. Merton's "parochial" academic, also became a "cosmopolitan." The life of learning also embraced a life of doing.

Reality Check: How True Is all This?

What's Here

Once in a blue moon one has an experience of such colossal impact that it becomes a major milestone on one's life journey. The most potent of my epiphanies occurred in 1958. When researching the relationship, during an election, between federal and provincial politicians of the same party, I interviewed activists in the provincial capitals across the country. The first stop on the Western expedition was Winnipeg, where I stayed at the YMCA. While there, I started reading the first draft of a thesis I had taken with me by of one of my M.A. students, A.D. MacKinnon. When trying to return to it in Regina a couple of days later, I realized that I must have left the thesis behind. I wrote the "Y" manager and asked him to send it to me c/o General Delivery, Vancouver. The first thing I did upon arriving there was to try to fetch the thesis at the post office. To my horror, there was only a letter from Winnipeg; the thesis had not been found. Hard drives, floppies and USB sticks were then unknown, and I thought that MacKinnon had not made a carbon copy. Had I wasted two precious years of a young man's life? The rest of my trip was ruined as I anguished over the inexplicable disappearance of the thesis draft.

My sighs of relief upon arriving back in Kingston were so deafening they could be heard all the way down the St. Lawrence to Montreal: the thesis was sitting on my study desk. I was aghast. Just before leaving for Winnipeg by train, I had telephoned for a taxi and while waiting, glanced at the thesis. I put it down exactly in the spot I had remembered, but later somehow transferred the desk to Winnipeg. How could my mind have played so grievous a trick? If ever called upon in a court of law to testify that I would utter only the truth, and nothing but the truth, I could henceforth not do so. The realization that my mind and its memory cannot be trusted was shocking and demoralizing—a moment of truth viscerally affecting my self-confidence.

You see what this leads to: the foregoing account of my past is the product of the flawed instrument just described which, on occasion, may distort. This being the case, what sort of documentary evidence did I call upon to verify the story? What files, diaries, correspondence, witness accounts, news stories back up what I say? Almost none, alas, because of the approach I took to reviewing the past.

My tatty database, housed in old shoe boxes.

My professional and personal files are, for the most part, deposited in the Queen's Archives. A very few have, for one reason or another (including my lack of discipline and disorderly ways) not made it there and still clutter up one of my two homes. But knowing some of my weaknesses I resolved, when beginning my story, NOT to go near my papers. Had I otherwise resolved, there would have been no book. I would not have been strong enough to stop far too much detail choking the text. The highlights, I assumed, were still in my head and would make a better story than well-documented and fully verified scholarly detail. I did not once consult my archived files and when, as rarely happened, some relevant document found its way into the text, it was because a letter or note had somehow escaped being deported for posterity. On January 26, 2012, however,

Teri-Ann, my intrepid editor, made a sortie to the fine Queen's Archives to ascertain and verify a couple of details.

I relied on one splendid source: my annual pocket diaries, starting in 1940. They have assisted in pinpointing dates, names and places, but have also often failed me. There are too many laconic entries like "Lunch, noon" without any indication of where and with whom. On the other hand, they reveal changing tastes, interests and activities. At certain times they bristle with reports on what birds, plants, flowers or animals I have come across and where or what creatures have come across me. Other times are filled with concerts, plays, exhibitions and the like. They record appointments, meetings, conferences, trips, swims, hikes, cross-country ski outings but avoid all detail. Many entries, names and places are now completely puzzling and some, indecipherable. But overall these slim Letts, Quo Vadis, U of T, U of London, and Queen's pocketbooks provided indispensable aid.

In pinpointing certain dates and places, I also used *all* my passports, starting with the Czechoslovak *cestovní pas*, issued in 1933 and renewed several times until I acquired the fraudulent Moroccan *passeport* (1940) enabling us to leave Casablanca, and concluding with ten successive Canadian exemplars, all of which, except the most recent (2012), were mutilated by the passport office at renewal time.

An additional help, and one new to me, was the Internet and particularly Google and Yahoo. These facilitated verifying dates, spellings of names and some historical details.

But despite the traumatic lapse of memory which so shook me in 1958, I relied on what I recalled I did and thought, what I remembered as my experiences. When I repeat a conversation it is what I remember of it, not what was recorded at the time. In the last 88 years, I managed to keep a diary on only three days!

Another caveat is in order. Truth and reality, as is well known, and as I noted from time to time, are often subjectively conceived. Remember Pirandello? Two witnesses to an event do not always see the same thing and even when they do, they may both overlook aspects which are defining to a third observer. So, to tell what is or was is a daunting task, not easily achieved in a relaxing text without references and footnotes.

The 5-HTTLPR gene may also muddy the waters. It, the "good humour" gene, you may recall, when present in one of its long forms, predisposes one to optimism. I tend to forget the bad things, and remember the good, thus perhaps infusing past panoramas with unrealistically rosy, Panglosian light.

All I claim, therefore, is that I have tried to report what I remember as accurately as I could, without embellishment or varnish or unseemly self-mortification, when admitting inadequacies. I sought to convey accurately what happened and what I thought and felt about it.

What's Missing?

As you saw, I have immensely enjoyed unearthing the past. In doing so, I was occasionally guilty of self-indulgent prolixity and of yielding to an irrepressible urge to record an incident or share an anecdote. I tried to tell not only a particular individual's story but also a good yarn. Quite frankly, I loved conversing with you. This led, unwittingly, to my fashioning a quasi-documentary of a passing age and institution—the university. The number of pages mounted like the rising tide, posing serious publishing problems. To keep the size down, I decided to redesign the book. It would provide an account of my childhood, coming to Canada, education and my academic career and my related dabble as a regulator.

Many proposed, as yet unwritten, chapters have been put aside. In a moment of lunacy (I am in my 89th year), I propose to come up with another volume, savouring the scraps on the cutting room floor.

What has been delayed? I planned to give an account of living in a bilingual society and my involvement with the Royal Commission on Bilingualism and Biculturalism, the Royal Society of Canada and the country's system of honours, the story of Colimaison, regular holidays in Austria, including, after Murie's death, my partnership with Hanna, reflections on the City of Kingston, excursions into philanthropy, and the joys and sorrows of aging. The whole was then to be topped by a concluding piece called "Canada: J'accuse—J'adore." A few of these have been written but most are still pupas waiting to emerge.

Hope springs eternal.

Stepping Stones

Of Czech origin, John Meisel was born in 1923 and came to Canada in 1942. He matriculated from Pickering College in Newmarket and received his university training at Victoria College (U of T), the University of Toronto and London School of Political Science and Economics. He has written extensively on various aspects of politics, notably on parties, elections, ethnic relations, politics and leisure culture, and, at the beginning of his academic career, international politics. He has been a pioneer in Canada of research on electoral behaviour, political parties and the relationship between politics and leisure culture, particularly the arts. Throughout his career he has examined the cohesion (or its absence) of the Canadian communities. He has also lectured and written about regulation, broadcasting, telecommunications, and the information society.

He is the Sir Edward Peacock Professor of Political Science Emeritus at Queen's University, a former President of the Royal Society of Canada and is a Companion of the Order of Canada. From 1980 to 1983 he was Chairman of the Canadian Radio-Television and Telecommunications Commission (CRTC). He also served on the Ontario Press Council. He taught at Queen's with only a few absences since 1949 and was the Chairman of the Department of Political Studies there in the '60s. In 1976-77 he was Visiting Professor at Yale University, and in 1978 he spent some time in Britain as a Commonwealth Distinguished Visiting Professor. He was a holder for five years of a Killam Award of the Canada Council—a grant equivalent to a Research Professorship providing, in addition, funds required for a large-scale study of the Canadian party system.

A former President of the Canadian Political Science Association and the Social Science Research Council of Canada, he has been an active member of the executives of various professional associations in Canada, the United States, and at the international level. He has honorary doctorates from Brock, Calgary, Carleton, Guelph, Laval, Ottawa, Queen's, Regina, Toronto and Waterloo universities. In 1981, he was an inaugural recipient of membership in the Class of 1842 — the highest honour Pickering College bestows on its alumni. He received the Centennial, Queen Elizabeth II Jubilee, and the 125th Anniversary of Canada Commemorative medals. The International Council for Canadian Studies bestowed on him the Northern Telecom International Canadian Studies Award of Excellence in 1991. Queen's Alumni have presented him with the John Orr, Agnes Benidickson and the Distinguished Service Awards, and the Montreal Medal. A Festschrift in his honour, entitled *Canada's Century: Governance in a Maturing Society* (eds. C.E.S. Franks, J.E. Hodgetts, O.P. Dwivedi, Doug Williams, and V. Seymour Wilson) was published in 1995.

In addition to his university responsibilities, John Meisel has pursued the field of political science at two other levels. First, he has been associated in various ways with Royal Commissions, Task Forces and Inquiries, examining problems such as biculturalism and bilingualism, national unity, the status of women, bias in news casting, and regulation; and he has advised a number of departments of both the Canadian and Ontario governments. Occasionally he also assisted various public inquiries in Quebec. He was a member of Premier Robarts's Advisory Committee on Confederation. Second, he has been active in an editorial capacity as a member of advisory boards of several political science journals in both North America and Europe and, until 1971, he was the first English-speaking co-editor of the *Canadian Journal of Political Science*. In 1979 he founded the *International Political Science Review* (the journal of the International Political Science Association) which he edited or co-edited until 1995. He was the founding editor of the series of books, sponsored by the Social Science Research Council of Canada, entitled Canadian Studies in the Structure of Power (University of Toronto Press).

At a more popular level, John Meisel has been a frequent media commentator. He lectured widely and gave seminars at academic and non-academic gatherings in Canada, the United States and Europe.

His chief recreational interests are the visual and performing arts, walking and tottering on cross-country skis, bird watching and wild flower admiring, indoor gardening and the printed word in any guise or form. From May to December, he rattles around in a round, spiral house in the middle of nowhere (but by a beautiful lake).

He can be reached at <meiselj@queensu.ca>.

Articles and Books by JM Cited in his Tale

Archives in Cyberspace etc... Presented at the Queen's University Archives Lecture. 2000.

Babies and Bathwater, or, What Goes Down the Deregulatory Drain. In O.H. Gandy, P. Espinosa & J.A. Ordover (Eds.), Proceedings from the Tenth Annual Telecommunications Policy Research Conference (pp. 5–29). Norwood, NJ: Ablex. 1983.

Bureaucrats and Reformers: A Remediable Dissonance? (The Alan B. Plaunt Memorial Lecture). Ottawa, ON: Carleton University Information Services. 1983.

Caesar and the Savants: The Socio-political Context of Science and Technology in Canada. In A.M. Herzberg & I. Krupka (Eds.), Statistics, Science and Public Policy (pp. 153–177). Kingston, ON: Queen's University. 1998.

The Canadian General Election of 1957. Toronto, ON: University of Toronto Press. 1962.

Cancel Out and Pass On: A View of Canada's Present Options. In R.M. Burns (Ed.), One Country or Two (pp. 139–169). Montreal, QC: McGill-Queen's University Press. 1971.
Also in Working Papers on Canadian Politics. Montreal, QC: McGill-Queen's University Press. 1972, 1973, 1975.

Continuities in Popular Political Culture: French and Anglo-Saxon Contrasts in Canada. Converse, Philip E.; Dupeux, Georges; Meisel, John. Paper presented at the International Conference on Comparative Electoral Behavior, Ann Arbor, MI. 1967.

Cultivating the Bushgarden: Cultural Policy in Canada (with Jean Van Loon). In Milton C. Cummings & Richard Katz (Eds.), The Patron State: Government and the Arts in Europe, North America, and Japan (pp. 276–310). New York, NY: Oxford University Press. 1987.

The Curse and Potential of Greed: Social and Political Issues Arising from Acquisitiveness (The Hagey Lecture). University of Waterloo. 2005. Available at
fauw.uwaterloo.ca/documents/hagey/HageyLecture_2005Meisel.pdf

The Decline of Party in Canada. In H.G. Thorburn (Ed.), Party Politics in Canada, 5th ed. (pp. 98–114). Scarborough, ON: Prentice Hall. 1985.

The Decline of Party in Canada. (revised). In H.G. Thorburn (Ed.), Party Politics in Canada, 6th ed. Scarborough, ON: Prentice Hall. 1991.

Dysfunctions of Canadian Parties: An Exploratory Mapping. In H.G. Thorburn (Ed.), Party Politics in Canada, 6th ed. (pp. 234–254). Scarborough, ON: Prentice Hall. 1991. Also appears in A.G. Gagnon & A.B. Tanguay (Eds.), Democracy with Justice/La Juste Démoctatie (pp. 406–431). Ottawa, ON: Carleton University Press. 1992.

L'évolution des partis politiques canadiens. Cahiers de la société canadienne de science politique, No. 2, pp. 55. 1966.

The Fear of Conflict and Other Failings. Government and Opposition [Anniversary Issue: A Generation of Political Thought], 15, 435–445. 1980.

Flora and Fauna on the Rideau: The Making of Cultural Policy. In K.A. Graham (Ed.), How Ottawa Spends, 1988/89 (pp. 49–80). Ottawa, ON: Carleton University Press. 1988.

J'ai le gout du Québec, but I like Canada: Reflections of an Ambivalent Man. In Richard Simeon (Ed.), Must Canada Fail? (pp. 291–307). Montreal, QC: McGill-Queen's University Press. 1977.

Language Continua and Political Alignments: The Case of French- and English-Users in Canada. Presented at the 7th World Congress of Sociology. Varna, Bulgaria. 1970.
Published under the title *Values, Language and Politics in Canada* in Working Papers on Canadian Politics. Montreal, QC: McGill-Queen's University Press. 1972, 1973, 1975.
Reprinted in Joshua A. Fishman (Ed.), Advances in the Study of Bilingualism. The Hague, Netherlands: Mouton. 1978.

The Larger Context: General Developments Preceding the Election. In H.R. Penniman (Ed.), Canada at the Polls: 1979 and 1980 (pp. 24–54). Washington, DC: American Enterprise Institute. 1981.

Living In a Bilingual Society (Chinese translation). In Chen Quineng (Ed.), Canadian Horizon. Beijing: Chinese Academy of Social Science. 1999.

Meteor? Phoenix? Chameleon? The Decline and Transformation of Party in Canada (with Matthew Mendelsohn). In H.G. Thorburn (Ed.), Party Politics in Canada, 8th ed. (pp. 163-178). Toronto, ON: Pearson. 1995.

Near Hit: The Parturition of a Broadcasting Policy. In K.A. Graham (Ed.), How Ottawa Spends, 1989–90 (pp. 131–163). Ottawa, ON: Carleton University Press. 1989.

Newspeak in the Information Society. (The Dunning Trust Lecture, Queen's University), Archivaria, 19, 173–184. Winter 1984-85.

Papers on the 1962 Election. (Ed.). Toronto, ON: University of Toronto Press. 1964.

The Party System and the 1974 Election. In Howard R. Penniman (Ed.), Canada at the Polls (pp. 1–28). Washington, DC: American Enterprise Institute. 1975.

Political Culture and the Politics of Culture. Canadian Journal of Political Science, 7, 601–615. 1974.

Religious Affiliation and Electoral Behaviour: A Case Study. Canadian Journal of Economics and Political Science, 22, 481–496. 1956. Reprinted in Bernard R. Blishen, Frank E. Jones, Kaspar D. Naegele, & John Porter (Eds.), Canadian Society. Toronto, ON: Macmillan. 1961.
and in J. Courtney (Ed.), Voting in Canada. Toronto, ON: Prentice-Hall. 1967.

Space Invaders: Some Canadian and International Implications of Telematics. (SNID Occasional Paper No.85-201). Kingston, ON: Studies in National and International Development, Queen's University. 1985. Revised version, under the title *Communications in the Space Age: Some Canadian and International Implications*. International Political Science Review, 7(3) 299–331. 1986.

Studies in the Structure of Power: Decision-making in Canada. (Ed.) Toronto, ON: University of Toronto Press. 1964–1980.

The United States and Canada: How Are They Governed? [Monograph].
    Washington, DC: The American Council of Education. 1956.

Working Papers on Canadian Politics. Montreal, QC: McGill-Queen's
    University Press. 1972, 1973, 1975.

Debts

Foremost among those who helped me tell my tale are my parents, although they did not live long enough actively to lend a hand. But I nevertheless owe them everything: no parents, no John; no John, no book. They also laid the critical foundations for the life portrayed here.

Closely behind stands Charles Gordon, my memoir guru. His encouragement, counsel and guidance, particularly in the early stages, pointed the way and kept me going. My niece Victoria, like Charley, provided much needed editorial expertise at the start and refreshed my memory about some family history. Sean Conway entered centre stage later on. His perusal of a few early chapters elicited so enthusiastic a response that it almost surpassed my own excitement over the project. Towards the end, it was Sean who toiled ceaselessly to bridge the seemingly insurmountable gulf between the manuscript and the volume in your hands. Here too, I can say no Sean, no book.

Ron Watts and Ken Cuthbertson read the whole manuscript and offered blue chip advice. Other friends, with special knowledge of certain areas, enriched the contents, caught gaffes and saved the reader from overloaded verbiage. In alphabetical order, they are James Eayrs, Jock Gunn, Hank Intven, Jean Laponce, Russ McMillen, Ken Russell, Rick Schultz, Victor Rabinovitch and Lisa de Wilde.

Hanna Dodwell, Beate and Istvan Anhalt, Heather Candler, Shirley Fraser, Peter Grant, Arthur Milnes, Peter Newman, Libuše Peichl and Julian Porter in various ways eased my path, as did the OED, Fowler, Roget, Google and Yahoo.

My thanks are also due to the many photographers and cartoonists who provided the illustrations accompanying our text. The identity of some, alas, has been lost in the fog of antiquity, including the gifted portraitist who caught me on my bike, holding the *Queen's Quarterly*, gracing the cover of this book.

This work occasionally strays into unconventional paths and so allows me to note two other debts, rarely acknowledged by authors.

At an early stage I intended to entitle the book *Thank You, Kaffee Hag* because the thought of writing a memoir occurred to me when suffering from a rare night of insomnia while on a hiking holiday in Austria. At the end of the preceding dinner, I ordered a cup of decaffeinated coffee, which in those parts is often referred to as Kaffee Hag. Like "Sanka" in the English-speaking world, the trade name of the brand grew into the generic term for decaf. The waiter must have brought me "real" coffee by mistake. Had it not been for this error, I might never have put my two typing fingers to work in your service. I toyed with the idea of weaving the story into the title, but ended up with a more congenial descriptive appellation. Nevertheless, I owe Kaffee Hag something.

Paradoxically, a truly colossal obligation is due the countless academic and trade publishers who showed no, or only minimal, interest in my book when approached to consider it. Their tepid manner (and some had no manners at all) made me notice an advertisement in the *Queen's Alumni Review*. Wintergreen Studios Press was inviting manuscripts. I had previously collaborated with Rena Upitis, the press's creative spirit, and was well aware of her originality, energy and unbridled enthusiasm for the many causes she espouses. Working with a boutique house in my backyard was uncommonly congenial and proved exhilarating beyond all expectations. Rena and her editor, Teri-Ann McDonald, miraculously identified with my musings as closely as I did myself and made innumerable suggestions for their improvement, not least the idea that there be illustrations. Claire Grady-Smith, Wintergreen's Marketing and Communications Director, also fell for the manuscript and became an inspired member of our little cabal.

The foregoing attests to my being in debt, often the greatest debt, to very many kindred spirits, but it would be churlish of me not to acknowledge Rena and Teri-Ann's giant role in endowing this work with its "feel," flavour and looks. My very first book, *The Canadian General Election of 1957*, was edited by Rik Davidson of the U of T Press, one of Canada's legendary editors and a soulmate. I never expected to experience again the joy of working with a linguistic alter ego, but was wrong. Rena and Teri-Ann restored my increasingly jaundiced view of Canada's publishing world.

Kohr and Schumacher long ago stressed that small is beautiful. How right they were! *Děkuji mnohokrát*, as I used to say in Zlín, many thanks.

John Meisel
Kingston, Ontario
December, 2011

Books, Films and Plays Mentioned Here

Books

Anthology of Canadian Poetry, edited by Ralph Gustafson. Penguin, 1942.

British Political Parties (Distribution of Power Within the Conservative and Labour Parties), by R.T. (Bob) McKenzie. Gregg Revivals, 1992.

The Bush Garden: Essays on the Canadian Imagination, by Northrop Frye. Anansi, 1995.

Canada's Century: Governance in a Maturing Society – Essays in Honour of John Meisel, edited by C.E.S. (Ned) Franks, J.E. (Ted) Hodgetts, O.P. Dwivedi, Doug Williams, and V. Seymour Wilson. McGill-Queen's University Press, 1995.

Closed Circuits: The Sellout of Canadian Television, by Herschel Hardin. Douglas & McIntyre, 1990.

The Comedians, by Graham Greene. Vintage Books, 2005.

Crazy Like a Fox, by Sidney J. Perelman. Vintage, 1973.

The Crisis of Democracy, On the Governability of Democracies to the Trilateral Commission, by Michel Crozier, Samuel P. Huntington, and Joji Watanuki. New York University Press, 1975.

The CRTC and Broadcasting Regulation in Canada, by Liora Salter. Carswell, 2008.

The Crucifixion of Intellectual Man: Incorporating a Fresh Translation into English Verse of the Prometheus Bound of Aeschylus, by Eric A. Havelock. Beacon Press, 1950.

Democratic Government and Politics, by James Alexander Corry. University of Toronto Press, 1960.

The Diefenbaker Interlude: Parties and Voting in Canada; An Interpretation, by Peter Regenstreif. Longmans, 1965.

Dynasties and Interludes: Past and Present in Canadian Electoral Politics, by Lawrence Leduc, Jon H. Pammett, Judith I. McKenzie, and André Turcotte. Dundurn Press, 2010.

Escape from Freedom, by Erich Fromm. Holt Paperbacks, 1994.

Exit, Voice and Loyalty: Responses to Decline in Firms, Organizations and States, by Albert O. Hirschman. Harvard University Press, 1970.

French Canada in Transition, by Everett C. Hughes. Oxford University Press, 2009.

The Gathering Storm, by Winston S. Churchill. Mariner Books, 1986.

Gentlemen, Players and Politicians, by Dalton Camp. Penguin, 1988.

Getting it Done, by Derek Burney. McGill-Queen's University Press, 2005.

The Great Transformation: The Political and Economic Origins of Our Time, by Karl Polanyi. Amereon, 2012.

A Guide to the Classics, or How to Pick the Derby Winner, by Michael Oakeshott. Oakeshott and Griffith, 1936.

Human Society, by Kingsley Davis. Macmillan, 1949.

An Illustrated History of Ottershaw Park Estate – 1761-2011, by John Athersuch. Peacock Press, 2010.

Das Kapital, by Karl Marx. Penguin Classic, 2004.

Language Matters: How Canadian Voluntary Associations Manage French and English, edited by David Cameron and Richard Simeon. University of Washington Press, 2010.

The Loss of Happiness in Market Democracies, by Robert E. Lane. Yale University Press, 2001.

Mice in the Beer, by Norman Ward. Douglas & McIntyre, 1986.

My Life and Work, A Happy Partnership: Memoirs of J.A. Corry, by James Alexander Corry. Queen's University Press, 1981.

A Nation Unaware: The Canadian Economic Culture, by Herschel Hardin. University of Washington Press, 1980.

1984, by George Orwell. Penguin UK, 2008.

One Country or Two?, edited by Ron Burns. McGill-Queen's University Press, 1971.

The Origin of Totalitarianism, by Hannah Arendt. Nabu Press, 2011.

A Party Politician: The Memoirs of Chubby Power, written by Charles G. Power. Edited by Norm Ward. Macmillan, 1966.

Party Politics in Canada, by Hugh Thorburn. Pearson Education Imports, 2003.

Political Ideology: Why the American Common Man Believes What He Does, by Robert E. Lane. The Free Press, 1967

Political Man, by Robert E. Lane. Simon and Schuster, 1972.

Politics of Democracy: American Parties in Action, by Pendleton Herring. W.W. Norton, 1965.

The Prophet, by Kahlil Gibran. Macmillan, 2010.

Protestant Ethic and the Spirit of Capitalism, by Max Weber. Dover Publications, 2003.

Religion and the Rise of Capitalism, by Richard H. Tawney. Hesperides Press, 2008.

Remembrance of Things Past, by Marcel Proust. Reprinted as *In Search of Lost Time.* Modern Library. 2003.

Social Theory and Social Structure, by Robert K. Merton. Free Press, 1968.

Sociology: A Systematic Introduction, by Harry M. Johnson. Routledge, 2011.

The Spirit of Russia, by Tomáš Masaryk. Translated by Eden Paul and Cedar Paul. General Press, 2010.

Two Innocents in Red China, by Pierre Trudeau and Jacques Hébert. Douglas & McIntyre, 2007.

The Vital Center, by Arthur M. Schlesinger, Jr. Transaction Publishers, 1997.

War and Peace, by Leo Tolstoy. Vintage Books, 2008.

When in Rome, by Ngaio Marsh. Harper Collins, 1999.

Films

Les Misérables, directed by Richard Boleslawski. Twentieth Century Pictures, 1935.

Last Year at Marienbad, directed by Alain Resnais. Cocinor, 1961.

To Catch a Thief, directed by Alfred Hitchcock. Paramount, 1955.

Smiley's People, directed by Simon Langton. BBC/Paramount, 1982.

Tinker, Tailor, Soldier, Spy, directed by John Irvin. BBC/Paramount, 1979.

Brideshead Revisited, directed by Michael Lindsay-Hogg and Charles Sturridge. Granada Television, 1981.

Casablanca, directed by Michael Curtiz. Warner Bros., 1942.

The Seventh Seal, directed by Ingmar Bergman. Svensk Filmindustri, 1957.

Plays

A chacun sa verité (To Each His Truth), by Luigi Pirandello. Gallimard, 1950.

The Birds, by Aristophanes. Oxford University Press, 2009.

The Dance of Death, by August Strindberg. Nick Hern Books, 2004.

Julius Caesar, by William Shakespeare. Simon and Brown, 2011.

Mother Courage and Her Children, by Bertolt Brecht. Methuen, 2010.

My Fair Lady, by Alan J. Lerner, based on *Pygmalion,* by George Bernard Shaw. Penguin, 1965.

Oklahoma!, by Richard Rodgers and Oscar Hammerstein II. Applause Theatre and Cinema Books, 2010.

Six Characters in Search of an Author, by Luigi Pirandello. Methuen Drama, 2001.

Tango, by Sławomir Mrożek. Grove Press, 1968.

Who's Afraid of Virginia Woolf?, by Edward Albee. NAL Trade, 2006.

Index

Wintergreen Studios Press is an independent literary press. It is affiliated with the not-for-profit educational retreat centre, Wintergreen Studios, and supports the work of Wintergreen Studios by publishing works related to education, the arts, and the environment.

www.wintergreenstudiospress.com
www.wintergreenstudios.com

Made in the USA
Charleston, SC
09 October 2012